WILLIAM FAULKNER
THE YOKNAPATAWPHA COUNTRY

by Cleanth Brooks

WILLIAM FAULKNER
THE YOKNAPATAWPHA COUNTRY

New Haven and London
Yale University Press

Library of Congress Catalog card number:
63–17023

ISBN: 0–300–00329–3 (cloth),
0–300–00028–6 (paper)

20   19   18   17   16   15   14   13   12   11

To Robert Penn Warren

Preface

THIS VOLUME attempts to deal with William Faulkner's character-istic world, the world of Yoknapatawpha County. How does one go about describing a world? Is there an inevitable way or even one best way? I think not, and the disposition of the chapters of this book represents no more than a possible—and I hope useful—way to explore Faulkner's world.

What I have rejected out of hand is any purely chronological arrangement. The order in which Faulkner wrote these novels and stories does not necessarily constitute the best order in which to discuss them. I have preferred to feel my way into the world of Yoknapatawpha and to let my book grow accordingly. But the arrangement of the chapters that follow is not haphazard.

The first three chapters are introductory. "Faulkner, the Provincial" attempts to connect Faulkner with the other provincial writers of our time and to suggest the relation of his special world to that of modern man. "The Plain People" provides some com-ment on the least understood stratum in Faulkner's social struc-ture. (The relation to the whole society of the other strata—the older families of planter stock and even the Negroes—is less likely to be misunderstood.) This large intermediate category, with its various subsections, is so important to his novels that I believe it deserves some detailed consideration at the beginning.

Although the next chapter, "Faulkner as Nature Poet," deals with material derived from novels to be discussed later in the book, especially *The Hamlet* and *Go Down, Moses,* there is some-thing to be said for examining that material in its own right, at the start, for it has to do with elements that form the background of much of Faulkner's fiction and is closely related to his attitude toward ethics and religion.

The first novel to be considered as a work in itself is *Light in August*, which is not only one of Faulkner's masterpieces—and I have preferred to begin with a mature work—but a novel in which many of the characteristic topics and themes of his fiction appear. To mention only a few: there is the role of the community, the theme of isolation and alienation, Puritanism under the hot Southern sun, the tension between the masculine and feminine principles, and the relation of the characters to the past. There is a great advantage in dealing with such themes as they interrelate with one another in a concrete work, rather than as isolated and abstract topics.

"The Old Order" (*The Unvanquished*) grows out of some of the themes considered in the study of *Light in August,* and in turn points toward Chapters 6 (*Sartoris*) and 7 *(Sanctuary).* In these three novels one sees, among other things, the contrast between the old order and the new, and the pressures exerted upon various individuals by the crumbling of the old and the shift from the past to the present.

The theme of honor, as developed in *The Unvanquished, Sartoris,* and *Sanctuary,* is transposed into the world of the poor white in the discussion of *As I Lay Dying,* Chapter 8. The poor white also dominates the next series of novels—*The Hamlet, The Town,* and *The Mansion*—though with *The Town,* in particular, other elements come into play when both the poorer whites and the members of the old aristocracy move into town and adopt town ways.

With Chapter 12, "The Story of the McCaslins," we return to an older period, to the countryside, and especially to the world of the Negro, or at least a world in which the Negro occupies an important place. Next, "The Community in Action" brings the story of one of the McCaslins, a Negro McCaslin, up to the present, and provides still another modulation on the themes of honor and the community.

Chapter 14, "History and the Sense of the Tragic" (*Absalom,*

Absalom!), takes into account the special heritage of the South, with the presence of the Negro, the powerful pressure of family and community, and the past experienced not only as a precious heritage but as a crippling burden. The young man of the present, Quentin Compson, who is fascinated by the story of Thomas Sutpen and attempts to make some sense of it, has great difficulty in making sense of his own life and times. In *The Sound and the Fury,* discussed in the fifteenth chapter, we find Quentin involved with the disintegration of his own family and the apparent meaninglessness of the modern world, in which the old values are gone, and with them, the possibility of any heroic action.

Absalom, Absalom! and *The Sound and the Fury* are generally regarded as Faulkner's greatest works, and there is something to be said for ending with an account of these masterpieces. Yet since my book is essentially a study of Faulkner's world, an examination of *The Reivers* provides an appropriate conclusion to it; for though Faulkner's last novel does not give us his world in its tragic depth, it does exhibit its breadth and range. Here, more than in any other Faulkner novel I can think of, the inhabitants of country, town, and city, whether they are Negroes, plain people, or members of the old aristocracy, are presented in all their various gradations. The richness and variety of Faulkner's world has received no more complete expression.

In a subsequent book I plan to deal with many aspects of Faulkner's work that have had to be omitted here, including the novels and stories which lie outside of the Yoknapatawpha County cycle. There I shall concentrate on Faulkner's development as an artist—his beginnings, the forging of his style, and the working out of the special fictional techniques associated with his name. In this connection I mean to examine some of the earlier drafts of his novels and to discuss his process of revision with reference to style and structure.

There remains the pleasant task of acknowledging the encouragement and assistance given by various groups and individuals. I wish to speak my thanks to the John Simon Guggenheim Memorial Foundation for a grant which enabled me to undertake this study, and to Random House, Inc., for permission to quote from the Faulkner texts. I owe thanks also to Malcolm Cowley, whose introduction to *The Portable Faulkner* gave powerful impetus and direction to the serious criticism of Faulkner; to Linton Massey, Faulkner scholar and collector, who has been particularly helpful in many matters; to John Cook Wyllie, librarian of the Alderman Library at the University of Virginia, for various favors; to Mrs. Ann Bowden, librarian of the Humanities Research Center at the University of Texas; to the Committee on the Use of Literary and Historical Manuscripts for permission to quote from the manuscript of *Absalom, Absalom!* in the University of Texas Library; to Mrs. Paul D. Summers, Jr., for her kind permission to quote from the manuscript and typescript of *Sartoris;* to Hervey and Anna Lewis for special services, including the preparation of the genealogical charts; and to Albert Erskine of Random House, with whom my conversations about Faulkner began many years before he became Faulkner's editor—conversations which have continued to my benefit.

Some of the chapters of this book had the advantage of a reading and criticism by Andrew Lytle, editor of *The Sewanee Review,* who has been especially perceptive as to Faulkner's conception of the social structure of the South, and by Robert Penn Warren, whose early essay on Faulkner proved to be seminal and remains today one of the best pieces of Faulkner criticism ever written.

Northford, Connecticut   CLEANTH BROOKS
July 1963

Contents

Editions Cited

I HAVE GIVEN page references where possible to Modern Library editions of the novels including two Modern Library paperbounds (though I have avoided citing the flimsier paperbound reprints). I have, however, taken care to check the quotations from the Modern Library edition of *Sanctuary* against the 1962 edition of that work, which incorporates corrections of the text.

The Modern Library edition is cited for the following books, listed here with the dates of first publication and original publishers:

> *The Sound and the Fury,* New York, Jonathan Cape, Harrison Smith, 1929
> *As I Lay Dying,* New York, Jonathan Cape, Harrison Smith, 1930 (The ML edition includes *The Sound and the Fury* in the same volume.)
> *Sanctuary,* New York, Jonathan Cape, Harrison Smith, 1931
> *Light in August,* New York, Harrison Smith and Robert Haas, 1932
> *Absalom, Absalom!,* New York, Random House, 1936
> *The Hamlet,* New York, Random House, 1940
> *Go Down, Moses,* New York, Random House, 1942

The Vintage paperbound edition, which includes some revisions by the author, is cited for *The Town* (first publication: New York, Random House, 1957).

Page references to the following books refer to the first editions:

> *Soldiers' Pay,* New York, Boni and Liveright, 1926
> *Mosquitoes,* New York, Boni and Liveright, 1927

Sartoris, New York, Harcourt, Brace and Company, 1929
Pylon, New York, Harrison Smith and Robert Haas, 1935
The Unvanquished, New York, Random House, 1938
The Wild Palms, New York, Random House, 1939
Intruder in the Dust, New York, Random House, 1948
Knight's Gambit, New York, Random House, 1949
Requiem for a Nun, New York, Random House, 1951
A Fable, New York, Random House, 1954
The Mansion, New York, Random House, 1959
The Reivers, New York, Random House, 1962

"Smoke," "Monk," "Hand upon the Waters," "Tomorrow," "An Error in Chemistry," and "Knight's Gambit" are included in *Knight's Gambit.*

Page numbers after quotations from the stories refer to *The Collected Stories,* New York, Random House, 1950. "Was," "The Fire and the Hearth," "Pantaloon in Black," "The Old People," "The Bear," "Delta Autumn," and "Go Down, Moses" are sections of *Go Down, Moses,* which Faulkner regarded as a novel rather than a collection of stories. Page references to all other stories are to *The Collected Stories* except for "Race at Morning" (which is included in *Big Woods,* New York, Random House, 1955) and the three following stories, which have never been collected:

"Thrift," *The Saturday Evening Post,* 203, September 6, 1930
Idyll in the Desert, New York, Random House, 1931
Miss Zilphia Gant, Dallas, The Book Club of Dallas, 1932

The editions cited in the Index of Characters are those cited in the text. I have not given page references in the Index to stories which were later integrated into the novels or to materials reprinted in *Big Woods.*

1

Faulkner the Provincial

MOST READERS associate William Faulkner with the South quite as automatically as they associate Thomas Hardy with Wessex, Robert Frost with northern New England, and William Butler Yeats with Ireland, and perhaps more naturally than they associate Dylan Thomas with Wales. The regions and cultures to which these writers are linked differ in character, but they all stand in sharp contrast to the culture of the great world cities of the twentieth century. They have in common a basically agricultural economy, a life of farms, villages, and small towns, an old-fashioned set of values, and a still vital religion with its cult, creed, and basic norms of conduct. Wessex is very different from Sligo; New Hampshire, from North Mississippi. But for all their differences, each provides its author with a vantage point from which to criticize, directly or perhaps merely by implication, the powerful metropolitan culture.

Thus Robert Frost has characteristically taken for his vantage point not the more populous, heavily urbanized southern half of New England but the gaunt, old-fashioned, and relatively poverty-stricken region of northern New England. It is a grave injustice to regard Frost as a local colorist, exploiting the attraction that the quaint and the folksy hold for a metropolitan audience. He can be, and has been, so misunderstood, but Frost is making a serious criticism of twentieth-century man, and his loving elaboration of the life of New Hampshire is no mere indulgence in picturesque sentimentality or the comedy of the American rustic.

So it is also with Yeats, whose Ireland stands over against London much as Faulkner's South stands over against New York. The parallels between the cultural situations of these two very different men are so interesting that they deserve detailed illustration. Like Yeats, Faulkner benefited immeasurably from the fact that his own country has shown a long cultural lag behind great commercial and intellectual centers like London and New York. Like Yeats again, Faulkner's sense of history and his sense of participation in a living tradition have been of the utmost importance. Faulkner's work, like that of the great Irish poet, embodies a criticism of the prevailing commercial and urban culture, a criticism made from the standpoint of a provincial and traditional culture.

An Irishman like Sean O'Faolain senses at once the similarity between the two provincial cultures (even though O'Faolain manages to misunderstand the use that Faulkner makes of his). From "what little I have seen of Mississippi," O'Faolain writes,

> and [from] all I have read about it, life there sounds very much like life in County Cork. There is the same passionate provincialism; the same local patriotism; the same southern nationalism—those long explicit speeches of Gavin Stevens in *Intruder in the Dust* might, *mutatis mutandis,* be uttered by a southern Irishman—the same feeling that whatever happens in Ballydehob or in Jefferson has never happened anywhere else before, and is more important than anything that happened in any period of history in any part of the cosmos; there is the same vanity of an old race; the same gnawing sense of old defeat; the same capacity for intense hatred; a good deal of the same harsh folk-humor; the same acidity; the same oscillation between unbounded self-confidence and total despair; the same escape through sport and drink.[1]

Such general likenesses are also discernible from this side of the Atlantic. Any Southerner who reads Yeats' *Autobiographies*

1. *The Vanishing Hero* (New York, Universal Library, 1957), p. 75.

is bound to be startled, over and over again, by the analogies between Yeats' "literary situation" and that of the Southern author: the strength to be gained from the writer's sense of belonging to a living community and the special focus upon the world bestowed by one's having a precise location in time and in history. But as the *Autobiographies* show, Yeats learned to distrust the sentimental patriot whose notions of literature worked through all the obvious symbols—shamrocks, pepper pots made in the shape of Irish round towers, harps, and books with green covers.[2] (In the South, for shamrocks and round towers read magnolias and Greek-revival porticoes.) Yeats learned too the fact that one's worst literary enemies are sometimes to be found among one's own people. He once consoled an English friend whose book of poems had been soundly trounced in a Dublin newspaper by telling her that Dublin reviews were to be discounted; for years he had instructed his London publishers not to send his books to the Dublin papers for review. In London he could take his chance, for the reviewer, if sometimes uncomprehending, had no special cause to serve. But too often the Dublin journalist had to prove his cosmopolitanism by giving the back of his hand to an Irish book.[3] In the last fifty years Southern authors also have discovered that their severest critics were to be found at home in the person of reviewers who meant to show themselves just as emancipated as the New York critics.

Through loyalty to his Irish provincialism—though it was never a blind loyalty—Yeats converted potential weakness into a position of strength. Faulkner has done something comparable, making the provincial society out of which he comes, and with which so much of his fiction deals, a positive resource—an instrument for developing and refining his meaning. But many readers evidently regard Faulkner's provincial subject matter as a sheer liability, or else they totally misconceive what he does with it. After all, what can a provincial have to say of any consequence to modern industrial man living in an age of electronics and nuclear power? Faulkner is preoccupied with the past and with a rural

2. *Autobiographies* (New York, 1927), pp. 250–54.
3. Allan Wade, ed., *The Letters of W. B. Yeats* (New York, 1955), p. 860.

setting, and what possible value can these have except perhaps as negative object lessons? Faulkner's treatment of history is, then, a confirmation of our disowning the past, Faulkner's famous county (obviously a rural slum) a way of reminding us how far we have progressed.

If one trusts one's impression of the bulk of Faulkner criticism, these would seem to be typical ways in which Faulkner is now being read. Much of it takes his fiction to be sociology—an amateur and nonacademic sociology characterized by powerful moral overtones. There is in such criticism a surreptitious commerce between sociological-historical fact and fictional meaning. Particular insights and moral judgments that the critic has derived from fictional contexts are smuggled across the frontier into the realm of historical fact and become generalizations about Southern culture. They are then cited as historical "fact" to prove the accuracy of the sweeping judgments of the Southern scene that are attributed to Faulkner.

Such shady methodological transactions are usually prompted by the highest motives. Whether they know it or not, most authors of Faulkner criticism are serious moralists, and they recognize that Faulkner is, in his own way, a moralist too. They want to take him seriously and this means that they are very much concerned with the factual substratum of Faulkner's mythical county.

In view of the situation, it might be wise to take a look at Faulkner's facts—at Faulkner as the sociologist of north Mississippi. For this purpose, one of the most useful articles I have ever encountered is that published a few years ago by Dr. Winthrop Tilley in the *American Journal of Mental Deficiency*.[4] In an article entitled "The Idiot Boy in Mississippi," he undertook to show that Benjy Compson of *The Sound and the Fury* is merely a "stuffed idiot," a "fabricated literary idiot," quite incredible on any literal level. Tilley maintains that on the basis of clinical evidence most idiots are "phlegmatic, indifferent, and comparatively unexcitable." Moreover, they are "low-geared sexually." Tilley finds it most unlikely that Faulkner's Benjy would ever have displayed toward the schoolgirls passing by his house the sexual interest which prompted his brother Jason to have him gelded.

4. 59 (1955), 374–77.

Tilley finds that Faulkner is just as wide of the legal facts. He points out that there are cogent reasons for doubting that Benjy's gelding would ever have been permitted. He cites the Mississippi code which makes mayhem a penitentiary offence, and he adds a footnote pointing out that though Mississippi did in 1928 (fifteen years after Benjy's alleged gelding) legalize sterilization for "certain institutionalized individuals," "castration was specifically forbidden in the statute. Sec. 6957." Besides, Benjy would have had to be sent to the State School for the Feeble Minded at Ellisville, Mississippi, the state code (see Section 6907) specifically stipulating that "mere idiots" shall not be admitted to the institution at Jackson.

All of this is sufficiently devastating evidence of how little Faulkner's story of the life and times of Benjy Compson is to be taken as a sound medical and legal account of what can happen to idiots in Mississippi. Though the present case is extreme, anything calculated to shake the reader's confidence in the literal accuracy of Faulkner's "facts" is probably to be commended. Faulkner's novels have too often been read not as fiction but as factual accounts, with the notion that they represent only slightly distorted pictures of Southern rural and small-town life.

But Dr. Tilley wrote his article not so much in defense of the good name of the state of Mississippi as in derogation of Faulkner's art, for he argues that Faulkner's failure to get his facts straight has seriously injured his novel. He can allow to *The Sound and the Fury* no higher praise than "interesting failure." The character of Benjy, he says, is too implausible to carry the fictional weight placed upon him.

This judgment is the more interesting in that most admirers of Faulkner would put *The Sound and the Fury* among his three or four finest novels, and many would account it—as apparently Faulkner himself did—his masterpiece. Moreover, many readers have felt Benjy to be quite convincing—including a colleague of mine who is a psychoanalyst. One does not know, he says, what really goes on in an idiot's mind, but Faulkner's dramatization of what goes on in Benjy's seems to him a plausible guess and in any case constitutes a convincing imaginative account.

What is of basic concern here is what is always of concern in literature: the relation of truth of fact to aesthetic value—of "truth of reference" to "truth of coherence." The relationship between the two truths is rarely a simple one. It is not a simple one in Faulkner's novels. Faulkner critics are prone to confuse matters by saying that since the fiction is good, the "facts" must be correct, or that since the facts are incorrect, the fiction is bound to be poor. Faulkner's novels and stories, properly read, can doubtless tell us a great deal about the South, but Faulkner is primarily an artist. His reader will have to respect the mode of fiction and not transgress its limitations if he is to understand from it the facts about the South—that is, he must be able to sense what is typical and what is exceptional, what is normal and what is an aberration. He can scarcely make these discriminations unless he is prepared to see what Faulkner is doing with his "facts."

This misplaced stress upon realism might seem to find its proper corrective in a compensating stress upon symbolism—not facts but what they point to, not Faulkner as sociologist but Faulkner as symbolist poet. Surely, such a general emphasis is sound, for no great literature is to be taken just literally, and even the simplest literature is symbolic in the sense that it is universal, representative, and finally exhibits Man, not merely individual men. But a good deal of Faulkner criticism has to be described as little better than symbol-mongering—and I mean by the term something morbid, excessive, and obsessed, a grotesque parody of anything like an adequate, careful reading. It magnifies details irresponsibly; it feverishly prospects for possible symbols and then forces them beyond the needs of the story. It views the novel not as a responsible context with its own network of interrelations but as a sort of grab bag out of which particular symbols can be drawn.

The symbol-mongers have been busy with Benjy, the idiot of *The Sound and the Fury*. Mrs. Compson, his mother, is a vain and superficial woman who feels it necessary to assert from time to time that her family is as good as that into which she has married. When it becomes plain that her child is condemned to idiocy, she insists upon changing his name from Maury to Benjy, since Maury is a name associated with her family, the Bascombs. Her motive is clear and, granted the nature of the woman, perfectly adequate. But one critic has seen in the name-changing evidence that the Compsons are really superstitious and primitive, since they evidently "assume that names have mysterious powers." [5] The Compson family's trouble, however, is not primitivism but decadence, not irrational belief but lack of belief. Mrs. Compson, for example, would be the better off for Dilsey's simple faith.

Again, because it would be "especially significant in the degradation of the Compsons," [6] another commentator has discovered that Benjy—and the evidence is the flimsiest possible—has committed incest with Caddy, his sister. That this notion completely distorts Caddy's character and her whole relation to her afflicted brother apparently did not seem to be a matter of any importance. Faulkner is concerned to show the degradation of the Compsons, so to discover another bit of degradation—it does not matter what kind—is to help the author along.[7] The "fact" (of incest) has been manufactured out of "symbolic" appropriateness.

Anthropology has been used on occasion to throw startling light upon the Compson family. In *The Golden Bough* we are told that in Burma adulterers kill a pig to atone for their crime and pray that the hills and streams will be healed. Now someone has noted that the Compsons kill a pig for their Christmas dinner, but that they do it without penitence and without expressing any wish for atonement.[8] This is so ingenious that the voice of common sense may seem that of a churlish spoilsport. Yet only one of the Comp-

---

5. Barbara M. Crossman, *"The Sound and the Fury:* The Pattern of Sacrifice," *Arizona Quarterly, 16* (1960), 11.

6. George R. Stewart and Joseph M. Backus, " 'Each in Its Ordered Place': Structure and Narration in Benjy's Section of *The Sound and the Fury,*" *American Literature, 29* (1958), 455 n. Carvel Collins has disposed of this notion in his "Miss Quentin's Paternity Again," *Texas Studies in Language and Literature, 2* (1960), 253–60.

7. Mr. Backus writes that "if Faulkner sought to picture Southern decadence, an incestuous affair between his heroine and her idiot brother provides the finishing touch." See his "Names and Characters in Faulkner's *The Sound and the Fury,*" *Names, 6* (1958), 228–29.

8. Crossman, pp. 12–13.

sons, Uncle Maury, is an adulterer, and Uncle Maury is not a Burmese. Shall there be no more innocent consumption of pork chops and spareribs in Yoknapatawpha County because someone has read *The Golden Bough?*

When Quentin, in his agony over Caddy's having given herself to her lover, proposes killing her and then killing himself, he takes out a knife and holds it to her throat. One critic suggests that Quentin "symbolically" wants to perform a hysterectomy—that is, to remove "the agent [sic] of Caddy's (and the family's) sin." [9] But there is something far-fetched about trying to make Quentin even symbolically a Jack the Ripper, and the suggestion is not rendered any more plausible by the portion of Caddy's anatomy at which Quentin points his knife.

Quentin's section of *The Sound and the Fury* is dated June 2. It has been proposed that perhaps he did not actually drown himself until after midnight, in which case his death would have occurred at an especially appropriate time, for June 3 is the birthday of Jefferson Davis, the president of the Confederacy.[10] The notion would seem to be that Quentin's downfall is somehow tied to the downfall of the Old South. But there is no hint in the novel that Quentin knew that it was the eve of Jefferson Davis' birthday or that he meant to postpone his death until 1:00 A.M. Eastern Standard Time. Faulkner could have saved Quentin the wait by simply assigning his section to June 3 in the first place.

These instances of symbol-hunting are extreme, but they are only a little more absurd than much respectable commentary on Faulkner. Any useful criticism must do more than provide an aimless and mechanical notation of symbols. It must make its account of symbolic events and scenes coherent and responsible by relating the alleged symbols to the total fictional context.

It might be supposed that sociologizing and symbol-mongering are antithetical faults, but they can, and do, occur side by side. Indeed, both aberrations have to be regarded as different ways of evading the central critical task: to determine and evaluate the meaning of the work in the fullness of its depth and amplitude.

9. Earle Labor, in *Explicator, 17* (1959), Item 29.
10. Stewart and Backus, *American Literature, 29,* 453, n. 10.

The excessive literalism which converts the fictional into factual events and thus yields "sociology" is a counterpart of the misguided yearning for universal meanings which produces the perversities of symbol-mongering.

Some knowledge of how life is actually lived (and has been lived) in Mississippi would have prevented the writing of much nonsense. An awareness of how fiction "works" would have helped even more. Faulkner, to be sure, has much to tell us about life in Mississippi and in the South generally. He is indeed concerned with human beings and human values. But his novels are neither case studies nor moral treatises. They are works of art and have to be read as such. It is as works of art that they will be treated in the pages that follow.

2

The Plain People:

YEOMAN FARMERS, SHARECROPPERS,

AND WHITE TRASH

THOUGH THE PLANTER families of the Old South and the Negroes
play a very important part in Faulkner's novels, the folk who
dominate much of his fiction are descendants neither of the old
ruling class nor of the slaves. They are white people, many of
them poor, and most of them living on farms; but they are not
to be put down necessarily as "poor whites" and certainly not
necessarily as "white trash." It is with characters such as these
that the non-Southern reader of Faulkner is likely to have most
trouble. He may too easily conclude that the McCallums and the
Tulls are simply poor white trash. Hasty or unobservant readers
may even see them all as allied to the infamous Snopes clan.

If the reader is likely to misunderstand the social situation of
those people, he has a long tradition of such misunderstanding
behind him. The usual account of the Southern social structure
as it existed just before the Civil War depicted a tripartite division: there were the Negro slaves, of course, and there were the
very wealthy plantation owners, and there were also the poorer
whites, who, according to this account, had been pushed off the
fertile land and back onto the pine barrens or onto the sterile
hills. Here they lived by small farming, the proceeds of which
they eked out with hunting and fishing. They were represented

as being in general a shiftless, illiterate, and often vicious group of people—the stereotyped picture to be found in Frederick L. Olmsted's *Journey in the Back Country* (1863), George M. Weston's *The Poor Whites of the South* (1856), and J. E. Cairnes' *The Slave Power* (1862). This well-established stereotype was a gross oversimplification, as more recent scholarship has made plain. But like other oversimplifications, it has proved perennially attractive and has been kept alive by much popular fiction and drama right down to the present day. Some of the sustaining fiction has been very popular indeed, as witness Erskine Caldwell's *Tobacco Road* and *God's Little Acre* and similar tales sold in paperback volumes in drugstores throughout the land.

It must be conceded that the antics of the shiftless poor white have from the beginning proved irresistible to writers. As early as 1728 one finds William Byrd of Westover describing the lazy woodsfolk who lived along the Virginia–North Carolina border, and they have figured ever since in humorous literature about the South. Augustus Baldwin Longstreet's *Georgia Scenes* (1835) is a typical instance. There is a long tradition in which the poor white figures as a comic character, though it should be said that the humor is not invariably at his expense, nor is he invariably presented as a kind of American Yahoo.

Faulkner was thoroughly alive to the comic possibilities of the type: witness I. O. Snopes, with his malapropisms and his jumbled proverbs, or Clarence Snopes, the state senator, with his cocksure brassiness and his animal cunning. But Faulkner frequently reveals his sympathies with the characters who come of poor-white stock, seeing in them an integrity, dignity, and sense of values which is not at all commensurate with their inadequacies in speaking or writing formal English. Faulkner is also very much aware of the niceties of a social structure which distinguishes the yeoman farmer from the tenant farmer and which sees within the category of the tenant farmer a variety of types ranging from the honest and often shrewd man of poor fortune to the embittered or numbed landless peasant and on to the happy-go-lucky buffoon or the thoroughgoing rogue.

Readers who want to understand Faulkner's treatment of these varying types and who need help in shaking off the inherited clichés would do well to read James Agee's *Let Us Now Praise Famous Men*,[1] a book which registered with considerable impact when it first appeared during the Great Depression and which has been recently reissued. A reviewer last year called it a "literary-sociological classic." In this book Agee writes of the life of the sharecroppers of northern Alabama with whom he sojourned for some weeks. His account is sensitively and intelligently written and often very moving. It must also be said that it is the work of a very angry and somewhat confused young man. Among other things, it manifests a deep sense of guilt, as the writer, from his little peak of relative affluence, looks down onto the lives of these utterly poverty-stricken people. Agee clearly states his fury at intellectuals in general and his lack of confidence in the ability of any literary man or any work of art to portray the terrible truth about human beings. His human sympathy is genuine, and at its best his prose rises to a kind of poetry.

In spite of its subjective bias, Agee's book can serve as a very useful makeweight for the reader who is tempted to dismiss the essential humanity of the poor white by reducing him to the usual stereotype. It can also be helpful in holding a kind of balance between the poor white's virtues and vices. It is an honest book. The sharecroppers of whom Agee writes so sympathetically are often, he has to admit, cruel to their livestock and other animals, and are wretchedly callous toward the Negroes. Even so, they are men, with essential dignity and worth, and their plight joins them to the company of all suffering humanity.

The social structure of the South has always been more fluid than outsiders suppose. One needs to recall that the President of the Southern Confederacy, Jefferson Davis, was, like Abraham Lincoln, born in a log cabin—indeed, born in a Kentucky log cabin not a hundred miles away from the birthplace of the President of the Union. When the Davises moved to the new country that was opening up around Natchez, Mississippi, plantation country with rich loess soil, the family prospered, and by 1861 young Davis had become a wealthy plantation owner and a United States

1. Boston, 1941.

senator. Some of the newly rich were looked down upon by the older Virginia and low-country South Carolina families, and Mrs. Jefferson Davis, when she became the president's wife, was sometimes referred to as "that coarse western woman." But the social system was, on the whole, fluid. People did move up and down the social scale, and, between the great plantation owners with many slaves and the landless poor white, there were great numbers of people representing almost every possible intermediate gradation. There were landowners who had a small number of slaves, others who owned only one or two slaves and worked in the fields beside them, and still other farmers who had no slaves, but did have considerable holdings in land and livestock. Lowest of all were the landless people, and yet many of these owned quantities of livestock and lived well. In brief, as the late Frank L. Owsley has shown in his *Plain Folk of the Old South*,[2] more and more people in the South were acquiring land right up to the very onset of the Civil War. He quite overturns the hitherto accepted view that the great plantation owners were getting more and more of the land and, as a consequence, the poor whites were being forced off the land. Owsley's study of church records, wills, county tax books, inventories of estates, deed books, and manuscript returns of the federal censuses are decisive on this point. As he sums up: "the core of the social structure [of the Old South] was a massive body of the plain folk who were neither rich nor very poor. These were employed in numerous occupations; but the great majority secured their food, clothing, and shelter from some rural pursuit, chiefly farming and livestock grazing."

Faulkner is writing fiction, not sociology or history, and he has employed all the devices for the heightening, special focus, and, in some instances, distortion that fiction demands and justifies. Still, the picture of the yeoman farmer and the poor white that emerges is perfectly consonant with the findings recorded in Owsley's study.

Faulkner's story "Shingles For the Lord" furnishes a particularly useful illustration of his treatment of the poor whites, if for no other reason than that it constitutes something of a balance

2. Baton Rouge, Louisiana State University Press, 1949.

for his more somber accounts of the poor white. Several of the characters in this story are also to be met with in *As I Lay Dying*. The Reverend Mr. Whitfield, who is Addie's lover in that novel, is here seen as the natural leader of his congregation and a man of some force and dignity. Other characters from the book—such people as Vernon Tull, Henry Armstid, Homer Bookwright, and Solon Quick—also appear in the story.

These people, along with the Griers—the little Grier boy tells the story—are hard-working farmers and small farmers at that. But they have dignity and self-respect, and though the action of the story has to do with reshingling the rural church, these farmers exhibit something more than ignorant and perverted religiosity. They are certainly not sanctimonious. Their relish of a good trade and the enjoyment they derive from driving a sharp bargain are clearly evident.

Actually, religion itself is seen in a genial light in this story. The characters are members of a congregation of Southern Baptists. When Res Grier, in trying to outwit one of his neighbors in a trade over a dog, manages—by accident—to set the church on fire, the happening gives Faulkner an opportunity for some of his best description in the tall-tale manner and for some of his most discerning commentary on human nature. But the occasion also gives him an opportunity to present Southern Protestantism not merely as a baleful and oppressive force but as a stable religion that has its own power and dignity.

The Reverend Mr. Whitfield keeps in the church, hanging on a special nail, an old long nightshirt which he wears when he conducts a baptizing, and the little boy who is telling the story remarks that "to a boy of ten it wasn't jest a cloth garment or even a iron armor; it was the old strong Archangel Michael his self, that had fit and strove and conquered sin for so long that it finally had the same contempt for the human beings that returned always to sin as hogs and dogs done that the old strong archangel his self must have had" (p. 40).

So the boy watches it "hanging there among the fire," reluctant to burn as if it had "knowed in its time too much water to burn easy, but like it had strove and fit with the devil and all the hosts of hell too long to burn in jest a fire that Res Grier started" (p. 40), until finally it does burst into flame and goes "kind of roaring on up and out against the stars."

The more humanly humorous view of the rural community, friendly and relaxed and firmly supported by its religious underpinning, does not of course cancel out other views of the same community as given in certain other works. There is no real reason why the Reverend Mr. Whitfield, seen here in his dignity and robust fervor, should not be the same man who, in a moment of weakness, became Addie Bundren's lover. Nor need one necessarily conclude that the little church depicted in "Shingles for the Lord" is not precisely the same sort of church at which Charles Mallison glowers because, as he remarks in *The Town*, it is composed of "incorrigible nonconformists, nonconformists not just to everybody else but to each other in mutual accord; a nonconformism defended and preserved by descendants whose ancestors hadn't quitted home and security for a wilderness in which to find freedom of thought as they claimed and oh yes, believed, but to find freedom in which to be incorrigible and unreconstructible Baptists and Methodists; not to escape from tyranny as they claimed and believed, but to establish one" (p. 307).[3]

The Mansion provides an account of people of this sort in the 1940s and in an urban setting by giving us the story of Mink Snopes' brief sojourn with the congregation of the Reverend J. C. Goodyhay. (Is his name a corruption of "Cudahy"?) The time is 1946. Goodyhay, who had been a Marine sergeant in the Pacific theater, is now building a church. The place where he lives, because of the piled second-hand materials which he has assembled to build the church, looks like a junkyard. When Mink comes up to Goodyhay's house, he finds himself looking at the mailbox, which is a kind of "metal hutch with the words *Bro J C Goodyhay* not stencilled but painted on it, not sloven nor careless but impatiently, with a sort of savage impatience." Goodyhay's wife, as one of his followers tells Mink, has recently run off "with a sonabitching Four-F potato-chip salesman before he even got back from fighting in the Pacific" (p. 267). His house has "an

3. See below, Notes, p. 369.

air of violent transience similar to the indiscriminate jumble of walls and windows and doors among which he and the other man worked: merely still nailed together and so standing upright" (p. 269). Just before bedtime, he has Mink kneel down with him "on the kitchen floor beneath the hard dim glare of the single unshaded low-watt bulb on a ceiling cord" (p. 271). Goodyhay is on his knees but "his head [is] up, the coldly seething desert-hermit's eyes not even closed" as he says "Save us, Christ, the poor sons of bitches" (p. 271).

In the short time that Mink stays at Goodyhay's, he attends one of his services and watches the congregation assemble. They come up to the little unpainted "box of a building" in five or six stained and battered cars and pick-up trucks. They are mostly men and women about the age of Goodyhay or a little younger. Among them is a big Negro woman—"a woman no longer young, who looked at the same time gaunt yet fat too" (p. 277). Mink inquires whether they "take niggers too" and is told: "We do this one. . . . Her son had it too just like she was a white woman, even if they didn't put his name on the same side of the monument with the others" (p. 277). (If this seems implausibly liberal—and the case, it must be granted, is special—I can testify that such cases do occur from time to time. I remember hearing, as a boy in 1915, a white man teased for regularly attending a Negro Holy-Roller meeting. His reply was that he had rather go to heaven with a lot of niggers than to hell with a lot of white folks.)

Goodyhay's sermon insists on the search for God. Man cannot simply wait for salvation. He must get up on his feet and hunt it, and if he cannot find it, then, Goodyhay exhorts his congregation, "by God make it. Make a salvation He will pass and then earn the right to grab it." But most of his sermon is simply the telling of a story—the story of something that had happened to him during the war. Goodyhay had experienced a meeting with Christ, a Christ who looked "like any other shavetail just out of a foxhole, maybe a little older, except he didn't have a hat, bucket: just standing there bare-headed . . . smoking a cigarette" (p. 280). The experience had transformed Goodyhay: it had worked a miraculous change in which a terrified man had found himself doing things which moments before lay beyond his powers.

The poor whites' religion in this shift to recent times has not changed at all. It embodies the same account of man and of his relation to God that has dominated this segment of society for two hundred years. It is highly personal. It emphasizes the will. It is finally a religion of the Holy Ghost in which power is communicated directly to men without any mediation of the sacraments and which calls for an answering response and resolve on the part of the sinner. But Goodyhay's is presumably no longer a Southern Baptist church; one supposes that it is a small Holiness group. It is partially urbanized, with battered and stained cars and pick-up trucks in place of the buggies and wagons that one would have seen forty years earlier. The poor whites too have seen something of the world and now they work in the small towns along the highways rather than on the farms in the hills. But the folkways and the basic folk character continue without very much change.

In this connection, it might be worth adding that Mink apparently observes the service with curiosity and some interest but without in the least becoming converted. Religion for him, as well as for most of these people, is a highly individual thing: Mink had already received his personal vindication and has his own peculiar faith. All he is really concerned with here is that Brother Goodyhay will make good on his promise to raise the ten dollars that he needs to get on to Memphis to buy the gun. But the side glance at this queer service which Faulkner gives us here has its importance for the novel: in many respects Mink is out of date in this world; yet some aspects of the culture in which he was bred are scarcely changed. Brother Whitfield would doubtless have had his differences with Brother Goodyhay, but he would have felt completely at home in the service.

The characters portrayed in *Light in August* are largely of poor-white stock. The Negroes figure in it only incidentally, and there are only casual references to some of the old aristocratic families of Jefferson. The Reverend Gail Hightower is the only real exception: he had gone to college and seminary and counts in this community as a learned man. But Hightower has been defrocked and, in effect, declassed. All the other characters in *Light in August* come from a different stratum of society. The mother of Joe Christmas is a poor girl. Lena Grove is an orphan, living with her brother who works in a small sawmill town. Her social position and her social aspirations are nicely reflected in her cogitations on her entertainment at the Armstid's. She says to herself: "I et polite . . . Like a lady I et. Like a lady travelling" (p. 23).

In her traveling, Lena walks barefooted, because it is more comfortable and to save her shoes. (So does Dewey Dell Bundren in *As I Lay Dying*. When the wagon approaches town, she gets out of it and puts on her shoes so that she can make a proper entrance.) Readers of Walter Scott will remember that Jeanie Deans, the heroine of *The Heart of Midlothian*, acts in exactly the same way. On her celebrated walk from Scotland to London she carefully ties up her shoes in a little bundle, saving them for town appearances, and preferring to make the actual journey barefoot.

One should note also that Mrs. Armstid (at whose house Lena spends the night), though she befriends Lena, looks at her swollen figure with obvious disapproval. The reader is not to conclude, as a casual perusal of Erskine Caldwell might suggest, that people of Lena's and Mrs. Armstid's class are lax and easygoing with regard to fornication. Young unmarried women might become pregnant, especially if they were poor and lived in a day in which contraceptives were less easily come by, but there is a strong Puritan tinge to these Southern farmer folk. Even the wild young men and the too-easygoing young women have behind them a stern moral tradition from which they have lapsed or against which they are in conscious revolt.

This Puritan tradition is represented in positive form by Byron Bunch, the man who falls in love with Lena and tries to act as her protector. Byron is a methodical man. When the other workmen at the sawmill head for town on Saturday afternoons in their Sunday clothes and neckties, Byron prefers to keep at work loading the finished boards into the freight cars. When Lena comes inquiring about her "husband," he checks the time by his huge silver watch to make sure that he knows how much to deduct from the working time for which his employer will pay him. Every Sunday, Byron leads the choir in a country church some thirty miles away, and one supposes that he is at least a deacon in the church.

A common denominator of the poor whites throughout Faulkner's work is that they are indeed poor. The South as a whole was wretchedly poor, upper classes as well as lower classes, right on from the Civil War period until the Second World War. The economy of the whole region was basically a colonial economy, manipulated from the outside. Even the so-called aristocracy, as Faulkner depicts them, had little wealth. The Compsons, for example, in 1909 had to sell land in order to send Quentin to Harvard, and in 1928 they are obviously in rather straitened circumstances, living in genteel poverty. But it is not lack of money as such that determines either character or social position among these people. This generalization holds for the plain people as well as the aristocrats. Anse Bundren is a shiftless, fatuous, and grotesquely selfish man, but it is his fecklessness and laziness that determine his relation to his neighbors, not his poverty as such. In any case, his neighbors, the Tulls and the Bookwrights, are not notably richer than he, though they are thrifty and provident.

Faulkner, it is true, does give us instances of the direst poverty. There is Mink Snopes, who has the greatest difficulty in buying buckshot shells with which to shoot his enemy, Houston, and who works at the rate of fifty cents a day—the year is 1908—in order to redeem his cow. But again, sheer poverty is not the determining factor in Mink's attitudes. There are other Faulkner characters as poor as Mink whose attitudes and behavior are very different from his.

One judges that the McCallums have very little in the way of ready money. They do have a great deal of independence, however. Presumably they own their own land and live with dignity and contentment. *Sartoris* provides a nice instance of the relation between yeoman whites of this sort and members of the older aristocracy like the Sartorises. When Bayard Sartoris goes out to visit the McCallums, he does so without condescension and is received with anything but servility. It is not even a case of each family knowing its place and being careful not to presume or to condescend. The relation is easy, natural, unself-conscious. If it occurred to either side to state a difference, it would probably be put in terms of living in town and living in the country. But the relationship between the yeoman white and the plantation owner is quite different in *Absalom, Absalom!* There Wash defers to, waits upon, and has a naïve admiration for Thomas Sutpen. Wash, however, is a poor white of rather different cut from the McCallums. He is a grosser man and a man with far less breeding or sense of family. And Sutpen himself comes originally from Wash's own kind of stock. Sutpen has force of character and he has wealth, or had wealth before the Civil War. Part of Wash's admiration for him is that another poor boy should have gone so far. Even so, Wash has his own independence and his own pride, and when Sutpen reveals his essential contempt for other human beings by refusing to provide even a decent bed for Milly, Wash raises the rusty scythe and cuts his erstwhile hero down.

The Unvanquished throws additional light on the relation of the squirearchy or aristocracy to the poor whites in the case of the hill man whom Colonel Sartoris shot. Bayard tells us that his father had thought that the man was trying to rob him, or that perhaps his father had been simply too quick to shoot. The man whom he killed had a wife and several children in a dirt-floored cabin back in the hills, and the next day Colonel Sartoris sent some money to the widow. Bayard remembers how she walked into the Sartoris dining room and flung the money in the Colonel's face. His is an obvious instance of condescension—though Colonel Sartoris, with his arrogance, is a rather special case—and the woman's action reflects the fierce independence of the humbler person who will not be condescended to. But there are subtler relationships displayed in this same novel. There is George Wyatt, who had served in the Colonel's troop during the Civil War and who meets Bayard Sartoris when he comes home at his father's death. Trying to befriend the boy, he offers to face the assassin himself in Bayard's place, though he expects to be refused and is refused. One Faulkner commentator has been so unwary as to refer to Wyatt and his friends as the "gentlemen" who expect Bayard to avenge his father. But George, as his loose and easy grammar hints, is not a gentleman in this sense. He is a good friend of the Colonel's and he is certainly no toady who grovels before his powerful friend, but George Wyatt would not presume to be the Colonel's social equal. On the other hand, one should add that George Wyatt would never allow anyone else to hint that he was not the Colonel's peer.

One of Faulkner's less effective stories, that entitled "Shall Not Perish," does at least put this matter—the relationship between the poor yeoman farmer and the wealthy townsman—with nicety and conviction. The story has to do with the Griers, who have lost a son in the Second World War. Mrs. Grier, hearing that Major De Spain has also lost his son, comes into town to comfort the stricken man. His grief makes him bitter and even rude to her. He asks the woman, "What do you want?" But she can answer, proudly and emphatically, "Nothing," and can go on to say: "We had nothing to bring you. And I don't think I see anything here"—though the litle boy who tells the story describes it as "a rich man's parlor"—"we would want to take away" (p. 107).

A common grief brings the woman to the man who has never called upon her and on whom she would never, in ordinary circumstances, think of calling. And a common tradition and a common community of feeling allows her to give him the comfort and advice that she knows he needs. In the end Major De Spain, touched and comforted, proposes to have his chauffeur drive Mrs. Grier back to Frenchman's Bend, but her reply is characteristic: "We came in Mr. Quick's bus. He comes in every Saturday." And when Major De Spain presses his offer, she thanks him but replies firmly, "We have already paid Mr. Quick. He owes us the ride back home" (p. 110).

The barrier of poverty can be a very real one, however, and a painful one. One of the most poignant instances occurs in *As I Lay Dying*. When Vardaman, the little boy, finds that the family is going to ride to Jefferson, the following play of thought goes through his mind:

Dewey Dell said we will get some bananas. The train [he is thinking of the toy train of which he has heard] is behind the glass, red on the track. When it runs the track shines on and off. Pa said flour and sugar and coffee costs so much. Because I am a country boy because boys in town. Bicycles. Why do flour and sugar and coffee cost so much when he is a country boy. "Wouldn't you ruther have some bananas instead?" Bananas are gone, eaten. Gone. When it runs on the track shines again. "Why ain't I a town boy, pa?" I said God made me. I did not said to God to made me in the country. If He can make the train, why can't He make them all in the town because flour and sugar and coffee.   [p. 385]

It is interesting, in this general connection, to consider the attitude of the Negro toward the poor whites and the poor whites' toward the Negro. On the part of the poor white there may be hostility and resentment of the sort that James Agee found among his Alabama tenant farmers. In Beat Four of Yoknapatawpha County, the upland hill section inhabited by such families as the Workitts and the Gowries, there are no Negroes to be found. Historically, this was never plantation country, and the white folk in Beat Four do not want Negroes around. But one must not make a hasty generalization: the relations between yeoman whites and Negroes may be amiable and friendly. Faulkner's stories and novels will yield plenty of examples.

On the part of the Negro, the attitude toward the poor white may be one of contempt—contempt for, among other things, an affected but baseless pretension to superiority. Lucas Beauchamp, with his pride in his descent from old Carothers McCaslin, is exceptional, perhaps too much so to support generalizations about the Negro. Yet his attitude toward the poorer whites is interesting and has its significance. In "The Fire and the Hearth" there is a nice example in Lucas' conduct toward the salesman from Memphis who hopes to sell him the money-finding machine. The white salesman is brash and brusque in his dealings with the old Negro. Lucas, on his part, is elaborately formal and quietly contemptuous. To the white sheriff, "Lucas was just another nigger and both the sheriff and Lucas knew it, although only one of them knew that to Lucas the sheriff was a redneck without any reason for pride in his forbears nor hope for it in his descendants" (p. 43). As for the machine salesman, Lucas—seeing his son-in-law George and the salesman squatting in the shade of a tree, "squatting on their heels without any other support"—thinks, "He mought talk like a city man and he mought even think he is one. But I know now where he was born at" (p. 80). Lucas knows how far he can go in his contempt toward the salesman and takes care never to go quite over the line, but in a short time Lucas has the situation completely under control.

Lee Goodwin, the bootlegger in *Sanctuary*, and Ruby, his common-law wife, are not altogether typical of the poor white class. The pair are not only poor; they are consciously outlaws, the woman no less than the man. Ruby, in her passionate devotion to her man, is perfectly willing to prostitute herself in order to raise money to help him. (Mink Snopes' wife in *The Hamlet* shows the same willingness.) But we must be cautious about generalizing from the case of the Goodwins. Lee Goodwin's ties with society have been cut so completely that he despairs of any help from society and is suspicious of the intentions even of his lawyer, Horace Benbow. Ruby is so certain that men do not act out of disinterested motives that she offers her body to Horace— to his shock and disgust—in order to pay for his services to her man. Such people exist, and Goodwin and Ruby give some sort of indication of the Southern rural underworld. (One gets another glimpse of it in the Bobbie episode in *Light in August*.) But the great majority of Faulkner's poor whites are members of a community and, according to their own lights, law-abiding.

This is true even of the Gowries in *Intruder in the Dust*. Though Crawford Gowrie is guilty of fratricide and hides his brother Vinson's body in the quicksand, the Gowries are not outlaws. They have their code of values, their sense of community, and their religion—embodied physically in the little frame church back in the hills which made such an impression upon Charles Mallison. He remembers it as

a plank steepleless box no longer than some of the one-room cabins hill people lived in, paintless too yet (curiously) not shabby and not even in neglect or disrepair because he could see where sections of raw new lumber and scraps and fragments of synthetic roofing had been patched and carpentered into the old walls and shingles with a savage almost insolent promptitude, not squatting nor crouching nor even sitting but standing among the trunks of the high strong constant shaggy pines, solitary but not forlorn, intractable and independent, asking nothing of any, making compromise with none and he remembered the tall slender spires which said Peace and the squatter utilitarian belfries which said Repent and he remembered one which even said Beware but this one said simply: Burn. [p. 157]

The church beautifully symbolizes the quality of the worshipers.

The society to which those worshipers belong is a society which —for all its essential Puritanism—does not frown too hard on certain faults. Whisky-making and bootlegging will go on, and crimes of passion and violence will be committed. But Crawford Gowrie's crime strikes at the very roots of any society, and this particular society, with its powerful clannishness, will regard fratricide with a peculiar horror.

Such is Faulkner's Beat Four. The settlement of Frenchman's Bend, where the events recorded in *The Hamlet* take place, is not noticeably different. Here is Faulkner's description of the people who settled Frenchman's Bend:

[They] came from the northeast, through the Tennessee mountains by stages marked by the bearing and raising of a generation of children. They came from the Atlantic seaboard and before that, from England and the Scottish and Welsh Marches, as some of the names would indicate—Turpin and Haley and Whittington, McCallum and Murray and Leonard and Littlejohn, and other names like Riddup and Armstid and Doshey which could have come from nowhere since certainly no man would deliberately select one of them for his own. They brought no slaves and no Phyfe and Chippendale highboys; indeed, what they did bring most of them could (and did) carry in their hands. They took up land and built one- and two-room cabins and never painted them, and married one another and produced children and added other rooms one by one to the original cabins and did not paint them either, but that was all. Their descendants still planted cotton in the bottom land and corn along the edge of the hills and in the secret coves in the hills made whiskey of the corn and sold what they did not drink. Federal officers went into the country and vanished. Some garment which the missing man had worn might be seen—a felt hat, a broadcloth coat, a pair of city shoes or even his pistol—on a child or an old man or woman. County officers did not bother them at all save in the heel of election years. They supported their own churches and schools, they married and committed infrequent adulteries and more frequent homicides among themselves and were their own courts, judges and executioners. They were Protestants and Democrats and prolific; there was not one Negro landowner in the entire section. Strange Negroes would absolutely refuse to pass through it after dark.

[pp. 4–5]

Perhaps the most difficult of the characters to place in the general social scheme are the Varners. The Varners are people of some wealth, but without breeding or gentility. Old Mr. Varner is a power in his part of the country and Mrs. Varner dominates the local church. In *The Hamlet* Faulkner describes Will Varner as "a farmer, a usurer, a veterinarian." (Judge Benbow, paraphrasing a line from Byron's *Don Juan*, remarks of Varner that "a milder-mannered man never bled a mule or stuffed a ballot box.") He "was shrewd secret and merry, of a Rabelaisian turn of mind and very probably still sexually lusty" (p. 5), though he is now sixty years old. Faulkner regards Will Varner somewhat indulgently, though he makes it very plain that he is coarse of mind and coarse of moral fiber. He is, indeed, a usurer, a man who reaps where he has not sown, and the Varners, Will and his son Jody, become involved with the Snopeses, to their loss, only because they try to get the better of them. Jody planned to allow Ab Snopes to sharecrop on the Varners' land until just before harvest time, when they would run him off and get his part of the crop by letting him know that they were aware of his past. Snopes had once been involved in burning a barn, and Jody is sure that a charge of arson will frighten him into leaving quickly.

With the Varners there is no fastidiousness of morals or manners. In *The Hamlet* the reaction of Will Varner and Mrs. Varner to the knowledge of Eula's pregnancy is treated in comic fashion. Though Jody, the son, wants to take violent action to avenge the family honor, his father is too practical to countenance such a vainly quixotic exhibition and finds a simpler solution by arranging for a husband who can be the presumptive father of Eula's child. As for Mrs. Varner, her immediate reaction to the news of Eula's pregnancy is one of fury—at being waked from her nap. With her "ordinarily cheerful opinionated face suffused and irate," she gasps out: "Hold him till I get a stick of stove wood. . . . I'll fix him. I'll fix both of them. [Eula] Turning up pregnant and [Jody] yelling and cursing here in the house when I am trying to take a nap!" (p. 144). This is admirable exaggeration of the sort that fits the atmosphere of *The Hamlet*. So conceived, the Varners are comic types, larger than life, not so much realistic portraits as caricatures.

Many years later, when Faulkner returned to the story of the Varners and the Snopeses in *The Town* and *The Mansion*, the quality of the comedy changed and the focus upon many of the characters, including the Varners, changed also. In the last two novels of the trilogy, Will Varner is much sharper in his hatred of his son-in-law, Flem Snopes. One could argue that things have occurred between him and Flem to make him hate Flem with greater intensity. But Faulkner has also doubtless remodeled his notion of the character: Will is now less merry, less Rabelaisian, more responsible, and more vindictive. The character of Mrs. Varner has been altered even more radically. In *The Town* (p. 276) she is not the woman of "cheerful opinionated face"; she is called "grim," and though she is not herself "church-ridden," she runs "the local church she belonged to with the cold high-handedness of a ward-boss." True, Gavin Stevens (p. 294) imagines Mrs.

Varner telling her husband that Flem has finally caught Eula in adultery and that he must hurry into town to stop Flem from filing a suit for divorce, saying to her husband: "We had enough trouble with Eula twenty years ago. I aint going to have her back in my house worrying me now." This last remark would be reminiscent of the character that we shall meet with in *The Hamlet*. But the Varners in *The Town* and *The Mansion* have, on the whole, less comic extravagance and more of the grim intensity of characters realistically conceived.

Yet in spite of the changes Faulkner has made in his conception of the Varners' characters, their social position is not really altered. They represent plain people of vigor and force, somewhat coarse of fiber and with no aspirations toward "society." They have managed by shrewdness and some chicanery to amass money with which to live comfortably. They are the only family in the Frenchman's Bend community who have Negro servants, and indeed almost all the Negroes in that part of the county work for the Varners. But the Varners do not move into town. Their felicity is not disturbed by social ambition. They are content to live comfortably in their own bailiwick.

In the older South the planter ideal was very important. A Mississippian like General Bedford Forrest, though himself a poor boy, uneducated and almost illiterate, was careful, as his own fortunes improved, to see that his younger brothers were educated as gentlemen. But this kind of ambition hardly touches the Varners.

The finest of Faulkner's characters of yeoman stock is of course Ratliff, the sewing-machine agent. In *The Town*, as a kind of romantic afterthought, Faulkner discloses that Ratliff's initials, V. K., stand not for something like "Victor Knight" or "Vincent Knapp" but for "Vladimir Kyrilytch." It seems that an ancestor of Ratliff's by this name had gone into the British army, and during the American Revolution was captured at Saratoga. Sent to Virginia, he escaped and met a Virginia girl who hid and fed him and finally married him. Her family name (which her husband adopted as his own) was originally Ratcliffe, but was finally reduced to Ratliff, because they forgot the original spelling and "just spelled it like it sounds." One son in the family has always been named Vladimir Kyrilytch though it is not made clear how they always remembered to spell correctly a name so much more difficult than Ratcliffe.

The account is pleasant enough, and one understands why Faulkner, himself an incorrigible romantic, wanted to have it so. But as far at Ratliff's relation to society, one must say that in eight or ten generations the Russian blood must have run fairly thin. Intermarriages would have been heavily Anglo-Saxon in Virginia, and later, in Mississippi. At any rate, Ratliff, insofar as background and stock are concerned, represents the plain people of the South. Insofar as curiosity, intelligence, sensitivity, good sense, and good humor are concerned, Ratliff is an individual, and an exceptional individual at that. He is sufficiently the individual to make his own shirts. This matter is rather easily accounted for, since he sells sewing machines and recounts to a friend that "the first thing I knowed I could run one too." But there is nothing effeminate about the robust bachelor. He is perfectly easy in his world, but he also stands a little outside it and a little above it. He is the detached sage of the folk society, which he knows, expresses, and yet judges. Ratliff is wise in his own right, but his wisdom is tinctured with the values of the Southern folk society whose intelligence and conscience he is.[4]

4. For further comment on the plain people of the South see below, Notes, p. 370.

3

Faulkner as Nature Poet

YEARS AGO, Malcolm Cowley called attention to Faulkner's "brooding love for the land where he was born and reared," [1] including the physical land as seen in all seasons and weathers. Indeed, he wrote, "No other American writer takes such delight in the weather." The observation is thoroughly just, as the sheaf of phrases which Cowley appended by way of illustration makes clear: "the hot still pinewiney silence of the August afternoon," "the moonless September dusk, the trees along the road not rising soaring as trees should but squatting like huge fowl," "the tranquil sunset of October mazy with windless wood-smoke," the "slow drizzle of November rain just above the ice point," and "those windless Mississippi December days which are a sort of Indian summer's Indian summer" (pp. 19–20).

This sensitive apprehension of the natural scene is everywhere in Faulkner's work. Here is a similar sheaf culled from *The Hamlet:* "the pollen-wroiled chiaroscuro of spring," "a gray day, of the color and texture of iron, one of those gray days of a plastic rigidity too dead to make or release snow," the "sun drew shadows on the frozen ground," "night-time roads across the mooned or unmooned sleeping land, the mare's feet like silk in the dust," and "the ordered stars seemed to glare down in cold and lidless amazement at an earth being drowned in dust."

1. *The Portable Faulkner* (New York, Viking Press, 1946).

In Faulkner's novels and stories nature is sometimes merely background, and attains its prominence in his work simply because so much of his work has its setting in the countryside. But nature is often much more than mere background and one can point to a number of functions that it performs.

Nature frequently reflects, and may even generate, a mood in man. In *As I Lay Dying* Addie Bundren finds her own sense of terror and loneliness mirrored in the landscape. Addie tells us (p. 466) that as she lay beside her husband she could hear "the dark land talking of God's love and His beauty and His sin; hearing the dark voicelessness in which the words are the deeds." In the same meditation the blood pulsing in her veins seems to her like "the red bitter flood boiling through the land." Addie is clearly projecting her own feelings upon the landscape, but Dr. Peabody (p. 369) suggests that it is the land which creates such feelings within the human being. Watching Vardaman sitting on the top step, "looking smaller than ever in the sulphur-coloured light," he thinks: "That's the one trouble with this country: everything, weather, all, hangs on too long. Like our rivers, our land: opaque, slow, violent; shaping and creating the life of man in its implacable and brooding image." In the story "Dry September" it is a moot question whether it is the weather which actually provokes the men to carry out a lynching, or whether the "bloody September twilight, aftermath of sixty-two rainless days," which had "gone like a fire in dry grass" (p. 169), simply reflects the agonized frustration of the men who drag out and kill Will Mayes. One of his murderers is seen at the end of the story ripping his shirt off his maddened body, "sweating again already," stooping to pick up his shirt to wipe the sweat off his body once more and standing "with his body pressed against the dusty screen . . . panting. There was no movement, no sound, not even an insect. The dark world seemed to lie stricken beneath the cold moon and the lidless stars" (p. 183).

But the reflection in the landscape of the individual's consciousness need not be violent. Here is the way the world looks to the placid Lena Grove as she stands by the road and listens to the approaching wagon, its clatter distantly reaching her through the "hot still pinewiney silence of the August afternoon." As the wagon comes along "like a shabby bead upon the mild red string of road," it moves so slowly that "in the watching of it the eye loses it as sight and sense drowsily merge and blend, like the road itself, with all the peaceful and monotonous changes between darkness and day, like already measured thread being rewound onto a spool" (p. 7). The author, supplying the vocabulary that the inarticulate Lena lacks, describes the way the approaching wagon might have appeared to some half-tranced observer: "So that at last, as though out of some trivial and unimportant region beyond even distance, the sound of it seems to come slow and terrific and without meaning, as though it were a ghost travelling a half mile ahead of its own shape" (p. 7).

Faulkner frequently uses nature not to reflect man's moods but to stand in sharp contrast to them. In *Sartoris,* for example, the somnolent Mississippi scene everywhere contrasts with the restlessness of the young aviator, home from the war. And in the opening scene of *Sanctuary* the world of leaf and bird song and flowing water points up by contrast the mechanical sleaziness of Popeye. "Delta Autumn" takes the contrast further still: nature is not only set over against man's restless violence; it becomes a judgment on that impious violence. Man's exploitation of the bottom lands of the Delta in this story is by no means treated as man's triumph over the "impenetrable jungle of water-standing cane and cypress, gum and holly and oak and ash," or a bringing of light and civilization to the Tallahatchie and the Sunflower, the "thick, slow, black, unsunned streams almost without current," which unite to become the Yazoo, "the River of the Dead of the Choctaws" (p. 340). For Faulkner's Uncle Ike the wilderness has been violated, the dark rich land has been looted. In place of its power and mystery there is now simply the meaningless litter of civilization: neon signs and shining this-year's automobiles and broad plumb-ruled highways and buildings constructed of sheet iron. The richness of the Delta has tempted men and they have proceeded to violate and exploit it, but as the outraged old hunter

31

says in this story: "The woods and fields [man] ravages and the game he devastates will be the consequence and signature of his crime and guilt, and his punishment" (p. 349).

This note is struck early in Faulkner's work. In 1925 he wrote: "The beauty—spiritual and physical—of the South lies in the fact that God has done so much for it and man so little." [2] Sometimes this note modulates toward a Wordsworthian lament for what man has done to man as well as what he has done to nature. Critics have been tempted to generalize such anguished perceptions into a philosophy of primitivism, a philosophy in which nature becomes the source of man's values and the norm by which man's actions are judged. But Faulkner's alleged primitivism deserves a closer look. He is certainly no simple follower of Rousseau, and if his villains are indeed all of them men who have in some sense denied nature, the converse is not necessarily true. The Faulknerian hero does much more than follow his natural impulses: he achieves his virtue by disciplined effort and difficult choice.

Though one ought to be chary of saying that Faulkner worships nature, his love for it is certainly powerful and deep-seated, and on occasion it rises up into great rhapsodic hymns that celebrate the power and continuity of nature, finally changeless through all its apparent changes. Thus when Isaac McCaslin, in the last section of "The Bear," visits the graves of Lion and of Sam Fathers, he has a vision of the boundless vitality of nature, a vitality that renders death unimportant and meaningless. The place across which he walks is not the abode of the dead, "because there was no death, not Lion and not Sam: not held fast in earth but free in earth and not in earth but of earth, myriad yet undiffused" (p. 328). The life which flourished in the great dog and in the old man has simply merged itself with the fountain of life; the drop has been swallowed up in the great heaving ocean of being.

Perhaps the most elaborately lyrical of all such passages in Faulkner, however, are those which have to do with the idiot and the cow in *The Hamlet*. As Faulkner describes the springtime scenes in which the idiot follows the cow over the hills, the cow

2. "Verse Old and Nascent" (April 1925), printed in *Salmagundi* (Milwaukee, 1932), p. 37.

becomes a kind of animal goddess. Like the cow-headed Egyptian divinity, Hathor, she is a principle of fertility, feminine and calmly joyous, and, as Faulkner describes her, she seems to be almost an exhalation of the natural scene. Faulkner's mode of presentation is very subtle. He has the idiot smell her before he can see her: "the whole mist reeked with her; the same malleate hands of mist which drew along his prone drenched flanks played her pearled barrel too and shaped them both somewhere in immediate time, already married" (p. 167). The idiot represents man so thoroughly merged into nature that he almost lacks consciousness, and becomes not much more than a stance of mindless adoration and worship—though it must be said that the idiot still has enough of the man in him to be able to care for, protect, and even sacrifice himself for the loved one.

Faulkner has not made the mistake, however, of overspecifying the divinity of Ike's goddess, or formalizing Ike's relation to her. The cow radiates her divinity as a kind of nimbus, just as her very form, in the idiot's rapt gaze, is sensed as a kind of evocation through the dawn mist by the creek's side. For the reader, too, she becomes a creature of the dawn light. Our senses are lulled and almost surfeited by the play of the sun upon the burgeoning earth through "the gradation from gray through primrose to the morning's ultimate gold" (p. 167).

The emphasis upon light transforms the ordinary world that we know: here we are made to see (as with the idiot's eyes) a radiant world which is like some Eden, "serene and one and indivisible in joy." The idiot discovers that dawn is not "decanted onto earth from the sky, but instead is from the earth itself suspired." The light makes itself felt as a kind of lambency exhaled from the stable earth: "it wakes, up-seeping, attritive in uncountable creeping channels: first, root; then frond by frond, from whose escaping tips like gas it rises and disseminates and stains the sleep-fast earth with drowsy insect-murmur; then, still upward-seeking, creeps the knitted bark of trunk and limb where, suddenly louder leaf by leaf and dispersive in diffusive sudden speed, melodious with the winged and jeweled throats, it upward bursts and fills night's globed negation with jonquil thunder" (p. 184). (Surely

Faulkner is remembering here "the dawn comes up like thunder outer China 'crost the Bay," but he has turned Kipling's rhetorical trumpery into poetry.)

The theme of powers surging up out of the earth is repeated, a few paragraphs later, with a description of the spring that the idiot has discovered: it is "a brown creep of moisture in a clump of alder and beech, sunless, which wandered away without motion among the unsunned roots of other alders and willows. He cleaned it out and scooped a basin for it, which now at each return of light stood full and clear and leaf by leaf repeating until [he and the cow] lean and interrupt the green reflections and with their own drinking faces break each's mirroring, each face to its own shattered image wedded and annealed" (pp. 185–86).

Faulkner's only direct allusion to the cow's divinity is modest and obliquely put. The allusion is not in fact to Hathor but to Juno, Homer's ox-eyed goddess. The idiot, looking into the cow's eyes, sees himself within "the mild enormous moist and pupilless globes." He finds himself "in twin miniature mirrored by the inscrutable abstraction; one with that [with] which Juno might have looked out" (p. 184). Throughout these pages Faulkner's rhetoric is intricate and *florid,* but in this context it is not excessive and certainly not careless, for the scene is described with the eye distinctly on the object, even though the eye here is the idiot's tranced and ecstatic organ of sight. Moreover, the rhetoric has a purpose and adapts itself perfectly to the purpose. The author is not attempting to prettify the world of nature; on the contrary, he means to take us, with our tired eyes and bleared vision, into a world miraculously charged with the power of animal innocence, miraculously fresh with all the sharpness of an animal's unjaded senses. The reader who feels that Faulkner's description of nature is uncontrolled and merely indiscriminately lavish, might profitably compare the great hymn to nature as it sings itself through the idiot's mind in *The Hamlet* to the hymn to nature that reverberates through the mind of young Isaac McCaslin in "The Bear." The descriptions of nature are in fact carefully discriminated, and each is adapted to the particular mind upon which the energies of nature play. In Isaac McCaslin's meditation, for example, time has the dimension of history; in the free association of the idiot's mind it does not.

In "The Old People," Isaac, as a boy of twelve, having gone through a rite of initiation in which his forehead is marked with the blood of his first buck, has a vision of the immortal quarry. He soon learns, however, that the buck he saw could not have been an actual animal. Troubled at the thought that what he had visualized so clearly must have been merely an illusion, a trick of his own imagination, he talks about it to his elder cousin, who stands to him in something of the relation of a father. His kinsman's speech to Isaac is a descant upon the difficulty that any creature has in breaking its tie with earth. The earth, Edmonds says, does not want to hide its dead; it throws them back toward the sun. Experience is good, "even suffering and grieving is better than nothing." But you cannot be alive forever and "you always wear out life long before you have exhausted the possibilities of living." Yet all these possibilities "must be somewhere; all that could not have been invented and created just to be thrown away" (p. 186). After all, why should there not be such things as these on the earth even if they "cant cast a shadow?" They could not be expected to prefer "the scoured and icy stars" (p. 186) when there is the earth itself for them to haunt—the beautiful and inexhaustible earth.

Faulkner also touches upon this theme in the "wawkin" episode in "Pantaloon in Black," in a cryptic reference to the fact that in spite of what the preachers say about how the dying leave the earth "not only without regret but with joy, mounting toward glory," actually everybody knows that the dead "either will not or cannot quit the earth yet although the flesh they once lived in has been returned to it" (p. 136). Thus Rider, hours after his wife's burial, sees her as plainly as he sees the kitchen doorway within which she stands.

Isaac's kinsman can think of no better place after death for earth's creatures (perhaps including himself) than the familiar earth—even if he could only haunt it as a shade. The inability to conceive of any heaven better than the earth is voiced by many a modern, whether in Frost's observation that "Earth's the right place for love: / I don't know where it's likely to go better," or in Robert Jordan's dying tribute at the end of *For Whom the Bell Tolls,* or more exuberantly in the poetry of Wallace Stevens and Dylan Thomas. A related theme is the boundless immortality of nature upon which man looks in joyful awe and in which he is willing to lose himself. One thinks of—in addition to Stevens and Thomas—certain sections of *Finnegans Wake* and of some of the later poems of Yeats. But this note is, of course, not new in the literature of the West and there is already a strong reverberation of it in Wordsworth. In his attitude toward nature, Faulkner is in some respects actually closer to Wordsworth than he is to his contemporaries or to the writers of the later nineteenth century. The truth of this observation will become clear if we explore some of the parallels between Faulkner and Wordsworth, especially the way in which the joy that both men take in nature springs ultimately from a Christian base. Because of the cultural "lag" of the South, Faulkner, like Wordsworth and unlike so many of his contemporaries, scarcely inherits a "post-Christian" world.

If Wordsworth shows a special concern in his poetry for the power of nature to shape and mold human character, and therefore tends to attribute to his children and peasants and idiots a special access to its beneficent and gracious influence, there are parallel elements in Faulkner's novels. Faulkner too makes much of the special qualities to be found in children and peasants, both black and white, and in idiots. Indeed, Faulkner's famous idiots go far beyond Wordsworth's treatment of Johnny in "The Idiot Boy," both in depth and in range. More than that, Wordsworth's concern for older men like the shepherd in "Michael" or the pedlar in *The Excursion* or the old leech-gatherer in "Resolution and Independence," men who have spent their lives close to nature and have imbibed a special wisdom from their long intercourse with it, is fully matched in Faulkner's work. One thinks, for example, of such a character as Sam Fathers, the old hunter, who radically shapes the life of his protégé, Isaac McCaslin, by teaching the boy how a man must conduct himself in relation to nature.

It is in virtue of Faulkner's characteristic treatment of his Negroes and his characters like Sam Fathers that he is called a primitivist. The term can do no harm if it simply means that many of the people whom Faulkner admires are simple in mind and spirit and have managed to maintain the kind of wholeness and integrity that we associate with childlike sincerity and lack of duplicity. But if primitivism means to us a reliance upon the instincts and a disparagement of discipline, then Faulkner is even less of a primitivist than was Wordsworth. Sam Fathers is a man whose life exhibits poise and restraint and discipline. The part-Indian Boon Hogganbeck is indeed an impulsive and highly emotional man, but Isaac is taught nothing by Boon, though he regards him with affection and enjoys him as a companion.

Some of Faulkner's noblest characters are Negroes, like Dilsey and Lucas Beauchamp, but they are not noble through some mystique of race. Dilsey is warm-hearted and gives of herself without stint, but she is no noble savage. She is a deeply religious person, and if her Christianity is one of simple faith, it is nevertheless Christianity—that is, hers is a religion which involves discipline and self-sacrifice and not simply a cultivation of the spontaneous impulses of the heart. I find nowhere in Faulkner the notion that man, if he would only know his true nature, could be at home and happy in the world, or any hint that the subtropical South was a kind of latter-day Garden of Eden in which men, had they not allowed their native ideas to be distorted, might have lived in an easy and harmonious rapport with nature.[3] Faulkner's men are not innocent in this sense. They are already fallen and alienated. In effect, then, Faulkner seems to accept the Christian doctrine of original sin. Men are condemned to prey upon nature. The only question is whether in doing so they will exercise some kind of restraint and love the nature that they are forced to use, or whether they will exploit nature methodically and ruthlessly in a kind of rape.

In spite of Faulkner's loving contemplation of nature, he expects man to struggle with it. Nature is the necessary theater of man's activity, the realm in which man must prove himself. In "Delta Autumn" old Uncle Isaac says that when God created man,

3. For further discussion of this matter see below, Notes, p. 371.

"He created the world for him to live in," and he goes on to say that he reckons that God "created the kind of world He would have wanted to live in if He had been a man—the ground to walk on, the big woods, the trees and the water, and the game to live in it" (p. 348). And what of man as predator, as violator of nature? Uncle Isaac deals with that matter too. Maybe God "didn't put the desire to hunt and kill game in man but I reckon He knew it was going to be there."

This observation is closer than one might have supposed to Milton's treatment of the problem in *Paradise Lost*. There, God creates for man a beautiful and fascinating world, and though He does not implant in man the attack upon nature which will occur when, having been driven out of the happy garden, man invents fire and kills beasts and clothes himself in their skins, Milton's God knows full well that man will do precisely this. It is so clearly foreknown that Milton thought that his reader needed to be assured by God himself that His "Foreknowledge had no influence on [the] fault" of Adam and Eve and that they had decreed "Their own revolt," not He.

Wordsworth's primitivism also has to be qualified in a somewhat similar way. For even though Wordsworth stresses the life of the affections, especially as that life is influenced by an unconscious nurturing of nature, some of Wordsworth's noblest characters have to struggle with difficulties and to exhibit an almost stoic power of endurance. The death of his brother in 1805 is usually taken to mark a watershed in Wordsworth's life. It was this "deep distress" that "humanized" Wordsworth's soul, shattered his dream that man could live merely in terms of his imaginative vision, and impressed upon him the need for some sterner and more external code by which to conduct his life. In his "Elegiac Stanzas, Suggested by a Picture of Peele Castle," Wordsworth bids farewell to "the heart that lives alone, / Housed in a dream, at distance from the Kind" and welcomes "fortitude, and patient cheer, / And frequent sights of what is to be borne!" [4] In 1805 also he wrote

4. E. de Selincourt and H. Darbishire, eds., *The Poetical Works of William Wordsworth, 4* (5 vols. Oxford: At the Clarendon Press, 1940–49), 260.

his "Ode to Duty," in which he tells his reader that "unchartered freedom" tires him and that from this hour he intends to seek the guidance of duty, since he longs for a "repose that ever is the same." Yet if one looks at Wordsworth's earlier poems, such as "Resolution and Independence" or "Michael," one finds that the sturdy ancients there seem already proficient in such a discipline. Whether or not they have imbibed their moral wisdom simply from intercourse with nature, they certainly show what could be called a stoical endurance—no grim Stoicism, it is true, an almost cheerful Stoicism—but it is a power that stays them and enables them to endure.

"They endured" is the resonant epitaph which Faulkner penned for his noblest Negro characters in the appendix he later supplied for *The Sound and the Fury.* Indeed, the ability to endure is the virtue which Faulkner most stresses in his simpler peasant types, whether black or white. In his long colloquy with his cousin in "The Bear," Isaac McCaslin, in urging his claims for the Negroes, says: "they will endure. They will outlast us" (p. 294). Endurance is the quality also celebrated in Faulkner's next-to-last novel, *The Mansion,* which tells how the curious little white tenant-farmer, Mink Snopes, waits out nearly forty years without crumpling up and abandoning hope, biding his time until he is released from the penitentiary and can carry out his act of vengeance.

Because Faulkner sets great store by endurance and courage and the related virtues, he is sometimes called a Stoic. Wordsworth, too, one remembers, has been called a Stoic, and not merely the aging poet, for Wordsworth was no more than thirty-five when he wrote his "Ode to Duty." There is considerable evidence of Wordsworth's indebtedness to Seneca and to Cicero and to Roman Stoicism generally though Wordsworth's Stoicism was not wholly of Roman origin: he drew, directly or indirectly, upon modern and romantic Stoics like Shaftesbury, Schiller, and Kant. That Faulkner drew directly and consciously on either the ancient or the modern writers in the Stoic tradition is rather unlikely. But the lines translated from Seneca that Wordsworth chose to insert in his *Excursion,*

> And that unless above himself he can
> Erect himself, how poor a thing is Man! [5]

could well serve as an epigraph to *Light in August* or *Absalom, Absalom!* But we need not be much puzzled as to how Faulkner came by the "Stoical" elements that we find in his work. As Professor John Hunt, of Earlham College, has aptly put it: the first step backward from Christian orthodoxy is usually into some version of Stoicism. That tradition is so pervasive and so thoroughly interwoven into the Christian tradition that when, under pressure, certain specific Christian doctrines recede or are displaced, Stoical elements almost automatically come into prominence. This likelihood is the greater when the Christian tradition that one inherits is strongly tinged, as Faulkner's was, with Puritanism.[6]

Pauline Christianity came close to the contemporary Stoicism in that both defined the truly human existence in terms of freedom. (All of Faulkner's characters yearn for such freedom. Joe Christmas says in effect: that was all I ever asked for. Isaac McCaslin proudly tells his kinsman: "Sam Fathers set me free," though later the author will comment, with reference to Isaac and all the rest of us, that no man is free.) The Stoic achieved his freedom by his own will, by learning to discipline his appetites and to live in the *Logos,* freed from the world of the flesh. But St. Paul insisted that such freedom could come only from God through an act of grace. Insofar as the concept of grace is weak or at least not very clearly evident in Faulkner's work, he often seems closer to the Stoic Epictetus than to the Christian Paul.

My principal reason for calling attention to parallels between writers so temperamentally antithetical as Wordsworth and Faulkner is to try to put Faulkner's "primitivism" and "Stoicism" into perspective. Wordsworth loved nature and associated that love of nature with his own moral and spiritual recovery from a period of disillusionment and severe depression, and his poetry shows his admiration for those men and women who reflected in their lives the beneficent shaping power of nature. To that power he at-

5. Ibid., 5, 119.
6. For further discussion of Faulkner's Stoicism see below, Notes, p. 372.

tributed the single-heartedness and sincerity of their reactions and the inner resources which provided a stay against the disappointments and defeats incident to life. But Wordsworth also came out of the Christian tradition, and though it has been argued that he moved away from it and in some ways moved contrary to it, there is a great deal of Christianity in the earliest Wordsworth, just as there remains in the later poetry of his most orthodox period a great deal of his love of nature and his "Stoical primitivism."

Something of the same kind of argument may be made with regard to Faulkner, and calling attention to Wordsworth's case may help to secure the reader's acceptance of the argument. In the light of certain passages in "The Bear," must we conclude that Faulkner is some kind of pantheist? And if we do, what are we to make of his statement to an interviewer that "within my own rights I feel that I'm a good Christian?" [7] Even if, as he makes quite clear, Faulkner is using the term without much reference to dogma, how can one square observations of this sort with the joy that some of his characters take in contemplating the surging energies of nature or with the religious awe with which he, as author, celebrates the immortality of nature? The parallel with Wordsworth may also make it a little easier for us to see how Faulkner was able to accommodate such views to a general scheme which is in some sense still Christian.

In this connection it is interesting to note Faulkner's observation that the Christian legend is part of the background of any Southern country boy. "My life," he says, "was passed, my childhood, in a very small Mississippi town, and that was a part of my background. I grew up with that. I assimilated that, took that in without even knowing it. It's just there. It has nothing to do with how much of it I might believe or disbelieve—it's just there." [8] This is a modest and perceptive description of his cultural "situation": there is a Christian framework within which his sensibility operates but against which at any particular time it may—and does—rebel.

7. *Faulkner in the University* (Charlottesville, University of Virginia Press, 1959), p. 203.

8. Ibid., p. 86.

Along with the more serious parallels between Wordsworth and Faulkner, one might mention an amusing though not trivial parallel. It has to do with the beggar in Wordsworth's early poem "The Old Cumberland Beggar" and the old Negro woman called Het in Faulkner's *The Town*. Wordsworth conceives of his beggar as the bearer of positive virtues, one who keeps alive in the community the "kindly mood" necessary to its spiritual life. On his begging rounds from door to door, he stirs up the community's sense of charity. After an admonishment not to deem "this Man useless," [9] since it is "Nature's law" that not even "the meanest of created things" should exist "Divorced from good," Wordsworth rather daringly specifies the old beggar's function. Even the poorest poor

> Long for some moments in a weary life
> When they can know and feel that they have been,
> Themselves, the fathers and the dealers-out
> Of some small blessings. . . .

The beggar is that necessary lowest rung on the ladder of charity. Since he is poorer than anybody else, his presence allows even the very poor to achieve the happiness of being "dealers-out" of blessings.

Faulkner's old Het serves for her community the same blessed role. After the hilarious mule-in-the-yard episode, when she asks Gavin Stevens for a dime, and he hands her a quarter, she remarks: "That's quality. . . . You talk about change to quality, what you gets back is a quarter or a half a dollar or sometimes even a whole dollar. It's just trash that cant think no higher than a nickel or ten cents." So much by way of compliment to her benefactor, but she does not grovel. She justifies her role as recipient: "There's some folks thinks all I does, I tromps this town all day long from can-see to cant, with a hand full of gimme and a mouth full of much oblige. They're wrong. I serves Jefferson too. If it's more blessed to give than to receive like the Book say, this town is blessed to a fare-you-well because it's steady full of

9. *Works, 4,* 236.

folks willing to give anything from a nickel up to a old hat. But I'm the onliest one I knows that steady receives. So how is Jefferson going to be steady blessed without me steady willing from dust-dawn to dust-dark, rain or snow or sun, to say much oblige?" (p. 245).

Faulkner does not risk Wordsworth's serious philosophic tone. The mode is comic, and if the recipient is to state her own justification rather than have the author state it for her, then it had best not be done with dead seriousness. But if we discount as self-serving old Het's justification of the benefit she confers, we would do well not to discount too heavily Faulkner's belief that the old Hets of the world have their function and play a not unworthy part in the human community.

That community is for Faulkner typically a small town or rural community. Like Wordsworth, he is not really at ease in the great city. Wordsworth's agrarianism—his conception of the good life lived on the land and his distrust of industrialism and urban life—has been very ably set forth in Kenneth Maclean's *Agrarian Age*.[10] Life in Cumberland and Westmorland in the first part of the nineteenth century may seem to be a long, long way from north Mississippi in the first half of the twentieth. But the cultural lag of the South does something to close the gap. In any case, Faulkner's distrust of the city and his familiarity with, and love for, life on the land is comparable to that of Wordsworth.

Another very interesting (and more seriously important) parallel between Faulkner and Wordsworth is the role that they both assign to the pedlar. In Wordsworth's poetry, the pedlar has a very important function: he not only provides articles for the peasantry as he makes his rounds, but he brings in news from the great world outside, carries messages from one person to another, and may even be appealed to for advice and counsel. Professor Frederick Pottle tells me that the pedlar had some such role in the countryside of the state of Maine as late as his own boyhood. Wordsworth was quite aware that pedlars could be wicked men, as his poem "Peter Bell" shows. But the pedlar who figures in his *Excursion* is a kind of lay saint, a man who has gone to school

10. New Haven, 1950.

to nature and from nature has imbibed not only a love of natural beauty but a discipline of the heart and a profound vision.

Faulkner's "pedlar" is the sewing-machine agent, V. K. Ratliff. Like Wordsworth's Wanderer in *The Excursion,* Ratliff moves through the country, purveying his goods and his counsel; but Ratliff, though a good man, is not invested with a saintlike aura. He is salty, of the earth earthy, with the ability to tell a story in the best tradition of the old Southwest. In personality he is far removed from Wordsworth's yeoman philosopher, who in the "silent faces" of the clouds touched by the sun "could . . . read . . . Unutterable love" and who was often rapt into "still communion that transcends / The imperfect offices of prayer and praise." [11] But Ratliff is, as we have seen, in his own way a philosopher too, the purveyor of a rich wisdom, and the conscience of the countryside. Ratliff does not talk much about nature, but he obviously enjoys it. The characters with whom Faulkner expects his reader to be sympathetic are usually men who love nature and live in some kind of close rapport with it. On the other hand, nearly all of Faulkner's villains are men who are guilty of violating it: Popeye, for example, has no natural vices. He cannot drink; he must use unusual means in order to accomplish his rape of Temple. He is afraid of the dark; the swooping owl terrifies him. He contemptuously spits in the spring.

Flem Snopes is impotent; his greed and lust for money condemn him to a life in which the senses are starved or dormant. Even Thomas Sutpen, the villain with the most heroic and tragic stature, sacrifices everything to his "design." One feels that he has no deep natural affections—certainly not for either of his wives, who have been chosen for a purpose and are ancillary to the design, and none even for his children. He apparently does not find it difficult to reject his son Charles because of his Negro blood, but he sacrifices to his abstract dream, just as coldly, his white children, Judith and Henry.

Many of Faulkner's characters obviously enjoy nature. They are alive to its every shading; but the kind of mystic communion with nature which the early Wordsworth seemed sometimes to ex-

11. *Works,* 5, 15.

perience is not vouchsafed to any character of Faulkner, nor do Faulkner's characters often find in nature the Wordsworthian healing for the distraught spirit. Joe Christmas seems to derive such solace when he returns, as though driven by compulsion, to "his native earth" (*Light in August,* p. 295). It is as though he wanted to see it "in all its phases for the first or the last time." For a week he lurks and creeps "among its secret places" and thinks "that this is what it is—the looking and seeing—which gives him peace and unhaste and quiet," but his surmise proves to be wrong: "suddenly the true answer comes to him."

Faulkner and Wordsworth are much closer in their interpretation of the way in which a life close to nature has molded their simple peasants and country people and in the way in which they interpret the desecration of nature—one remembers Wordsworth's poem entitled "Nutting" and Faulkner's "Delta Autumn"—as a revelation of the perversity of the human heart.

One cannot leave this matter of nature without a further glance at Faulkner's Puritanism. Faulkner, it is plain, resents the Puritan emphasis on sober living and strict Sabbath observance, its frowning upon the pleasures of conviviality, and its tendencies toward spiritual pride and self-righteousness. Though he is capable on occasion of discerning in a Puritan service a fine simplicity and moral integrity (see, for example, "Shingles for the Lord" or his account of the burial of Rosa Millard in *The Unvanquished*), on the whole, Faulkner is appalled at the grim constrictions of Puritanism even when he is not enraged by its spiritual aggressions. But Faulkner seems to share with Puritanism one cardinal belief: the sense of the importance of the human will. Having rejected the notion of a teaching church and having subordinated the sacraments, the Puritan laid supreme importance on the unmediated encounter between man and God. Man must gain his salvation by individual effort—by an agonizing wrestle with the angel.

Faulkner's characters wrestle with the angel too. Man defines himself through his striving—for Faulkner as well as for Calvin. Man cannot simply vegetate—cannot simply be. He must become, and he will become what he ought to be largely through his own effort. For Faulkner, therefore, there can be no easy subsidence into nature. True, men run the risk of distorting themselves if they reject nature in a cold and callous asceticism, and they become monstrous if they vent their hatred of nature, if their appropriation of nature becomes a kind of rape. But love nature though man should, and respect it though he must, he is alienated from nature and must never presume upon an easy union with it if he wishes to call himself a man.

4

The Community and the Pariah

(LIGHT IN AUGUST [1])

WHAT HAS BEEN SAID in the two last chapters has a very special bearing on *Light in August,* for nearly all the characters in this novel are drawn from the ranks of the plain people and most of them exhibit a Puritan ethic. They are in tension with nature, and some have even been deformed and perverted in a struggle against it. The theme of man strained away from nature, however, is only one of several significant Faulknerian themes to be found in *Light in August.* Because it is a mature novel, these themes receive full development and yet are thoroughly embedded in the fictional structure. The reader does not encounter them as abstractions. They have their full dramatic weight as renderings of characters in action. There is therefore good reason for choosing such a masterpiece as the first of the novels to explore in some depth. But *Light in August* also provides examples of the typical difficulties that many people experience in reading Faulkner.

One of the most characteristic is that of finding a principle of unity. No novel of Faulkner's exhibits more brilliant writing or abounds in a greater number of memorable individual scenes, and no reader would fail to respond to most of them. There is, for example, the very touching scene at the orphanage in which a young girl named Alice, who is departing for the home of her

1. For the meaning of this title see below, Notes, p. 375.

new foster parents, wakes the sleepy child Joe Christmas to tell him good-bye. She has mothered the little boy and now she weeps. "He didn't know that she was crying because he did not know that grown people cried, and by the time he learned that, memory had forgotten her. He went back into sleep while still suffering her, and the next morning she was gone. Vanished, no trace of her left, not even a garment, the very bed in which she had slept already occupied by a new boy" (p. 119).

There is the scene in which the boy Joe Christmas and his foster father McEachern face each other, both of them silent and obstinate, over the Presbyterian catechism. There is the scene in which Joe as an adolescent confesses, shyly but almost proudly, to Bobbie the waitress-prostitute, his belief that he has some Negro blood. There are the several scenes in which Joe faces Joanna Burden, among them the one in which she tells Joe about her father and grandfather and relates the incident in which her father showed her, a four-year-old child, the secret graves of her grandfather and her brother. There is the equally wonderful scene—but so different in tone—in which the grim and damned woman, clutching the old cap-and-ball pistol, demands that Joe kneel down with her and pray. There are the quietly charged scenes in which Byron sits opposite the Reverend Gail Hightower in Hightower's little cottage and tells him about Lena and her plight, and later calmly makes the terrible proposal that Hightower should save the murderer Christmas with a lie. He tells Hightower that if he will only say that Joe Christmas spent the night of the murder with him at his house: "Folks would believe you. They would believe that, anyway." There is the account of Percy Grimm running lightly and surely with the automatic in his hand and suddenly discovering what it is that he wants. These are only a few of the tremendously moving and exciting scenes to be found in the novel.

The difficulty has never been that such individual segments of the narration lacked vividness and power. The difficulty has always come with the attempt to relate the various episodes so as to show a coherent pattern of meaning. Critics so generally sympathetic as Conrad Aiken and George Marion O'Donnell find the novel a failure because of lack of unity. This is the basic complaint of Richard Rovere in his introduction to the Modern Library edition.

As for typical misreadings, two in particular seem to recur. Since either can affect the meaning of this novel, it may be well to dispose of them at the outset. The first has to do with Joe Christmas' alleged Negro blood. Most commentators refer to his mixed blood and several call him a mulatto (technically, one-half Negro), though Joe easily "passes" as white. But what is the evidence for Joe's mixed blood? Two special passages seem to have fostered this supposition. The first is Joe's flaunting of his alleged Negro blood —as when he tries to shock the white prostitute by telling her that he is a Negro. The second is the hypothesis put forward by Gavin Stevens as he tries to account for the events that occur just before Joe's death. Stevens sees Joe's last actions as involving a clash between his white blood and his black blood: the "black blood drove him first to the Negro cabin. And then the white blood drove him out of there, as it was the black blood which snatched up the pistol and the white blood which would not let him fire it" (p. 393), etc. Because many readers are disposed to consider Stevens Faulkner's mouthpiece in the novel, his comments about Joe's Negro blood may seem endowed with special authority. But Faulkner says specifically in the interviews he gave at the University of Virginia [2] that the scholarly and somewhat romantic Stevens is not his mouthpiece. Stevens, who evidently has no more facts than we have, is merely spinning a theory.

What do we really know about Joe's ancestry? The fanatical old Doc Hines is quite certain that his daughter, Joe's mother, is lying when she tells him that her lover is a Mexican. But that conviction is part and parcel of his fanaticism. He "knows" that the man is a Negro just as he knows many other things—by a special revelation that short-circuits any need for evidence. It is true that Mrs. Hines admits that after her husband's trial for his murder

2. "Question: Sir, if he . . . does not definitely have Negro blood, well, what is the significance of Gavin Stevens's surmise at the end . . . that there's a conflict of blood? . . . Answer . . . That is an assumption, a rationalization which Stevens made." *Faulkner in the University,* p. 72.

of Joe's father, "the circus owner come back and said how the man really was a part nigger instead of Mexican, like Eupheus said all the time he was. . . ." But she adds, a sentence or two later, "it was just that circus man that said he was a nigger and maybe he never knew for certain" (p. 330).

Is Mrs. Hines here allowing hope to warp her judgment? Or was the circus owner, in admitting that Joe's father was part Negro, simply humoring the *idée-fixe* of the old monomaniac? At any rate, we are never given any firm proof that Joe Christmas possesses Negro blood, for the sufficient reason that Joe would have become what he became whether he had an infusion of Negro blood or not. The pressures that mold him into an Ishmael have, as Faulkner knows, nothing to do with biology as such. The decisive factor is the attitude that the world takes toward Joe and the attitude that he takes—toward other men and toward himself.

Faulkner has made this point very powerfully in a number of scenes. There are those in the orphanage in which old Hines as janitor watches the child Joe and broods over him in malignant hate, silently gloating when the children begin to call Joe "nigger." The author tells us that the child, with "more vocabulary," might have thought "That is why I am different from the others: because he is watching me all the time" (p. 121). There is the scene in which the child follows a Negro workman around, fascinated by him, "until at last the nigger said, 'What you watching me for, boy?' and he said, 'How come you are a nigger?' and the nigger said, 'Who told you I am a nigger, you little white trash bastard?' and he says, 'I aint a nigger,' and the nigger says, 'You are worse than that. You dont know what you are. And more than that, you wont never know. You'll live and you'll die and you wont never know' " (p. 336). Or there is the scene in which Joe is talking with Joanna Burden. To her question whether he has any idea who his parents were, he tells her only that "one of them was part nigger." (It is significant that he says "one of them," not "my father" as he might have done had he even as much information as Old Hines believed that he had.) When Joanna asks him how he knows that, he "didn't answer for some time. Then he said: 'I dont know it' " (p. 222).

The Negro workman's reply touches the matter of real importance. Joe does not know what he is. Throughout his life, he lashes out at both the white community and the Negro community. But the warping of his mind and spirit—Faulkner has been at great pains in this book to show just how it has been done—is the result of the way in which he has been reared from infancy. The biological matter is quite irrelevant.

The second misreading that recurs in comments on *Light in August* is less important but betrays a bias worth noting. Many readers assume that Joe Christmas is lynched at the end of the novel. Joe is killed by Percy Grimm when, during his trial, he breaks away and tries to escape.[3] Percy sees him enter Hightower's house, finds him in the kitchen armed with a pistol, barricaded behind an overturned table, and shoots him five times with his automatic. Then with a knife picked up in the kitchen he emasculates Christmas.

Grimm is unaided. Three men who had been deputized to prevent disorders and who had joined in the chase followed Grimm into the house, but they evidently do not participate in the violence, and when they see what Grimm is doing, one of them cries out and begins to vomit.

A lynching is defined as the concerted action by private individuals who execute summary punishment outside the forms of the law. Can a lynching be carried out by one person? The jurists who framed the proposed federal statute on the subject evidently did not think so.[4] Christmas is murdered, not lynched, and even the charge of murder would seem to be obviated insofar as Grimm was a properly deputized officer, attempting to apprehend a fugitive from justice who turns out to be armed. Grimm could have claimed (doubtless later he must have claimed) that he had to fire first, since he had every reason to believe that this desperate man did not mean to be taken. What gives away Grimm's storm-

3. For a discussion of Joe's attempt to escape see below, Notes, p. 375.
4. Congressman Emanuel Celler, for example, in discussing House Bill 4683 (introduced in the first session of the 81st Congress) said that the proposed antilynching act stated in its definition that "a lynching may be committed by an assemblage of two or more persons." See also below, Notes, p. 377.

trooper mentality is what he says to the dying man and his act of mutilation.

Something more than a mere quibble about a term is involved. If we use the word "lynching" loosely and carelessly, we shall be in danger of missing the relation of Joe Christmas to the community he has defied, and more importantly, that of Percy Grimm to the community he claims to represent. There is, in fact, every reason to think that Grimm's whole *conscious* motivation is to ensure that the good name of the town not be marred by a lynching—even though the community itself is not apprehensive of a lynching. The Commander of the American Legion post to whom Grimm appeals does not think that a special force is needed to preserve order and frowns upon vigilante tactics, even in a good cause. Even if force were needed, he tells Grimm, "We would all have to act as civilians. I couldn't use the Post like that" (p. 396). And the sheriff is just as emphatic in opposing Grimm's idea. There has been no hint of trouble and he can't have fifteen or twenty people "milling around the square with pistols in their pants" (p. 398). But Grimm's utter seriousness and complete dedication to the concept of order prevails against these counsels. Obviously, the sheriff does not know what Grimm's real motivation is; but then, Grimm does not himself know what it is until, with his blood up, his pistol ready, fired by the excitement of the chase, he faces Joe Christmas across the overturned table. I shall have something to say later in this chapter about Grimm's relationship to Joe and to the community. But Grimm's action does not commit the community, and although it involves the community powerfully it does so only in a very special way.

The community demands special consideration at this point,[5] for the community is the powerful though invisible force that quietly exerts itself in so much of Faulkner's work. It is the circumambient atmosphere, the essential ether of Faulkner's fiction. But for many a reader, the community is indeed invisible and quite imperceptible: it exerts no pressure on him at all—and lacking any awareness of this force, he may miss the meaning of

5. See below, Notes, p. 377.

the work. Such readers find *Light in August* quite baffling simply because they are unaware of the force of community that pervades it and thus miss the clue to its central structure.

Yet a little reflection will show that nearly all the characters in *Light in August* bear a special relation to the community. They are outcasts—they are pariahs, defiant exiles, withdrawn quietists, or simply strangers. Miss Burden, the daughter of carpetbagger intruders, has lived for years within what can be described only as a kind of cultural cyst. The community has tried its best to expel the Reverend Mr. Hightower, though having failed in the attempt it has finally accorded him a sort of grudging acceptance. Joe Christmas is, of course, Ishmael himself, actively defying the community. Even Byron Bunch fits into this pattern of alienation. Byron, with his methodical earnestness and his countrified asceticism, is regarded as a kind of eccentric—a "character." For "seven years [he] had been a minor mystery to the town" (p. 369).

But the community itself, the great counterforce to which these characters are attracted or against which they are reacting, has no special representatives in the novel and need have none. For the community, everywhere in the novel, is visible to the reader who is prepared to see it. It expresses itself through Mrs. Armstid emptying her china bank and knotting the coins into a sack for Lena; through the sheriff kicking the ineffectual bloodhounds or ordering the thrill-seekers away from his examination of the Negro witness; through the second-hand furniture dealer who relates the closing episode of the novel; and through a dozen other minor or anonymous characters.

Sometimes the author makes an explicit comment upon the community, as he does in the long and brilliantly handled account of Gail Hightower in chapter 3. After Mrs. Hightower's shameful death, the community is sure that Hightower will resign his church. When he does so at last, after persistent moral pressure, the town is glad. "Then the town was sorry with being glad, as people sometimes are sorry for those whom they have at last forced to do as they wanted them to" (p. 60). But Hightower still would not leave the town, and the community was furious with him for his stubbornness. Finally, some men took him out and

53

beat him, and the townspeople, now horrified, offered "to prosecute the men who had done it" (p. 62). But Hightower refused to tell who his assailants were. "Then all of a sudden the whole thing seemed to blow away, like an evil wind. It was as though the town realized at last that he would be a part of its life until he died, and that they might as well become reconciled." Neighbors once more began to leave baskets of food upon his porch—"though they were the sort of dishes which they would have sent to a poor mill family. But it was food, and wellmeant" (p. 63).

One way in which to gauge the importance of the community in this novel is by imagining the action to have taken place in Chicago or Manhattan Island, where the community—at least in Faulkner's sense—does not exist. As far as the general plot is concerned, everything in the novel could be easily accounted for: The frustration and rage of Joe Christmas, the murder of the lonely old maid, Miss Burden, and the moral impotence and isolation of Hightower are situations and events that occur frequently enough in the setting of our great modern world cities. The plight of the isolated individual cut off from any community of values is of course a dominant theme of contemporary literature. But by developing this theme in a rural setting in which a powerful sense of community still exists, Faulkner has given us a kind of pastoral—that is, he has let us see our modern and complex problems mirrored in a simpler and more primitive world. *Light in August* is, in some respects, a bloody and violent pastoral. The plight of the lost sheep and of the black sheep can be given special point and meaning because there is still visible in the background a recognizable flock with its shepherds, its watchdogs, sometimes fierce and cruel, and its bellwethers.

Yet the reader of *Light in August* may still question the relation of the fact of community to the meaning of the novel. Granted that the community is a living force, what does that have to do with the meaning of the novel? And he can scarcely be blamed if he goes on to ask whether *Light in August* is a novel at all. What possible relation is there between the two main characters, Lena and Joe Christmas, who never meet and who go their separate ways, the one placidly, the other violently? There is obviously the bare fact of contrast; but is there anything more? Do not these characters between them rend the book in two? [6]

Both questions are in order. A proper answer to the first (the relation of the community to the meaning of this novel) will suggest an answer to the second (the unity of the novel). But the answer to the first cannot be succinct, and in any case we must begin by considering more fully the relations of the various characters—to each other and to the world around them.

Lena and Joe Christmas, as everyone has seen, stand in obvious contrast to each other. Their very likenesses stress their basic differences. Both are orphans; both escape from home by crawling out a window; both are betrayed by their first loves; both in the course of their wanderings come to Jefferson. But how different they are in relation to society! Every man's hand is sooner or later lifted against Joe Christmas; he demands that it be so. But Lena, heavy with child, on an obviously ridiculous quest to find the father of her child, leads a charmed life. Even the women who look upon her swollen body with evident disapproval press their small store of coins upon her, and the community in general rallies to help her. As Mrs. Beard remarks to Byron Bunch: "Aint you and that preacher and ever other man that knows about her already done everything for her that she could think to want?" (p. 368). In the person of Bunch, her quixotic errand actually raises up for her an authentic though clumsy knight-errant, who becomes her protector and fights her battles.

Joe repels, Lena attracts the force of the community into which they both come as strangers. But the point is not that Lena is "good" and Joe "bad." Joe's alienation from the community is not simply "willed"—there are deep-seated reasons for it, and, moreover, his is only the most extreme of a whole series of such alienations.

Faulkner has documented each history of alienation rather carefully, and has done so in great detail with those of Joe Christmas and Gail Hightower. Hightower, because of certain warping influences in childhood, becomes fettered to the past. Because of

6. See, for example, Richard Rovere's introduction to the Modern Library edition.

certain traumatic experiences in childhood, Christmas is cut off from any meaningful past. Hightower toward the end of the novel comes to the bitter realization that he has hardly lived at all. The son of middle-aged parents (his father fifty, his mother forty), brought up in an austere house, he came as a child to dote upon the memory of his Confederate cavalryman grandfather, who represented all that his father was not. Hightower regards his father as an enemy. As he puts it, "I skipped a generation" (p. 418). He is able to invest his grandfather's death (he was shot while robbing a henhouse on some foraging expedition) with romantic glamour. His sermons mix up in an incredible farrago the charging cavalry with the word of God. Late in the novel he comes to admit to himself that "for fifty years" he has "not even been clay: I have been a single instant of darkness in which a horse galloped and a gun crashed. . . . my dead grandfather on the instant of his death" (p. 430). But his friend Byron Bunch has realized the truth about him long before, thinking to himself: "it's the dead folks that do him the damage. It's the dead ones that lay quiet in one place and dont try to hold him, that he cant escape from" (p. 65).

But Christmas has no "dead ones" to hold him, no family, no past. The orphanage, where he was conscious that the grim old man was watching him "all the time," and life with his foster father, the dour Calvinist McEachern, lock him into himself. He is cut off from ties of any sort, and he learns to suspect and resent any appeal to sentiment or tenderness. Part of that suspicion of tenderness comes from his experiences with sex. Faulkner has most skillfully traced this development through the well-known toothpaste episode, the experience with the Negro girl, and the affair with the prostitute-waitress Bobbie, but he has not forced the development to extremes. Joe is not made into an overt homosexual. But his distaste for women and his fear of them is accounted for, and this antifeminine attitude becomes, as we shall see, a meaningful part of the novel. It is parallel to the attitude of Hightower, who does not understand women and comes to shrink from them and all that they represent. Doubtless the community was viciously wrong in accusing Hightower of homosexual practices; yet there is a latent tendency in him just as there is in

Christmas. There is this much justice in Grimm's bitter accusation when Hightower, attempting to give Christmas the alibi for which Bunch had pleaded, says, "He was with me the night of the murder" (p. 406).

It is Joe's latent homosexuality that involves him with Joanna Burden. When he forces himself upon her, there is "no feminine vacillation, no coyness of obvious desire. . . . It was as if he struggled physically with another man for an object of no actual value to either, and for which they struggled on principle alone" (p. 205). It is when Joanna's masculinity finally dissolves into nymphomania and that in turn gives way to feminine religiosity that Joe kills her. He cannot bear having her pray over him.

Joanna Burden is one of the most interesting of Faulkner's characters. Some years ago Maxwell Geismar protested that Faulkner had made "this decent and well-meaning abolitionist spinster" the "special object of his venom." He accused Faulkner of hating her because she is a modern woman and a "Northern" woman and of subjecting her to humiliations that he spares the Southern women in his novels. This comment is obviously silly. Faulkner endows Joanna Burden with pathos and even tragic dignity. She is lonely, cut off from her kind, shunned by the community; and she has been crippled (very much as Hightower has been) by her personal inheritance. But she has courage, a quiet power of endurance, and a remarkable lack of bitterness at her plight.

Joanna is one of Faulkner's masculinized women, but Faulkner is no harder upon Joanna than he is on his other masculinized women including Drusilla Hawk, the Southern girl who rode with a Confederate troop of cavalry. It is inaccurate to say that Faulkner is hard on either of them: he thinks, rather, that life has been hard on them. He has treated both Drusilla and Joanna with great sympathy and understanding.

Joanna has been warped by the pressure of events away from the fulfillment of her nature. She has been forced to bury a part of herself; but the needs and desires are there, and when they are awakened too late for normal fulfillment in children and a home, something very terrible happens to her. Joe Christmas is perceptive enough on this point. He says to himself early in their relationship: "At least I have made a woman of her at last" (p. 207), though later, less certain of the fact, he thinks: "She's trying to be a woman and she dont know how" (p. 210). But Joe is not prepared for the torrent that is released when the "New England glacier [is] exposed suddenly to the fire of the New England biblical hell" (p. 225). Later he observes, when she sometimes stares at him "with the wild, despairing face of a stranger," that "she wants to pray, but she dont know how to do that either" (p. 228).

Faulkner is pitiless in recounting the details of Joanna's sexual discovery of herself and in indicating the man's revulsion from her—his feeling that he was "being sucked down into a bottomless morass" (p. 227). But there is never any question that Joanna is essentially the victim—of sex too long repressed, of sex driven up into the head—or of her being compelled to her actions by a self that she had scarcely known existed. To witness Joanna's one love affair is like watching a stunted autumnal plant frantically trying to bloom and seed itself before the killing frosts—"something of dying summer spurting again like a dying coal" (p. 228). Compare also: "hair just beginning to gray drawn gauntly back to a knot as savage and ugly as a wart on a diseased bough" (p. 241).

At the end, Joanna reverts to her ancestral religion—as in some sense she has known all the time that she must. ("Dont make me have to pray yet," she prays. "Dear God, let me be damned a little longer, a little while" (p. 231). When she becomes once more the religious woman, the solicitous mother figure, the woman who would counsel the child and do him good, Joe finds that he has to kill her, and does—though not before Joanna has tried to kill him, for she serves a just God who will not be mocked, whose judgments are very sure, and she is ready to be that God's instrument. The last point is very important: Joanna's final gesture is not the spiteful reaction of a jilted woman. There is something almost impersonal about it. As she has told Joe when she asked him for the last time to kneel and pray with her, "It's not I who ask it" (p. 247). She is the dedicated instrument of her God, whether in saying "kneel with me" or in pulling the trigger.

Joanna Burden's frantic exploration of sex contrasts with Joe's attitude toward sex. Joe's life, as the author observes, had been, "for all its anonymous promiscuity . . . conventional enough, as a life of healthy and normal sin usually is" (p. 227). And on another level, Joanna is contrasted with Lena in her attitude toward sex, for Lena, with her uncomplicated urge to foster life, is not so much normal as an embodiment of the very norm itself.

Most of all, however, Joanna invites comparison with Hightower. Faulkner has pointed to the parallels between these two characters in a number of ways. Both are recluses. Both have been rejected by the community for good and sufficient reason. Both are dominated by the past, since the family past has impinged upon both of them in a special way. Because of all this, the incautious reader might even leap to the conclusion that it was something in the personal heritage of these two people that destroyed them, leaving them unfulfilled and incomplete. In contrast to Joe Christmas, who has no roots in anything, Joanna and Hightower may seem too deeply rooted, helplessly fettered by their personal traditions—the one of militant abolitionism, the other of the galloping Confederate cavalry leader. But neither's is a live tradition. It does not connect past with present. It is absurdly doctrinaire and abstract or absurdly romantic. That, incidentally, is how the community judges both these obsessions.

The ancestors of both Gail Hightower and Joanna Burden were able to fulfill themselves. Calvin Burden, Joanna's grandfather, was lusty, full-blooded, completely alive. He was a fire-eating abolitionist, coming home "especially on Saturday nights . . . still full of straight whiskey and the sound of his own ranting. . . . [But he] was no proselyter, [no] missionary" (p. 212). His peer is Hightower's grandfather, a "hale, bluff, rednosed man with the moustache of a brigand chief" (p. 412), triumphantly at home in his world.

Joanna's father Nathaniel, after an exciting youth spent in the Southwest, becomes an austere grizzled man who settles in Jefferson immediately after the Civil War. There his father and his son are shot down in a Reconstruction period election. But with all his justification for bitterness, and though isolated as a hated alien, he has an understanding of the values of the community. As Joanna herself reconstructs it: "We were foreigners . . . that thought differently from the people whose country we had come into without being asked or wanted. And [father] was French, half of him. Enough French to respect anybody's love for the land where he and his people were born and to understand that a man would have to act as the land where he was born had trained him to act" (p. 223).

Like Joanna's father, Hightower's father was an abolitionist, though a Southern abolitionist. But he entered the Confederate army and "took an active part in a partisan war and on the very side whose principles opposed his own" (p. 414). He taught himself surgery during the war, retained his idealism, and, as Faulkner puts it, "the other part of him, which lived in the actual world" (p. 415), was as successful as any man and more successful than most. Thus, though Joanna's and Hightower's fathers were as unlike their own fathers as they could be, they too were able to fulfill themselves. Both the grandfathers and the fathers of Joanna and Hightower were whole men, fully related to the world outside them, fully alive. The issue is not that of a Northern or Southern heritage or even that of a sensual or ascetic temperament: both traditions and both temperaments are represented in their ancestors. The real issue is whether one's relation to one's heritage permits participation in life or isolates one from life—whether it connects past with present or is simply a private obsession.

The most fascinating instance of the alienated person that occurs in the novel is that of Percy Grimm. Faulkner says: "I wrote [*Light in August*] in 1932 before I'd ever heard of Hitler's Storm Troopers," [7] and thus had described a storm trooper without knowing it. Faulkner's claim that he had described the breed without help from the newspapers is quite justified; but because of hazy and inaccurate notions of the rise of Nazism, some readers will not realize just how accurate Faulkner's account is. In the

7. *Faulkner in the University*, p. 41.

first place, it may seem strange to them that one should regard Percy Grimm as an alienated character at all. Yet Faulkner has gone to great pains to show that Grimm is cut off from the community and is thoroughly conscious of being cut off from it. Indeed, Faulkner has been almost as careful in working up the background of Percy Grimm's spiritual starvation and alienation as he has with that of Gail Hightower.

Grimm had been born too late to take part in the First World War. Because he had missed out on being a soldier, the boy had received a kind of psychic blow. As Faulkner puts it: "The boy was suffering the terrible tragedy of having been born not alone too late but not late enough to have escaped first hand knowledge of the lost time when he should have been a man instead of a child" (p. 394). At another point, Faulkner makes the comment that Grimm had no one "to open his heart to." In short, Percy Grimm is a man who needs desperately to be felt a part of the community. He needs it so much that he attempts to seize the community values by violence. He yearns to wear a uniform marking him as the community's representative and defender. Whereas Christmas repudiates the customs and institutions of the community, Grimm insists upon seeing them in peril and demanding the right to take up arms in their defense. We shall miss the point badly if we entertain any doubts as to Percy Grimm's sincerity of motives in trying to prevent a lynching. He wants to ensure that Joe Christmas, murderer though he be, shall have a fair and proper trial.

So much for Grimm's conscious motives. What his unconscious motives are becomes plain enough when he confronts Joe Christmas at the end of the chase. Faulkner makes it clear that only in the heat of the chase does Grimm suddenly feel released, happy, fulfilled. Grimm runs "with a kind of fierce and constrained joy." Later, "above the blunt cold, rake of the automatic, his face had that serene, unearthly luminousness of angels in church windows" (p. 402). It is probably only at the very end that the dammed-up sadism is revealed even to Grimm himself, bursting forth in a full tide as he fires the shots into the overturned table and seizes the butcher knife.

A lesser artist would have made of Grimm a kind of caricature, merely brutalized and bestial. It is a mark of Faulkner's insight that even in his "Storm Trooper" he sees lurking beneath the fury and brutality the emotionally starved, lonely, terrified little boy.

In a sense we may say that Joe Christmas and Percy Grimm are closely akin—mirror images of each other in their relation to the community. This is why it makes good artistic sense that the stricken and wounded Hightower, in a final moment of truth about himself, should see the faces of Christmas and Grimm blurred together. In this vision there appear to him the faces of his wife, the townspeople, the members of his congregation, and those of Byron Bunch, Lena, and Joe Christmas. But one "face alone is not clear. It is confused more than any other, as though in the now peaceful throes of a more recent, a more inextricable, compositeness. Then he can see that it is two faces which seem to strive . . . in turn to free themselves one from the other, then fade and blend again" (p. 430). Suddenly, he realizes whose the second face is: " 'Why, it's . . .' he thinks. 'I have seen it, recently . . . Why, it's that . . . boy. . . . who fired the . . .' " (p. 431).

The theme of alienation from the community is in this novel closely connected with an emphasis on a kind of hell-fire Protestantism. In much of his work Faulkner reveals himself to be a Protestant anticlerical, fascinated and also infuriated by some of the more violently repressive features of the religion that dominates his part of the country. But in *Light in August* his criticism of the harsher Protestantism is not a gratuitous gesture that disturbs the work of art: it is absorbed into the total pattern of meaning.

Many of the characters in *Light in August* are doctrinaire by temperament and by training. The specific doctrines that they hold are forms of "Calvinism," but naturally there is a wide variation in content and stress. For McEachern the doctrines are quite literally those of the Westminster Confession, though McEachern overstresses the self-regarding and repressive virtues and conceives of God primarily as a god of wrath who administers an inexorable justice. In old Doc Hines there is definite distortion and perversion. His fury at "bitchery and abomination" is the fury of a crazed man. What is particularly bloodcurdling is Hines' confidence that he is privy to God's plans and purposes. There is the wonderful passage in which he relates how God "said to old Doc Hines, 'You can go too now. You have done My work. There is no more evil here now but womanevil, not worthy for My chosen instrument to watch.' And old Doc Hines went . . . But he kept in touch with God" (p. 338).

In her conversation with Bunch and Hightower, Mrs. Hines states quite precisely what has happened to her husband: he began "then to take God's name in vain and in pride to justify and excuse the devil that was in him" (p. 326). His attribution of his furies to God is quite literally a taking of God's name in vain, blasphemy. The tendency to call one's own hates the vengeance of a just God is a sin to which Protestantism has always been prone. But not merely Southern Protestantism and not merely Protestantism as such. Norman Cohn's *The Pursuit of the Millennium* shows how deep-rooted is this element in our culture. In fact, most of the millennial movements, including the revolutionary movements, of the West share in this tendency to attribute the desires and hates of an individual or a group to God or to the dialectic of history or to the nature of reality. Doc Hines' distortions of this aspect of some of the Protestant sects, though they are those of a madman, are meaningful, for they constitute a serious caricature of views held by people who are quite "normal."

Joanna Burden's grandfather should be mentioned in this company. He was the son of a Unitarian minister, but when he ran away to the West he became a Catholic and lived for a year in a monastery. On his marriage he repudiated the Catholic Church, choosing for the scene of his formal repudiation "a saloon, insisting that every one present listen to him and state their objections" (p. 211). But in repudiating Catholicism, he did not repudiate religion. Though he could not read the English Bible— he had learned from the priests in California to read Spanish—he began to instruct his child in the true religion, interspersing his readings to the child in Spanish with "extemporized dissertations composed half of the bleak and bloodless logic which he remembered from his father on interminable New England Sundays, and half of immediate hellfire and tangible brimstone" (p. 212). Perhaps he differs from the bulk of doctrinaire hellfire and brimstone Protestants in not being a proselyter or a missionary. But everything else marks him as truly of the breed: his intensity, his stern authoritarianism, and his violence. He has killed a man in an argument over slavery and he threatens to "frail the tar" (p. 212) out of his children if they do not learn to hate what he hates —hell and slaveholders.[8]

Hightower's father differs sharply from Calvin Burden, but the doctrinaire element in him is also unmistakable. He "was a man of Spartan sobriety beyond his years" (p. 414). His bibulous father, the Confederate cavalryman, teases him a little for being a "sanctimonious cuss" who requires for a wife only somebody who "can sing alto out of a Presbyterian hymnbook" (p. 413), though Faulkner also makes it plain that the father has a great deal of respect for his sober-minded son and that the son is in many respects an admirable man. But to the neurotic boy, Gail Hightower, this man of principle, his father, is more than a stranger, he is an enemy. To the child he seemed to "fill the room with rude health and unconscious contempt" (p. 416). The relation between them makes a certain parallel with the relation between Joe Christmas and his foster father McEachern. The parallel is far from exact, but it is discernible. It is only another of the several ways in which Hightower and Christmas resemble each other.

Gail Hightower, of course, is the only one of these Protestants who has had formal theological training. Because of that fact, one might expect him to be the most doctrinaire of all. He is not. He seems at the beginning of the book the most tolerant and pitying of all the characters, the one who recoils in horror at man's capacity for evil and man's propensity to crucify his fellows, the man whose only defense against violence is nonresistance. One may be inclined to say, therefore, that Hightower has rebelled against his Calvinist training and repudiated its jealous and repressive God; and certainly, there is truth in this notion. High-

8. For the Burdens' attitude toward slavery and the Negro see below, Notes, p. 378.

tower is a disillusioned man and a man who has learned something from his sufferings. But there is a sense in which he has never broken out of the mold: he still stressses a God of justice rather than a God of mercy, for his sincerest belief is that he has somehow "bought immunity." He exclaims: "And after all, I have paid" (p. 429)—in confidence that God is an honest merchant who has receipted his bill and will honor his title to the precious merchandise he has purchased at such cost. But although he cannot entirely free himself from his intellectual heritage, he has broken with his earlier Calvinism, and his indictment of the Church is an indictment of "the professionals who control it" because they have seen to it that its steeples are "skypointed not with ecstasy or passion but in *adjuration, threat,* and *doom*" (p. 426; italics mine).

Lastly, there is Joe Christmas, the most violent rebel of all against hellfire Protestantism. As a child, he is conscious that he is being hounded by the fanatically religious old Doc Hines; he resists stubbornly the discipline imposed by his foster father McEachern, whom he finally brains with a chair; and when his paramour, Joanna Burden, threatens him with hell and insists that he kneel with her and pray for forgiveness, he decapitates her. Yet there is a most important sense in which Joe Christmas is the sternest and most thoroughly dedicated "Calvinist" in the book.

He has imbibed more from the training of his foster father than he realizes. For all that he strains in fierce resistance against him, he "could depend" on "the hard, just, ruthless man." It is the "soft kindness" of the woman, his foster mother, that he abominates. If one mark of the "Calvinists" in this novel is their fear and distrust of women and their hatred of the female principle, then Joe Christmas is eminently qualified to take a place among them. He even has affinities with his old childhood ogre, Doc Hines, and with Hines' fury at the bitchery of women and abomination of Negro blood. Joe, hearing the "fecundmellow" voices of Negro women, feels that he and "all other manshaped life about him" had been returned to the "lightless hot wet primogenitive Female" (p. 100) and runs from the scene in a kind of panic.

Christmas too wants not mercy but justice, is afraid of the claims and obligations of love, and yearns only for a vindication of his identity and integrity—a vindication made the more difficult by his not knowing precisely what he would vindicate. When he puts aside the temptation to marry Joanna and win ease and security, he does it by saying: "If I give in now, I will deny all the thirty years that I have lived to make me what I chose to be" (p. 232). Finally, Joe is something of a fatalist, and his fatalism is a kind of perversion of Calvinist determinism.[9] On his way to murder Joanna, "he believed with calm paradox that he was the volitionless servant of the fatality in which he believed that he did not believe" (p. 244). But so "fated" is his act of murder that he keeps saying to himself "I had to do it" (p. 245)—using the past tense, as if the act had already been performed.

In *Light in August* some of the characters who have become cut off from the community—and from life—become reintegrated with it, fully or partially. Such a character is Byron Bunch. He has suffered no traumatic experience in his youth; he has received no special conditioning from the past; nor has he violently rebelled or been violently rejected by the community. He is rather the methodical little "settled" man with no vices, the perpetual bachelor, who is somewhat withdrawn from the tides of life. We are told how he came to fall in love and, through this love, became involved in matters of life and death, crime and scandal. We are also told how Hightower, who had tried so desperately hard to avoid involvement ("I have bought immunity") is also drawn back into decision and responsibility. Hightower, as Bunch's confidant and in some sense his spiritual adviser, fears that Bunch is risking his "freedom," and counsels him to avoid involvement. But finally, through Bunch, he himself once more becomes involved in life and death; he delivers Lena's baby, since the doctor has not got to her in time, and he makes a desperate last-minute attempt to save Joe Christmas just before he is shot to death in the next room.

The involvement of Bunch comes through a woman, and that

9. For Joe as a Christ-Symbol see below, Notes, p. 379.

fact itself is significant. For the alienation of many of those separated from the community has come about through their attitudes toward woman and sex—or at least reveals itself in those attitudes. It is so with Christmas, with Hightower, and with Byron Bunch. One might include Joanna Burden here, for though she is a woman, her masculinization is the badge of her loneliness and the means through which she is destroyed. Hightower makes the connection very definitely. As he passes the charred timbers of her house he says: "Poor, barren woman. To have not lived only a week longer, until luck returned to this place. [Lena's child has just been born in a cabin on her place.] Until luck and life returned to these barren and ruined acres" (p. 357). Joanna's own barrenness is precisely to the point, and conversely Lena's fertility is connected not only literally with life but also with luck, good fortune.

Lena, by the way, is the only one of the strangers—the outsiders who have come into the community—who does not suffer from frustration and alienation. The others suffer from the characteristic disease of modern life, its sick hurry and divided aims. One can recognize in the situation of Christmas or Hightower themes characteristic of other writers of our time such as Eliot and Joyce. To all of them one might apply John Crowe Ransom's telling description of modern man as a being unable "to fathom or perform his nature." Since Christmas does not know who he is, he can express himself only in fits of compulsive violence. Gavin Stevens thinks that perhaps just before his death, Christmas did come to know who he was, and there are rather clear indications that Hightower fathoms his nature at the end, but this knowledge comes very late. Lena is almost alone in not suffering from this modern defect. She can perform her nature because she does not need to fathom it: she *is* nature.

Lena (along with Eula of *The Hamlet*) has sometimes been called an "earth goddess." The description does have a certain aptness when applied to Eula, especially in some of the more rhapsodic passages of *The Hamlet*. But it is a little highfalutin for Lena. It is more accurate to say that Lena is one of Faulkner's several embodiments of the female principle—indeed, one of the

67

purest and least complicated of his embodiments. Her rapport with nature is close. She is never baffled as to what course of action to take. She is never torn by doubts and indecisions.[10] There is no painful introspection. This serene composure has frequently been put down to sheer mindlessness, and Lena, to be sure, is a very simple young woman. But Faulkner himself undoubtedly attributes most of Lena's quiet force to her female nature. Faulkner may indeed have had a rather romantic idea of woman. He certainly had an old-fashioned idea of her. In the Faulknerian world men have to lose their innocence, confront the hard choice, and through a process of initiation discover reality. But women are already in possession of this knowledge, naturally and instinctively. That is why in moments of bitterness Faulkner's male characters —Mr. Compson in *The Sound and the Fury,* for example—assert that women are not innocent and have a natural affinity for evil. It would be more acurate to say that Faulkner's women lack the callow idealism of the men, have fewer illusions about human nature, and are less trammeled by legalistic distinctions and the niceties of any code.

In *Light in August,* however, the male-female contrast is stressed in a rather different way. Here, the principal male characters suffer alienation. They are separated from the community, are in rebellion against it—and against nature. But Lena moves serenely into the community and it gathers itself about her with protective gestures. Its response to her, of course, is rooted in a deep and sound instinct: Lena embodies the principle upon which any human community is founded. She is the carrier of life, and she has to be protected and nurtured if there is to be any community at all.

A basic theme in *Light in August* is man's strained attempt to hold himself up in rigid aloofness above the relaxed female world. Many of the men in the novel take up this stance, notably Hightower and Christmas. The crazed fanatic Doc Hines and the dour Presbyterian McEachern are to be numbered here too; perhaps also, though with an obvious difference, Hightower's father, Jo-

10. On Lena Grove as an embodiment of the female principle see below, Notes, p. 380.

anna Burden's father, and Joanna (as masculinized woman) herself. Byron Bunch, when we first see him, is aligned with this group. He is timid with women, and his religiousness has just a hint of the anchorite in it. Even Lucas Burch ought to be mentioned in this company—if only for comic relief (though he does have a quite literal claim to be admitted: in his own terms, he is not the marrying kind, and we last see him frantically escaping from Lena and her baby and his responsibilities to them).

Lena's function in the novel ought now to be clear. Faulkner uses her to affirm a kind of integrity and wholeness by which the alienated characters are to be judged. But Lena has more than a symbolic function. She is the means through which Byron Bunch is redeemed from his pallid half-life and brought back into the community. And she is the indirect means through which Hightower is redeemed. This coming back into the community is an essential part of their redemption. Unless the controlling purposes of the individual are related to those that other men share and in which the individual can participate, he is indeed isolated and is forced to fall back upon his personal values, with all the risk of fanaticism and distortion to which such isolation is liable.

The community is at once the field for man's action and the norm by which his action is judged and regulated. It sometimes seems that the sense of an organic community has all but disappeared from modern fiction, and the disappearance accounts for the terrifying self-consciousness and subjectivity of a great deal of modern writing. That Faulkner had some sense of an organic community still behind him was among his most important resources as a writer.

If in Faulkner's work the community can still serve as a positive norm, does that mean that in his fiction there is no room for the roles of the prophet and the saint? Can one ever find implicit approval of the individual's effort to amend or transcend the values held by the community? The answer is yes, and often. Faulkner was always fascinated by rebels and has usually accorded them a full measure of dramatic sympathy. But his fiction also reveals keen awareness of the perils risked by the individual who attempts to run counter to the community. The divergent individual may invite martyrdom; he certainly risks fanaticism and madness. In *Light in August* Faulkner's emphasis is primarily on the distortion and perversion and sterility which isolation from the community entails, though even here there is a clear recognition of a heroic element in Hightower, Joanna Burden, and Joe Christmas.

The term "redemption" may seem to claim too much for Hightower. Yet by the end of the novel he has been powerfully changed. After he has successfully delivered Lena's baby, he feels "a surge of something almost hot, almost triumphant" and thinks "I showed them! . . . Life comes to the old man yet" (p. 355). And he goes home to read not Tennyson but *Henry IV*, "food for a man" (p. 355). When he hears that Byron has left, he says to himself: "So he departed without coming to tell me goodbye" (p. 363). And then, with a conscious and purposed inversion of the usual phrase, "After all *he* has done for *me*. Fetched to me. Ay; given, restored, to me" (italics mine). Later, it is true, Hightower has to experience Christmas' attack upon him, the futile attempt to stop Grimm with a lie offered too late to save Christmas' life, and the blood-letting in his own house. But he has dared the opprobrium and told the generous lie, and in the long reverie which closes Faulkner's account of him he has admitted to himself that he "was the one who failed" (p. 426), that he was responsible for his wife's death, that he has been "a charlatan preaching worse than heresy" (p. 427), and that, bound by his romantic fixation on his grandfather's death, he has himself been neither dead nor alive. In this hour of truth he has his vision of the faces, and sees them for what they are, and he hears once again the phantom cavalry, the mystic experience with which he has sustained himself in the past, but this time he hears with a difference "the clashing sabres and the dying thunder of hooves," for he himself has finally dared something and has broken out of his self-centered dream.

Most readers have assumed that Hightower, old and exhausted, his head bandaged after Christmas' blows, dies as he hears "the dying thunder of hooves." But Faulkner, in his University of Virginia discussions, indicated that Hightower "didn't die." [11] This is obviously highly interesting; but as far as the larger scheme of

11. *Faulkner in the University*, p. 75.

the book is concerned, it hardly matters: whether Hightower died or lived on, he had broken out of the circle in which we find him at the opening of the story.

And what of Byron Bunch? Is he also "redeemed?" Can we say so in view of the curious and somewhat ambiguous ending of the novel in which Lena has not accepted marriage with Byron but, with Byron in tow, pursues her ridiculous quest for the father of her child, the unspeakable Lucas Burch? An answer to this question necessarily brings up for consideration Faulkner's attitude—not only to the characters in this episode but to all the happenings in the book. What shall we call the predominant mode? Tragic or comic or neither?

Finally and generally, I believe, the mode is that of comedy. To say so in the light of some of the terrible episodes may seem perverse. But Faulkner's comedy is frequently a makeweight to the terrible. The tender-minded reader may feel that Faulkner frequently uses a savage humor; but his is never a cynical and nihilistic humor. Its function is to maintain sanity and human perspective in a scene of brutality and horror. For example, there is the wonderful passage in which the countryman who has discovered the fire in Miss Burden's house enters and finds her body with the head almost severed, a condition which presents him with a problem in getting the dead woman downstairs. He is afraid to try to pick her up and carry her out "because her head might come clean off." But the fire forces the issue and he has to pick her up and bring her out as best he can. When he deposits the body on the ground, however, the cover in which he had hastily wrapped her "fell open and she was laying on her side, facing one way, and her head was turned clean around like she was looking behind her. And he said how if she could just have done that when she was alive, she might not have been doing it now" (p. 80).

This is comic and we may call it a grotesque and savage comedy, but we miss the point if we think that the countryman is being rude or cynical. It does not occur to him to leave the body in the burning house, and he has done his best under the circumstances to observe the decencies. His wry and sardonic humor is not disparaging or irreverent, though it speaks to the issue and keeps, amid the horror, a tenacious grip on common sense. Faulkner's work is full of this kind of comedy. *The Hamlet* and *As I Lay Dying* abound in it, and there is not a little of it in *Light in August*.

One can look at Faulkner's comedy in still another way. We may say that Faulkner tends to take the long view in which the human enterprise in all its basically vital manifestations is seen from far off and with great detachment. If the view is long enough and the perspective full enough, the basic attitude is almost inevitably comic. James Joyce comes to mind. His *Ulysses*, though it has much pathos and horror in it, is also finally a comic work. In *Light in August* Faulkner observes even the tragic events that involve Joanna Burden with detachment and in a full perspective. It is Lena and her instinct for nature, Lena and her rapport with the community, Lena as a link in the eternal progression from mother to daughter who provides the final norm for our judgment. In this connection Faulkner's abiding concern with man's endurance and his ability to suffer anything—compare the Nobel Prize speech—is worth remembering. Tragedy always concerns itself with the individual, his values, his tragic encounter with the reality about him, and the waste which is suffered in his defeat. Comedy involves, on the other hand, the author's basic alignment with society and with the community.

In calling *Light in August* a pastoral we have already suggested something of the comic mood. The pastoral, on the whole, aligns itself with comedy, not with tragedy. The suggestion made earlier that *Light in August* is a kind of pastoral has not been made whimsically. The last chapter of the book, with the adventures of Byron Bunch and Lena, is almost conventionally pastoral, and pastoral with an authentic comic note, for Byron is comically balked of his reward. The little man has done quite nobly. He has befriended and protected Lena, and now Lena obviously should marry him; but as the book closes, Lena is still hitchhiking across Tennessee in pursuit of Lucas Burch. Yet Byron finds it impossible to abandon her.

Our last glimpse of Lena is given through the eyes of a character whom we have not met before in the novel. Faulkner introduces him most casually. The last chapter simply opens to the statement that there lives in the eastern part of the state a furniture repairer and dealer "who recently made a trip into Tennessee to get some old pieces of furniture which he had bought by correspondence." On this trip the furniture dealer picked up the hitchhikers Lena, her baby, and her strange little bachelor companion. The oddity of the group piques his curiosity. Later he senses what is going on and the situation stirs his amusement, though it is an amusement not without insight into Lena's coquetry and not without a trace of pity for Byron's abashed devotion.

The reader may resent the casual and last-minute introduction of the new narrator and he may be disposed to dismiss this incident as simply another of Faulkner's tricky fictional devices. Yet if he has been able to see the importance of the community in this novel, he should have little difficulty in hearing and recognizing the voice of the community once more in the furniture dealer's narration. It is not important that we do not know his name or that we have not met him before or that we shall not meet him again. He can be for us the anonymous, earthy, genial, experienced, tough-minded representative of a corporate body of values, insights, and beliefs.

As such a representative, he finds Byron's plight amusing, and he obviously enjoys having so good a story to relate to his wife when he gets home. But his humor is not cruel and his insights into the relation of man and woman, the nature of chivalry, and the connection of love with honor are not untouched by a certain wisdom. In any case, we can observe that this last chapter of *Light in August,* with its comic overtones, does not really represent an abandonment of the theme that I ventured earlier to characterize in a phrase borrowed from John Crowe Ransom. For Byron Bunch too is a man unable "to fathom or perform his nature"— still unable, that is, in our last glimpse of him, to bring Lena to terms. He has acted unselfishly and gallantly, but he cannot do now what the furniture dealer knows that he ought to do: force the issue and persuade Lena to accept him as lover and husband.

On the first night they camp out together, the furniture dealer thinks that Byron has nerved himself to the act. He watches

Byron quietly entering the truck where Lena is sleeping and, as he observes to his wife, "I says to myself, 'Old boy, if you'd a just done this last night, you'd a been sixty miles further south than you are now, to my knowledge" (p. 440). But Lena repels Byron's advances with the exclamation: "Why, Mr. Bunch. Aint you ashamed. You might have woke the baby, too." And the furniture dealer tells his wife: "I be dog if I dont believe she picked him up and set him back outside on the ground like she would that baby if it had been about six years old" (p. 441).

Byron had retired in confusion, but when the furniture dealer started the next day's journey with the imperturbable Lena and her child, Byron was waiting around the next curve in the road, and got back in the truck with the explanation: "I done come too far now. . . . I be dog if I'm going to quit now." Lena answers him with: "Aint nobody never said for you to quit" (p. 443).

The furniture dealer evidently has no doubt that eventually Lena will marry Byron. He says to his wife, in explaining Lena's continuation of her obviously foolish quest, "I think she was just traveling. I dont think she had any idea of finding whoever it was she was following. I dont think she had ever aimed to, only she hadn't told him [Byron] yet. . . . I reckon she knew that when she settled down this time, it would likely be for the rest of her life. That's what I think" (p. 444).

Gail Hightower, too, had earlier made the same prophecy when he imagined that Lena would continue to bear children, fulfilling her nature, but, in the future, children sired by Byron. Eventually, one supposes, Byron came to realize that Lena wanted to be possessed and mastered. For though Faulkner counsels that man should stand in awe of nature, and, loving and respecting it, should forbear to violate it, he does not expect man to stand perpetually aloof from nature, completely passive and lacking a field for action. Byron needs to learn the mean between a rape and Platonic love. But Faulkner did not chose to give us here the story of the marriage of Byron and Lena. He preferred to end his novel on the dominant theme of man's inability to fulfill himself, though the theme is treated here not tragically but with humor and amused irony—even as social comedy.

5

The Old Order

The Unvanquished has suffered more than any other of Faulkner's novels through having been dismissed as a sheaf of conventional Southern Civil War stories. Readers suspect that Faulkner
is playing the old romantic Confederate game on them, with
valiant cavalrymen dashing to the rescue, undaunted matriarchs
keeping the old plantation going, and "good" Negroes helping
bury the family silver against the coming of the Yankees; and
many have rejected these stereotypes with a stereotyped response
of their own. So far as I am aware, there have been only one or
two commentators who have had anything of importance to say
about *The Unvanquished*. Andrew Lytle, out of his deep knowledge of the older South and out of his interest in and concern for its
social system, has made some discerning observations on the
book.[1] Most critics, however, have been willing to dismiss *The
Unvanquished* as a series of stories which Faulkner wrote for *The
Saturday Evening Post* and then shuffled together into book form.

Thus a typical comment reads: "The volume is composed on
the one side of slick magazine stereotypes of the Confederate
soldier and the unquestioned romanticizing of the Sartoris [2] males,
but on the other it contains a few nightmarish scenes of the an-

1. See below, Notes, p. 382.
2. For the name Sartoris see below, Notes, p. 383.

guished days of the South's defeat and, at the book's end, a very cold, quizzical view of the old order." [3] This is, however, to get the point by missing the point. Faulkner's attitude toward his characters and events is much more than a glib romanticizing that cannot be sustained and finally breaks down into cold quizzicality. His attitude toward his characters is one of the most interesting and complicated aspects of this novel.

The issue at stake here is not, of course, whether the dashing Confederate cavalryman did in fact exist. General William Tecumseh Sherman, a sound witness in this matter, testifies that he did. In 1863 he wrote to General Halleck about the part played in the Southern armies by the

> young bloods of the South: sons of players and sportsmen, men who never did work and never will. War suits them, and the rascals are brave, fine riders, bold to rashness, and dangerous subjects in every sense. They care not a sou for niggers, land or anything. They hate Yankees, *per se,* and don't bother their brains, about the past, present, or future. As long as they have good horses, plenty of forage, and an open country, they are happy. This is a larger class than most men suppose, and they are the most dangerous set of men that this war has turned loose upon the world. They are splendid riders, first-rate shots, and utterly reckless. Stuart, John Forrest, and Jackson, are the types and leaders of this class. These men must all be killed or employed by us before we can hope for peace.[4]

The real issue is whether, in depicting his Colonel John Sartoris,[5] Faulkner is able to realize him in his human complexity, and in recognition of this complexity, treat him with more than simple and uncritical admiration. Faulkner is not uncritical: as

3. William Van O'Connor, *The Tangled Fire of William Faulkner* (Minneapolis, University of Minnesota Press, 1954), pp. 100–01.

4. As cited by Edmund Wilson, *Patriotic Gore* (New York, Oxford University Press, 1962), p. 195.

5. For parallels between the Colonel and Faulkner's own grandfather, see below, Notes, p. 384.

author, he maintains a large measure of detachment, and, with special reference to Colonel Sartoris, he is pointed in his censure.

Early in the novel, to be sure, Colonel Sartoris is presented as a heroic figure, and rightly so, since the narrator is his son. The events related in the section entitled "Ambuscade" occurred when Bayard Sartoris was a boy of twelve and a boy who worshiped his father. But even in the early sections of the book John Sartoris is no mere stereotype. He is presented in a realistic setting and allowed a realist's wisdom. Bayard, looking back to this period, now knows as he tells the story that what he then took in boyish ignorance to be the smell of powder and glory was "only the will to endure, a sardonic and even humorous declining of self-delusion which is not even kin to that optimism which believes that that which is about to happen to us can possibly be the worst which we can suffer" (p. 11).

Colonel Sartoris' library reflects its owner. It contains a complete Walter Scott, a complete Fenimore Cooper, and a paper-bound Dumas, but it also contains a Coke on Littleton, a Jeremy Taylor, and a copy of Napoleon's Maxims. In the section entitled "Retreat," Colonel Sartoris captures sixty Yankees through stratagem and daring, and later on, when Yankee troops surround his house, he makes a romantic getaway. Yet we also see him in the first part of the book building the stock pen in the creek bottom "with his coat off now" and "with a sapling under each arm" (p. 13). The Colonel, even as seen through the eyes of his adolescent son early in the novel, is not a paper paladin: he is a portion of sweating humanity. And in the hard and difficult years after the fighting had ceased, the boy did not always see him as the perfect gentle knight.

In his encounter with the carpetbaggers Colonel Sartoris is treated with a great deal of detachment. He reveals himself here as the hard, ruthless man who believes that he is quite justified in shooting the carpetbaggers and in seizing the ballot box. Obviously he regards the whole event as an extension of the war, which has for him ended only formally. Yet even in this encounter with the carpetbaggers he is careful to observe the code by which he lives. He tells George Wyatt, who had served under him in the war, "I let them fire first. You all heard. You boys can swear to my derringer" (p. 238). But he is ruthless and in the last part of the book, "An Odor of Verbena," Faulkner has very carefully underlined this callousness. Bayard watches him clean the derringer and reload it after he has killed "a hill man," almost a neighbor, "who had been in the first infantry regiment when it voted" him out of the command. Bayard observes that we were "never to know if the man actually intended to rob Father or not because Father had shot too quick" (p. 255). The Colonel next day sent some money to the widow living with her several children in a dirt-floored cabin in the hills, but two days later the woman walked into the house while, as Bayard relates it, "we were sitting at the dinner table and flung the money at Father's face." Bayard makes no comment on the event and quietly goes on with his story, but his manner of reporting the incident is its own witness to the depth of its impact.

In some respects Colonel Sartoris is most attractive in his dealings with Drusilla. There he is understanding and sympathetic and high-hearted. He reveals a kind of generous consideration when he realizes that Drusilla's mother is using pressure on Drusilla to induce her to marry him. He is sensitive to the girl's plight and deeply sympathetic, but it is obvious to Bayard that his father is scarcely in love with Drusilla. Years later, long after the marriage, his courteous treatment is maintained, but it is coupled with a kind of indifference. This becomes clear when Drusilla kisses her stepson, and Bayard, a young man of punctilious honor, tells his father what has happened, but finds that his father, in his preoccupation with his affairs, does not attend to and perhaps cannot really take in what he has been told. Bayard ruefully remarks: "I looked at him, watched him fill both glasses and this time I knew it was worse with him than not hearing: it didn't even matter" (p. 266). At this point in the novel the Colonel is a colder and a partially corrupted man. Some readers, however, have missed the delicacy of what Faulkner has been doing throughout. They are not able to see that young Bayard still loves his father even though he is aghast at his father's abstraction and obsession with power.

Consider the fine scene in which Bayard looks at his dead father. His appearance was, as Bayard says, "just as I had imagined it . . . but with that alteration, that irrevocable difference which I had known to expect yet had not realized" (p. 272). Bayard peers with "illimitable grief and regret" upon the face he had known— the nose, the hair, "the eyelids closed over the intolerance—the face which I realized I now saw in repose for the first time in my life." And as he looks at the empty hands in their stillness, he senses beneath them "the invisible stain of what had been (once, surely) needless blood" (p. 272). Bayard feels a grief that is the more poignant because it cannot refuse to see the intolerance, the fierceness, and the stain of blood that should not have been shed.

Faulkner's refusal to "romanticize" his characters and his searching appraisal of their motives and moral values comes out even more strikingly in his treatment of Drusilla Hawk, who marries Colonel Sartoris after the War and who, though only eight years older than Bayard, becomes his stepmother.[6] In the earlier sections of the novel she is a bewildered young woman buffeted by events, frustrated by life, yet sensible and brave and successful in maintaining her dignity. Faulkner, it is true, gives Drusilla a bravura scene in which she defies the Yankee troopers and saves her horse. As her admiring younger brother tells it to Bayard, when she found that she could not get Bobolink away in time, she "jumped down in her Sunday dress and put the pistol to Bobolink's ear and said, 'I can't shoot you all, because I haven't enough bullets, and it wouldn't do any good anyway; but I won't need but one shot for the horse, and which shall it be?' So they burned the house and went away!" (p. 102).

But Drusilla's bravery and dignity come out in more telling ways. When Bayard sees her on his visit to Hawkhurst, she is sunburned and "her hands were hard and scratched like a man's that works" (p. 103). She has been down to the river to see the Negroes who swarm along the roads trying to cross over Jordan into the Promised Land. Jordan is now an Alabama river guarded by the Federal army. When her mother says to her, "But we cannot be responsible. The Yankees brought it on themselves; let

6. See below, Sartoris Genealogy, p. 450.

them pay the price," Drusilla answers: "Those Negroes are not Yankees, Mother" (p. 105).

Drusilla confides to her young cousin Bayard her wish to join John Sartoris' troop. She begs him to intercede with his father, saying: "Tell him I can ride, and maybe I can learn to shoot" (p. 115). In the conversation between them at night outside the cabin, she indicates quite clearly why she has come to this decision. In her bitterness she says:

> I've quit sleeping. . . . Who wants to sleep now, with so much happening . . . Living used to be dull, you see. Stupid. You lived in the same house your father was born in, and your father's sons and daughters had the sons and daughters of the same Negro slaves to nurse and coddle; and then you grew up and you fell in love with your acceptable young man, and in time you would marry him, in your mother's wedding gown, perhaps, and with the same silver for presents she had received; and then you settled down forevermore while you got children to feed and bathe and dress until they grew up, too; and then you and your husband died quietly and were buried together maybe on a summer afternoon just before suppertime. Stupid, you see. [p. 114]

She has lost her fiancé at Shiloh. With this bitter commentary she is really repudiating the whole of the traditional life of a woman. Now, she tells Bayard, it's all fine, for "you don't have to worry about getting children to bathe and feed and change, because the young men can ride away and get killed in the fine battles; and you don't even have to sleep alone, you don't even have to sleep at all."

How Drusilla persuaded her cousin, Colonel John Sartoris, to accept her as a soldier, we are not told. One assumes that it was not an easy matter to get his consent; but she must have got it, for the next we hear is that she was with his cavalry troop for the last months of the war. Had Faulkner indeed been interested in mere romantic stereotypes, this was an opportunity to show the brave maiden in battle or on a raid. But there are no such scenes in *The Unvanquished;* Faulkner was apparently uninterested in this kind of glamour. Drusilla was doubtless brave enough, yet it was not bravery that made her a combatant.

Later in the book, in the section called "Skirmish at Sartoris," we see more of Drusilla's bravery, but what she defies is not the Federal army but the conventionality of the older women. Her mother and other relatives are naturally outraged at her unfemi-nine and, to them, scandalous conduct, and once the war is over and she has returned home, they demand that she marry Colonel Sartoris immediately. When her mother had learned that Drusilla was in Colonel Sartoris' troop, Drusilla had "not only showed neither shame nor remorse but actually pretended she did not even know what [I] was talking about; how when [I] told her that she and [John Sartoris] must marry at once, Drusilla said, 'Can't you understand that I am tired of burying husbands in this war? That I am riding in Cousin John's troop not to find a man but to hurt Yankees?' " (p. 220).

But Drusilla is a woman, after all, and in a traditional society all the more vulnerable to the pressure of the older women. It is vain for her to assume identity with the men with whom she has fought. She bursts into tears, exclaiming: "That John and I—that we—And Gavin dead at Shiloh and John's home burned and his plantation ruined, that he and I—We went to the war to hurt Yankees, not hunting women!" (p. 227). The wording of the last clause reveals how completely she has identified herself with the men. But the guardians of society, the matriarchs, are too much for her. They make her leave off tending the sawmill; they put skirts on her; they push her into marriage. Colonel Sartoris finally goes to persuade her that she must give in. As Bayard tells the story: "So Father came out too and we went down to the spring and found Drusilla hiding behind the big beech, crouched down like she was trying to hide the skirt from Father even while he raised her up. 'What's a dress?' he said. 'It don't matter. Come. Get up, soldier' " (p. 231).

It is a moving passage, but Faulkner is not playing here for easy sentimental effects. The judgment on Drusilla's tragedy is already implicit. The girl marries not because she is a young woman in love with a man but because, like a good soldier, she obeys her commanding officer. Their wedding underscores Drusilla's alienation from her sex. Her mother and the other women relatives are so concerned to get her promptly made an honest woman that they are unaware that the day they have chosen for the wedding is election day in Jefferson. The election is one in which Colonel Sartoris and the other Confederate veterans are much concerned: they mean to defeat the carpetbaggers, even at the risk of violence. With her mother's clamor in her ears, Drusilla and the Colonel go into town to be married as quickly and quietly as possible, but Drusilla promptly reacts as a soldier rather than a bride. When John Sartoris shoots the carpetbaggers and seizes the ballot box, Drusilla returns with it in her arms, her wedding gown torn, her veil ruined, and her twisted wreath hanging from her hair by a few pins.

Her mother is scandalized: " 'So you are not married,' she said. 'I forgot,' Drusilla said. 'You forgot? You *forgot?*' " (p. 239). So the bride and groom have to ride back into town, crooked wreath, torn wedding dress and all, to be married at last. Aunt Louisa's exasperation sometimes takes the form of scolding her daughter for wearing trousers and thereby unsexing herself, and at other times for having used her sex wantonly and thus having become a lost woman. Yet Aunt Louisa, in spite of her silliness and her Victorian conventionality, happens to be right in both instances. There is a sense in which Drusilla has unsexed herself and she is indeed a lost woman—though not in Aunt Louisa's meaning of the term.

Our last sight of Drusilla in the novel is that of a young widow, for the body of her assassinated husband lies in the parlor. More than half in love with her stepson, but most of all in love with "honor," the hysterical priestess of a rite, a destructive force, she urges upon Bayard the dueling pistols with which to avenge his father.

Yet all the portraits of this woman ring true. Drusilla has the defects of her virtue. Faulkner has not tried to portray a kind of Confederate Joan of Arc. She is not so much valiant as hopeless, and she does not hate her country's enemies so much as she hates her own life and her womanhood. She is, at the end, a warped figure, feverish in her pursuit of honor, masculine in her concern for the code and her obsession with the dueling pistols. And she is judged pitilessly. Aunt Jenny Du Pre calls her "a poor hysterical young woman" (p. 276), and after the final scene between Drusilla and young Bayard, it is evident that it will be impossible for her to remain any longer in this house. She is packed away to her relatives in Alabama.

Faulkner has not been easy on this woman, but he has not robbed her of her dignity. He has made her a believable character and has endowed her with a real pathos, because even her final hysterical transport is made intelligible to us. We know why she became what she became.

Like Joanna Burden, she has risked an essential distortion of her nature and she pays the penalty, though of course a very different kind of penalty from that paid by Joanna. Both women can throw light upon Faulkner's conception of womanhood and not least upon his typical instances of womanhood—Lena and Eula Varner and Aunt Jenny Du Pre. The difference between Aunt Jenny and Drusilla is not merely a difference in age. (Unless Faulkner has confused his dates, Aunt Jenny is only three or four years the elder.) Aunt Jenny's attitude toward the code of honor which binds Bayard is quite typical of Faulkner's women. She loves her young kinsman and she can sympathize with his position as a man. Indeed, at the end she is terribly proud of what he does in honoring the code. But as a woman, she can be counted on to see through codes of any kind. Drusilla shows her masculinization nowhere more than in becoming a priestess of a rite and exalting the code above all the more instinctive and "natural" claims on human beings.

We shall miss the point completely, however, if we take Aunt Jenny's deprecation of the code to represent Faulkner's own view. One commentator says that *The Unvanquished* "ends with the recognition that heroics, in the words of Aunt Jenny, are 'for small boys or fool young women.' " [7] These are indeed Aunt Jenny's own words and they represent what most of Faulkner's mature

7. O'Connor, *Tangled Fire*, p. 103.

women will feel. But Bayard cannot possibly take the view that Aunt Jenny takes, for he is a man; and as a man he must undergo his initiation and prove himself worthy. At the end of *The Unvanquished* Bayard meets the test through an action that is much more than a mere repudiation of the code of retribution, that is in fact the most quixotic bit of heroics to be found in this novel. His final action is the culminating step in his initiation into manhood and moral responsibility. That it should be so is entirely appropriate, for *The Unvanquished* is a novel about growing up— it is the story of an education.

Some readers will need to be reminded that every section of this novel is told by Bayard himself. In the first section he is a boy of twelve; in the last section, a man of twenty-four. The intervening dozen years span the period from early adolescence to young manhood. Where the telling involves a romanticizing of persons and events, we must remember that it is the romanticizing of an adolescent boy. Later qualifications of interpretation and corrections in judgment are those which come to a man who looks back at his earlier experiences and reassesses them. The moral judgments made upon his stepmother and his father, though they are the judgments of a young man who is bound to them by the closest bonds of attachment, are severe. The end of the novel, then—"the cold, quizzical view of the old order"—is no afterthought. Faulkner is not attempting to retrieve for morality a piece of slick-magazine romantic claptrap, for Bayard's final judgments are implicit in the earlier parts of the novel and emerge as Bayard comes into his manhood and is able to see his family and himself with more objectivity.

The experiences which most powerfully affect Bayard's development, of course, are those that occur in the last third of the book, roughly after Bayard became sixteen; yet some of his very early experiences are also important for his moral education, and these are very delicately handled. Ringo, a little Negro boy of his own age, and Bayard are playing at war. They are fighting the battle of Vicksburg with a trench scraped in the earth to represent the Mississippi and with chips from the wood pile to represent the various regiments. As they play, Loosh, Ringo's uncle, who knows what the boys do not know, that Vicksburg has already fallen, suddenly stoops and with his hand sweeps the chips flat, saying "There's your Vicksburg." His wife, Philadelphy, rebukes him, but "Loosh squatted, looking at me with that expression on his face. . . . I didn't know triumph; I didn't even know the word" (p. 5). Faulkner beautifully suggests the troubling effect on the boy to whom Loosh is an adult, even though a slave, and whose slumbering revolt is felt rather than understood, and whose triumph, which he would have to conceal from a white adult, he can intimate to the boy.

The world in which the boy grows up is the exciting world of war, a world in which the two boys can try to shoot a Yankee soldier, in which the boy's father can appear as if by magic out of the woods, or in which enemy troops can suddenly emerge from nowhere. Once when Ringo, Bayard, and Mrs. Millard are on a journey, enemy troops suddenly surround the wagon, cut the mules out of their traces, and leave Bayard's grandmother and the boys sitting there thunderstruck. Even a world so topsy-turvy as this is presented with a great deal of authenticity.

When Bayard and Ringo shoot at the Yankee soldier and have to take refuge beneath Miss Rosa's skirts, they are terrified. But their confidence in the grandmother and the very psychology of a twelve-year-old boy keep the event from becoming a traumatic experience. It is perhaps no more so than, let us say, a spectacular automobile wreck in which no one is hurt might be to a modern boy. In "Raid," Bayard's interest in the railroad and the consequent glamour which surrounds even the torn-up ties and the rails that have been heated and hooped around trees help to provide a realistic counterbalance: that is, Bayard finds very "romantic" some things that a modern reader regards as dull; and, conversely, Bayard is able to treat with a kind of matter-of-fact realism events that the modern reader regards as "romantic."

The harrowing experience which has so much to do with Bayard's later development comes with the long pursuit of the bushwhacker Grumby, a chase which ends in Grumby's death. This is a commission that should not have been laid upon a fifteen-year-old boy, but Bayard feels that his grandmother's murderer ought to be brought to justice. It is not primarily a question of the boy's personal commitment to a code of retribution. Grumby must be punished; yet the country is absolutely lawless; there are no constituted authorities to whom he could appeal had he wished. As Bayard describes the long chase and finally the killing of Grumby, there is very little in the telling to indicate the scarring of his psyche that evidently occurred. He narrates the story tersely and objectively, with few, if any, comments on his own emotions, but at the end of the episode the boy's exhaustion, emotional as well as physical, is eloquent of his state of mind.

Another indication lies in the remark that Drusilla makes on the last page of the episode entitled "Vendée." When Uncle Buck, in his exultation, says that Bayard and Ringo have not only tracked down but "brought back the actual proof of it to where Rosa Millard could rest quiet," and Joby asks "Fotch back the which?", Drusilla says "Hush! Hush! That's all done, all finished" (p. 213). But she is not able to hush Uncle Buck, who proceeds to tell what he and John Sartoris and Drusilla saw when they rode up to the old cotton compress: "the first thing we see was that murdering scoundrel pegged out on the door to it like a coon hide, all except the right hand." And he adds that if anyone wants to see that, "just let them ride into Jefferson and look on Rosa Millard's grave!" This comment throws back a startling light upon an earlier passage, in which Bayard tells how he and Ringo returned to Miss Rosa's grave to find the earth had sunk in it "almost level now," as if Granny "had not wanted to be dead either but now she had begun to be reconciled." He tells how they unwrapped "it" from the "jagged square of stained faded gray cloth and fastened it to the board. 'Now she can lay good and quiet,' Ringo said. 'Yes,' I said. And then we both began to cry" (p. 211).

The nailing of the murderer's body to the door of the cotton compress, the severing of his hand, and the bringing of it to the grave—all of these are acts too savage to be those of a fifteen-year-old boy. Bayard is not essentially callous and brutal. Moreover, he has been gently nurtured. His sensitivity has been suggested in a number of the earlier episodes of the novel. The killing and mutilation of Grumby thus measures the stress of the times and their pressures on Bayard. But we cannot realize fully the impact of the episode on Bayard's mind and spirit until we have read the last section of the novel.

This last section, "An Odor of Verbena," opens with the news brought to Bayard away at law school that his father has been assassinated by a political opponent, Ben Redmond.[8] It is characteristic of Faulkner that he does not tell us in so many words of Bayard's decision not to avenge his father. Since Faulkner rarely dramatizes the agony of choice—the process by which the character actually arrives at his decision—some readers assume that Faulkner's characters make no decisions at all and are merely driven and determined, helplessly adrift on the tides of circumstance. André Gide has said something to that effect, and he is only one of many. The notion, however, will not bear inspection. Bayard has very consciously chosen a course of action, though in this story Faulkner has preferred to dramatize Bayard's sustaining his choice—maintaining his decision against every pressure—rather than to give us the stages by which he arrived at the decision.

A number of things enter into Bayard's decision besides this matter of his having once already taken vengeance into his own hands. A most important factor is Bayard's knowledge that his father had pushed Ben Redmond much too hard. Though George Wyatt, the rough and forthright soldier, will urge the revenge upon Bayard, Wyatt himself has some months earlier said to Bayard: "Right or wrong, us boys and most of the other folks in this county know John's right. But he ought to let Redmond alone. I know what's wrong: he's had to kill too many folks, and that's bad for a man. We all know Colonel's brave as a lion, but Redmond ain't no coward either and there ain't any use in making a brave man that made one mistake eat crow all the time. Can't you talk to him?" (p. 260). And Bayard himself has observed his father's growing abstraction and obsession with power in the scene already commented upon, in which Bayard tries to tell his father that Drusilla has kissed him and finds that his father has not even taken in what he has told him. In refusing to punish

8. He is called Redlaw in *Sartoris*. See below, Notes, p. 384.

Redmond, Bayard is in effect judging against his father, who, in his determination to get his railroad built and running, has acted ruthlessly.

Yet it can be argued that Bayard, in refusing to avenge his father, is actually following his father's example. Two months earlier his father had told him: "I shall do a little moral house-cleaning. I am tired of killing men, no matter what the necessity nor the end" (p. 266). But however we are to interpret his action, there can be no doubt that Bayard loved his father and is grieved for him: the intense scene in which he views his father's dead body is sufficient testimony to that. If the scene also testifies to Bayard's candid admission to himself that his father has been fiercely intolerant and ruthless in his life, the fact but stresses the complexity of his relation to his father. His decision to refuse to kill his father's assassin stems not at all from any rejection of his father, but rather from a love for, and understanding of, him.

Bayard's attitude toward his father is analogous, in its duality, to his attitude toward the community. It is possible to misread the story by underestimating the claim of the community upon Bayard's loyalty or by regarding this claim as simply a baleful and degrading inertia. The cultivated reader of our time may feel that to kill a man is so obviously a terrible thing that he wonders that the decision not to do so could have cost Bayard anything at all. (The same reader will usually have no such trouble with the revenge code in *Hamlet*.)

Bayard, however, has a hard choice to make, and what he actually does is more than a simple repudiation of the code of vengeance. Here then, as in *Light in August,* it is very important to see the importance of the community. As a member of a close-knit community, Bayard from the beginning and at every point feels its pressure upon him. There is the feverishly wrought-up Drusilla; there are George Wyatt and the other members of his father's old troop, all quite convinced that someone must put a bullet into the assassin. Though George Wyatt is sincere in offering to act for Bayard, he expects Bayard to reserve for himself the post of honor. To this list must be added even Professor Wilkins, a good and compassionate man, who believes in the law and certainly would be shocked to think that he did not believe in the Gospel. He is filled with pity for the young man as he says to him, "Bayard. Bayard, my son, my dear son" (p. 244). Yet Professor Wilkins offers Bayard his pistol as well as his horse.

One must not forget Ringo either. Though Ringo stands outside the white code and, like Aunt Jenny, will feel that the code is rather silly, he has no doubt that vengeance should be executed. " 'We could bushwhack him,' he said [to Bayard]. 'Like we done Grumby that day. But I reckon that wouldn't suit that white skin you walks around in' " (p. 251). And even Aunt Jenny, though she thinks that all men's codes are excessive and though she pretends to be infuriated by the congenital quixotic folly of the Sartorises, does not try very hard to dissuade Bayard from the confrontation. When Bayard tells her that he is going to town, with the explanation, "You see, I want to be thought well of," she answers "I do [think well of you]. Even if you spend the day hidden in the stable loft, I still do" (p. 280). But he needs more than her good opinion.

Bayard does not resent the community's pressure; he dreads the thought of being dishonored in its eyes. His action, then, is to be thought of not as the rejection of a wrongheaded code of conduct but as the transcendence of that code in a complex action that honors the community's demand that he should call his father's assassin to account, while at the same time acknowledging the higher law embodied in "Thou shalt not kill." But to transcend the code in this fashion is of course to risk death, and though Bayard seems to have some youthful confidence that he will not die (see p. 250), he has no real reason for believing that Redmond will not shoot him on sight. The pressure upon Bayard to honor the code is not, however, merely external. For Bayard himself sufficiently embodies the community's values to hold himself to the code. When Aunt Jenny tells him, "I know you are not afraid," he replies, "But what good will that do? What good will that do? . . . I must live with myself, you see" (p. 276). Unless he confronts Redmond, he will never really be sure that his refusal to call him to account was not, after all, motivated by cowardice.

Bayard, of course, is fortunate, for Redmond, whom George Wyatt had called a brave man, is also a decent man. If, egged on past endurance, he has shot his political enemy, he has resolved not to kill the son. As Bayard walks steadily toward Redmond, he can see the slant of the barrel and he says: "I . . . watched that foreshortened slant of barrel which I knew was not aimed at me." From the beginning Bayard knew "it would miss me though his hand did not tremble" (p. 286). (Faulkner could not have made clearer the fact that Redmond has deliberately shot to the side. There is no question of a "misfire," as some careless readers have described the incident.)

The significance of what Bayard has done is not lost upon the community. George Wyatt, having heard the two shots, demands of Bayard: "You took the pistol away from him and then missed him, missed him *twice?*" (p. 288). Then George answers himself: "No; wait. You walked in here without even a pocket knife and let him miss you twice. My God in heaven." But he adds a moment later: "You ain't done anything to be ashamed of. I wouldn't have done it that way, myself. I'd a shot at him once, anyway. But that's your way or you wouldn't have done it" (p. 289). And even Drusilla, obsessed though she is, leaves a token of her recognition of his bravery, for Bayard finds on his pillow that night a single sprig of verbena "filling the room, the dusk, the evening with that odor which [Drusilla] said you could smell alone above the smell of horses" (p. 293).

Aunt Jenny, of course, has sensed all along what Bayard intends to do and, understanding him, has tried to say what she could to sustain him. But her manner of receiving him when he comes home after his confrontation with Redmond has caused some readers to mistake her meaning. She makes him kneel down in front of her chair and begins to chide him: "So you had a perfectly splendid Saturday afternoon, didn't you? Tell me about it." But she cannot keep up the pose and bursting into tears she exclaims, "Oh, damn you Sartorises! Damn you! Damn you!" (p. 292). In this outburst, relief and admiration, love and exasperation at the necessary folly of men are all intermingled.

This culminating section of *The Unvanquished* has in it some of the very finest passages that Faulkner has ever written. To mention only a few, there is the scene in which Drusilla greets Bayard dressed not in black but in a yellow ballroom gown, her eyes lighted up with fierce exultation and her voice "silvery and triumphant" (p. 271), quite as mad as Medea. She is acting out a ceremony but is so completely caught up in it that she becomes something rapt and terrible. There is the scene in which George Wyatt meets Bayard in town and gives him some technical advice as well as moral support. Here the dialogue reveals beautifully the character of the man, as when George comments on the derringer as a weapon. He remarks that "they are tricky things to fool with. Couldn't nobody but Colonel ever handle one right" (p. 284). But suddenly sensing that Bayard may not be intent on killing Redmond, George is swept with a surge of outrage: "By God, if you don't kill him, I'm going to." Then when he receives what he takes to be Bayard's assurance that he means to act, the fierceness fades from George's eyes—so it seems to Bayard—"exactly as you turn a lamp down," and George apologizes to his young friend: "You'll have to excuse me, son. I should have knowed you wouldn't do anything that would keep John from laying quiet. . . . And remember: [Redmond's] a brave man, but he's been sitting in that office by himself since yesterday morning waiting for you and his nerves are on edge" (p. 285).

There is the compelling bit of description in which the boy, with sensibility heightened in the excitement of walking toward his death, picks out the details of the approach to Redmond's office: "I looked once at the small faded sign nailed to the brick *B. J. Redmond. Atty at Law* and began to mount the stairs, the wooden steps scuffed by the heavy bewildered boots of countrymen approaching litigation and stained by tobacco spit, on down the dim corridor to the door which bore the name again, *B. J. Redmond* and knocked once and opened it. He sat behind the desk, not much taller than Father but thicker as a man gets who spends most of his time sitting and listening to people, freshly shaven and with fresh linen; a lawyer yet it was not a lawyer's face" (p. 285). And finally, there is the passage in which we follow Redmond after the shots are fired, a half-dazed man stumbling down the stairs and walking past the outraged cries of Wyatt and his friends to the station where the southbound train was just coming in, preparing to leave Jefferson forever.

Brilliant as "An Odor of Verbena" is considered as a story in its own right—it has frequently been printed as such in anthologies—it is much enriched when read in the context of the whole novel. Moreover, it completes the novel by drawing together the themes of the preceding sections and by marking the culmination of Bayard's development in one significant dramatic action. It is the concluding act in his long initiation into the moral responsibility that goes with manhood.

If one of the themes of *The Unvanquished* is that of a boy compelled to undertake a man's job, there is the related theme of the woman forced into a man's role. The case of Drusilla we have already discussed; but there is also that of "Miss" Rosa Millard who, finding that she has a method of getting mules from the Union army under forged orders, believes that it is her duty to furnish work animals to her poor neighbors. Finally, overreaching herself, she gets involved with the scalawags and is led to her death by Grumby. Miss Rosa is not, like Drusilla, unsexed, but she is forced into a role too difficult and dangerous for her. Both women are definitely casualties of the war.

The harm that they suffer has special point because in a traditional society such as this, women are assigned a definite and special role. This warping of the woman from her proper nature and function is one aspect of what is the overarching theme of the novel: the need for order and the disastrous effects on everyone of a breakdown in the civil order. In *The Unvanquished* we have a traditional society brought to lawlessness by becoming a sort of no man's land during the war. Drusilla and Bayard react to the breakdown in different—and characteristic—ways.

An obvious expression of this breakup is the exodus of the slaves who believe that the year of jubilee has come and take to the roads, moving blindly toward their Utopian dream. They are obsessed with a deeply human aspiration: they have taken seriously one of the basic promises of the religion that has been preached to them, and they believe quite literally what their emancipators have proclaimed. Now their embarrassed liberators do not know what to do with them as they destroy themselves like a horde of lemmings moving blindly and compulsively toward the sea. Their former masters cannot possibly cope with the situation. Miss Rosa does what she can: when she comes upon the young mother, burdened with her child, who has fallen by the road, she gives her food and tells her to go home. But the advice is meaningless. The woman cannot go home. Home has disappeared for her; she has no means for getting back, and the plantation from which she came may by this time be burned. But in any case, her very notion of home has been blotted out in the millennial glow. The Negro woman says: "Hit's Jordan we coming to. Jesus gonter see me that far" (p. 96). There is nothing for Miss Rosa to do but take her into the wagon and down the road, until she asks to be put down when they come upon another party of Negroes. Society is dissolving into pure formlessness.

Andrew Lytle's discussion of the character of Miss Rosa is illuminating.[9] Far from seeing her as primarily the heroic grandmother, fabulous and improbable, defeating the Yankees with her frail hand and imperturbable spirit—the Thomas Nelson Page stereotype for once, through some shocking lapse of taste, taken seriously by an otherwise great writer—Lytle tends to see her as a symbolic, almost allegorical figure, whose blindness to the real nature of the war allows her to set out upon the preposterous quest to recover her silver and horses and slaves. For Lytle her daring has in it as much blindness as bravery, and her exploits have their comic as well as their tragic aspect. He actually sees her death as brought on by her own greed and can even refer to her "fall." This, I believe, is to make Miss Rosa much more of a symbolic figure than the novel allows, and is to press the moral issues far too hard. Still, Lytle has provided a useful corrective to the dismissal of Miss Rosa as a stock figure in the old-fashioned Civil War novel.

One of the most revealing things about Miss Rosa is her re-

9. *Sewanee Review, 63* (1955), 114–37.

ligion. Her essential beliefs bear upon Faulkner's notion of Puritanism and his conception of the nature of woman, for Miss Rosa is typical of those who undergird and sustain the traditional society revealed in this novel. Specifically, she dominates Bayard's early life: she mediates his morality to him.

The problem of her ultimate creed is put forcibly by the Yankee lieutenant who, having discovered how clever she has been at forging requisitions, asks her not to tamper with the record on which his name is to appear. He pleads with her: "I have a family; I am a poor man. . . . And if in about four months the auditor should find a warrant in the records for a thousand dollars to Mrs. Rosa Millard, I would have to make it good" (p. 166). He is afraid to rely upon her mere promise not to do so, and wishes he could find a binding oath: " 'Confound it, I don't mean promise. If I just knew what you believed in, held—' He cursed again."

What does Miss Rosa believe in? Unquestionably, she believes in a god, but what god? Hers is evidently a god to whom she can and does talk back, even when, guilty of forgery and falsehood, she feels the need to confess. She declares: "I have sinned. I have stolen, and I have borne false witness against my neighbor, though that neighbor was an enemy of my country" (p. 167). But she calls God's attention to the fact that she did not sin for gain or greed: "I did not sin for revenge. I defy You or anyone to say I did. I sinned first for justice. And after that first time . . . I sinned for the sake of food and clothes for Your own creatures." She ends her strange prayer with the following words: "What I gained, I shared with them. It is true that I kept some of it back, but I am the best judge of that because I, too, have dependents who may be orphans, too, at this moment, for all I know. And if this be sin in Your sight, I take this on my conscience too. Amen."

In many ways this is an admirable prayer. There is absolutely no cringing; she puts the question honestly and she is willing to take full responsibility. But it is a prayer notably lacking in awe and reverence and humility. Ringo admires Miss Rosa's praying and catches its spirit exactly: "She 'cide what she wants and then she kneel down about ten seconds and tell God what she aim to do, and then she git up and do hit" (p. 105).

One of the features of Miss Rosa's religion is her high sense of rectitude and her severity with herself. It is she, not the community, who insists that she make public confession before the company gathered in the little country church.

Miss Rosa is another of Faulkner's Puritans—that is, she has not much concern for ritual or devotion as such; she has a strongly practical bent; she believes powerfully in good works; and she believes in God's justice (though toward the end of the war, her belief in His justice totters). More important still, Miss Rosa has very little metaphysical sense. To her, goodness means the nurturing and fostering of children, mercy for the helpless, aid for the poor, and, one is tempted to say, very little more. Here Miss Rosa is representative: Faulkner's women, when religious, tend to have either a kind of nature religion like that of Lena Grove, or something not unrelated to it—a worship of the gods of hearth and home. For the most part, they are content to leave theology and conscious ethical codes to men, who need such intellectual schema as women do not.

A disturbing problem of tone in this novel has to do with Miss Rosa's war against the Yankees. Could she possibly have managed to get the loot that she does get from them? Is it in the least likely that any Federal officer would have given her an order calling for the return of 110 Negroes, 110 horses, and 10 trunks of silver? If we are not to dismiss Colonel Dick's doing so as part of a farcical action, what serious motive can we assign to him? His liking for Miss Rosa, or his sense of exasperation at the state of affairs— "Damn this war," he exclaims—or possibly his sense of humor?

As a matter of historical fact, the Federal army was embarrassed by the presence of the Negroes, and some of the officers in that army might have happily welcomed any means to get rid of them. For example, Sherman on his march through Georgia reported to the War Department: "We . . . have gathered a large supply of negroes, mules, horses, etc . . . my first duty will be to clear the army of superfluous negroes, mules and horses." [10] And the Reverend F. Senour, who in 1865 published an account of Sherman's march, writes:

10. *Memoirs of Gen. W. T. Sherman* (New York, 1891), p. 201.

Gen. Sherman invites all able-bodied negroes (others could not make the march) to join the column, and he takes especial pleasure when they join the procession, on some occasions telling them they are free. . . . Thousands of negro women join the column, some carrying household truck; others, and many of them there are, who bear the heavy burden of children in their arms, while older boys and girls plod by their sides. All these women and children are ordered back, heart-rending though it may be to refuse them liberty.[11]

Faulkner thus has historical justification for the situation, including Colonel Dick's desire to get some of the Negroes off his hands. But Faulkner has been willing to treat the situation in terms that risk absurd exaggeration. A good share of the humor is at Miss Rosa's expense. She has been very careful to stipulate exactly what she wants back. She describes her chest of silver which is tied with a hemp rope—a *new* hemp rope. She mentions the names of the two slaves, Loosh and Philadelphy. She even gives the names of her mules: Old Hundred and Tinney. Colonel Dick has told her that he will be glad to give her twice the silver and mules just for taking "that many niggers." But by the time the order is finally executed, there are ten chests tied with hemp ropes and Old Hundred and Tinney have multiplied themselves into "a hundred and ten mules."

Perhaps the best justification of this wildly improbable incident is to say that Miss Rosa's mule-requisition game is not the matter of central consequence in the novel. The author might have easily trimmed it down toward probability by allowing Miss Rosa to take back her one trunk of silver, her slaves, and perhaps a dozen mules. And as for Miss Rosa's later actions in spoiling the Egyptians with her forged requisitions for mules and horses, it would have been sufficient to allow her two or three successful ventures before her downfall. Two or three would have been enough to show all that was needed about Miss Rosa's character

11. *Maj. Gen. William T. Sherman, and His Campaigns* (Chicago, 1865), pp. 330–31.

and her relation to Ringo and her grandson, and to account for her involvement with Snopes and her subsequent death.

But even the grotesque and farcical humor does not crowd out comedy of a very different kind. As Lytle has pointed out, when Miss Rosa, in her blind confidence in the basic decencies and in her almost religious respect for property, starts off on her quixotic errand, she "does not consciously see the war for what it is. To her it is the usual folly of man raised to its highest power. Her silver and mules and negroes have been stolen, not levied upon formally as the Articles of War allowed as late as the Revolution. She sets out to the proper authority to get them back, on the assumption that it is a crime against property."

She starts off as if she were going to make a social call or perhaps a business call, but with social overtones. "She sends for a more formal hat, since her call is to be formal; she 'borrows' the team; she carries rose cuttings as if everything was going on as usual . . . This is the usage of social order, small evidences of manners . . . of the decent behavior she knows. It is comedy, but it becomes a grim irony as the action progresses. More and more the nature of the war shows itself. Her house is burned along with the others." [12] When the wagon approaches the river, she finds herself in a world gone completely mad, in which all the conventions are overturned, where even decency and kindness assume almost monstrous terms, since the Union soldiers do not merely make restitution of what she has a right to demand back but give her a tenfold return, which in its exaggeration is a mockery of property rights.

The grim comedy associated with Miss Rosa's journey is far more indicative of Faulkner's attitude toward his characters than is the more obvious comedy in such scenes as that in which Miss Rosa makes the little boys, when they utter the word "bastard," wash out their mouths with soap; or that having to do with the humors of the colored servants; or that occasioned by the frustration of the Yankee soldiers, burdened with Negro refugees whom they do not want, or snarled in red tape, unable to cope with the

12. Lytle, *Sewanee Review, 63,* 131.

formidable Miss Rosa. So also is the comedy that runs through the section entitled "Skirmish at Sartoris." It is social comedy—a comedy of manners. Though the society has been engulfed by violence, Drusilla's mother and her embattled women-friends are as jealous as ever of the claims of respectability. They are bent upon saving Drusilla's reputation by seeing that John Sartoris makes her an honest woman. Drusilla's mother may possibly be deeply hurt by the danger to which her daughter has been physically exposed and by the blighting effects of such an experience upon her spirit. But what is certain is that she has been shocked by Drusilla's violation of the conventions. That is the wound that rankles. As Bayard and Ringo spell out the letter she wrote to Miss Rosa on wallpaper stationery with pokeberry juice for ink, Mrs. Hawk's conventional respectability appears in every phrasing. She tells her sister that Drusilla "was now living in a word that [she] would not even repeat but that [her sister] knew what it was, though at least thank God that Father and Drusilla were not actually any blood kin, it being Father's wife who was Drusilla's cousin by blood and not Father himself" (p. 219). Mrs. Hawk, Bayard's Aunt Louisa, relates in her letter that after Drusilla had been gone from home for six months, she had finally returned *"in the garments not alone of a man but of a common private soldier* and told them how she had been a member of [Colonel Sartoris'] troop for six months, bivouacking at night surrounded by sleeping men" (p. 220). When Drusilla had tried to explain that she was "riding in Cousin John's troop not to find a man but to hurt Yankees," Aunt Louisa's reply was: "At least don't call him *Cousin* John where strangers can hear you" (p. 220).

When Drusilla has finally been badgered into giving her consent to marry John Sartoris, there is the matter of planning the ceremony: "It was to be a big wedding; all Jefferson was to be invited and Mrs. Habersham planning to bring the three bottles of Madeira she had been saving for five years now when Aunt Louisa began to cry again. But [the ladies] caught on quick now; now all of them were patting Aunt Louisa's hands and giving her vinegar to smell and Mrs. Habersham saying, 'Of course. You poor thing. A public wedding now, after a year, would be a public notice of the . . .' So they decided it would be a reception, because Mrs. Habersham said how a reception could be held for a bridal couple at any time, even ten years later" (p. 235).

The element of social comedy—and it bulks rather large in *The Unvanquished*—points to the importance of the women in this novel, and three of them are very important—Drusilla, Miss Rosa, and Miss Jenny. Miss Jenny, it is true, appears only in the last section, "An Odor of Verbena," for she does not come to live with the Sartorises until 1869. But her presence in the story is crucial. She serves as a counter to Drusilla. Like Drusilla, she has lost a young husband in the war, though, as Bayard observes, she differs from Drusilla in the fact that she had at least been able to spend a few nights with him before he was killed. But she is everything that Drusilla is not and she is able to give Bayard precisely the sort of understanding which in his crisis he requires. When she looks at him before he goes to meet Redmond, her eyes are "intent and grave and (she was wise too) without pity" (p. 280). If she lacks Miss Rosa's obvious heroism, she also avoids the comedy associated with Miss Rosa's ridiculous adventure to retrieve her silver. We shall see Miss Jenny in other novels and stories as an old woman and a much more acid person than she is here. But there as here, she represents stability and sanity. She is not, like Miss Rosa, pulled out of her proper orbit by untoward events, nor like Drusilla, embittered and unsexed. She continues to be the nurturing and sustaining force on which a society rests.

6

The Waste Land: Southern Exposure

(SARTORIS)

TWO OF THE CHARACTERS who figure in *The Unvanquished* appear in the novel *Sartoris:* Bayard Sartoris (who is referred to in this novel as "old Bayard") and Mrs. Jenny Du Pre. The events that occur in the last section of *The Unvanquished* took place in 1873 or 74 (though the dating as given in *Sartoris* is 1876). In 1874 Bayard was twenty-four years old.[1] But *Sartoris* opens with a Bayard who is sixty-nine or seventy years old, for most of the events in this novel occur in 1919. Old Bayard's aunt, "Miss Jenny," who came to Mississippi in 1869 at the age of thirty, is now a very old woman indeed.

It may be difficult to recognize the Bayard Sartoris of *The Unvanquished* in the rather crotchety old banker who is fussed over by Aunt Jenny and by his coachman Simon, and who sputters or blusters at Simon in return, putters about his office, and exchanges reminiscences with old man Falls. One may be tempted to say that since *Sartoris* (Faulkner's third novel, published in 1929) appeared five years before *The Unvanquished,* the author had not at that time thought about the dilemmas of character and courage to which he would expose the young Bayard when he came to write *The Unvanquished.* This way of accounting for the discrepancies may well be sound, though it is perhaps risky to assume

1. See below, Sartoris Genealogy, p. 450.

that Faulkner would not have had in mind at a very early date the events in "An Odor of Verbena." Faulkner apparently carried many novels in his head for years before he actually wrote them down. But in any event, the more interesting way of handling this problem—and one tidier in terms of aesthetic theory—is to say that a young man who has his heroic hour may very well subside into a lifetime of rather conventional duties, and that in any case the man of seventy, however heroic his conduct at twenty-four, will seem stodgy to those who know him only as an old man. To have read *The Unvanquished* before reading *Sartoris* should enrich the latter book, not necessarily contradict it.

In the course of the years, Miss Jenny too has changed, and in perfectly natural ways. She is more tart, more acid of tongue, more the old matriarch set in her ways, and yet it is possible to recognize in her the young widow of "An Odor of Verbena."

A whole generation has dropped out between the events of 1874 and those of 1919. Though we are not told anything about old Bayard's wife, he has in the meantime married, his wife has died, and their son, John Sartoris, has been dead for some eighteen years. Indeed, besides old Bayard and Miss Jenny, the only Sartoris now alive is old Bayard's grandson, "young Bayard," who is now about twenty-five years old. He and his twin John had volunteered for the Royal Air Force and John had died in combat in July of 1918. A few months later, while young Bayard was still at the front, his wife and infant son had also died. Now in 1919 the grandfather and the great-great-aunt are awaiting young Bayard's return. He does return, but like a thief in the night; he slips off the train and prowls about for hours before he finally presents himself to his grandfather. Once he is home, he is restless and at loose ends, eaten up with guilt because in some irrational way he feels himself responsible for his twin brother's death, and unable to find any purpose or meaning on which he can base his peacetime life.

Within a few months young Bayard marries Narcissa Benbow, but he cannot settle down with his second wife; the marriage is precarious. Having killed his grandfather in an automobile accident—Bayard has a mania for driving too fast over the country roads—Bayard leaves Jefferson and a few months later himself dies in an airplane accident, as a test pilot flying an experimental plane. But his young widow is with child, and at the end of the novel she has borne another male Sartoris to carry on the line, though of the older generation only Miss Jenny now remains, as a link with the past.

The fortunes and death of young Bayard constitute one large element of the plot. The other has to do with his wife, Narcissa Benbow, and her brother Horace. The Benbows come of good family, one comparable to the Sartorises, but at the beginning of this novel neither brother nor sister has married. Horace is thirty-three years old, his sister is twenty-six, and the pair are very close to each other, unnaturally close. Horace too is returning from the war. He has been a YMCA secretary in the army, a role which earns him the jeers and catcalls of the returning veterans because of the widespread feeling among the troops in World War I that the YMCA, since it had been persuaded to run the army canteens, was a profit-making organization.

Horace is a somewhat finicky young man, very much the introvert, bookish, with a streak of the aesthete in him, a dabbler at the arts. (He has brought back with him from Europe a glass-blowing machine and hopes to learn how to make Venetian glassware.) Soon after his return, he becomes involved with a married woman, Belle Mitchell, and Belle subsequently goes to Reno to get a divorce from her husband Harry. By the end of the novel, Horace, to the disgust and alarm of his sister Narcissa, has married Belle.

Faulkner nowhere says that the breakup of the traditional society of antebellum times and the abandonment of its code was in essence a breakup of the family, with children bereft of proper fathers or mothers, reared as orphans, thrown too much upon their own resources, or deprived of the healthy atmosphere of a big family. Yet such dislocations seem to be the basic difficulties besetting all the younger people in the novel. If there is a decadence, it seems to be conditioned by, and to take its characteristic form from, this kind of childhood rearing.

Young Bayard and Horace constitute a neatly opposed pair of romanticists. Bayard is not in the least bookish; he would scorn any noncombatant's place in the war. He is the man of action; his anodyne is speed. Indeed the only release that he can get from his emotional difficulties is in courting danger, in taking the dare to ride an unbroken stallion, or in racing an automobile too high powered for the country roads. (By contrast, Horace does not own a car and has never learned to drive one.) Apart from his courting of danger, Bayard seems most at home on a hunt with simpler characters like some of the Negro servants about the place or with the McCallums, a family of yeoman stock who still live a life close to that of frontier days.

Miss Jenny refers to young Bayard's recklessness as something in his blood. The Sartorises are "savages, every one of 'em" (p. 298). And there is much in the novel to emphasize this particular interpretation. But in spite of Miss Jenny's old-fashioned notions of racial inheritance, Bayard's trouble is in great part referable not to his family or to his blood but to his experiences as a war-time aviator. In *Faulkner in the University* (p. 23) Faulkner comments on what happened to the airplane pilots of the First World War. He says: "In a way they were dead, they had exhausted themselves psychically . . . anyway, they were unfitted for the world that they found afterward." And on a later page he comes back to the theme with the comment: "I do know that the flying people out of that war, most of them would have been better off if they had died on the eleventh of November, that few of them were any good to try to take up the burden of peace, and this man [he is speaking of Jock in the story "Death Drag"] was lost and doomed." [2] Young Bayard is lost and doomed in just this sense, and the fact that he has Sartoris blood in his veins would seem to make very little difference.

It is a curious fact that the impact made upon our writers and intellectuals by the first World War seems to have been much more profoundly shattering than that made by the second. In

2. See p. 48; see also "Ad Astra," *Collected Stories* (New York: Random House, 1950), pp. 407–29.

September 1914 D. H. Lawrence, in a hitherto unpublished letter to a friend, made what proved to be a true prophecy:

> The war makes me depressed, the talk about the war makes me sick, and I have never come so near to hating mankind as I am now. They are fools, vulgar fools, and cowards who will always make a noise because they are afraid of the silence. I I don't even mind if they are killed. What I do mind is that those who are sensitive, will receive such a blow from the ghastliness and mechanical, obsolete, hideous stupidity of war, that they will be crippled beings further burdening our sick society. Those that die, let them die. But those that live afterwards—the thought of them makes me sick.[3]

This theme has, of course, received brilliant treatment in the fiction of Ernest Hemingway, as, for instance, in the story of Harold Krebs in "Soldier's Home." The difference between Bayard and Krebs is that the society to which Bayard returns is a traditional society, and that very fact heightens Bayard's sense of alienation. Young Bayard is remorseful and hagridden with vague guilt, but here we must be careful not to misconstrue his Southern heritage. It is not, for example, his sense of an ancestral responsibility for slavery that is gnawing at him. He is restless and disturbed, but his plight reflects the stunning effect of the war rather than the decadence of the Southern aristocratic tradition or the burden of a family curse.

We have noted that both Bayard and Horace Benbow are romanticists, though diametrically opposed in their personalities. Yet Horace in his own way is as much a product of his time as is Bayard. He is indeed one of the sad young men of the period, an inhabitant of the cultural waste land. When we meet Horace Benbow for the first time (p. 161) his "wretchedly-fitting khaki . . . but served to accentuate his air of fine and delicate futility." When he lies in his bedroom that night (p. 179) he voyages "in lonely regions . . . beyond the moon, about meadows nailed with firmamented stars to the ultimate roof of things, where unicorns

3. In the possession of the author.

filled the neighing air with galloping, or grazed or lay supine in golden-hooved repose." One of the ladies at Belle's party remarks that "Horace is a poet" (p. 184), and indeed he is, a poet of the nineties, a rather poor poet in a lushly decadent way. But Horace has the good sense, or perhaps simply the good taste, not to put his poetry on paper except as it spills over in letters written to his sister Narcissa.

Horace will write to Narcissa in this fashion: "Perhaps fortitude is a sorry imitation of something worth while, after all, to the so many who burrow along like moles in the dark, or like owls, to whom a candle-flame is a surfeit. But not to those who carry peace along with them as the candle-flame carries light. I have always been ordered by words, but it seems that I can even restore assurance to my own cowardice by cozening it a little. I dare say you cannot read this, as usual, or reading it, it will not mean anything to you. But you will have served your purpose anyway, thou still unravished bride of quietness" (p. 352). In these words we hear the accents of a less sophisticated J. Alfred Prufrock.

Earlier versions of *Sartoris* (preserved in manuscript and typescript) show that originally Faulkner stressed even more heavily the themes and mood of Prufrock and the waste land. Much attention is given to the nature of Horace's special relationship to his sister and to Horace's colloquies with himself. His mood is fatalistic. The draft preserved in manuscript tells us that the "still unchanging days" just after his return from the war "were doomed days; he knew it . . . during this period not only did his immediate days become serenely inevitable, but the dead thwarted ones with all their special and ludicrous disasters . . . grew luscious in retrospect and without regret, and those to come seemed as undeviating and logical as mathematical formulae." The manuscript version stresses Horace's shyness and moral indolence: "All he wanted anyway was quiet and dull peace and a few women, preferably young and good-looking, and fair tennis players, with whom to indulge in harmless and delicate intrigues." The manuscript draft tells us, incidentally, that Horace, on leaving Oxford, had almost decided to become an Episcopalian clergyman before family responsibilities imposed by his father's illness pushed him into the law. The early versions contain a great deal of Horace's decadent poetic prose, such as the following: "you ought to run in a cheese-cloth shimmy on hills under a new moon. . . . No, not the moon; but in a dawn like pipes green and gold, and maybe a little pink. Would you risk a little pink?" In the typescript Horace is described somewhere as having a "thin face brilliant and sick with nerves." [4]

When the book was prepared for publication, a good deal of Horace's decadent poetry was wisely trimmed away, many of his introspective reflections were pruned, and his conscious acknowledgment of a quasi-incestuous relationship with his sister was toned down; but even in the printed version Horace remains very much the middle-aging man filled with nostalgia for a world of dreams and with disillusionment for the present.

One can argue, of course, that Horace represents the decadence of the Southern aristocratic tradition, but the specific models for Horace's distemper are Eliot's deracinated young men among the Boston teacups or the protagonist of *The Waste Land* walking along the autumn-stricken Thames. In any case, these figures are sufficient proof that the blight was generally Anglo-American and not specifically Southern. But Horace Benbow's mood is adapted—naturally—to his own special world, and there is much in that provincial world to give body and flesh to the mood: the sense of a quiet backwater removed from the great current of events, the memory that once, however, even in this quiet backwater, there occurred deeds of violence and glory, and, most of all, Horace's consciousness that he is a weak and ineffectual dreamer incapable of the power and authority of his ancestors.

Yet there is the presence of young Bayard to indicate that the situation is not so simple as Horace's plight would imply; for Bayard's love of action and rapport with violence do not suffice either. Indeed, Horace and young Bayard are neatly reversed images of each other. Neither of them has a life purpose; neither has a true vocation. Both are somehow cut off and lost. But as with

4. I quote from the typescript. The manuscript version reads somewhat differently: "hills blanched by the moon . . . dawn all green and gold, and pink a little, maybe. Would you risk pink?"

Horace, so with Bayard: his plight is set off the more sharply because it has for its background a traditional society in which there is a true community, which means that there is a community of values as well as an organic society.

One can, however, be more specific still: the sick and agitated violence of Bayard and the morbidly effete dreaminess of Horace Benbow contrast with the stability of the other characters in the novel. There are the older people who have played a heroic role in the past and represent the force of the older tradition, notably old Bayard and Miss Jenny. There are the Negroes, with their power of endurance and their own vitality. There are white men like Surratt and the McCallums, who represent the folk tradition —still sane, vigorous, and very much alive. (Even the Snopeses have a sense of purpose, though it resembles animal cunning.) And there are the women—though some of them have become corrupted in the new order of things.

Except for *Sanctuary,* no Faulkner novel brings the war between the sexes more clearly into the open or stresses more sharply what Faulkner conceives of as the basically different attitudes of men and women. As elsewhere in Faulkner, the men are romantic, obsessed with their foolish codes, quixotic schemes, and violent follies. It is the women who are practical, concerned with the concrete actualities and committed undeviatingly to first principles, though the women in *Sartoris* vary greatly. Belle Mitchell, who betrays her rather silly husband and entraps Horace, is a real bitch. She is seen by Aunt Jenny at once for what she is, and Narcissa describes her, with loathing and hatred, as "dirty." Horace himself is aware of Belle's cruelty and selfishness.

Miss Jenny and Narcissa are much more interesting and more complicated than Belle. In calling his sister an "unravished bride of quietness," Horace speaks more accurately than he could have known, for there is indeed something incorrigibly virginal about Narcissa. She is terribly afraid of men. What seems early in the novel to be simple shyness, a rather attractive little-girl bashfulness, turns out to be a deep-rooted coldness and a considered inability to make any concessions to men. Miss Jenny says to Narcissa half-seriously, half-jokingly, that Horace is "making an old maid out of you." She shrewdly adds, however, that if Horace had waited another five years "to play the fool [with Belle], there wouldn't have been anything left for you except to give music lessons" (p. 259). The marriage between Narcissa and Bayard does ensue, but though Narcissa becomes a mother, she never really becomes a wife, and at the end of the novel we find her resolute in her war against men, marshaling all her forces to protect her child from ever becoming what his father was.

Narcissa thinks to herself "that there would be peace for her only in a world where there were no men at all" (p. 245). Thinking so, why does she ever marry Bayard Sartoris? In part, because she is fascinated by him; her fear and disapproval of him act as magnets. In part, because Miss Jenny is quietly making the match. But most of all, because Horace, in preparing to marry Belle Mitchell, is breaking up the cozy nest they have shared.

One must be sympathetic with Narcissa. She does try hard to make a go of her marriage. She tries to follow her desperate young husband, physically, on some of his night hunts, spiritually, in his lonely malaise. But it would take a more womanly woman, a wiser and also a more passionate creature than Narcissa is, to reclaim Bayard. Miss Jenny once asks Narcissa: "Are you worrying because maybe he don't love you like you think he ought to?" And Narcissa gives her an honest and a perceptive answer: "It isn't that. He doesn't love anybody. He won't even love the baby. He doesn't seem to be glad, or sorry, or anything" (p. 298). Miss Jenny refers this callousness to the Sartoris blood, but the numbness of spirit is, as we have seen, what Faulkner attributes to many people of Bayard's generation and experience.

One of the most revealing things about Narcissa is her attitude toward the anonymous love letters that are sent to her by the bank clerk, Byron Snopes. Narcissa has no idea who is writing these passionate, illiterate, and obscene letters. She shows one of them to Miss Jenny, with the explanation that showing it to someone else will perhaps make her feel less filthy. Miss Jenny wonders why she should feel filthy at all, since no misconduct has invited the letters. Were the letter not a possible clue to discovering the sender, Miss Jenny would burn it at once. But Narcissa shrinks from Miss Jenny's suggestion that she turn it over to Bayard.

Narcissa is a shy girl, diffident, anxious to maintain her reserve, and yet something more than shyness and inertia is probably involved. Miss Jenny more than hints as much. She herself would have known what to do. She would have turned the letters over to some man in the family who would have located the villain and horsewhipped him. Or she would have dropped them immediately in the fire as fast as they appeared. Certainly they would not have made her feel filthy.

Narcissa, rather perversely, keeps the letters—until they are stolen from her bedroom. In the short story "There Was a Queen" we are told how Narcissa, years later, recovered them. When the letters turn up in the possession of a Federal agent, Narcissa gets them back by the simple and practical expedient of yielding her body for a night as the price for their return. Respectability triumphs over virtue. Better to be for once the kind of person the letters beseech her to be rather than remain innocent and virtuous with the possibility that other men may read the letters and *think* that she is not virtuous. When Miss Jenny learns how Narcissa got the letters back, it is the end of Miss Jenny: she is found a little later sitting up straight like the patrician that she is, dead in her chair—and high time, when women who bear the name of the family are so anxious to be known as ladies that they will prostitute themselves for the name's sake. But all this occurs some ten years after the events that take place in *Sartoris*, and it could be argued that the Narcissa of "There Was a Queen" is not necessarily the same person as her younger and earlier self.

Narcissa's inner contradictions hint of a deep-seated malaise, but Miss Jenny has none: she is not at odds with herself. She is clearly at home in her world. She affects to hold in contempt the wild follies of the Sartoris clan, but she obviously loves them. She enjoys telling the story of her brother's exploits in the Civil War, even his madcap prank of riding back after the anchovies "with all Pope's army shooting at him" (p. 17). Some of her waspishness is genuine enough. Being a true woman, she cannot help seeing through the folly of man's quixotic conduct. But some of her exasperation at the Sartoris menfolk is clearly assumed, a pose that she has cultivated through the years. Narcissa, on this point a sound witness, evidently thinks so. Narcissa admires Miss Jenny and thinks how much braver Miss Jenny is than her male relatives, how much finer is the "uncomplaining steadfastness of those" women like Miss Jenny "than the fustian and useless glamour of the men that obscured it." Yet she is suspicious of her, for as Narcissa hugs her child to her, she thinks: "And now she is trying to make me one of them; to make of my child just another rocket to glare for a moment in the sky" (p. 358). Miss Jenny is a Sartoris after all.

Narcissa's case against her husband and the Sartorises defines itself for her as she looks at a miniature of her husband Bayard as a child. She finds in the little picture "not that bleak arrogance she had come to know in Bayard's [face], but a sort of frank spontaneity, warm and ready and generous." As she looks at the picture, "there shone like a warm radiance something sweet and merry and wild." Sensing this, "she realized as she never had before the blind tragedy of human events" (p. 356). It is from such a transformation that she vows she will protect her unborn child.

If the younger aristocratic generation, male and female, young Bayard and Horace, and Narcissa as well, are shaken and baffled, divided and alienated, the folk society remains sane and strong. V. K. Surratt (who will be renamed Ratliff in later novels) and the McCallums are not confused by the times. They maintain the elemental human decencies and sympathies. Surratt is a sewing-machine salesman of good sense, salty converse, and philosophical disposition. The McCallum boys live with their father well out from town. They love the woods, are great hunters, and their lives have a Spartan simplicity. But their lives also have the natural dignity of all lives that possess a certain form and discipline.

Surratt and the McCallums represent a very different social stratum from that occupied by Bayard. But it is typical of the easygoing social relations within the Southern community of the period that there should be a comfortable association between Bayard and these friends of yeoman stock, who have had far less formal education than he has had and who have rather different social aspirations from his, but who are not sensitive on that score and who have no misgivings about their own worth and dignity.

A nice little touch, significant of some of these social differences, occurs in the incident in which Bayard goes with Surratt to get a drink and have some conversation. They take the jug down to where "the spring welled from the roots of the beech, into a wooden frame sunk to its top in white sand that quivered cease-lessly and delicately beneath the water's limpid unrest" (p. 138). Surratt and his friend Hub squat on their heels while drinking, and Bayard sociably "squatted also on his heels against the bole of the beech tree" (p. 139); but Bayard soon feels his legs grow numb and has to straighten them, whereas Surratt and Hub "appeared to be able to sit tirelessly and without discomfort on their heels" (p. 141). This ability to squat comfortably on one's heels is a trait of Southern country people. It is the trait that gives away to Lucas Beauchamp, in "The Fire and the Hearth," the origin of the tricked-out Memphis salesman who is trying to sell him the money-finding machine.

Later on, when Bayard has killed his grandfather by his reck-less driving, he is ashamed to go home and rides out into the country to stay with the hospitable McCallums. The walls of the McCallums' house "were of chinked logs. On them hung two or three outdated calendars and a patent medicine lithograph in colors. The floor was bare, of hand-trimmed boards scuffed with heavy boots and polished by the pads of generations of dogs; two men could lie side by side in the fireplace. In it now four-foot logs blazed against the clay fireback, swirling in wild plumes into the chimney's dark maw" (p. 309). It is against this background of solid values and purposeful life that Bayard sees "the recent months of his life coldly in all their headlong and heedless waste-fulness." But Bayard cannot find refuge with the McCallums for long, for he knows that they are soon bound to hear of his grand-father's death and he is ashamed for them to know how he died. Accordingly, when the McCallum wagon takes its trip to town, Bayard makes an excuse and leaves. That evening—it is Christmas Eve—he takes lodging for the night, on the pretext that he has lost his way, at a Negro cabin he has found by chance.

The scene in the cabin is beautifully realized. Here Christmas is celebrated in the direst poverty. There are the three little children in nondescript garments, with their poor and trivial toys and their bit of peppermint candy. There is the Christmas dinner —"possum with yams, more gray ash cake, the dead and tasteless liquid in the coffee pot; a dozen bananas and jagged shards of cocoanut, the children crawling about his feet like animals, scenting the food" (p. 347). Bayard realizes at last that the Negro couple are waiting until he has finished eating, "but he overrode them and they [all] dined together."

Though Faulkner nowhere makes the point explicitly—and it does not need to be made explicitly—the Negro family represents genuinely, if in its humblest form, the precious thing that Bayard has forfeited. After the dinner, Bayard induces the Negro to drive him, even though it is Christmas day, to the nearest station, and he takes the train, nevermore to return to Jefferson.

In his introduction to the Signet edition (1953) of *Sartoris*, Robert Cantwell makes much of the fact that *Sartoris* is a key volume among Faulkner's works, "the one that sets the pattern for them all" (p. vii). Among other things, he tells us, this novel introduces the two great families that figure so powerfully in Faulkner's novels, the Sartoris family, who represent the declining aristocratic tradition, and their opposites and opponents, the Snopes family. But the Snopeses have little to do with the action of this novel. There are references to Montgomery Ward Snopes, who had gone away to war with Horace Benbow, and to Flem Snopes, already vice-president of the Sartoris bank. But only Byron Snopes, who works in the bank and writes the obscene letters to Narcissa, affects the basic plot.

As was pointed out in chapter 3, one must not assume that the yeoman farmers or even the poor-white farmers are necessarily Snopeses. Surratt and the McCallums are of quite another breed. Whereas Flem Snopes is the complete predator, single-minded in his drive for money and power, the McCallums are perfectly self-sufficient, covet no man's property, are certain of their standards of honor and conduct, and live in a thoroughly stable world. They and their world may be doomed to become obsolete, but they do not represent any portion of a sick society.

A last group, set in contrast to the disoriented Bayard and Horace, is that of the Negroes. Faulkner's treatment of them in this novel, however, will be the part of it most difficult for the reader of our mid-century to accept. He may object to what he regards as the use of stereotypes: Simon, the old family retainer, fussed at and petted, able to wheedle his way with his white folks, but swaggering and blustering among his own people; or Caspey, the "uppity" Negro who comes back from France with new ideas and has to learn his place once more; or Elnora, the typical mellow-voiced, hymn-singing Negro cook. Since 1929, when this novel was first published, the whole matter of the proper treatment of Negro characters in fiction has become a highly charged issue. The easiest way out, of course, would be simply to concede the presence of stereotypes here, and to plead that Faulkner in his later work has treated the Negro with great sympathy and dignity, and that some of his most admirable characters are Negroes. But the treatment of the Negro in *Sartoris* need not be allowed to go simply by default.

Reference has already been made to the beautifully handled scene in which Bayard eats Christmas dinner with the Negro share-cropper's family. In this scene the Negroes are treated with a scrupulous fidelity to the facts of the situation, and it is they who come off well in the scene, not the deracinated Bayard. (Bayard himself is evidently touched by what he sees and, for once, makes the proper response.) There are other scenes in which the Negro is used to set off Bayard's folly or cruelty—that, for example, in which Bayard takes old Simon with him in the car and, jamming the accelerator to the floor, tries to scare Simon out of his wits. Later Bayard "felt savage and ashamed" (p. 119). One should also mention the episode in which Bayard and his friends take three Negro musicians in the car with them to serenade the ladies. In the course of the evening they share their jug with the Negroes, though at the beginning Bayard, not having a cup handy, takes the breather-cap from the engine of the car and has the Negroes drink from that. But later, after more music and more whisky, when the breather-cap has been lost, "all six of them drank fraternally from the jug, turn and turn about" (p. 157).

Sartoris is not an argument about what the relation between the two races ought to be, but a rendering of the actuality of its time, in which the relationship is presented as it was in all its complexity and with all its aspects: good, bad, and indifferent; pathetic, cruel, or tender.[5]

One may sum up by saying that of all Faulkner's novels, *Sartoris* most resembles, on the one hand, a novel by Ernest Hemingway, and on the other, an old-fashioned Southern novel of the turn of the century. The combination is odd, but it is characteristically Faulknerian. The special problems of the twenties and a good deal of the mood of the waste land are here placed in a small Southern town that is still suffused with the atmosphere of the post-Civil-War period. But the troubles of neither young Bayard nor Horace Benbow have much to do with the "downfall of the Old South," even though Faulkner has chosen to present these men of the lost generation against the background of a traditional society.

If Faulkner has chosen conventional—and even stock—characters for heightening the theme of the lost generation, the writing itself is not at all stock writing. *Sartoris* is an extremely well-written novel. There are purple passages, to be sure, as when Faulkner at the end of his novel can write of the name "Sartoris": "For there is death in the sound of it, and a glamorous fatality, like silver pennons downrushing at sunset, or a dying fall of horns along the road to Roncevaux" (p. 380). And sometimes literary allusions are used a little trickily, as in the last sentence of the novel: ". . . beyond the window evening was a windless lilac dream, foster dam of quietude and peace." But the staple of the writing is crisp and sure. Here is a mean boarding house, for example: "The hall smelled of damp, harsh soap, and the linoleum carpet gleamed, still wet. He followed it and approached a sound of steady, savage activity, and came upon a woman in a shapeless gray garment, who ceased mopping and looked at him across her gray shoulder, sweeping her lank hair from her brow with a reddened forearm" (p. 106). Or here is an account of a hangover in the waste land: "His head was clear and cold; the whisky he had drunk was completely dead. Or rather, it was as though his head

5. For further discussion see below, Notes, p. 385.

were one Bayard who lay on a strange bed and whose alcohol-dulled nerves radiated like threads of ice through that body which he must drag forever about a bleak and barren world with him. . . . Three score and ten years to drag a stubborn body about the world and cozen its insistent demands. Three score and ten, the Bible said. Seventy years. And he was only twenty-six" (p. 160). Or here is a passage in which some Negroes on a wagon discover the car that Bayard has just overturned:

> The mules flapped their jack-rabbit ears and lurched the wagon into motion and they descended among cool, dappled shadows, on the jarring scrape of the locked wheel that left behind it a glazed bluish ribbon in the soft red dust. At the foot of the hill the road crossed the bridge and went on mounting again; beneath the bridge the creek rippled and flashed brownly among willows, and beside the bridge and bottom up in the water, a motorcar lay. Its front wheels were still spinning and the engine ran at idling speed, trailing a faint shimmer of exhaust. [p. 206]

Sartoris teems with literary echoes. When, for instance, Faulkner writes: "and the very earth itself might have found voice, grave and sad, and wild with all regret" (p. 333), he is remembering Tennyson's "Tears, Idle Tears." But the world evoked in this novel is not a world of romantic shadows. It has depth and substance and solidity. It is a world hot and dusty in the sun, and if the author sometimes betrays a wistful romanticism toward the Sartoris family, this is not the prevailing tone of the novel. There is too much realism, too much savage humor, for us to feel that the basic mood is nostalgic or the key minor. Bayard may be a lost soul, Horace an ineffectual dreamer; the one can only destroy himself by violence; the other, waste himself away with futility. But the folk society that lies around them goes on in its immemorial ways. It is neither sick nor tired. It has all the vitality of an old and very tough tree.

7

Discovery of Evil

(SANCTUARY and REQUIEM FOR A NUN)

THE THEME OF *Sanctuary* is the discovery of the nature of reality with the concomitant discovery of evil, and it recurs throughout Faulkner's work. In *The Unvanquished* Bayard Sartoris triumphantly passes the crucial test of courage in which his initiation culminates. But in *Sanctuary* the initiation of Horace Benbow has a much more somber ending. Instead of victory and moral vindication, Horace receives a stunning defeat. Horace is, of course, a different kind of man from Bayard and furthermore the times have changed. The traditional society has given place to a modern world in which amoral power is almost nakedly present.

Here, as in *Sartoris*, Horace is the man of academic mind, who finds out that the world is not a place of justice and moral tidiness. He discovers, with increasing horror, that evil is rooted in the very nature of things. Horace represents a type that appears often in Faulkner's work, not only in the early novels but again prominently in his last novels. He is an "intellectual." He has a great capacity for belief in ideas and a great confidence in the efficacy of reason. In *Sanctuary* Faulkner has made Benbow ineffectual in his contest with evil, but Faulkner has succeeded so well that many of his readers accord Horace something less than his due. Yet he must have his due, for if Benbow is a mere weakling, one loses the very point of the novel, which is a sense of the horrifying power of evil.

The truth of the matter is that a stronger man and a more aggressive lawyer than Horace Benbow might have failed under the circumstances. Horace demonstrates a good deal of pertinacity, shrewdness, and vigor. Having interested himself in Lee Goodwin and his wife, he works steadily to try to get his clients to talk. Lee Goodwin's own fatalism and his specific fear of the gangster Popeye's gun make it very difficult for Horace to get any help from his client. Later on, however, Ruby does give him a hint, namely that there was a girl on the Old Frenchman's Place the day that Tommy was shot. Horace tries to track down this mysterious girl, who may become his key witness. His getting the tip from Clarence Snopes has, of course, to be put down to sheer luck, but he follows up the tip vigorously and even wins the sympathy of Miss Reba, the madam of the brothel. This in itself is no small accomplishment. With her help, he persuades Temple Drake to agree to testify in favor of Lee Goodwin.

Horace takes what measures he can to ensure that Temple will remain in Memphis, where he can keep in touch with her as he awaits Goodwin's trial. This last point, by the way, is worth some comment, for at least one critic has reproached Benbow for waiting "until the night before the trial before he can decide to expose her as a witness. By that time it is too late." [1] But Horace calls up Miss Reba about a week after he had visited Temple, some nine or ten days before the trial,[2] "just to know if she's still there. So I can reach her if I need to" (p. 321). Miss Reba replies that Temple is still there all right, "but this reaching. I dont like it. I dont want no cops around here unless they are on my business." But Horace does call once more, the day before the trial, and this time finds that Temple has suddenly disappeared.

Horace is not, however, paralyzed by Temple's failure to show up at the trial. He carries on without her and has good hopes of success. (Had his sister, Narcissa, not betrayed him to the district attorney, he probably would have won his case.) What Horace, understandably, was not prepared for was Temple's *volte-face*—

1. Peter Lisca, "Some New Light on Faulkner's *Sanctuary*," *Faulkner Studies*, 2 (1953), 8.

2. See below, Chronology of Events in *Sanctuary*, p. 387.

her appearance on the second day of the trial with perjured testimony against which almost any attorney would have contended in vain. It is true that Horace does collapse after this body blow. The fight has been taken out of him, his rebellion against family pressures is over, and he goes back to the wife whom he should never have married and whom he has tried to leave. But as Faulkner has plotted this novel, a man much more practical, hard-headed, and belligerent than Horace Benbow would have been defeated.

One has also to remember that *Sanctuary* shows the stamp of its time and of its genre. It is a gangster novel of a sort: [3] the brilliance of the writing cannot conceal that fact. In a gangster story it is almost impossible to get the witnesses, including the gangster's victims, to testify against him. The gangster leads a charmed life, for the lethargic community, the corrupt public official, and the ordinary citizen, paralyzed with fear, allow him to escape punishment. All this is as true of stories laid in Cook County, Illinois, as of Yoknapatawpha County, Mississippi. In this connection, it may be worth noting that the real fatalist is the man on trial, Lee Goodwin, the rough-hewn hill man, and not his attorney, Horace Benbow, the son of a distinguished judge, with a love for Venetian glass and world-weary poetry. Lee Goodwin is certain that he is "doomed" and that Popeye, whether by a bullet through the jail window or by some other means, will see to it that he does not go free. By contrast, it is Benbow who remains hopeful to the end.

Sanctuary is not only a gangster novel; it is, as André Malraux has suggested, also something of a detective novel,[4] in that the meaning of certain events is not revealed until the end, and the author builds suspense, complicates his plot, and presents his reader with sudden and surprising developments. Indeed, there is something of a puzzle about just what does happen in the courtroom scene at the end of the novel; and some readers have been puzzled also by Popeye's conduct after he has been arrested for murder.

3. See below, Notes, p. 391.
4. *"Sanctuaire,* c'est l'intrusion de la tragédie grecque dans le roman policier." In "Préface à 'Sanctuaire' de W. Faulkner," *Nouvelle Revue française, 41* (1933), 747.

Part of the difficulty arises because the author is obviously concerned with something more important than a mere story of crime, with its plot suspense and exciting action. But some of the difficulty is to be referred to certain of Faulkner's methods of presentation. For one thing, he deliberately refrains from entering into the minds of his characters at the moments when they make their decisions. For another, he refuses—perhaps for fear of killing the psychological suspense—to fill in certain gaps in the action. The result is that the motive for an act is often merely implied, and sometimes the act itself is merely implied. The reader may therefore be confused, not only as to why something happened but as to what actually did happen.

Faulkner's chosen methods are very effective for presenting scenes of action with almost intolerable immediacy, for rendering psychological states, and for building up a sense of foreboding and horror. In his concern with this mode of presentation, however, he has slighted the analysis of motive, the articulation of action with thought, and the usual methods for working out the plot. We are not, for example, allowed inside Popeye's mind as he awaits his execution. The scene is vividly rendered: the curious little man methodically crushing out his cigarettes and carefully arranging the butts in a neat line to form a sort of calendar marking the days that have elapsed. But what is going on inside his head? Why is it that he will not summon a lawyer? Has he resolved upon a kind of suicide? Or is it that he simply cannot believe that he is to be hanged? The author does not show us—or if he does, it is only through hints and suggestions. In fact, a great deal of the power of the novel comes from the naked objectivity of such scenes as this of Popeye in prison or that of Temple Drake in the courtroom. They are rendered in compelling detail, though without explicit reference to the inner thoughts of the characters.

Having in mind Faulkner's use of this kind of technique, one may be tempted to call *Sanctuary* a mood piece rather than a novel proper. The interpretation of the situation is often mediated to the reader poetically rather than through the more normal modes of fiction. Consider what the author accomplishes in the mere description of a room in Miss Reba's brothel (p. 185):

The light hung from the center of the ceiling, beneath a fluted shade of rose-colored paper browned where the bulb bulged it. The floor was covered by a figured maroon-tinted carpet tacked down in strips; the olive-tinted walls bore two framed lithographs. From the two windows curtains of machine lace hung, dust-colored, like strips of lightly congealed dust set on end. The whole room had an air of musty stoginess,[5] decorum; in the wavy mirror of a cheap varnished dresser, as in a stagnant pool, there seemed to linger spent ghosts of voluptuous gestures and dead lusts. In the corner, upon a faded scarred strip of oilcloth tacked over the carpet, sat a washstand bearing a flowered bowl and pitcher and a row of towels; in the corner behind it sat a slop jar dressed also in fluted rose-colored paper.

The style is what Joyce would have called "scrupulously mean." But though the mode is apparently that of naturalism, the whole passage glows with meaning. The physical picture is convincing and even compelling in its detail, but there is much more than the physical picture, and much more than a vague aura. The author relentlessly exposes the pretentious sleasiness of the room and the faked respectability that emanates from the machine-made lace curtains, the crazed "wavy" mirror, and the slop jar, swathed in rose-colored paper.

Another obvious example of Faulkner's descriptive power occurs in his celebrated view of Popeye at the spring: "His suit was black, with a tight, high-waisted coat. His trousers were rolled once and caked with mud above mud-caked shoes. His face had a queer, bloodless color, as though seen by electric light; against the sunny silence, in his slanted straw hat and his slightly akimbo arms, he had that vicious depthless quality of stamped tin" (p. 2).

The prose never becomes shrill, the attitude remains thoroughly detached, but the damnation is absolute. Here two figures of speech do most of the work of interpretation. They rob Popeye of substance and make him a sinister black silhouette against the spring landscape. "As though seen by electric light" justifies the

5. Corrected to "stodginess" in 1962 ed.

description of his queer, bloodless color, but it does more: juxta-
posed as it is to the phrase "against the sunny silence," it introduces the sense of the contrived and artificial, as though Popeye
were a kind of monstrous affront to the natural scene. At the least
it sets up notions of a sort that will be confirmed at the end of
the sentence with the phrasing "depthless quality of stamped tin."
Popeye is here not merely described physically, but interpreted
and judged.

Thus the author, through the very rendering of scene and action, supplies the interpretation of its meaning. But has Faulkner
done so sufficiently in the trial scene? Why does Temple Drake
break her promise to Horace Benbow and commit perjury by accusing Lee Goodwin of the rape and the murder of which he
was innocent? What is her motive? We are never told directly,
nor are we allowed to follow the play of her thoughts and emotions, either at the time at which she decided to perjure herself or
during the scene in which she actually gives her false testimony.
Instead, there is only a powerful reporting of the trial scene as a
spectator might have observed it. Detail after detail is picked out
in a hard light. Some of Temple's responses to the district attorney are given verbatim, but others are simply implied; furthermore, many of the questions put to her are merely implied or sum-
marized.

There are, to be sure, scenes in the novel in which we are allowed to see what goes on in Temple's mind. When she tells Horace
Benbow the long and horrifying story about what happened at the
Old Frenchman's Place, we are put very definitely and emphatically
inside her mind and so inside her cringing and outraged flesh. But
in this crucial scene of the trial we merely observe her from the
outside. The psychiatrist Dr. L. S. Kubie notes that Faulkner
makes no effort to explain "why [Temple] sacrifices Goodwin . . .
to the furies of the mob and saves Popeye, her impotent malefactor." [6]

One theory which has won a considerable measure of acceptance
holds that Temple's perjury is the result of pressure from her

6. "William Faulkner's *Sanctuary*," *Saturday Review of Literature, 11* (1934), 211,
224–26. See below, Notes, p. 392.

family.[7] According to this interpretation of the novel, Clarence Snopes, the corrupt state senator, having discovered Temple's hiding place in a Memphis brothel, looks up Temple's father, Judge Drake, and sells him this information. Judge Drake then collaborates with the district attorney in concocting the lie that Temple is persuaded to tell on the witness stand. The father's motive for having his daughter tell the lie is to protect the family honor: it must not come out that Temple has been living in a brothel from the time of the murder until the time of the trial. If Popeye committed the rape and murder, then the truth about his having kept Temple in the brothel will have to come out "either through necessity or [through] Popeye's malice"; but if the rape and murder can be fastened on Lee Goodwin, the man on trial, then the fact of Temple's having lived in the brothel can be concealed.

But this reasoning does not convince. If Temple Drake's father was indeed stage-managing her testimony, why does he have Temple disclose the rape at all? Why not, since the story is being fabricated out of whole cloth anyway, make it simply a story of murder? Popeye would not care. His only concern is that the murder should be pinned on another man. If Judge Drake is arranging the testimony in this manner to protect the good name of his daughter, then he is not only a corrupt judge, he is also a very stupid man.

There are a number of other things wrong with this account. In the first place, there is considerable evidence to indicate that Judge Drake had not seen his daughter until the day of the trial. According to Lisca's theory, Clarence Snopes came back from Jackson, Mississippi, after having conferred with Judge Drake, two days before the trial—that is, on June 18.[8] But Popeye and Temple had already left Memphis—had at least left Miss Reba's— when Horace Benbow telephoned on the day before the trial (June 19), and there is every reason to believe that they had left two days before that, on the evening of the 17th, the day on which

7. See Lisca, *Faulkner Studies*, 2, 5–9. This theory is apparently accepted by Olga Vickery in her *Novels of William Faulkner* (Baton Rouge, 1959). See also below, Notes, p. 392.

8. See below, Chronology. p. 389.

Popeye had shot Red. When Horace Benbow called Miss Reba on the night of the 19th to speak to Temple, Miss Reba told him that "they" had gone, and since she says that they left owing a week's rent, theirs must have been a sudden departure. Miss Reba goes on to remark to Horace: "Dont you read no papers?" (p. 322). The only possible meaning of this question is that the newspapers had attributed the death of Red to Popeye, and that if Horace Benbow had read the Memphis papers, he would not now expect to find Popeye and Temple in her house.

If, as Lisca implies, Clarence Snopes returned from a visit to Judge Drake in Jackson just two days before the trial (June 18), Judge Drake could not have used information given as late as that for the purpose of establishing contact with his daughter. For it is perfectly plain that Clarence Snopes did not know in advance that Popeye was going to shoot Red on the 17th and therefore could not have predicted the flight of Popeye and Temple. Popeye, of course, had not supplied a forwarding address.

Be this as it may, according to the theory we are examining, "the district attorney established a socially acceptable account of Temple's actions between the rape and the trial." The district attorney asks Temple: " 'Where did he [her father] think you were?' 'He thought I was in school.' [a lie, as we have seen] 'You were in hiding, then, because something had happened to you and you dared not—' " Thus goes the passage in *Sanctuary* (p. 343), with Mr. Lisca's interpolations in brackets. But we need to look at the paragraph that immediately precedes the passage he has quoted. The district attorney asks Temple: " 'Where have you been living since May twelfth of this year?' Her head moved faintly, as though she would see beyond him. He moved into her line of vision, holding her eyes. She stared at him again, giving her parrotlike answers. 'Did your father know you were there?' 'No.' "

As I read it, the clear implication is that Temple *did* tell the district attorney where she was living. When he puts the question, she tries to avoid his eyes; but he forces her to look at him, and then evidently she answers him. For the district attorney's next question, "Did your father know you were there?" surely implies that Temple has confessed that she was at Miss Reba's house in Memphis. Temple's answer is "No," and the attorney then goes on to inquire: "Where did he think you were?" Temple evidently had not been provided with a "socially acceptable account" of her actions between the murder and her appearance in court. In spite of his pretensions of sympathy, the district attorney fully exposes her shame.

There are two further matters that must be taken into account by anyone who means to describe what happens at the trial. The first of these has to do with the Memphis "Jew lawyer," who turns up in the courtroom on the second day of the trial, June 21. The second is the action of Horace's sister, Narcissa, in visiting the district attorney and telling him that Clarence Snopes possesses some important information bearing upon the case.

As for the Memphis lawyer, it is significant that Horace Benbow is not really surprised when he sees him in the courtroom. On page 338 we are told that Horace stopped just within the door. "It's a lawyer," he said, a "Jew lawyer from Memphis," and he evidently expects that now he will see Temple in the courtroom. Indeed he says, "I know what I'll find before I find it . . . She will have on a black hat" (p. 339).

Evidently, when he heard from Miss Reba that Popeye and Temple had suddenly fled, Horace had rather expected that something like this might happen. It is significant that the Memphis lawyer apparently takes no part in the courtroom scene at all, and this can only mean that he has conferred already with Eustace Graham, the district attorney. For Eustace Graham knows exactly what to bring out and what to say.

Graham's information as to what happened at the Old Frenchman's Place is detailed. He knows that Temple has been raped. Where did he get his information? From whom unless from Temple herself or a representative of Popeye's? Obviously, he did not get it from Horace Benbow; nor did he get it from the man on trial, Lee Goodwin, or from his common-law wife Ruby. He could not have got it from Narcissa directly, for when Narcissa called upon him (see p. 317), she tells him: "Three nights ago that Snopes, the one in the legislature, telephoned out home, trying to find him. The next day he [Horace] went to Memphis. I dont know what for. You'll have to find that out yourself. I just want Horace out of this business as soon as possible."

Presumably, as soon as Eustace Graham had been given the tip-off by Narcissa, he did get in touch with Clarence Snopes, and by using bribes or simply the various pressures available to him, extracted from Snopes all that he knew about Temple, including her Memphis address. Narcissa spoke with Eustace on the 4th of June.[9] One supposes that Eustace wasted very little time in getting in touch with Temple and perhaps with her protector, Popeye. At any rate, he had plenty of time to do this before the 17th of June, the day on which they fled. Did Eustace exact from Temple a promise to appear in the courtroom and testify against Goodwin? And then after the murder of Red, did Popeye insist that Temple go on and keep her date with the district attorney in the courthouse? One can only speculate, but it would be hard otherwise to see how Eustace Graham could know so well just what to say and do. This hypothesis also provides a role for the Memphis lawyer, who presumably was commissioned by Popeye to see to it that Temple duly appeared in the courtroom.

There remains, however, the problem of why Clarence Snopes, who had some days earlier talked about going to Jackson on business, should turn up in Jefferson on the morning of the 18th, showing the marks of having been recently beaten up. What happened to Clarence? Who gave him the beating? Again we can only conjecture. When Clarence read the Memphis papers and found out that Popeye was alleged to have killed Red and had left town, did he then rush to Judge Drake to try to milk him of a hundred dollars, receiving the money but also a beating, possibly from one of Temple's brothers? But if so, why then is he screaming his revulsion at the "Jew lawyer" (p. 319): "We need laws against them. . . . When a jew lawyer can hold up an American, a white man, and not give him but ten dollars for something that two Americans. . . ." (Obviously, Clarence is referring to Judge Drake and Horace Benbow, each of whom had evidently paid him a hundred dollars.) Judge Drake would scarcely have hired a lawyer

9. See below, Chronology, p. 389.

from Memphis, nor, with his legal connections, would he have employed this obviously raffish mouthpiece of the underworld. Moreover, the ten dollars paid to Clarence by the Memphis lawyer was evidently not paid on behalf of Judge Drake, who had already paid ten times that amount. Actually, it is difficult to see why the Memphis lawyer should have paid Clarence Snopes anything at all. Did Popeye's henchmen beat up Clarence when he came asking for money, and is Clarence lying about having been paid the ten dollars? Or was he given the ten dollars contemptuously after the beating? There is simply not enough evidence presented in the novel to allow any clear answers to these questions.[10]

Again, we can do no more than speculate about the circumstances that brought Judge Drake to the trial. Someone had evidently told him that his daughter would appear in the courtroom at Jefferson. The way in which Temple reacts to her father and cringes from her brothers suggests that this is her first meeting with any of them since her disappearance. Perhaps Eustace Graham had at the last minute let Judge Drake know that his daughter would appear at the trial. (Graham would lose nothing by informing him on the eve of Temple's appearance, and to have failed to inform him at all would certainly have created resentment—resentment that Graham would not want to provoke in a man with powerful political connections within the state.)

What, then, was Temple's motive for perjuring herself? Did she do so out of fear of Popeye? Or because she had been corrupted by Popeye? Faulkner leaves the answer for the reader to infer, but everything in the novel suggests that in her lassitude and docility she was willing to carry out Popeye's command. At the trial she appears to be drained of energy, listless, like a person drugged. Apparently she had cared something for Red, and now that he is dead, she is so emptied of volition that she has no concern for anything. She may be so listless as to acquiesce even in the wishes of Red's murderer, Popeye. Certainly, that is the general impression that we get of her as the novel closes: Temple on a gray day at the end of a gray year, sitting in the Luxembourg Gardens, yawning behind her hand, taking out her compact, looking at

10. See below, Notes, p. 393.

her face, "sullen and discontented and sad" (p. 379), listening to the dying brasses of the army band.

When Faulkner, some twenty years later in *Requiem for a Nun*, reconsidered the character of Temple Drake, he made it quite plain (p. 126) that it was Popeye's hold upon Temple that caused her to testify against Goodwin. The Governor tells Temple that he remembers her from newspaper accounts, as the young woman who disappeared and reappeared "six weeks later as a witness in a murder trial in Jefferson, produced by the lawyer of the man who, it was then learned, had abducted her and held her prisoner—" In *Requiem* Faulkner thus makes it clear that the facts about Temple's rape and her stay in the Memphis brothel did get into the newspapers, where the Governor read them. Temple does not disagree with the Governor. She apparently accepts his version of the affair, namely that she was "produced" in the courtroom by the lawyer of the man who had abducted her.

I have been careful, however, to base my argument as to what happens in *Sanctuary* upon evidence found in that novel itself, for *Requiem for a Nun* may well present Faulkner's revised conception of the story. But at the least, the interpretation of Temple's actions that Faulkner gives in *Requiem* does not make it any easier to maintain that Temple's perjury was forced upon her by her father.

Sanctuary is clearly Faulkner's bitterest novel.[11] It is a novel in which the male's initiation into the nature of evil is experienced in its most shattering and disillusioning form. After Horace has left Temple in the Memphis brothel, he thinks "perhaps it is upon the instant that we realize, admit, that there is a logical pattern to evil, that we die" (p. 265), and he thinks of the expression he had once seen in the eyes of a dead child and in the eyes of the other dead: "the cooling indignation, the shocked despair fading, leaving two empty globes in which the motionless world lurked profoundly in miniature."

In nearly every one of Faulkner's novels, the male's discovery of evil and reality is bound up with his discovery of the true na-

11. See below, Notes, p. 394.

ture of woman. Men idealize and romanticize women, but the cream of the jest is that women have a secret rapport with evil which men do not have, that they are able to adjust to evil without being shattered by it, being by nature flexible and pliable. Women are the objects of idealism, but are not in the least idealistic.

In the novel *Sartoris* Horace's younger sister, Narcissa, is depicted as a rather sweet girl, shy, quiet, and dependent upon her brother. But nine years later, the Narcissa of *Sanctuary* reveals a depravity that the reader, and certainly Horace himself, finds shocking. She is much upset that her brother has concerned himself with such people as the Goodwins, and midway through the novel Horace is forced to realize that it is his sister who has stirred up the "church ladies" to see that Ruby is evicted from the cheap room in which he had found lodgings for her. Horace, who has returned to his sister's house after trying to find another place for Ruby Goodwin, exclaims: "Just because she happens not to be married to the man whose child she carries about these sanctified streets. But who told them? That's what I want to know. I know that nobody in Jefferson knew it except—" (p. 219). Miss Jenny Du Pre puts in, "You were the first I heard tell it." Obviously, since only she and Narcissa have heard it from Horace, it is Narcissa who has arranged the eviction.

On the very next day Narcissa asks Horace who the district attorney is, and as she urges Horace to be quit of the murder case, it becomes perfectly plain to Horace how shallow and cruel Narcissa actually is. With regard to the murder, she exclaims: "I dont see that it makes any difference who did it. The question is, are you going to stay mixed up with it?" (p. 221). At this point, however, Horace could hardly have suspected that she would betray his case to the district attorney. (We are not told in the novel whether Horace ever does learn of her betrayal.) Next to Popeye, Narcissa is the most frightening person in this novel, as she pitilessly moves on to her own ends with no regard for justice and no concern for the claims of truth.

One most important facet of Horace's discovery of the true nature of woman involves his stepdaughter, Little Belle. In the powerful scene which closes chapter 23, Horace has been looking at Little Belle's picture. Her face "dreamed with that quality of sweet chiaroscuro" (p. 267). But suddenly the room is filled with the odor of invisible honeysuckle and "the small face seemed to swoon in a voluptuous languor." Then "he knew what that sensation in his stomach meant." He hastily puts down the photograph and hurries to the bathroom, but as his stomach begins to retch, he has a terrible vision of Little Belle. Or is it Temple? "She" could be either: ". . . bound naked on her back on a flat car moving at speed through a black tunnel, the blackness streaming in rigid threads overhead, a roar of iron wheels in her ears." In the vision the car shoots out from the tunnel "in a long upward slant . . . toward a crescendo like a held breath, an interval in which she would swing faintly and lazily in nothingness filled with pale, myriad points of light. Far beneath her she could hear the faint, furious uproar of the shucks" (p. 268). In the last sentence Little Belle has not only been fused with Temple; she has fused with Horace himself, who in an agony of empathy has felt himself into the raped girl's ordeal.

This passage has been interpreted by several critics as a revelation to Horace of the evil within himself—incestuous feelings which he suddenly realizes he has for his stepdaughter. In Horace's unconscious mind there may indeed lurk such feelings, but I believe it would have required a psychiatrist to reveal them to Horace. (Toward his sister Narcissa, however, he clearly does have them and may well be aware of them.) But what troubles Horace in this scene are other matters: the evil to which a sweet young girl is exposed and, more darkly, the disposition to evil which lurks within such a girl. Earlier, Horace had told Miss Jenny that he thanked God that Little Belle wasn't his own flesh and blood. "I can reconcile myself to her having to be exposed to a scoundrel now and then, but to think that at any moment she may become involved with a fool" (p. 199). This is after he had learned the consequences of Gowan's folly. As for a girl's own propensity to evil, Benbow has already been aware of that. He "looked at the familiar image [of Little Belle] with a kind of quiet horror and despair, at a face suddenly older in sin than he would ever be, a face more blurred than sweet, at eyes more secret than soft" (p. 200). This is why, when Horace returns from his shocking interview with Temple at Miss Reba's house and looks once more at Little Belle's photograph, the nausea rises in his stomach.

Horace's tendency to idealize women also receives a rather shattering blow from another quarter. He admires Goodwin's common-law wife, Ruby, for her loyalty, her power of endurance, her willingness to suffer anything in order to aid the man she loves. She tells Horace that she had once prostituted herself to raise money for her man when he was in jail. She makes it plain to him that she is willing to do so again, and indeed that she assumes that Horace means to demand her body as a fee for his legal services. He cries out in exasperation: "O, hell! Can you stupid mammals never believe that any man, every man—You thought that was what I was coming for? You thought that if I had intended to, I'd have waited this long?" (p. 330). Finally Horace whispers to her: "Good God. What kind of men have you known?" The term that Horace uses in addressing Ruby is revealing: "you stupid mammals." Women are peculiarly mammals, creatures that give suck, and to Horace, the appalled and outraged idealist, these human beings, whose function is so invincibly animal, are nowhere more so than in their unwillingness to believe in ideals.

Horace's grudge against women, against nature, against the irrational brutality of reality, comes out rather plainly when, after the verdict, he starts home. Narcissa has invited him into the car and asks him whether he wants to go "to the house" (that is, to Horace's house) or "out home" (that is, where she and Miss Jenny Du Pre live). Horace answers, "I dont care. Just home" (p. 349). A little later in the car "he began to cry, sitting in the car beside his sister" (p. 350). There was still a little "snow of locust blooms" on the drive. " 'It does last,' Horace said. 'Spring does. You'd almost think there was some purpose to it.' "

Sanctuary here shows the mark of the period in which it was written. Horace Benbow is not so much a product of a decadent Southern culture as a bookish, middle-aged inhabitant of the modern waste land. "April is the cruelest month, breeding" lilacs and locust blossoms "out of the dead land." It is the cruelest month because it promises a rebirth that is fraudulent and meaningless. And this is Horace's complaint here, "You'd almost think there was some purpose to it."

The reader may well ask whether Temple does not have some part in these rites of initiation or whether Faulkner regards them as strictly the prerogative of the male. Temple's discovery of evil is horrifying enough, but it takes a very different form from Horace's. In spite of the terror and violent affront that the girl feels, the experience is not so much a disillusionment as a discovery of her own capacities, resources, and deepest drives and desires. To say this is not to rely entirely upon *Requiem for a Nun*, in which Temple, eight years later,[12] is very hard on herself and confesses that she discovered that she liked evil. Even in *Sanctuary* there is plenty of evidence to support this conception of her. Horace, for example, notices as Temple tells him the story of the rape that there is a kind of detachment and even pride in her account.

Her story is overpowering in its vividness. In the telling Temple seems to become a pure medium through which the sense of horror is being transmitted directly and with a terrifying immediacy. For example, describing Popeye's touch upon her skin, the girl says: "and my skin started jumping away from [Popeye's hand] like those little flying fish in front of a boat. It was like my skin knew which way it was going to go before it started moving, and my skin would keep on jerking just ahead of it like there wouldn't be anything there when the hand got there" (p. 262). Yet this appalling story is told, as it seems to Horace, "in one of those bright, chatty monologues which women can carry on when they realize that they have the center of the stage." Suddenly Horace realizes that Temple "was recounting the experience with actual pride, a sort of naive and impersonal vanity, as though she were making it up, looking from him to Miss Reba with quick, darting glances like a dog driving two cattle along a lane" (p. 259). The masterful simile at the end beautifully describes what Temple is

12. See below, Notes, p. 394.

doing or at least what it seems to Horace that she is doing. The searing experience is already mixed up with posturing and histrionics.

Or consider the episode in which the girl is being taken to Memphis by Popeye. She has been brutally raped, and as they drive through the spring landscape Temple begins to scream. But when the traffic thickens she is willing to hush, and when Popeye stops at a filling station in a small town, Temple does not scream. "She watched him go up the street and enter a door. It was a dingy confectionery" (p. 166). When Popeye comes back to the car, Temple has gone, but she has not rushed down the street in order to escape. Instead, Popeye finds her in the filling-station yard, cowering between a barrel and the wall. She whispers in terror to Popeye: "He nearly saw me! He was almost looking right at me!" When Popeye asks who, Temple tells him, "A boy. At school. He was looking right toward—" (p. 167). The desire not to be seen in these circumstances by someone she knows apparently drives out of her head any notion of escape. It is this kind of inordinate respectability that corrupts Narcissa, Benbow's sister, as well as Temple Drake. Later, in *Requiem for a Nun,* Faulkner is to make Temple realize this trait for what it is. She tells the Governor "I had two legs . . . and I could have simply screamed up the main street of any of the little towns we passed" (p. 139).

The fatal adaptability, the "social sense," the ability to accommodate to circumstances—any circumstances—these are the things that paralyze any impulse on Temple's part to flee the scene or to resist the evil. Having made her accommodation to evil, she will find that she has a positive liking for it.

But the liking comes later. It is one thing to say that Temple's very terror and self-consciousness serve to arouse the men at the Old Frenchman's Place and that the one mode of ingratiation which she has learned by her eighteenth year turns out to be precisely the worst behavior that she could use. It is, however, a very different thing to say that the terrified girl is actually trying to lead the men on and to provoke the sexual assault that finally occurs. Poor Temple's "grimace of taut, toothed coquetry" (p. 56) is not intended as an invitation to Popeye but as a way of placating him. So also with her cringing yet grinning demeanor, which elicits from Popeye simply the comment, "Make your whore lay off of me, Jack" (p. 58).

Ruby Goodwin, in her fury with respectable women and in her very lively concern lest Temple arouse Lee's lust, is very sharp with Temple and proceeds to read into her actions motives of which Temple was surely not conscious.[13] But later, in talking to Horace, Ruby testifies to Temple's utter terror and her compulsive efforts to escape. What Temple discovers is that the world of nightmare evil is real. She tells Ruby, "Things like that dont happen. Do they? . . . You're just like other people" (p. 64). Temple's mind is thoroughly conventional—that is, good and evil do not exist; only what is proper and improper exist. It is a world which can be arranged if one has the money and the proper position, and the real shock to Temple is that she has suddenly fallen into a place in which money and position no longer avail. This is why she can do nothing but practice her little foolish grimaces of coquetry and protest, "My father's a judge; my father's a judge" (p. 60).

Faulkner has presented what happened at the Old Frenchman's Place with a multiple focus. Beginning with chapter 5 and extending through chapter 14, we have the omniscient author's third-person account with a good deal of conversation and occasional presentation of the various characters' inmost thoughts and feelings. But later on, in chapter 19, Ruby gives Horace her own account of what happened that night, with special reference to Temple's actions. Horace is very much concerned to make sure that the girl has not been touched. (Ruby evidently knows nothing of the rape, or, if she does, chooses not to tell Horace anything about it.) Their interview concludes with Horace's statement: "You know she was all right" (p. 197).

But there is still another focus on these same events. In chapter 23, when Horace visits Miss Reba's establishment, Temple tells her own story, with special reference to her fears and apprehensions. Hers is naturally a highly subjective account. The curious

13. See below, Notes, p. 395.

thing to Horace is that Temple seems fixated upon the night that she spent in the ruined house, "from the time she entered the room and tried to wedge the door with the chair, until the woman came to the bed and led her out. That was the only part of the whole experience which appeared to have left any impression on her at all: the night which she had spent in comparative in-violation" (p. 257). As for Horace's attempts to get her to talk about the crime itself, "she would elude him and return to herself sitting on the bed, listening to the men on the porch, or lying in the dark while they entered the room." " 'Yes; that,' she would say. 'It just happened. I dont know. I had been scared so long that I guess I had just gotten used to being' " (p. 257).

What it is to be scared as Temple was scared has been brilliantly dramatized by Faulkner. The psychology is convincing to the reader but frequently puzzling to the victim herself. Consider the passage in which Temple "thinks" herself into a boy's body, or in which she imagines herself in a spiked chastity belt. She says to Horace: " 'Oh, yes; this was something else funny I did' " (p. 261). It is the strange way in which she reacted when she felt Popeye approaching her bed. As she lay in the dark and sensed him ap-proaching, she was silently saying to him: "Come on. Touch me. Touch me! You're a coward if you dont. Coward! Coward!" And she goes on to tell Horace, by way of explanation: "I wanted to go to sleep, you see. And he just kept on standing there. I thought if he'd just go on and get it over with, I could go to sleep. So I'd say You're a coward if you dont! . . . and I could feel my mouth getting fixed to scream, and that little hot ball inside you that screams" (p. 262).

In discussing Faulkner's brilliant handling of the psychology of terror, one should not fail to mention the phantasy in which Temple sees herself in the coffin. She tells Horace: "I did a funny thing. I could see myself in the coffin. I looked sweet—you know: all in white. I had on a veil like a bride, and I was crying because . . . they had put shucks in the coffin. I was crying be-cause they had put shucks in the coffin where I was dead" (p. 263). A depth psychologist could doubtless do a lot with this passage, but the sensitive layman is able to get much of the force of it without professional help: death and loss of virginity fuse in this phantasy, with its overtones of self-pity, but the death has been robbed of dignity by a cruel joke—the dry rustling corn husks in the coffin, and their associations with the girl's unnatural rape in the corn crib.

Temple's respectability, conventionality, and pliability all have their part in her final betrayal of Lee Goodwin at the trial. But not least important in this matter is the ambiguity of her attitude toward Popeye. If she hates Popeye—and perhaps just because she does hate him for his power and authority—she finds in him something of a father. In *Requiem for a Nun* (p. 140) Temple tells the Governor that Popeye "was worse than a father or uncle. It was worse than being the wealthy ward of the most indulgent trust or insurance company." But this theory of her relationship to Popeye is not necessarily an afterthought on Faulkner's part, for in *Sanctuary* itself there are hints of a "fatherly" role. While Temple lives at Miss Reba's, Popeye showers her with gifts of all sorts and frequently simply sits by her bed: "Often in the night she would wake to smell tobacco and to see the single ruby eye where Popeye's mouth would be" (p. 270). She resents the close guard that Popeye keeps over her, and when she is angry at him she taunts him for not being a man; but when she tries to wheedle something out of him she calls him "Daddy," and when she fears that he is preparing to shoot her lover Red, she tries to get the pistol away from him by saying to him "Give it to me . . . Daddy. Daddy" (p. 284). If "Daddy" as used here could be the slang of the twenties for one's lover, nevertheless it carries in this context some sense of the father image too.

The comic scenes in this novel have won deserved praise. The adventures of Fonzo and Virgil trying to find a cheap hotel and, in their country innocence, putting up at Miss Reba's establishment and for two weeks speculating as to what Miss Reba does for a living are all very funny. So also, though in a different mode, is the account in chapter 25 of the wake that is held for Red and the subsequent beer party at Miss Reba's, in which the two other madams, Miss Myrtle and Miss Lorraine, philosophize about life and love and the difficulties that confront "us girls."

The comic scenes are not, however, extraneous to the novel. They provide, among other things, depth and substance to the nightmare. The evil in which Temple is involved is no shadowy specter; it has blood and bone and belly. Daylight, common sense, and humor can exorcise the mere nightmare. But the evil that can live in the daylight world of common sense is substantial. Insofar as *Sanctuary* has to do with Horace's initiation, the comic scenes associated with Miss Reba's establishment supply more than comic relief from horror; they comment upon his idealism and thus play their part in the initiation.

The meaning of the title, *Sanctuary*, has excited various conjectures. A student of mine once suggested that Faulkner must have had in mind the following passage in Joseph Conrad's *Chance* (p. 311 of the Uniform edition):

> A young girl, you know, is something like a *temple*. You pass by and wonder what mysterious rites are going on in there, what prayers, what visions? The privileged man, the lover, the husband, who are given the key of the *sanctuary* do not always know how to use it. For myself, without claim, without merit, simply by chance I had been allowed to look through the half-opened door and I had seen the saddest possible desecration, the withered brightness of youth, a spirit neither made cringing nor yet dulled but as if bewildered in quivering hopelessness by gratuitous cruelty; self-confidence destroyed and, instead, a resigned recklessness, a mournful callousness.
> [italics mine]

This passage about the girl named Flora de Barral is spoken by Conrad's Marlow, but it might very well have been spoken by Horace Benbow with reference to Temple Drake. In the long interview with Temple in Miss Reba's brothel, Horace had looked through a half-opened door and had seen, as Conrad has put it, "the saddest possible desecration." In that experience there was "gratuitous cruelty" indeed. Temple's conduct at the end of the book answers brilliantly to Conrad's phrase "a resigned recklessness" if we think of her at the trial of Lee Goodwin, and to a "mournful callousness" if we think of our last sight of her in the Luxembourg Gardens. One grants, of course, that if Horace Benbow had spoken these words with reference to Temple Drake, he would have been speaking of a very different situation from that recounted by Conrad and would have been using the words not wonderingly but bitterly. Indeed, Horace's creator, William Faulkner, may have felt that Conrad had understated woman's general situation and probably had misunderstood it—that in some instances a look within the "sanctuary" would have proved too shocking for Conrad to have credited, and that his own novel to be entitled *Sanctuary* might provide instruction in what indeed such a Temple could contain.

Did Faulkner then derive the title of his novel and the name of his heroine from this passage? Faulkner's titles are highly subjective and often whimsical. I think it certainly possible that the title *Sanctuary* came from Conrad's *Chance;* but in any case, the view of woman held by Conrad and expressed so explicitly in this novel certainly reminds one of the view entertained by Faulkner. For example, Marlow (p. 281) describes what he calls "the pathos of being a woman." Though a man can struggle, a woman's part is passive: "they are not made for attack. Wait they must. I am speaking here of women who are really women. . . . Nothing can beat a true woman for a clear vision of reality; I would say a cynical vision if I were not afraid of wounding your chivalrous feelings—for which, by the bye, women are not so grateful as you may think, to fellows of your kind." A disillusioned Horace might be speaking here.

I observed earlier that the Faulknerian male's discovery of evil and reality is bound up with his discovery of the true nature of woman. Women, though idealized by men, are themselves hardheaded realists. As is said of Narcissa, "Fiddlesticks. You dont wonder. You just do things and then stop until the next time to do something comes around" (p. 223). This is a bitter but quite just comment upon Narcissa, but it is a comment made by another woman, by Mrs. Jenny Du Pre. Yet if Narcissa and Temple terrify Horace with their lack of any final morality, one must remember that there are also in the novel women like Ruby and Miss Jenny, women who, for all their great differences and dissimilar attitudes, are both feminine and yet both fundamentally decent. Even Miss Reba has a kind of decency. After Temple's confession, Miss Reba begs Horace to take her away and not let her come back: "I'd find her folks myself, if I knowed how to go about it. But you know how . . . She'll be dead, or in the asylum in a year, way him and her go on up there in that room" (p. 265).

Yet if *Sanctuary* is in some respects Faulkner's most pessimistic novel, it is certainly one of his most brilliant,[14] and the psychology of Temple as she goes through her various experiences is hair-raising in its power of conviction. No one knows just what would go through a girl's head were she to undergo Temple's experience, and yet most readers will feel that the account in *Sanctuary* carries conviction. However incredible the events narrated, Temple's reaction to them is compellingly credible, and the reader will acknowledge the veracity of Faulkner's searching look into her mind and heart.

Whatever its final meaning,[15] the story of Temple Drake evidently remained with Faulkner as a fascinating problem. In *Requiem for a Nun* he asked himself what might have happened to people like Gowan and Temple. What Faulkner supposes to have happened does thorough credit to his sense of reality. Their marriage could hardly have been a really happy one. Temple would have found it difficult not to resent what Gowan had got her into and his pusillanimous conduct at the Old Frenchman's Place. Moreover, Temple would have been too conscious of the fact that he had married her because he had felt that this was the only honorable thing to do and thus would have been too conscious of the fact that he had done the decent thing. There was too much to be forgiven and too much for which to be grateful.

Faulkner as a good realist knows that Temple had, in her sojourn in the Memphis brothel, gone on past the tepid decencies of suburbia. As she puts it herself (p. 135): "Temple Drake liked evil." In fact, she liked it so much that she longs for a confidant, and so chooses for a maid, Nancy, the Negro prostitute dope-fiend. Nancy can talk her language, and Temple can confide in her. Be-

14. See below, Notes, p. 396.
15. See below, Notes, p. 397.

cause Temple Drake really likes evil, she finds herself unprepared to resist when Red's younger brother comes up out of the past to blackmail her with the love letters that she had written to Red several years before. As Temple tells the Governor (p. 134): "You've got to be already prepared to resist [evil], say no to it, long before you even know what it is." This is a comment shrewd enough to have come from the lips of a Jesuit confessor.

Faulkner's basic conception of his sequel, then, is perfectly sound. He is too good a realist to believe that it would have been very easy for either Temple or her husband to gloss over the fact of Temple's past. Before there could be any enduring bond between them, they would have had to be able to forgive each other the past, and that would have meant accepting the fact of the past. For either one to be capable of doing that would require some bitter and difficult struggle. Nancy Mannigoe's violent attempt to save Temple's home is thus justified, for Temple's case is one requiring the most drastic remedies. But Faulkner's choice of drastic remedies sets some very special and difficult problems. Most readers will be hard put to maintain complete sympathy with Nancy as she murders one of Temple's children in order to save the home for the other child. The difficulty is compounded by the fact that Faulkner has chosen to render all the action through a strict use of the dramatic mode. Thus there is no direct means for our getting inside Nancy Mannigoe's head or for looking into her heart as she goes about the terrible deed dictated to her by love. Her own speeches do not help too much, for she is not allowed many speeches; besides, she is a simple person, relatively inarticulate, and a great deal must therefore be left to the reader's inference.

Under the circumstances, Faulkner has done very well indeed. The play as performed carries a certain amount of power and conviction, particularly the last scene, in the jail, in which Nancy appears and speaks her good-bye to Temple, the woman for whose sake she is going to her death. But a measure of power and conviction is not enough to bring off this most ambitious work. By limiting himself to dialogue, and rather clipped and terse dialogue at that, Faulkner has pretty well cut himself off from the poetic resources that are really necessary if *Requiem for a Nun* is to succeed. To be sure, he has put a great deal of poetry into the book; but the poetry has been introduced in a very special way: before each block of dramatic matter, Faulkner has given us a long section of bardic prose on the courthouse, the scene of Nancy Mannigoe's trial; the statehouse, in which the Governor meets Temple and Gavin Stevens to hear Temple's plea for Nancy; and the jail, where Temple goes to see Nancy for the last time. These three sections are brilliantly written, particularly that entitled "The Courthouse," which gives us the early history of Faulkner's Jefferson. But though they evoke a general background rich in history for the events that take place in the play, they do not solve Faulkner's specific dramatic problems. The use of this material in just this fashion constitutes the most daring but perhaps the least successful solution of the structural problems attempted by Faulkner in any of his novels.

There is much that could be said for the ethical and psychological insights given us in *Requiem for a Nun,* and a great deal has to be said for the fine last scene. Here Nancy, illiterate and humble yet quietly confident, addresses herself to the problem of evil and the problem of suffering, and tries to answer Temple's anguished question: "Why do you and my little baby both have to suffer just because I decided to go to a baseball game five years ago? Do you have to suffer everybody else's anguish just to believe in God? What kind of God is it that has to blackmail His customers with the whole world's grief and ruin?" (p. 277). Nancy's answer is that God "don't want you to suffer. He don't like suffering neither. . . . He don't tell you to suffer. But He gives you the chance. He gives you the best He can think of, that you are capable of doing. And He will save you" (p. 278).

Nancy has faith, the kind that moves mountains, and for some readers she will have established the fact that she killed Temple's baby indeed because she loved it. But for others the credibility of Nancy's motive is more difficult. Their difficulty will be not so much with Nancy's theology, which is probably sound enough, but with the dramatic presentation, which may not be quite full enough, articulate enough, convincing enough to bring the whole work to success.

8

Odyssey of the Bundrens

(AS I LAY DYING)

THE AUTHOR'S FONDNESS for *As I Lay Dying* is easily understood. The writing in this novel is as good as Faulkner has ever done, and the book constitutes a triumph in the management of tone. Faulkner has daringly mingled the grotesque and the heroic, the comic and the pathetic, pity and terror, creating a complexity of tone that has proved difficult for some readers to cope with. To ignore this complexity is to find in the novel simply an exploitation of horror for the sake of its shock value or for the sake of a grotesque comedy. Even the reader who is able to see that the novel concerns itself with a heroic action is likely to have his difficulties. Appreciating the heroic, he may wonder whether his comic response is appropriate, or, sensing the comic value of the absurd and anticlimactic incidents, he may come to doubt his earlier intimations that the action was in fact heroic.

The heroic act, because it does involve the violation of common-sense notions and conventional responses, is always, at some level, vulnerable to the comic squint. That which is larger than ordinary life is likely to seem exaggerated and fantastic, and thus always risks inviting the mock-heroic attitude. The journey which the Bundren family undertake to bury Addie is preposterous, and they persist in it in obvious violation of common sense.

In view of the prevailing tendency to "sociologize" Faulkner, it may be just as well to say here and now that Faulkner is not portraying a quaintly horrifying Southern folkway. Few, if any, families in rural Mississippi would have attempted to do what the Bundrens did. Consider how all the non-Bundren characters within the novel regard the expedition. They are shocked and horrified—the women especially. Lula Armstid exclaims: "It's a outrage. [Anse] should he lawed for treating her so" (p. 475). Rachel Samson bursts out to her husband: "You and [Anse] and all the men in the world that torture us alive and flout us dead, dragging us up and down the country—" (p. 420). Samson thinks to himself: "I got just as much respect for the dead as ere a man . . . and a woman that's been dead in a box four days, the best way to respect her is to get her into the ground as quick as you can" (p. 419).

A primary question, therefore, must be why the Bundrens carry out their strange and difficult task, for it not only cuts across the community's sense of what is fitting, but runs counter to the shiftless husband's lethargy and irresponsibility, is opposed by at least one of the brothers, and involves the whole family in hardship, loss, danger, and injury. The reader will not find an obvious answer. When neighbors remonstrate with Anse, he replies that "it's Addie I give the promise to. Her mind is set on it" (p. 418), though we do not take very seriously Anse's concern for his wife. Early in the novel we learn of other motivations for taking Addie's body to Jefferson: Anse longs for a set of store-bought teeth and Darl imagines Anse saying, when Addie dies, "God's will be done. Now I can get them teeth" (p. 375). The daughter, Dewey Dell, who knows she is pregnant, is desperately anxious to get into town so that she can buy an abortion drug. And there are things in town which tempt even the moderate Cash and the child Vardaman. Did the Bundren family, then, simply drift into its heroic action? Did they accomplish it unwittingly and for the least heroic of motives?

One would like to postpone for the time answers to such questions, but I suggest that as we look about for answers, we will be forced to consider the possibility that one of Faulkner's principal themes in *As I Lay Dying*—perhaps the principal theme—is the nature of the heroic deed, with an examination both of what fosters it and of the various things that would inhibit it, including not only common sense, selfishness, and cowardice, but romantic self-consciousness.

Yet we should not dismiss out of hand the claims of honor, heavily as we may be constrained to qualify them in view of Anse's character. The code of honor receives heavy stress in this novel. The need of the male to prove himself—we have commented upon it in earlier chapters—comes to a high focus in this story of the Bundren family. It is not enough simply to bury the mother reverently and with some show of decent grief; the promise she has exacted must be honored to the letter: come fire or flood, hell or highwater, her body must be taken to the spot which she has designated as her final resting place, and no circumstance, not even the most frustrating, is allowed to cancel the obligation. By any rational test, the undertaking is quixotic, but in carrying it out, two of the children, Cash and Jewel, exhibit true heroism—Cash in his suffering, Jewel in his brave actions. Both brothers go far beyond the claims of rationality and common sense. Their brother Darl, of course, does not. His role is that of the critic of the action, who does not believe in honor and has the supreme lucidity of the mad.

The general importance of honor in the novel deserves stress, especially since many readers associate a concern for honor only with Faulkner's aristocrats and are not sufficiently aware of the sensitivity on that score exhibited by Faulkner's poor whites. An episode late in the book will illustrate, and the comic overtones need not obscure the seriousness of the issues here for the Bundrens. The wagon with its stinking burden is just approaching Jefferson. A passer-by, shocked by the odor, exclaims: "Great God, what they got in that wagon?" (p. 507). Jewel whirls toward him with the cry: "Son of a bitches." It is a term which cannot be ignored, and for a moment it looks as if Jewel and the stranger will fight: Jewel swings at him and the stranger promptly draws a knife. It is interesting to see what happens. Darl apologizes for Jewel by explaining that he is ill and not himself. When this excuse does not suffice, he adds: "[Jewel] thought you said something to him" (p. 507). This explanation opens a way for mutual accommodation, but in what follows the touchiness of the code of honor is nicely illustrated.

Darl promises that Jewel will take back the offending words but insists that the retraction must not be made under duress, for when the stranger demands that Jewel take back the words, Darl says: "Put up your knife, and he will" (p. 508). The stranger does so, and now Darl conjures Jewel to tell him "you didn't mean anything." "I thought he said something," Jewel says. "Just because he's—" But Darl hushes him and says: "Tell him you didn't mean it." And Jewel at last makes the necessary concession by saying that he didn't mean it. The angered man then remarks: "He better not. Calling me a—" (p. 508). But the Bundrens must not seem to concede too much and it is now Darl who quickly asks: "Do you think he's afraid to call you that?" Whereupon there is a slight retreat on the other side as the stranger cautiously replies: "I never said that." Jewel follows up the advantage with: "Don't think it, neither." But Darl, now that honor has been saved, orders Jewel to "shut up" and urges his father to drive on. The code involved is quite as elaborate as that humorously described in the fifth act of Shakespeare's *As You Like It*. It has its own degrees corresponding to such niceties as Touchstone's "Reproof Valiant" and his "Countercheck Quarrelsome."

The episode is significant in another way. Though we are by this time in the novel perfectly aware of the hostility that exists between Jewel and Darl, and though in another hour or so Jewel will be leaping upon Darl to turn him over to the officers, at this moment Darl is quite as much involved as any other member of the family in preserving the family honor and seeing to it that no stranger takes liberties with it. Even Darl, who does not believe in the quixotic journey and who sees the absurdity of any literal fulfillment of the promise made to his mother—even Darl responds automatically to a defense of the family honor.

Because Darl is by far the most articulate of the Bundrens, because his speech is endowed with a certain poetry, and because he voices what is probably the reader's own revulsion against the Bundrens' foolish and horrible journey, it is very likely that Darl will appear to be the representative intelligence of the novel and the mouthpiece of the author. By contrast, the decent, patient, unimaginative Cash—the good workman, proud of his work and careful of his tools—may well appear as dull and unfeeling, hopelessly prosaic. Nor is the typical reader likely to find Jewel other than antipathetic. For Jewel is the high-strung man of action, impatient, ardent, flamboyant, and heroic, but only in some kind of terribly brainless way. Yet the reader will be mistaken if he accepts Darl's account of things as necessarily true and if he sees in Darl's judgments and valuations necessarily those of the author. The novel is not nearly so simple.

With regard to the burial journey, Darl, the lunatic, is indeed the only one of the three older brothers who is thoroughly "sane," and in general he is the one who knows the truth—about Dewey Dell's secret thoughts, about his mother's special attachment to Jewel, and about the various secret motivations of the members of his family. But Darl's truth is corrosive and antiheroic, and in its logic perhaps finally inhuman. Does he really grieve for his mother at all? It would be hard to say. In a sense, he knows too much about her and too much about the absurdity of reality to have any emotional commitment.

Darl represents, among other things, the detachment and even callousness which we sometimes associate with the artist. Darl is pure perception. He intuits almost immediately Dewey Dell's pregnancy, and his sister, realizing this, resents and fears him. Darl sees through his father's clumsy pretenses. He chides Jewel for his childishly immoderate attachment to his horse. Twice he tries to stop the outrageous journey to the Jefferson cemetery. In general, in spite of all his poetry, he is a rationalizing and deflating force—the antiheroic intelligence.

Vernon Tull puts the issue to his wife in forceful, if homely, terms in telling her how in the flooded river "Darl jumped out of the wagon and left Cash sitting there trying to save [the coffin] and the wagon turning over, and Jewel that was almost to the bank fighting that horse back where it had more sense than to go" (p. 448). Tull teases her for having said that "Darl is the queer one, the one that ain't bright," remarking that Darl was "the only one of them that had sense enough to get off that wagon. I notice Anse was too smart to been on it a-tall." Indeed, though we are disposed to think of Darl as being the poet of the group, it might be argued that Jewel represents more truly the poetic temperament, though his is the poetry associated with high-heartedness and the heroic gesture—the poetry of action rather than that of contemplation.

It is important to notice the author's own detachment in this matter. Though Darl, with his gift for language and his penchant for almost clairvoyant observation, must represent much that is dear to Faulkner himself, Faulkner is, as we shall see, perfectly willing to judge against Darl on point after point. Indeed, Faulkner, probably more than any other author of our time, is willing to see the limitations of the artistic temperament and to refuse to believe that it has a monopoly upon truth. Or perhaps Darl as artist has too much truth—sees the complexity of human motivations so thoroughly that all action is paralyzed and all risks rendered quixotic because no motivation is so pure and no goal so desirable as to be worth the necessary risk.[1] There are passages in the novel that would seem to support this interpretation, and yet there are other passages in which Darl's prophetic and preternatural vision gives way to a bitterness and pettiness as in his baiting of his brother Jewel.

Yet Darl, even if we are not to assume that he has all the truth, certainly does possess some of the truth, and Faulkner avails himself of Darl's imagination nineteen times in the novel. Far more passages are given to Darl than to any other character in *As I Lay Dying*. Moreover, it is in these passages—in which we are within Darl's mind—that Faulkner employs some of his most interesting technical devices and departs furthest from a merely naturalistic presentation of events. The scene of Addie's death, so meticulous in its detail, so convincing in its realism, is actually a fictitious construct imagined by Darl as he rides on the wagon with Jewel, miles from home. (This is not to say, of course, that Darl's vision of what happened was necessarily untrue.) So also is the fine scene in which Darl imagines Cash working into the

1. See below, Notes, p. 398.

night through the rainstorm on their mother's coffin. Even after Darl has suffered his breakdown and is on the train headed for the state insane asylum, laughing with the laughter of the mad, his description of the scene in which two deputies sit by him on the train is brilliantly done. Such clarity of vision is not impaired by Darl's madness and may even find in that special kind of madness its necessary condition.

That this last section is attributed to Darl may at first glance seem a mistake for it begins: "Darl has gone to Jackson. They put him on the train . . . ," and Darl is spoken of in the third person throughout. But then one suddenly realizes that the attribution is correct: at this point the disintegration of Darl's personality has beome complete. Darl now sees himself as object as well as ego —as object rather than ego.

The one woman who occupies a seat in the Bundren wagon, the daughter of the family, Dewey Dell, does not oppose the journey. One might suppose that, like Faulkner's other women characters, she would be too "practical," too concrete and immediate in her relation to reality, to approve of something so quixotic. But the contradiction is only apparent, for Dewey Dell's motive in urging the journey *is* practical. She knows that she is with child; she must find a way to prevent the birth of the child; and the trip to Jefferson offers an opportunity to solve her urgent problem.

The last of the Bundren progeny is the child Vardaman. Like Jewel and Cash, Vardaman runs counter to the claims of common sense; but he does so in the way in which a child, confused and disturbed, would. He is suffering from a traumatic shock. Because the two exciting experiences, the catching of the big fish and his mother's death, happen so close together, the events somehow coalesce in his mind and he can say "my mother is a fish." [2] Vardaman bores holes in his mother's coffin in order to give her air. His attempt to liberate her from the coffin is "crazy" of course, but it has nothing to do with Darl's kind of madness.

Though only Darl opposes the journey, its successful prosecution depends upon the positive efforts of two of the children, Cash and Jewel. They are willing to pay the price for honoring their

2. See below, Notes, p. 399.

mother's request. Anse, it is true, appears to honor it. He evidently enjoys refusing to let his neighbors talk him out of the trip to Jefferson with his wife's body. He explains to Tull, "I give my promise. [Addie] is counting on it" (p. 438). Anse can enjoy this display of his nice sense of honor, for he thinks that it will cost him nothing. (He does lose a team of mules in making the journey, though he induces Jewel to make up part of the cost of replacing it.) Anse is the selfish man who has a lifetime habit of leaning on other people. Anse knows that he can depend on his children to make good his promise. His statement to Cash, "There is Christians enough to help you," is characteristic. In this general connection it is interesting to note what Darl has to say about him. Darl imagines his father leaning above his mother's deathbed and pictures him thus: "his humped silhouette partaking of that owl-like quality of awry-feathered, disgruntled outrage within which lurks a wisdom too profound or too inert for even thought" (p. 372).

One is tempted to say that in this novel Addie and Anse have exchanged roles. It is Anse who has the profound inertia that Faulkner usually associates with woman, who is apparently unaggressive, pliant, and resilient, but with tireless persistence tends toward her elected goal and is never finally deflected from it. Addie one is tempted to call another example of Faulkner's masculinized women. Like Drusilla, but unlike Aunt Jenny, she insists upon the impractical and heroic gesture, and though she could hardly have foreseen how difficult the journey with her coffin would be, it is obviously her still-vital, implacable energy that enables her family to complete their mission and holds them together as a family until her body is finally deposited in the stipulated grave. But the word "masculinized" risks distorting Addie's character. She is completely feminine to the extent that she expresses herself in and through her children. She has fulfilled herself in breeding up and nurturing the children whom she is forcing to become heroes.

Addie is also feminine in Faulkner's sense in being completely committed to the concrete fact. She has seen through all illusions. She despises words. One thinks of the one long, terrible expression allowed her in this novel in which she tells the story of her life. What Addie lacks, and what she yearns for, is some kind of communion. Even before her marriage to Anse, she has felt this emptiness of despair. She switches the children she teaches, in a desperate attempt, as she puts it, to say to them: "Now you are aware of me! Now I am something in your secret and selfish life, who have marked your blood with my own for ever and ever" (p. 462).

Addie's malady is what a recent psychologist [3] has called the loss of the experience of community. With Addie, the loss of community is at the same time a loss of communication. Language seems to her empty and drained and ineffectual. She relates: "I would think how words go straight up in a thin line, quick and harmless, and how terribly doing goes along the earth, clinging to it, so that after a while the two lines are too far apart for the same person to straddle from one to the other; and that sin and love and fear are just sounds that people who never sinned nor loved nor feared have for what they never had and cannot have until they forget the words" (p. 465).

Since Addie does not believe in the spiritual—not, at least, in any of its conventional senses—she can make the assertion of her identity only in terms of the body. Her body then becomes of inordinate importance to her, first through her children—two of whom she jealously claims as a peculiar expression of her body, having no part of Anse but "being of [her] alone"—and now that she is dead, as a token of her final repudiation of Anse. Her dead body becomes a monstrous token—the only available token—of her fierce identity when, through the pledge that she forces from her shiftless husband, she manages to endow it with an almost vampire-like personal will. The body will die only on its own terms: it will not rest—or allow her family rest—until it has been delivered to its chosen resting place.

Addie's grim but exultant confession ends with a significant sentence: "One day I was talking to Cora. She prayed for me because she believed I was blind to sin, wanting me to kneel and pray too, because people to whom sin is just a matter of words, to them salvation is just words too" (p. 468). Addie's salvation was

3. See below, Notes, p. 399.

not of mere words. It involved the substantiality of the body. The Jordan which it had to cross in order to enter into salvation was the flooded river from which Cash and Jewel save her coffined body. The fire of hell which she had to escape was the quite literal fire of the burning barn from which Jewel lugs the coffin. The salvation was a tangible one, not that of some wordy prayer that was to bring her before a heavenly Father but the actual placing of her now foul body beside the bones of her literal earthly father. When Cora Tull had reproached Addie for her partiality to Jewel, saying, "There is your sin. And your punishment too. Jewel is your punishment. But where is your salvation?" Addie had replied, "He is my cross and he will be my salvation. He will save me from the water and from the fire. Even though I have laid down my life, he will save me" (p. 460). Cora Tull, as she confesses later, did not at first understand what Addie was saying, supposing that Addie was speaking of God until she suddenly realized that "he" whom Addie trusts to save her was not God but Jewel. Addie's prophecy of course, is made good.

Cora says, "I realized that out of the vanity of her heart she had spoken sacrilege." And Cora begs her to kneel down and open her heart and cast out her vanity. "But she wouldn't. She just sat there, lost in her vanity and her pride, that had closed her heart to God and set that selfish mortal boy in His place" (p. 460). Cora is, to be sure, a conventional woman with fatuous notions and no real insights into Addie Bundren's situation. It is plain that she knows nothing of Addie's sin with Whitfield nor that Jewel is the son of Whitfield, and she lacks any real comprehension of Addie's spiritual agony and isolation. Yet Cora is here literally correct. Addie is guilty of blasphemy and sacrilege.

Addie has good reason for her disgust at mere words—not only from her experience with her husband but also from her experience with her lover. The passage assigned to Whitfield follows immediately after Addie's. In it Whitfield tells what went on in his mind when he heard that Addie was dying and when, as her pastor, he was summoned to her bedside. His colloquy with himself beautifully illustrates Addie's point about those who live by mere words. When the minister hears of Addie's impending death, he wrestles with his spirit and finally gathers strength to make a full confession to the deceived husband; but in spite of his talk about feeling that he has now been received again into God's holy peace and love, it is plain that he continues to dread the confession that he must make. Thus, when he reaches Tull's house and hears that Addie is already dead, he is greatly relieved. He says to himself: "I have sinned, O Lord. Thou knowest the extent of my remorse and the will of my spirit. But He" (and the shift from second to third person is significant) "is merciful; He will accept the will for the deed, Who knew that when I framed the words of my confession it was to Anse I spoke them, even though he was not there. It was He in His infinite wisdom that restrained the tale from her dying lips as she lay surrounded by those who loved and trusted her . . . Praise to Thee in Thy bounteous and omnipotent love; O praise" (p. 470).

Whitfield's confession,[4] then, is only a matter of words. It is never fulfilled in deeds. Whitfield enjoys the credit of full confession and reacceptance without undergoing any of the suffering and opprobrium that would have ensued from an actual confession to Anse and Anse's neighbors. The point is underlined by Vernon Tull's comment upon the sermon that Whitfield preaches at Addie's funeral. In order to get to the Bundrens', Whitfield, coming on horseback, had had to cross the flooded river. Tull's comment alludes to this fact as he remarks on the discrepancy that he feels between Whitfield as voice and Whitfield as man: "His voice is bigger than him. It's like they are not the same. It's like he is one, and his voice is one, swimming on two horses side by side across the ford and coming into the house, the mud-splashed one and the one that never even got wet, triumphant and sad" (p. 404). Even Tull can sense that the sermon is sentimental rhetoric.

The various commentators on *As I Lay Dying* have made rather heavy work in dealing with Addie.[5] She is sometimes seen as a "good" woman, much put upon, whose story is one of pathos and suffering, and sometimes as a wicked woman, deliberately punish-

4. See below, Notes, p. 400.
5. See below, Notes, p. 401.

ing the members of her family by playing a horrible joke upon them. Neither of these views is very perceptive. Addie is indeed a destructive force, but she is responsible for whatever of heroic temper the Bundrens achieve. She is a wicked woman, if you like (certainly a woman who has been warped and perverted), and she uses her energies for questionable purposes, but the Lady Macbeths and the Medeas—to name more celebrated and august members of Addie's sisterhood—have all been such mixed cases.

Though Addie Bundren has so small a speaking part in this novel, she possesses something of tragic complexity as well as tragic intensity. If she is perverted, her energy, her willingness to suffer, and her complete honesty with herself provide complicating virtues. In any case, she possesses a tremendous intensity, and her corrupting body is throughout the nine days' journey, in some sense, the most vital thing that rides upon the Bundren wagon.

Faulkner has employed various devices to suggest her vitality within the coffin. Anse will say not that Addie's mind "was" set on it but "is" set on it. The confused child Vardaman worries that she may suffocate in the box that Cash has made for her. The madman Darl tells Vardaman to put his ear to the coffin so that he can hear their mother talking—this eight days after her death —and Vardaman says that he can hear her, only he "can't tell what she is saying" (p. 495). Even the rather stolid countryman Vernon Tull at Addie's funeral has the feeling that "her eyes and her voice were turned back inside her, listening" (p. 404). Though Dr. Peabody, on the day of her death, says to himself that the still-breathing woman "has been dead these ten days" (p. 368), Addie maintains her vital power over her family for nearly another ten, until in fact she has finally been lowered into her grave.

In her increasing alienation from her husband, Addie sees as the difference between them the trickery of words and the implacability of deeds, but she soon comes to put the difference in terms of death and life. She says that she discovered that Anse was "dead." As she puts it: "And then he died. He did not know he was dead. I would lie by him in the dark, hearing the dark land talking of God's love and His beauty and His sin; hearing the dark voicelessness in which the words are the deeds, and the other words that are not deeds, that are just the gaps in peoples' lacks, coming down like the cries of the geese out of the wild darkness in the old terrible nights, fumbling at the deeds like orphans to whom are pointed out in a crowd two faces and told, That is your father, your mother" (p. 466).

The romantic poets like Byron and Shelley, whom Addie may have read—she was a schoolteacher—would have understood very well what she was talking about. Byron, one remembers, yearned to find "words which are things." Addie resents mere words, for emptied of substance as they are, they stand as a fence between her and experience. She craves some more direct expression—the naked and bleeding deed: the welt raised by the switch on the limbs of schoolchildren, or the pain of childbed, or the intimate communion that is possible between a woman and the child at her breast. She says, for example, that Cash, as a baby, "did not need to say it to me nor I to him" (p. 464).

It is a romantic and idealistic passion in which Addie is caught up. She was not for nothing the lost and lonely child of a father who used to tell her that the "reason for living was to get ready to stay dead a long time" (p. 461). Addie's concern for deeds and the fierce energy she associates with the earth may disguise her idealism, but it is idealism nevertheless, though of a passionate and devouring kind. What she has done is to transpose the spiritual (and, specifically, the Christian spiritual) into secular terms. Man must not simply vegetate—must not merely grow up like a plant and in due course flower, yield his fruit, and subside again into the nurturing soil. Addie believes that man must assert himself through some unique gesture to indicate that he has lived. She is in an agony to do so. Like the Ancient Mariner, she would gladly bite her arm and suck the blood in order to cry out in a language that will have meaning—a language of deeds and not words.

Other Faulkner characters exhibit this trait. Judith Sutpen in the novel *Absalom, Absalom!* tells Mrs. Compson that one tries to make some kind of impress upon life, then suddenly "it's all over and all you have left is a block of stone" upon which someone has scratched your name, and a stranger doesn't even know "what the scratches were trying to tell. . . . And so maybe if you could go to someone, the stranger the better, and give them something"— she is bringing Mrs. Compson a letter—"something, anything, it not to mean anything in itself and them not even to read it or keep it, not even bother to throw it away or destroy it, at least it would be something just because it would have happened, be remembered even if only from passing from one hand to another, one mind to another, and it would be at least a scratch, something, something that might make a mark on something that *was* once for the reason that it can die someday, while the block of stone cant be *is* because it never can become *was* because it cant ever die or perish" (pp. 127–28).

Addie cannot be fully understood, however, unless we take into account her husband. Anse Bundren is one of Faulkner's most accomplished villains. He lacks the lethal power of a Popeye and the passionate intensity of a Percy Grimm, but the kind of force that he embodies has to be reckoned with. It is deceptively slight, as delicately flexible as a root tendril but, like the tendril, powerful enough to break a boulder. Anse resembles most nearly Flem Snopes—in his coolness, his sheer persistence, his merciless knowledge of other human beings and of how much they will put up with. A nice example is the way in which he gets from Dewey Dell the money her lover has given her for an abortion drug. The girl frantically tries to save her money. But Anse is like a ferret working his way toward the trapped rabbit. When Dewey Dell in her desperation tells her father, "If you take it you are a thief," Anse has his rhetoric ready at command: "My own daughter accuses me of being a thief. My own daughter." And reminding her that he has fed her and sheltered her, he laments that "my own daughter, the daughter of my dead wife, calls me a thief over her mother's grave" (p. 528). Besides, it is only a loan. "God knows, I hate for my blooden children to reproach me. But I give them what was mine without stint. Cheerful I give them, without stint. And now they deny me. Addie. It was lucky for you you died, Addie" (p. 529).

This scene stands as the prelude to Anse's coup which ends the novel. As the innocent but not imperceptive Cash describes it:

"Pa was coming along with that kind of daresome and hangdog look all at once like when he has been up to something he knows ma ain't going to like, carrying a grip in his hand, and Jewel says, 'Who's that?' " (p. 531). The luggage belongs to a duck-shaped woman with "hard-looking pop eyes," and Anse, his store-bought teeth now in his mouth, approaches the wagon and introduces his bride to her stepchildren: " 'It's Cash and Jewel and Vardaman and Dewey Dell,' [he] says, kind of hangdog and proud too, with his teeth and all, even if he wouldn't look at us. 'Meet Mrs. Bundren,' he says" (p. 532).

Our attitude toward Anse—fury at his cheapness and pusillanimity, disgust for his essential callousness and cruelty, baffled admiration for the stubborn vitality which like that of some low order of organism allows him to fatten on what would starve nobler creatures and survive blasts that would kill more sensitive organisms, and, not least, a sense of simple awe at the sheer thickness of his skin—all of these attitudes qualify and determine the kind of comic figure that Anse is. But we must not underestimate him. He is not contemptible, a mere insect that one could and would like to squash underneath the foot. He represents a force probably necessary to the survival of the human animal though it is terrifying when seen in such simple purity.

The grim comedy that attaches to Anse does not, however, call in question the heroic quality of the Bundren adventure. Indeed, this novel beautifully exemplifies how comic elements such as Anse, the human buzzard, and horrifying elements, such as the actual buzzards, are in fact used to undergird the epic mode. The account of the river-crossing, surely one of the finest descriptive achievements in American literature, will illustrate.

Faulkner was skillful in his choice of the people who describe the crossing. It is a fine stroke to have Tull, the practical, earthy, and common-sense countryman, tell part of it. Tull is cynical about the Bundrens' motives for insisting on crossing the river: "Just going to town. Bent on it. They would risk the fire and the earth and the water and all just to eat a sack of bananas" (p. 438). But Tull can make us see the flooded stream: "The water was cold. It was thick, like slush ice. Only it kind of lived. One part of you knowed it was just water, the same thing that had been running under this same bridge for a long time, yet when them logs would come spewing up outen it, you were not surprised, like they was a part of water, of the waiting and the threat" (p. 436).

But Faulkner also has Darl, whose perceptions are always instinct with poetry, describe the scene: "What had once been a flat surface was now a succession of troughs and hillocks lifting and falling about us, shoving at us, teasing at us with light lazy touches in the vain instants of solidity underfoot" (p. 444). And Darl, describing the catastrophe says: "Cash looked back at me, and then I knew that we were gone. But I did not realize the reason for the rope until I saw the log. It surged up out of the water and stood for an instant upright upon that surging and heaving desolation like Christ" (p. 445). Why like Christ? It would be hard to say, though the similitude seems inevitable and right. Is Darl remembering the passage in which the alarmed fishermen on Galilee see their Master incredibly walking upon the waves? But with the difference that this erect object, incredibly footing the water, moves toward them not to reassure but to threaten and astound? Perhaps so, or perhaps the force of the similitude is more general. The log, standing for an instant upright, is like Christ simply in its hint of supernatural portent, an astonishing assertion out of the mere flux of anonymity. (Later, Cora is to call the log "the hand of God.")

The passage that follows, which details the destruction caused by the log as it bears down upon the team and which depicts Jewel's surging horse and the mules for a moment shining black out of the water just before they are overturned—all of this is done with the fidelity that one expects from the dedicated observer, the habitual spectator, for that, as we have seen, is all that Darl is. Cash and Jewel agonize and struggle; Darl does not.

It is also a fine stroke on Faulkner's part to have the child Vardaman describe what happened just after the drowning of the mules and the coffin's slipping off into the water. Vardaman's account has the clarity of detail of the innocent eye, but also the confused subjectivity of Vardaman's anxiety. For the child it will be intolerable if Darl doesn't catch the coffin. Surely he will come up with it out of the water. His failure to do so will be unbearable: "Then his hands came up and all of him above the water. I can't stop. I have not got time to try. I will try to when I can but his hands came empty out of the water emptying the water emptying away" (p. 448). But we also need, for our total comprehension, Tull's objective account as he tells his wife about it later. He puts it laconically: "How Darl jumped out of the wagon and left Cash sitting there trying to save it and the wagon turning over" (p. 448).

The same brilliance of description and narrative effect shows in the barn-burning episode. This account of Jewel's rushing into the burning barn and getting out first the animals and then the coffin is related principally by Darl. The descriptions are vivid: Jewel silhouetted against the burning barn appears "like a flat figure cut cleanly from tin against an abrupt and soundless explosion as the whole loft of the barn takes fire at once, as though it had been stuffed with powder" (p. 498). When Jewel and the Gillespies come to rescue the cow, "she is backed into the corner, head lowered, still chewing though rapidly." The men break an opening through the planks of the barn and in a moment the cow rescues herself: "with a single whistling breath she rushes between us and through the gap and into the outer glare, her tail erect and rigid as a broom nailed upright to the end of her spine" (p. 500).

Once the animals are saved, Jewel returns for the coffin. As he does so, it seems to Darl that the "hall-way looks like a searchlight turned into rain" (p. 500). Jewel rushes into the barn, crouches to the far end of the coffin and "for an instant he looks up and out at us through the rain of burning hay like a portière of flaming beads" (p. 501). In a moment or two Jewel emerges with the coffin, "riding upon it, clinging to it, until it crashes down and flings him forward and clear and Mack leaps forward into a thin smell of scorching meat and slaps at the widening crimson-edged holes that bloom like flowers in his undershirt." This is sensitive reporting of a very high order indeed, and the more realistic elements in the account, including the grotesque detail of Gillespie's nightshirt borne ahead of him "on the draft, ballooning about his hairy thighs" (p. 499) do not cancel out the poetry. They ballast and stabilize the poetry.

After the rescue, Vardaman watches Dewey Dell put butter and soot onto Jewel's blistered back and then finds Darl out under the apple tree lying on the coffin. "The moonlight dappled on him too. On her it was still, but on Darl it dappled up and down. 'You needn't to cry,' I said. 'Jewel got her out. You needn't to cry, Darl' " (p. 503). Darl's tears, of course, are shed because Jewel did get her out. Darl had hoped to end the horrible journey by cremating his mother's body.

The force exerted by the dead woman in holding her family together is underscored by our sense of the divisions within the family. One might argue that each of the Bundren children is making the journey alone, each shut up in his own consciousness and unable to communicate with the others. Jewel cannot understand Cash and is exasperated by what he takes to be Cash's insensitivity and callousness. He is outraged that Cash chooses to work on his mother's coffin near a window through which his mother can see him at his work.[6] Between Jewel and Darl there is active hostility. Darl is bitter and even cruel in taunting Jewel for having a horse for a mother. The intensity of Jewel's love for his horse and the sacrifice that he has made to obtain it give special edge to the taunt. Yet there is no question that Jewel loves his mother and even Darl recognizes this, as, for example, when he observes what he calls "the furious tide of Jewel's despair" (p. 408).

The lack of communication extends through the family. Dewey Dell is unable to speak to anyone about her plight. There is a desperate need to talk to someone about her problem and yet there is literally no one to whom she can talk. The only person who is aware of her pregnancy is Darl, and him she fears and hates with a blind fury. Once their mother's body has been put into the grave, Dewey Dell joins Jewel in leaping upon Darl as they seize him in order to turn him over to the officers.

Jewel, too, is a passionate person who has no one with whom he can talk. Granted that there is a kind of nameless understanding

6. See below, Notes, p. 401.

between him and his mother, still it is nameless and unuttered, and his inarticulate poetry, the ardor and passion which he can express only through violent action, find no release in words—in part because there is no one with whom he can converse.

Cash, of course, has no poetry in him, articulate or inarticulate, and perhaps in him of all the family there is the least need for expression or for a sympathetic and understanding listener. Yet if Cash bears his relative isolation with patience and with no special sense of pain, he is nevertheless a baffled and lonely man. He reflects that he was born almost ten years before the three youngest children and therefore feels closest to Darl, but it is plain that he and Darl have very little in common. Cash shakes his head in puzzled reproach when he learns that it was Darl who set fire to Mr. Gillespie's barn. He is shocked when Dewey Dell and Jewel leap upon Darl in fury to turn him over to the officers, and when Darl breaks down into his crazy laughter, Cash is indeed at a loss. He says: "I be durn if I could see anything to laugh at" (p. 514).

The essential isolation of the characters is unobtrusively enforced by the fact that each part of the novel is presented through the consciousness of a particular character. We are always within one mind, never in some domain of objectivity and commonly held values. Often we are in the minds of sensitive observers like Darl and the child Vardaman. Darl has nineteen sections; Vardaman, ten. The sections assigned to all the rest of the family amount to only fourteen, and of these, Jewel, the heroically active son, has only one.

Faulkner's method of presentation allows us, on occasion, not only to penetrate into the depths of a character but to see him externally as others see him. Sometimes this external view is that of another member of the family; at other times, that of an outsider like Dr. Peabody or the druggist MacGowan. This technique of multiple presentation has everything to do with the solidity and power of *As I Lay Dying*. The author does not commit us to the experience and sensibility of one character whom we see only from the inside and whose world we apprehend only from his point of view. Instead, Faulkner has attempted the much more difficult role of putting us in some kind of sympathetic rapport with an individual character and yet constantly forcing this character back into the total perspective of the world—the world of the family and the larger world of the community.

The presentation of Dewey Dell will illustrate. She looks at first glance like a rather stupid and selfish young woman, as in some sense she is. Yet in spite of her somewhat bovine simplicity, Dewey Dell has her secret terrors, her pathos, and even her shy dignity. When Dr. Peabody comes to see her mother, she yearns toward his knowledge: "he could do so much for me and he don't know it" (p. 380). But she is afraid to tell him what her problem is and feels to the full her alienation: "It's because I am alone" (p. 379). Later she reflects: "I don't know whether I am worrying or not. Whether I can or not. I don't know whether I can cry or not. I don't know whether I have tried to or not. I feel like a wet seed wild in the hot blind earth" (p. 384).

Incidentally, the reader must not be put off because Dewey Dell —and all the other characters for that matter—frequently in these interior monologues use words and expressions which we feel are beyond their education and background. This is one of the conventions which must be accepted in a reading of *As I Lay Dying*. The language with which the author provides the character to express his innermost thoughts is not necessarily the same language the author has him use when he speaks to another character. It would certainly not occur to Dewey Dell to *tell* anyone that she felt like a "wet seed wild in the hot blind earth."

On the wagon Dewey Dell, obsessed with her own problem, is conscious of being unable to indulge her grief for her mother. She says: "I wish I had time to let her die"—meaning, I wish that I were not too distracted to think of her dying. "I wish I had time to wish I had. It is because in the wild and outraged earth too soon too soon too soon. It's not that I wouldn't and will not it's that it is too soon too soon too soon" (p. 422). And in her despair she says to herself "I believe in God, God. God, I believe in God" (p. 424).

But Faulkner allows us to see Dewey Dell through other eyes— those, for example, of the rather straight-laced Motson druggist, who notices that "she was pretty in a kind of sullen, awkward way," and who finally has to tell her that he wishes her "precious

Lafe had come for it himself; that's what I wish. . . . Me, a respectable druggist, that's kept store and raised a family and been a church-member for fifty-six years in this town. I'm a good mind to tell your folks myself, if I can just find who they are" (p. 487). He finally dismisses Dewey Dell with an admonition: "I haven't got anything in my store you want to buy, unless it's a nipple. And I'd advise you to buy that and go back home and tell your pa, if you have one, and let him make somebody buy you a wedding license." The author also lets us see Dewey Dell through the eyes of MacGowan, the less scrupulous druggist in Jefferson, who sees her as looking "pretty good" for a country girl, "one of them black-eyed ones that look like she'd as soon put a knife in you as not if you two-timed her" (p. 517). The account of MacGowan's prescription for what Dewey Dell has called the female trouble and of the "treatment" he gives her is comedy in the tradition of the medieval fabliau, but I find that it intensifies the pathos of the situation rather than canceling it.

Jewel, too, has an inner life—though little of it is revealed in interior monologue. He is high-strung and fractious, youthfully intolerant, lacking imaginative sympathy, shortsighted, and ignorant. Yet because of its real ardor and passion, his inner life has its beauty. The horse that Jewel finally sells so that his father can buy the team to complete the journey to Jefferson is his most precious possession. We cannot know how much this sacrifice costs him until we have from Darl the story of how Jewel paid for his horse, slipping out each night to work by lantern light in a neighbor's field and the next day working in his father's field. Darl says: "I have seen him go to sleep chopping; watched the hoe going slower and slower up and down, with less and less of an arc, until it stopped and he leaning on it motionless in the hot shimmer of the sun" (p. 429).

Darl first thinks that Jewel's nightly expedition has to do with a woman, but Cash, to whom Darl confides the secret, follows Jewel one night and learns the truth. But Cash does not let the rest of the family know what Jewel is doing; he just quietly takes over some of Jewel's work. The secret is not divulged until the morning that Jewel rides up on his pony. Anse is quick with his reproaches:

"You went behind my back and bought a horse" (p. 434). But Addie is overcome: " 'I'll give—I'll give—give—' Then she began to cry. She cried hard, not hiding her face, standing there in her faded wrapper, looking at him and him on the horse" (p. 434). And that night Darl finds his mother sitting beside the bed where Jewel was sleeping in the dark. "She cried hard, maybe because she had to cry so quiet" (p. 435). In saving the coffin from the river and from the burning barn, Jewel acts in character and makes use of his special talents. His sacrifice of his horse is less expected. In a sense it is the most heroic thing that he does.

It is Cash, however, who gains most from a multiple focus on his personality. Jewel possesses something of the poetry of action. Darl has the lucidity of the mad. But Cash's dignity and integrity scarcely shine forth—they are virtues too dull to shine—and we are hardly in a position to appreciate them until we have regarded Cash from a number of angles. More than one critic has been misled by Cash's inarticulate expression and his homely metaphors, drawn from the carpenter's trade, into taking him at the lowest discount. But Cash is no materialist; he is simply a very quiet and limited man, whose ideals are not showy but who has great power to endure and a great capacity to suffer without whining or complaining.

Cash also possesses more imaginative sympathy than may at first be evident. We have remarked upon the way in which he simply assumes a number of Jewel's duties when he realizes that his younger brother, in his passion to possess the horse, is attempting something beyond his powers. And Cash is sympathetic with Darl. He almost grasps the motives for Darl's actions on the journey. He says to himself: "I thought more than once . . . how it would be God's blessing if He did take her outen our hands and get shut of her in some clean way, and it seemed to me that when Jewel worked so to get her outen the river, he was going against God in a way, and then when Darl seen that it looked like one of us would have to do something, I can almost believe he done right in a way. But I don't reckon nothing excuses setting fire to a man's barn" (p. 510). But comprehension is not Cash's strong point. And Darl, after all, is insane.

The real difficulty with depicting a character like Cash, so patient, so uncomplaining, so passive in his acceptance of hardship, is that the reader may regard him as simply weak and stupid, and may laugh rather than sympathize with him. Faulkner's solution is to allow us to laugh at Cash. He does not play down the irreverent and mocking attitudes, but stresses them, makes them part of the total view, and thus wrests Cash's dignity out of the very jaws of comedy.

There are only five sections attributed to Cash, and the first three of these are brief and quite objective: Cash's justification for making the coffin "on the bevel," a short scrap of his conversation with Jewel, and an additional remark about the coffin's not balancing. The only meditative and ruminative passages allowed him are two that occur quite late in the novel.

Cash, then, begins as a kind of flat caricature, like a character in a humors play. We see him first working away at the coffin to the chuk, chuk, chuk of his adze, just outside the room in which his mother is dying. He is still a comic figure of a sort when he lies injured beside the flooded river, his tools carefully arranged beside him, with the wretched Anse muttering, "A fellow might call it lucky it was the same leg he broke when he fell offen that church" (p. 458). The horror of the grotesque contends with the comedy of the grotesque when the family, under Anse's direction, pour sand and cement around Cash's broken leg in order to set it in a crude cast. Later, when Cash is in agony, Darl recounts: "So we poured the water over it. His leg and foot below the cement look like they had been boiled. 'Does that feel better?' we said. 'I'm obliged,' Cash said. 'It feels fine'" (p. 495).

The problem of tone comes to a head in the exchange between Cash and Dr. Peabody. The doctor, having managed to get the homemade cast off the leg and having reset the broken bone, proceeds to say what he thinks of the way in which Cash has been treated. He remarks that a man might conceivably get into a position where he would let a veterinarian like Bill Varner patch him up as if he were a mule (this has happened earlier in the novel) but, he continues, "I be damned if the man that'd let Anse Bundren treat him with raw cement ain't got more spare legs than I have" (p. 515). Cash gives the soft answer, defending even the unspeakable Anse: "They just aimed to ease hit some." But Peabody tells Cash not to lie there and try to tell him that he has ridden for six days on a wagon without springs, "with a broken leg and it never bothered you." When Cash replies that "It never bothered me much," Peabody remarks sardonically, "You mean, it never bothered Anse much." And he goes on to refer to what has happened to Darl: "No more than it bothered him to throw that poor devil down in the public street and handcuff him like a damned murderer. Don't tell me."

Continuing his questioning, Peabody learns that Anse is now returning the spade that he borrowed and he remarks: "Of course he'd have to borrow a spade to bury his wife with. Unless he could borrow a hole in the ground. Too bad you all didn't put him in it too. . . . Does that hurt?" (p. 516). Cash replies: "Not to speak of," though Peabody notices sweat drops "big as marbles running down his face and his face about the colour of blotting-paper." As the doctor works grumpily over the leg, he assures Cash that maybe next summer he can hobble around fine on this leg: "Then it won't bother you, not to speak of. . . . If you had anything you could call luck, you might say it was lucky this is the same leg you broke before." And Cash answers: "Hit's what paw says" (p. 516).

What does the doctor feel toward Cash? Pity? Admiration? Sheer amazement at his patience, irritation at his stolidity? Perhaps something of all of these. But not contempt, I should think. Cash has earned his right to be allowed to suffer in his own way. He is too sturdy and too solidly based to deserve any emotion elicited by weakness or moral pettiness.

The truth of the matter is that Dr. Peabody would probably not himself be able to describe precisely what his attitude toward Cash is. Our attitude toward Cash, of course, is not necessarily Dr. Peabody's, nor is our attitude toward any other member of the family that of our attitude toward Cash. And yet the problem that we have just been considering is a sort of paradigm of the larger problems raised by the novel. As Vernon Tull or Samson might put it, the Bundrens' exploit leaves us not knowing whether to laugh or to cry. And more is involved than simple indecision or a stalemate between these opposed attitudes. Both the pathetic and the comic have scope in this situation: folly intermingles with heroism, and the total perspective in which we are invited to view the Bundrens' odyssey accommodates what would usually be regarded as hopelessly conflicting attitudes.

In the total perspective the contradictions prove to be only apparent. The surface of the Bundren life shows squalor, crassness, selfishness, and stupidity, but beneath the surface there are depths of passion and poetry that are terrifying in their power. The very drabness of the surface is the guarantee of the genuineness of the passion. These people are not rhetoricians who talk themselves into their transports. One of them has the poetry of madness; one of them, the poetry of the child. But the others are almost inarticulate, and the two brothers who dare most and suffer most lack the wordiness that their mother despised.

Faulkner has been concerned in all his books with what the human being can endure, what he can dare, what he can accomplish. The story of how the Bundrens managed the burial of Addie Bundren affords him a very special vantage point from which to contemplate the human capacity for both suffering and action. The heroic adventure involves a mixture of motives and a variety of responses. There is the child who only partially comprehends what is occurring and responds to what he sees with astonishment and fear. There is the young woman so much obsessed with her own problems that she can reflect upon the adventure only as a possible answer to her own need. There is the parasite Anse, who does not even know that he is asking his children to be heroes, and if he could understand it would not care. There is Darl, who knows too much and feels too much to take in more more than the nauseating horror and fear that the act costs. There is the patient Cash, who never sees that he is doing more than his bounden duty. There is Jewel, perhaps the least reflective member of the group, violent and even brutal, whose heroism is so pure and unself-conscious that he is not aware that it is heroism. It burns like a clean flame that exhausts itself in the process, leaving no sooty residue.

As a commentary upon man's power to act and to endure, upon his apparently incorrigible idealism, the story of the Bundrens is clearly appalling—appalling but not scathing and not debunking. Heroism is heroism even though it sometimes appears to be merely the hither side of folly. Man's capacity to spend himself in a cause is always a remarkable thing and nowhere more so than when it springs from an unlikely soil and when it is not aware that it is remarkable. For a summarizing statement on *As I Lay Dying*, one might appeal to one of the choruses in *Antigone:* "Wonders are many, and none is more wonderful than man." *As I Lay Dying* provides a less exalted but not unworthy illustration of Sophocles' judgment.

9

Faulkner's Savage Arcadia:
Frenchman's Bend

(THE HAMLET)

MORE THAN ANY other novel of Faulkner's, *The Hamlet* introduces us to a strange and special world. Frenchman's Bend, the little settlement built up around Will Varner's general store and cotton gin, together with the small farms that spread out from it through the hill country, constitutes a world of the poor white. The Negro has hardly any part in it. The Varners, it is true, have one or two Negro servants and there is a Negro fireman at the sawmill, but Negroes do not live in the community of Frenchman's Bend. There are none to be seen there after dark. Relations between white and black, which figure so powerfully in many of Faulkner's novels, have almost no place here.

In this regard *The Hamlet* resembles *Light In August* and *As I Lay Dying*. But *Light In August* is a novel about the town, and though countrymen constantly come into town, and though the townsfolk themselves are imbued with the folk culture, the atmosphere is quite different from that of *The Hamlet*. With respect to the social class of its characters *The Hamlet* more nearly resembles *As I Lay Dying*. A number of those who figure in *As I Lay Dying*, men like Tull and Bookwright and Quick and the Reverend Mr. Whitfield, also appear in *The Hamlet*. But the latter novel is not keyed to agonized activity. In it, to be sure, there are figures of passionate intensity, like Jack Houston or Mink Snopes or Labove, and some of the things that go on in it are as fantastic as the Bundren family's epic battles with fire and flood. But *The Hamlet* is worked out more expansively and on a wider canvas. It is like a great folk legend in which bawdy anecdote is intermingled with myth and stories of prodigies. Something like an antic paganism peeps out from the Protestant purlieus of Frenchman's Bend, and the comedy has a different note and serves a somewhat different purpose.

Before going into the novel, therefore, it will be useful to examine a little more narrowly the world conjured up by *The Hamlet* and to notice some of the special devices through which Faulkner has controlled the reader's view of it. A good place to start is with what might be called "distancing" devices, by means of which the reader views a scene as through a telescope: the detail is magnified; the reader's attention is caught and slowed as he is forced to take in the scene bit by bit; and yet, in spite of the clarity of his view, the reader is made to feel that he is not really close up to the scene. An instructive instance occurs very early in the novel.

Jody Varner has come to talk with his new tenant, Ab Snopes. As he nears the house, he hears "the mournful measured plaint of a rusted well-pulley" and two "flat meaningless loud female voices" (p. 20). When he passes beyond the house he sees the figures at the well—"the narrow high frame like an epicene gallows, two big absolutely static young women beside it, who even in that first glance postulated that immobile dreamy solidarity of statuary . . . even though one of them had hold of the well-rope, her arms extended at full reach, her body bent for the down pull like a figure in a charade, a carved piece symbolizing some terrific physical effort which had died with its inception, though a moment later the pulley began again its rusty plaint." The scene is made larger than life and yet at the same time remote from ordinary life.

Every detail is given with high definition and sharp focus. Because the scene is analyzed for the reader bit by bit, the action is decelerated as by a slow-motion camera. In describing the young women at the well Faulkner, to be sure, has a special purpose in wanting to slow the action, freezing it to a virtual tableau: he is suggesting something of the shiftless inertia of the poor white. He calls the young women "static" and attributes to them something of the "dreamy solidarity of statuary." Yet one element in the description—the "distancing" effect—is not special here but is typical of the whole novel.

In addition to such distancing devices, there are all sorts of ways in which the characters and scenes are formalized and stylized as in a Dutch genre picture. Character after character is described with a kind of meticulous accuracy, as if the author were introducing the reader to beings who were so much out of the way as to be exotic. Will Varner, for example, is depicted as sitting "in a home-made chair on the jungle-choked lawn of the Old Frenchman's homesite. His blacksmith had made the chair for him by sawing an empty flour barrel half through the middle and trimming out the sides and nailing a seat into it, and Varner would sit there chewing his tobacco or smoking his cob pipe . . . against his background of fallen baronial splendor" (p. 6). Eula Varner is described as "a soft ample girl with definite breasts even at thirteen and eyes like cloudy hothouse grapes and a full damp mouth always slightly open" (p. 10). Jody Varner doing clerical work presents this picture: "he sat at the roll-top desk in the rear of the store, hunched, the black hat on the back of his head and one broad black-haired hand motionless and heavy as a ham of meat on the paper and the pen in the other tracing the words of the contract in his heavy deliberate sprawling script" (p. 12).

Even when the action is trivial and the talk casual, earthy, and realistic, the nature which forms the background of the talk and the action is realized in a poetry that makes it seem vibrant and charged with power, portentous and awesome in its potentialities. For example, Ratliff is talking with Quick and Freeman on the evening before the spotted-horses auction. He observes that "a fellow can dodge a Snopes if he just starts lively enough" (p. 281), a far from poetic remark, but the men with whom he is talking stand out as black silhouettes "against the dreaming lambence of the moonlight beyond the veranda." The moonlight transforms the world. Across the road from them there is a pear tree "in full and frosty bloom," with its "twigs and branches springing not outward from the limbs but standing motionless and perpendicular above the horizontal boughs like the separate and upstreaming hair of a drowned woman sleeping upon the uttermost floor of the windless and tideless sea" (p. 281). The pear tree seems to rise "in mazed and silver immobility like exploding snow" (p. 312). The world, for all its brilliantly realized description, wears an eerie quality, and in the atmosphere of such a world it is easy to think of the human beings who move through it as more simple, more strange, and more elemental than are the ordinary human beings we know.

In the scene just described, the casual and humorous talk has as its background a nature that is remote and almost dreamily exotic. But this quality is no mere delicate frothiness: it is a powerful solvent that is able to turn the violent half-wild horses into phantoms. Seen by the "treacherous and silver receptivity" of the moonlight, the horses "huddled in mazy camouflage, or singly or in pairs rushed, fluid, phantom, and unceasing, to huddle again in mirage-like clumps from which came high abrupt squeals and the vicious thudding of hooves" (p. 280). In a moment there comes a "high thin squeal" from the lot and one of the horses emerges. "It seemed not to gallop but to flow, bodiless, without dimension. Yet there was the rapid light beat of hard hooves on the packed earth." There is the realistic and matter-of-fact detail—the sound of hooves drumming upon the solid earth—but the detail is associated with a creature that seems in no way earthbound, but rather wraithlike, "bodiless, without dimension." Devices of this sort, used constantly throughout *The Hamlet,* build up the sense of the marvelous and almost supernatural quality of beings and happenings in a remote, entranced world.

The "mythic" atmosphere of *The Hamlet* depends chiefly, however, on a special heightening of characters and incidents—a heightening achieved directly by the author through his own description and narration, or else indirectly through letting the reader see the characters and events as mirrored in the imagination of a Labove or a Ratliff. In *The Hamlet* Eula becomes a kind of rustic Aphrodite. Her power to arouse men is attested in various ways—through her bachelor brother's irritating consciousness of her power as he takes her behind him on horseback to school every day, or through the way in which the swains of Frenchman's Bend gather each Sunday afternoon on the Varner porch, or through the heroic actions of her one successful lover, Hoake McCarron. But much of this sense of her divinity is transmitted through her effect on Labove—specifically, through the descriptions of her which are associated with the young schoolteacher, whose head is full of his classic reading and whose veins are on fire. Some of the rather ornately rhetorical descriptions come, it is true, from the author in his own person. Eula's appearance, we are told, suggests something out of the old "Dionysic times— honey in sunlight and bursting grapes, the writhen bleeding of the crushed fecundated vine beneath the hard rapacious trampling goat-hoof" (p. 95). Eula's listening "in sullen bemusement, with a weary wisdom . . . to the enlarging of her own organs" is also the author's contribution. But other passages of such rhetoric— Eula's bringing into the "poorly-heated room dedicated to the harsh functioning of Protestant primary education a moist blast of spring's liquorish corruption" (p. 114)—are associated with the obsessed mind of Labove. So it is throughout this whole section of the novel: even the descriptions that are not part of Labove's own words tend to follow the play of his thoughts and feelings.

The mythic quality of the world of the novel is further built up through the character of Ratliff, but in a quite different way. Ratliff is not, like Labove, an obsessed man. He is practical and humorous; but he loves to embroider a tale, and his recounting of some of the stories about Flem and Flem's forebears achieves the dimension of myth. Ratliff achieves it most obviously in the passage in which he imagines Flem's entrance into hell. Flem, having entered into a Faustian compact with the devil, proves himself, with his own cool legality, far more than a match for the prince of darkness. As a cold retelling of the Faust legend, the story would, in its presumption, fall flat. But told as Ratliff can tell it, and with Ratliff taking the responsibility for the heightenings and exaggerations, the story comes off brilliantly. It gives us Ratliff's own shrewd, yet at the same time awed, conception of Flem, and thus does a great deal to turn Flem into a prodigy.

Flem and Eula are thus, in their very different ways, creatures not to be measured by the ordinary standards of this world. Eula is a woman of fabulous beauty and seductive power, though unself-conscious and almost unaware of that power. She becomes the archetypal feminine—at least in the eyes of the young fanatic Labove, and in a sense she becomes such for the whole community. And Flem, in his sheer concern for money and the power that it brings, becomes something fabulous too. Ratliff takes a kind of pride in Flem's prodigious character as he would have taken pride in the fact that Frenchman's Bend had produced a six-legged calf. Thus the impotent Flem, who is pure single-minded acquisitiveness, and Eula, who is the unself-conscious and almost mindless personification of the fecundity of nature, are almost like goddess and ogre, a positive and a negative power, and the yoking of them together takes on the quality of an allegorical event. What keeps the story from becoming transparent allegory, and thus a too bald commentary on the modern scene, is the richness of detail and the sheer power of fact which locate these two creatures in a community that is still close enough to nature to have nymphs and trolls walk within it and not so self-conscious as to have to rationalize them out of existence.

Yet, though the author uses characters like Labove and Ratliff in order to generate the atmosphere of a special world, his point of view is not identical with that of any of his characters. His attitude is closest, of course, to that of Ratliff, and Ratliff significantly views the world with a good measure of detachment and has his own joy in observing the behavior of human beings and the parade of human folly. The author relishes Ratliff and admires him, but he is not content to see Frenchman's Bend through Ratliff's eyes: the author's vision of Frenchman's Bend includes the figure of Ratliff himself.

One might try to characterize Faulkner's attitude in this fashion: he finds human beings fascinating, so fascinating that the fact that his characters are ignorant rustics in no wise diminishes interest in them. He is not willing to set any limits to what they will do in terms of trickery, mad folly, or even heroism: the human being is obviously capable of almost anything. This conviction springs not from a weary cynicism but from a profound conviction of the powerful mystery that resides in human nature. Faulkner simply does not condescend to his characters, not even—to use a currently fashionable term—by feeling compassion for them. His interest in his characters goes far beyond all the modes of condescension.

To sum up: the tone of *The Hamlet* is a compound of irony and wonder, but with somewhat more stress upon wonder than upon irony. Irony and wonder are of course related: when the poet or the novelist reveals to us that what we had thought to be a meaningless clutter really constitutes a pattern, or when he shows us beneath the commonly accepted appearance the true configuration, he can emphasize the ironic difference between appearance and reality or he can emphasize the fresh wonder of discovered truth. We tend to regard the revelation of the wonder of the world as romantic, and the ironic qualification of conventional judgments as antiromantic and satirical, but the two attitudes are related to the same basic act, in which the mirror of truth is wiped clean. There is no reason why elements of both attitudes should not occur together. In *The Hamlet* the ironic element frequently takes the form of a kind of folk humor, and the wonder tends toward the mythic extravagance of the tall tale. But the tall-tale tradition, though it can help us in trying to define the general tone of *The Hamlet,* provides only a partial definition. In the author's attitude toward the inhabitants of Frenchman's Bend, there is an element of genuine wonder—at the marvelous cantankerousness and devilment and energy of the human being— yet the wonder is tempered not only by folk humor but by an irony edged with the knowledge of the inadequacies and contradictions to be found in the usual notions about human nature.

In *The Hamlet,* as in novels like *Light in August* and *As I Lay Dying,* the pastoral mode is used to underscore this double effect of irony and wonder. Wordsworth's account of his peasants moves primarily in the direction of wonder—wonder at the depth and beauty of their human impulses and sympathies—but even Words-worth is quite aware that the great world finds it hard to credit peasants—the men, women, children, and idiots of Wordsworth's poems—with fine feelings and delicate sensibilities.

Faulkner's pastoral mode is, of course, more earthy and violent than Wordsworth's, and Faulkner's pastoral scene is, much more than Wordsworth's, consciously set off from the dominant urban culture of its time. In the community of Frenchman's Bend human nature operates without the refinements and restraints that we associate with a modern urban world, but also without its inhibitions and disguises. Because the world of *The Hamlet* is—at least at an initial glance—so different from the reader's normal experience, Faulkner's first problem is to make it credible to his reader. It cannot be presented as normal and everyday, but must be made to seem, in its very strangeness, solid and lifelike. Thus we find that Faulkner has stylized and formalized his world of Frenchman's Bend almost as much as Jonathan Swift stylized and formalized the country of Lilliput, but again like Swift, he has rendered it in almost microscopic detail. One might say that the narrator of *The Hamlet* has a touch of Gulliver in him, but scarcely a hint of the modern anthropologist investigating the customs of the Trobriand Islanders. Instead, he gives us typically the color and gusto of a tale told in something of Ratliff's man-ner: this is the staple ingredient.

The Hamlet is ostensibly the story of the rise of Flem Snopes—from a shiftless sharecropper's indigent son to the financial power of the community—who, at the end of the novel, has carried all before him and has defeated even Ratliff, the countrified St. George, the sole hope against this cold-blooded dragon. *The Ham-let* is thus a sort of sardonic Horatio Alger story, a tale of com-mercial success in which the poor but diligent young man marries the boss's daughter and becomes a financial power. But though the story of Flem's rise provides the line of plot that links the various episodes into a whole, Flem is far from being the most interesting of the characters, and some readers will feel that his story does not really provide a unifying element.

Certainly, *The Hamlet* is characterized by a prodigality of subplots and incidental actions. Indeed, this novel shows Faulkner's inventiveness and boundless energy at its best. One thinks of the exuberant story of horse-trading, which tells how Flem's father became soured on the world when he was worsted by the doughty horse-trader Pat Stamper, or of the episode in which Ab Snopes burned Major de Spain's barn, or of the way in which Mink Snopes found the woman that he married, or of the tale of Labove, the austere football star, who equips his poor-white hill family, including his grandmother, with cleated football shoes, though his sense of honor forbids him to claim a pair from the athletic locker when his team loses.

These stories are told with great gusto, sometimes by that born raconteur Ratliff, sometimes by the author in his own person. To many readers, therefore, the novel has seemed to be no more than a loose collection of spectacular yarns and anecdotes, and since some of these are among the finest that Faulkner has ever written, that fact might be held to aggravate rather than mitigate the sense of episodic looseness.

One of the most interesting subplots is the story of Labove. It may be significant that we never learn his first name. He comes into Frenchman's Bend merely because Will Varner, needing a new schoolteacher to replace the bibulous old "professor" who can no longer keep order in the schoolroom, happens to hear of Labove and his athletic prowess. Labove has a great talent for football, though he does not like the game. He plays it merely as a way of getting through the university and securing the degree that he craves. He does not even like the books that he studies, but simply believes "that he must read, compass and absorb and wring dry" their information "with something of that same contemptuous intensity with which he chopped fire wood" (p. 111). He is a man of tremendous and dogged ambition, capable of driving himself through any kind of difficulties, a man who has a great deal of the ascetic in him: Faulkner tells us that in an earlier age his face would have been that of a monk, "a militant fanatic who would have turned his uncompromising back upon the world with actual joy" (p. 106). Faulkner's account of Labove is another of his many studies of Southern Puritanism. Looking back over the range of Faulkner's work, one can see Labove's points of kinship with people like Joe Christmas or Byron Bunch or Jewel Bundren or even Gail Hightower. As one might expect, in view of his Puritan heritage, Labove is a man of tremendous natural integrity. He performs his promises and carries out his commitments, whether in the poor schoolroom at Frenchman's Bend or on the University of Mississippi's football field.

It is Labove's fate to fall in love with Eula Varner. "Love," of course, is not the proper term. His is a special kind of lust, a lust in the head as well as in the glands, and it is perverse and obsessive. At any rate, the young ascetic is captivated by Eula. He lives for her presence. Though at one time Labove had thought of marrying her when she grew up, he soon discards that notion. He doesn't really want a wife at all, and knows that he does not, in any case, want Eula as a wife. "He just wanted her one time as a man with a gangrened hand or foot thirsts after the axe-stroke which will leave him comparatively whole again" (p. 119). This notion is mad, and Labove's madness is acknowledged by the author. It is, in effect, acknowledged by Labove himself. But the madness is not rendered the less compulsive by the victim's admitting it to himself.

One day, after school has been dismissed, Labove finds himself alone with her in the schoolroom. Her brother is late in coming for her and it is too cold on this winter afternoon for her to wait outside. The opportunity is too much for Labove. In a frenzy, he tries to rape her. But the girl, unexpectedly strong, manages to throw him from her, and standing over him "breathing deep but not panting and not even disheveled," says to him: "Stop pawing me. . . . You old headless horseman Ichabod Crane" (p. 122). The tag from the Washington Irving story is the only thing that Labove can be sure that she had ever learned in her five years in the schoolroom. But it is enough. Her schoolgirl's scorn reduces him to impotence.

When she walks back into the schoolroom a moment later to recover her book satchel, Labove makes no further move to touch her. But, because in his own fashion he is a man of honor, he waits in the schoolroom for her brother to come and shoot him. When, after an hour and more, Jody finally does walk in and shows by his conduct that Eula has told him nothing at all, Labove realizes his full defeat. He says to himself: "She didn't even forget to [tell him]. She doesn't even know anything happened that was worth mentioning" (p. 127). And with this, Labove shuts the schoolroom door, drives a nail into the wall beside the door, hangs the key on the nail, and takes the road out of Frenchman's Bend and out of the story forever.

The Labove episode is brilliantly done—done with so much conviction that it could conceivably stand alone as a short story. But, obviously, it gains from the context in which it is set. The "world" of *The Hamlet* helps us to believe in the characters, enhances the plausibility of the incidents, and deepens the irony and pathos of the young schoolmaster's plight. What the reader of the *The Hamlet* needs to notice, however, is what episodes like that just described contribute to the total context. The Labove episode, for example, sounds two basic themes of the novel, the themes of love and honor. Labove's "love" for Eula is only one of the several sharply contrasted kinds of love—and Labove's "honor," only one of a half dozen variants of honor—exhibited in this novel. The structure of the novel is not so much a narrative progression as a kind of elaborate counterpointing of love and honor, counterpointing which adds density and bulk to the novel and provides it with a poetic body of great specific gravity. The Labove incident, then, in conjunction with the others, develops and defines the world of *The Hamlet,* especially in its dimension of value and meaning.

A different sort of love is that between Mink Snopes and his wife. We first see this pair when Ratliff drives up to their broken-back cabin of two rooms in order to sell them a sewing machine. Mink orders his wife back into the house. She shouts out her bitter words at him, but finally, as he advances menacingly, she breaks and runs from him. Yet this pair began their relationship in very different circumstances, and with the woman clearly dominant.

Mink had met her in a logging camp run by her father, "a roaring man of about fifty" (p. 240), who now lived "openly with

a magnificent quadroon woman most of whose teeth were gold"
(p. 241). His daughter, whom Mink was to marry, lived in a
separate wing of the house, with an entrance of its own, and
from time to time she summoned men from the camp for her
pleasure. In time Mink is summoned and sees in her "not a
nympholept but the confident lord of a harem." When Mink came
into her room, he entered "not the hot and quenchless bed of a
barren and lecherous woman, but the fierce simple cave of a
lioness" (p. 242). Shortly after, with the collapse of her father's
enterprise, she and Mink walked to the nearest county seat and
were married by a justice of the peace. Apparently she was the
woman for him in spite of the thirty or forty men with whom she
had slept; and he was—and still is—the man for her, though Mink
now beats her and their two children. He does so on the night on
which he kills Houston, and he actually drives all three away from
the house. Later, when she sees Mink again, she shows that she is
passionately anxious to save him. She pleads for him to stay in
hiding and presses upon him the ten-dollar bill that she has evidently prostituted herself to secure. Theirs is a relationship apparently founded upon pure passion, but it exerts a kind of intense idealistic hold upon her which has nothing to do now with
bodily gratification.

Or consider the love affair of Jack Houston, the man whom
Mink shoots from ambush. The woman Jack marries is not beautiful, almost homely, and he lives with her for only six months before she dies; yet "he grieved for her for four years in black,
savage, indomitable fidelity" (p. 208). Though they had known
each other all their lives, there was no easy courtship and early
marriage, though in a sense the girl claims him for her own from
the beginning. She even tries to do his schoolwork for him.
Houston resents her solicitude. He does not wish to be chosen,
and finally, in his desperation, he leaves and actually lives away
from home for thirteen years. For some seven years he stays with
a woman he had taken out of a Galveston brothel, a woman whom
he might have married had she been able to bear him a child, in
spite of the fact that she had been a prostitute and in spite of his
"inherited southern-provincial-Protestant fanaticism regarding

marriage and female purity" (p. 215). And then one day, almost without knowing why, he divides his money, gives half of it to the woman with whom he has been living, and despite her curses and pleadings, comes back to Mississippi and accepts the future that he had run away to escape. Within a few months after their marriage, his wife is killed by the stallion that Houston had bought, the beast that "represented that polygamous and bitless masculinity which he had relinquished" (p. 218). Later, on moonlight nights, the man would "lie rigid, indomitable, and panting" (p. 220).

It is a strange story, one that obviously could be developed, and for full understanding probably needs much more development than Faulkner cared to give it here. Yet one can understand enough of it to see why it has a place among these examples of human love. At points it matches the relation between Mink Snopes and his wife: in both instances it is the woman—though how different the two women—who chooses and even makes the first advances to the man. But it also complements and contrasts with the story of Mink Snopes and his wife. For Mink's marriage confirms his masculinity; he treats his wife harshly and, in doing so, perhaps answers her need; whereas Houston, for all his high-strung masculinity, is made gentle by his wife's maternal domesticity and, once bereft of her, finds himself inconsolable in his yearning for the thing which he spent thirteen years trying to escape.

Both Houston's wife and the wife of Mink Snopes are utterly different from Eula. Eula cares nothing for men, is unaware of the storms that she stirs up in them, and is totally without coquettishness or pride in her power. But on at least one occasion Eula is roused to passion. When her other suitors decide to ambush Hoake McCarron at the ford, Eula springs to McCarron's defense. One of the suitors was later to tell that "it was the girl who had wielded [the butt of the buggy whip], springing from the buggy and with the reversed whip beating three of them back while her companion used the reversed pistol-butt against the wagon-spoke and the brass knuckles of the other two" (p. 139). On this same night, after Eula and McCarron had returned to the Varners', and old

Will Varner, who has had veterinary training, had set McCarron's broken arm, Eula gives herself to her lover. When McCarron reaches home, the bone of his arm has to be set once more though Eula had tried to "support, with her own braced arm from underneath, the injured side" (p. 141).

It is perhaps not love. McCarron flees the country when he learns that Eula is with child and so do two of her other suitors, hoping "by fleeing too," to put in "a final and despairing bid for the guilt they had not compassed, the glorious shame of the ruin they did not do" (p. 141). If Eula felt more than an overpowering gust of passion for McCarron, it is not revealed in this novel. But at least there has been on her part, for once, an answering response to heroic potency.

Not least important in this group of love affairs is the most grotesque and terrible of them all, that of the idiot Ike Snopes for the cow. There is more here than the mere needs of blind animality. The idiot, for example, when he sees the smoke from the overgrown hill beyond the creek three miles away, makes his way as fast as he can to find the cow, rushes through the flame to her, and effects a rescue. He steals food for her and eats the cow feed with her.

Around Ike's wanderings with the cow Faulkner has lavished his poetry. The idiot conducts the cow with all the gallantry with which a knight might conduct his lady. Faulkner is aware of the grotesque character of the relationship and for this very reason insists upon associating it with the poetry of nature and the poetry of a love that is in absolute rapport with nature. For example:

> There is the one fierce evening star, though almost at once the marching constellations mesh and gear and wheel strongly on. Blond too in that gathering last of light, she owns no dimension against the lambent and undimensional grass. But she is there, solid amid the abstract earth. He walks lightly upon it, returning, treading lightly that frail extricable canopy of the subterrene slumber—Helen and the bishops, the kings and the graceless seraphim. When he reaches her,

she has already begun to lie down—first the forequarters, then the hinder ones, lowering herself in two distinct stages into the spent ebb of evening, nestling back into the nest-form of sleep, the mammalian attar. They lie down together.
[p. 189]

If the horror of this relationship cannot be masked, and indeed is intensified, by the poetry, the horror is not gratuitous. It is used to set off a deeper horror and a greater perversity, that of Flem Snopes. For Ike's cousin Flem has no poetry in him and no love at all. He is pure, graceless acquisitiveness, untrammeled by honor and unredeemed by love. It is fitting that he should be impotent, unable to bed the wife for whom all the other men long, and with no love for, and no rapport with, the nature over which he exerts more and more control.

The counterpointing of the different kinds of love (and, as we shall see, of honor) does add a dimension of value and meaning to the novel and helps to develop the special world that the novel presents. But the episodes which develop the love-honor themes initially demand more from the world of the novel than they contribute to it. They depend for their very credibility upon the atmosphere of that world, for most of them depict extreme cases which we would not readily accept in the world of our ordinary experience.

All that has been said earlier about the way in which Faulkner develops a special world bathed in a special atmosphere bears upon the fabulous quality of Eula and Flem. They are, as Faulkner has described them in the novel, quite literally out of this world, and therefore Faulkner has had to create a special kind of world to contain them. Eula is, as we have seen, a kind of goddess, and Flem is a kind of gnomelike monster. Eula sums up a central aspect of the love theme that runs, with variations, throughout *The Hamlet*. Flem points up the whole problem of honor, and his triumph at the end of the novel comments sardonically upon what life is like when devoid of honor.

Since Flem is essentially the trader, the man who buys cheap and sells dear and pockets the profit, and, most of all, the usurer, he may be taken to represent the commercial spirit in its purity —a spirit that is completely corrosive of all human ties and decencies. Yet it ought to be observed that *The Hamlet* as a novel makes no indictment of commerce as such. Ratliff, for example, is a man who loves the contest of wits involved in driving a bargain. He rejoices in his own prowess as a trader, and derives an especial pleasure in matching his talents with Flem's. Indeed, his first encounter with Mink Snopes is simply part of a complicated and carefully thought out plan by which he hopes to get the better of Flem.

When he goes out to Mink Snopes' rickety house in the country, his scheme is to see whether by selling a sewing machine to Mink, he can force Flem to pay the bill. The plan also involves the buying and selling of some goats, a transaction in which Ratliff means to concede Flem a pawn in order to win a piece. Ratliff's plan succeeds and he gets the better of Flem, but it is significant that he actually realizes no profit. Having discovered Ike Snopes, the idiot, and touched with the pathos of this creature who is completely in the power of someone like Flem, he burns Flem's promissory note to Ike, but gives its value and the profit he has made on the goat transaction to Mrs. Littlejohn to be held for Ike. He has sought his contest with Flem out of a sporting instinct to prove his superiority in the game of wits and is content with his moral victory over Flem: the money he cheerfully consigns to Ike's benefit.[1]

The incident which soured Flem's father, Ab Snopes, is not presented as an indictment of the ethics of sharp trading. Stamper, the horse trader, is something of a conjurer and a magician: he has a great reputation throughout this whole end of the state and on up into west Tennessee. And even the ineffable Ab is not motivated by love of money. Rather, he wants to vindicate "the entire honor and pride of the science and pastime of horse-trading in Yoknapatawpha County" (p. 35). The story of how Stamper outwitted Ab Snopes, as told by Ratliff in the best tall-tale tradition, is the story of a spirited contest for honor. Even the exasperation of Ab's first wife at her husband's folly does not—at least in Ratliff's telling of

1. For a discussion of Ratliff's bargaining with Flem see below, Notes, p. 402.

the story—dampen the tale. She does get her cream separator after all, even though, since Ab has lost the $24.68 she had saved up to buy it, she has to trade her cow to pay for it. But with borrowed milk, Mrs. Snopes can enjoy the high whine of the separator as she runs the gallon of milk through it over and over again.

Even the Texan who, at the end of the novel, auctions off the obviously untamable spotted horses has his sense of honor. He exerts all the wiles of a sideshow barker at a street fair, but he plays his game with men, and he refuses to take Mrs. Armstid's hard-earned five dollars. It will be Flem who will refuse to return the sum to her.

The scruple of honor is of the greatest consequence throughout the novel. There is Houston, a man who is high-strung and irritable, completely masculine, who takes pride in his stallion and his lean blue-ticked Walker hound. His quarrel with Mink, the quarrel that brings about his death, is not for the food that Mink's animal ate but for the principle of the thing. When he rides up to tell Mink about the yearling: "He was not shaking, trembling, anymore than a stick of dynamite does. He didn't even raise his voice" (p. 91), but he makes plain his warning. When Mink makes the sharp retort "they cursed each other, hard and brief and without emphasis, like blows or pistol-shots, both speaking at the same time and neither moving, the one still standing in the middle of the steps, the other still squatting against the gallery post. 'Try a shotgun,' Snopes said. 'That might keep it up'" (p. 92). But the shotgun is not used by Houston to keep off a stray heifer. It is actually used by Mink himself, and from ambush, to get his revenge upon Houston.

Ratliff observes about Mink that "this here seems to be a different kind of Snopes like a cotton-mouth is a different kind of snake," and in the sequel to *The Hamlet, The Town,* Ratliff remarks that Mink is "the only out-and-out mean Snopes we ever experienced." Later, Faulkner was to devote the better part of a whole novel (*The Mansion*) to the story of Mink, but even in the foreshortened account of Mink given in *The Hamlet,* Mink has, with all his bitterness and viciousness, a sense of honor. It may be little better than a cross-grained pride, but it is at least that. Having really nothing else, Mink has to hold on to this. And the implication is that because it is human it is better than the kind of honor that I. O. Snopes or Flem Snopes displays.

On the occasion when Ratliff decides to get rid of the cow and thus put a stop to the disgraceful exhibition of the idiot,[2] Faulkner treats the Snopes' concept of honor with a kind of Rabelaisian humor. The schoolmaster, I. O. Snopes, is unconcerned until Ratliff implies that his job as schoolmaster may be jeopardized by the family's conniving at the exhibition. When this point sinks in, I. O. does call a family conference (Flem is still away in Texas) and becomes concerned for the Snopes name, which, he says, "aint never been aspersed yet by no living man. [It's] got to be kept pure as a marble monument for your children to grow up under" (p. 207). But this last burst of eloquence is addressed to his cousin Eck Snopes, for it has occurred to I. O. that since Eck has a wife and three children, with another child on the way, Eck is five times as much involved in purifying the family name as he is, and therefore ought to pay five times as much as I. O. toward the purchase of the cow.

There is in *The Hamlet* another fine instance of the scruple of honor, and in this case it is tied in with the theme of love. When it is discovered that Eula Varner is with child and that three of her suitors have fled, her much older and bachelor brother Jody is furious and tries to force Eula to say which of the young men is the father-to-be. His caterwauling disturbs their mother, who proceeds to shut him up.

The episode is worked out in the comic mode, but the basic issues are nonetheless made perfectly clear. Varner inertia and practicality triumph. When Jody puts the question to his parents: "You mean you aint going to do *nothing*? Not anything?" his father points out that there is nothing that can be done. It is much too late to catch "them damn tomcats," who are obviously halfway to Texas by now. He tells his son to go on out to the barn and sit down and cool off, adding, "If this family needs any headholding-up done, I'll tend to it myself" (p. 145). And he does attend to it, by making out a considerable check in favor of Flem,

2. For a discussion of Ratliff's behavior see below, Notes, p. 407.

by recording a deed to the Old Frenchman's Place to Flem and Eula Varner Snopes, and by buying Flem and Eula a wedding license and packing them off to Texas. Ratliff remembers Eula's face: "It had not been tragic, and now it was not even damned, since from behind it there looked out only another mortal natural enemy of the masculine race. And beautiful: but then, so did the highwayman's daggers and pistols make a pretty shine on him; and now as he watched, the lost calm face vanished" (p. 151).

Eula's honor is saved because of a commercial transaction in which Flem has obviously driven a good bargain and presumably is concerned only that the bargain be good enough. So love itself comes down to a matter of bargaining. But the betrayal of honor which makes the sharpest impression on the community—at least on some of its more thoughtful members—is Flem's refusal to aid his cousin Mink. Bookwright, for example, remarks that "even Flem Snopes aint going to let his own blood cousin be hung just to save money" (p. 270). And later Bookwright is still maintaining that there "aint no man, I dont care if his name is Snopes, going to let his own blood kin rot in jail. . . . Flem aint going to let [Mink] go to the penitentiary" (p. 325). But Bookwright has misjudged his man. That is precisely what Flem does.

It is, however, in the great "spotted horses" episode that the true meaning and menace of Flem Snopes is most effectively dramatized. Many readers know the episode as an anthology piece that has often been reprinted because it is a fine example of story telling in the tradition of the Old Southwest, with brilliant dialogue and description. But the tale of the spotted horses fits perfectly into this story of the rise of Flem Snopes. It is an account of the world of advertising and Madison Avenue, in this instance set down in a little backwater of a community in the far-away days of the dawning twentieth century. The people of Frenchmen's Bend are stirred up to buy what they do not want and cannot afford and will not be able to use. It is Flem, of course, who is the entrepreneur. He has seen no reason why he shouldn't make some money out of his Texas honeymoon, and obviously it is he who has brought the Texas ponies back with him. But though the spotted ponies, clattering over the wooden bridges and running down the moonlit roads, have spread destruction throughout the county, there is no way to prove that Flem is legally responsible for them.

Flem is in complete command of the problem of public relations and he is on the hither side of the law. As for the first: when Mrs. Armstid, "gaunt in the shapeless gray garment" with her "stained tennis shoes hissing faintly on the boards," comes to Flem to get back the five dollars for the horse that the Texan refused to sell to Henry Armstid, Flem blandly tells her that the Texan "took all the money with him when he left" (p. 320). While the woman stands there before him, at a loss, waiting in the awkward silence, Flem adds "I reckon he forgot it" (p. 321). But as she leaves, Flem asks her to wait a moment and then appears with "a small striped paper bag" and hands it to her. "A little sweetening for the chaps," he says. The woman is too much beaten down to throw it in his face; she has had to absorb too much punishment in her lifetime to carry on what is obviously a hopeless fight for her money; so all that she can do is to say, "You're right kind," and to excuse herself: "I reckon I better get on and help with dinner," and she moves away like "a gray and blasted tree-trunk moving, somehow intact and upright, upon an unhurried flood" (p. 322). The clerk in the doorway, in his admiration for Flem, slaps his thigh and says, "By God, you cant beat him."

As for Flem's relationship to the law, this is uproariously dramatized in the episode in which Mrs. Vernon Tull sues Flem Snopes for damages. One of the spotted ponies belonging to Eck Snopes had frightened Tull's team, and Vernon Tull was injured when the team ran away. When the justice trying the case asks Eck whether the horse is his, Eck, who is the one decent Snopes, admits ownership, and is beginning to ask the justice how much he has to pay when Mrs. Tull, exulting in the knowledge that Eck can't deny ownership, interrupts to say that "at least forty men heard that Texas murderer give that horse to Eck Snopes. Not sell it to him, mind; give it to him" (p. 335). At these words the justice pricks up his ears, for if Eck has had the horse given to him and given to him only by word of mouth, the justice is forced to point out that it is highly questionable whether Eck does indeed own the horse. The justice, who is trying to abide by the law of the land, points out to Mrs. Tull that by her own testimony Eck never did own the horse. For in the law "ownership cant be conferred or invested by word-of-mouth. . . . By your testimony and his both, he never gave that Texan anything in exchange for that horse, and by his testimony the Texas man never gave him any paper to prove he owned it, and by his testimony and by what I know myself from these last four weeks, nobody yet has ever laid hand or rope either on any one of them" (p. 336). He tries to reason with Mrs. Tull, pointing out that if one could transfer ownership simply by uttering a few words, Eck himself "could have transferred all his title and equity in [the horse] to Mr Tull right there while Mr Tull was lying unconscious on that bridge" (p. 336).

As the situation gradually dawns on Mrs. Tull, her indictment of the inadequacy of the law becomes eloquent. "Her voice was still calm, quiet, though probably no one but Tull realized that it was too calm and quiet. 'My team is made to run away by a wild spotted mad dog, my wagon is wrecked; my husband is jerked out of it and knocked unconscious and unable to work for a whole week with less than half of our seed in the ground, and I get nothing' " (p. 337). But worse outrage is yet to be spoken, for the justice, still striving to be properly legal about an impossible situation, tells her that the damages are fixed by statute; that if there is a suit for damages such as this, and if the owner of the animal cannot, or will not, assume liability, the damaged party can find recompense in the body of the animal: "And since Eck Snopes never owned that horse at all, and since you just heard a case here this morning that failed to prove that Flem Snopes had any equity in any of them, that horse still belongs to that Texas man. Or did belong. Because now that horse that made your team run away and snatch your husband out of the wagon, belongs to you and Mr Tull."

This indeed is too much and Mrs. Tull begins to shout. "The horse! We see it for five seconds, while it is climbing into the wagon with us and then out again. Then it's gone, God dont know where and thank the Lord He dont! And the mules gone

with it and the wagon wrecked and [this, to her husband] you laying there on the bridge with your face full of kindling-wood and
bleeding like a hog and dead for all we knew. And he gives us the
horse! Dont hush me! Get on to that wagon, fool that would sit
there behind a pair of young mules with the reins tied around his
wrist! Get on to that wagon, all of you!" (p. 338). The last outburst is too much for the old justice, who cries out: "I cant stand
no more! I wont! This court's adjourned!"

Flem is truly impervious. In the first of the two legal actions
against him, he had been helped by the apt perjury of one of his
kinsmen. The perjury is obvious though it cannot be legally
proved. But in the second action against him, Flem receives most
aid from the law itself, which becomes the very shield by means
of which he wards off the claims of justice. Faulkner does not press
the issue. The comedy of the situation and the gusto with which
the whole episode is recounted provide the proper undercutting
of any argument put too seriously or symbolism set forth too
nakedly.

The law cannot accomplish the downfall of Flem, but Ratliff
decides to engage him once more. This time, however, Ratliff is
defeated, taken in by the oldest ruse of all: the salted gold-mine.
Flem has planted enough money in the grounds of the Old
Frenchman's Place to lure Ratliff, Armstid, and Odom Bookwright into buying it from him. It would seem too simple and
obvious a device to catch the astute Ratliff, but the incidental
baiting of the trap is well done, and moreover there is a kind of
poetic justice in what occurs. For Ratliff apparently can defeat
Flem Snopes only when he is acting in disinterested fashion for
the sake of honor or for the sake of someone else, like the idiot
Ike. When he himself sniffs the scent of easy money, he loses
his caution and eventually finds that he has been trapped.

For Ratliff, of course, this is no final disaster. He and Bookwright are able to jest a little about what has happened to them. It
is little Henry Armstid who lacks both inner as well as outer resources and who has, by the end of the novel, gone quite mad,
having turned on his fellows—telling Ratliff when he leans down
and touches his shoulder, "Get out of my hole. Get outen it" (p.

368). Even when Flem's trick has been exposed, Armstid persists in digging for the buried treasure, and soon children gather to watch Armstid spading the earth steadily "down the slope of the old garden." After he has been at it for some two weeks, one bystander says: "He's going to kill himself. Well, I don't know as it will be any loss" (p. 372). And then the speaker's companion returns to the subject of Flem Snopes. "Couldn't no other man have done it," he says in admiration. "Anybody might have fooled Henry Armstid. But couldn't nobody but Flem Snopes have fooled Ratliff."

Flem, having pulled off his last and most successful coup, is, as the novel ends, preparing to move into Jefferson in order to find a larger ambit for his powers. On his way there, Flem passes the halted wagons and the women holding the nursing children and the men along the fence who have stopped to watch Henry Armstid digging away for the treasure. Henry did not "glance up at the sun, as a man pausing in work does to gauge the time. He came straight back to the trench, hurrying back to it with that painful and laboring slowness, the gaunt unshaven face which was now completely that of a madman. He got back into the trench and began to dig" (p. 373). But Flem does not pause to look at his victim. He merely turns his head, spits over the wagon wheel, then jerks the reins slightly to put his team in motion toward the town.

In almost any other writer the symbolic tableau on which the curtain descends would be much too pat, a kind of labored cartoon illustrating the theme of the novel. There are few other writers of our time who would have been able to prevent the novel from breaking down into blatant abstraction here, but Faulkner still keeps our attention upon the body of his world—its sights, smells, and sounds, the gestures and postures, the quality of the folk community which is so far removed from our own that it seems simple to the point of fabulousness, and yet which is in its essence so thoroughly and humanly ourselves that we continue to believe in it and find ourselves reflected in it. Perhaps it is really a distortion mirror, which turns our faces into grotesquely comic caricatures, but Faulkner's mirror nevertheless has its truth: it returns to us, past any doubting, the image of ourselves.

The last point is worth stressing, for *The Hamlet,* one must insist, finally implies a definition of man. This observation is substantially true even though Faulkner has preferred to work in terms of polarities: Flem and Eula, for example, stand at the extremities of the human situation and bound on either hand the world of human relationships. Flem is naked aggression, undiluted acquisitiveness. Though the Varners are shrewd traders, their knavery has limits. Ratliff has a zest for trading, but for him the bargaining is a game, and sportsmanship and honor have their place in it. Not so with Flem, whose acquisitiveness is a chemically pure essence. Flem himself is very close to being a quintessence and therefore scarcely human: hence his aura of myth. Eula represents the feminine principle, the end and object of desire, again in an almost chemically pure form. She would be a parody of femininity if Faulkner had not managed to make her so nearly as he does a convincing goddess. The truth of the matter is that Eula is at once caricature and goddess, for in his treatment of her Faulkner does not let his sense of humor desert him. Even as a child of six, Eula, carried by the Negro manservant who accompanies her mother, is sufficiently female to make the little group seem like "a bizarre and chaperoned Sabine rape" (p. 96). At school Eula brings with her, and placidly devours, a cold potato, but sitting on "the sunny steps" she reminds Labove of "one of the unchaste . . . immortals eating bread of Paradise on a sunwise slope of Olympus" (p. 124).

The idiot, Ike Snopes, is also a kind of pure quantity—pure adoration, pure love of nature, pure responsiveness, without inhibitions, responsibilities, or self-consciousness. On one level, Ike is, of course, quite incredible: how can a creature who is so nearly animal in his lack of intellect have the depth of emotion and sheer intensity of poetry with which Faulkner endows him? It is the poetry itself which provides the solution, for insofar as the reader participates in the poetry, he gains an imaginative vision of the world in which the idiot lives, moves, and has his being. Even if the reader's vision of that world is only fleeting and intermittent, it reveals itself as a realm not absolutely cut off from the reader's ordinary experience, merely heightened, subtilized, and intensified, and the idiot's essential humanity is thus vindicated as the reader comes to realize that the idiot isolates in relative purity aspects of a world common to—or at least potentially available to —all human beings. Even so, the idiot, living out his unself-conscious poetry, constitutes the most extreme case of all—a being even more mythic than Eula or Flem.

Flem, Eula, and Ike, then, mark some of the boundaries of the total human experience which *The Hamlet* undertakes to explore. These three characters are scarcely to be detached from the world in which Faulkner makes them live, a world that accepts them— even takes them for granted. Yet though it does so, it is not a realm of fantasy. On the contrary, it is solid and substantial and earthy. Because we believe in it, we can accept what it believes in. But there is another factor in securing our belief: the sense that the prodigies are not exhibited for their own sakes. They simply project past the ordinary human limits certain elements of experience with which we are all familiar. They are not exhibits in a freak show. They are there to tell us about ourselves.

10

Passion, Marriage,
and Bourgeois Respectability

(THE TOWN)

THE READER WHO puts down *The Hamlet* and picks up the second volume in the trilogy,[1] *The Town,* faces an obstacle at the very start. The characters whom he encounters in *The Town* are much the same, and he even finds himself being told, in summary, matters about which he has been reading in the earlier novel. But if he begins reading *The Town* with the expectation that it is a simple continuation of *The Hamlet,* he is bound to be disappointed. He may, if he likes, attribute his disappointment to the fact that most sequels are disappointing; that, after all, *The Town* was published seventeen years after *The Hamlet;* that the author has forgotten some of the things with which he dealt so brilliantly in *The Hamlet;* and that he has changed his mind—for the worse —about others. He may thus have to regard *The Town* as an example of Faulkner's waning powers as a novelist.

There is, however, another way to go about a reading of *The Town.* Faulkner may or may not have been the victim of waning powers, and perhaps he had forgotten some details of the earlier novel and deliberately changed others. But in any case, and for whatever reason, *The Town* is a different kind of novel from *The Hamlet.* It has another atmosphere; it is set in another key; and

1. See below, Notes, p. 410.

we shall do well to try to read it by its own light and to judge it by its own standards. If we do so, we may still feel it a lesser work than *The Hamlet* (as I think we must), but we may be better prepared to find the kind of value that is there.

The Hamlet is mythic and heroic. It is placed in a time which is becoming more and more remote, and the physical setting—the hamlet that gives the novel its name—is one that few modern urban and suburban Americans know anything about at first hand and about which they are perfectly willing to believe anything—particularly because it is set in the South and populated by poor whites. The association that most citizens have with such a community is likely to be through Al Capp's cartoons of Dogpatch. The setting of *The Town,* on the other hand, will seem familiar to many readers, perhaps because of its association with another powerful stereotype. By daring to bring his rustic Helen (or Semiramis or Lilith) and his countrified Faustus out of the brooding countryside into a small town, Faulkner immediately risks trimming them down to size. They are compelled to breathe the air of a cozy world of little rivalries and social feuds, scandals and church suppers, jokes and cheerful gossip such as pervade any small town. By his choice of narrators, Faulkner has pretty well immersed us in this kind of atmosphere. There is Charles Mallison, the lively and observant boy of one of the town families. There is his uncle Gavin Stevens, the town's intellectual, who is later to go away to study at Harvard and later still to study in Europe. When Flem Snopes moves into Jefferson in 1909, Gavin is about nineteen or twenty.[2] He is young enough and callow enough to fall under the spell of the beautiful but underbred Mrs. Snopes. V. K. Ratliff, the third narrator, is, to be sure, of another stripe. But even with Ratliff as a powerful makeweight, the balance is swung far over toward a bemused, romantic, or youthful account of what happened in Jefferson.

What is likely to prove the worst stumbling block to the reader of the novel is the possibility—especially if he has read much Faulkner criticism—that he may take Gavin to be Faulkner's mouthpiece. His previous reading of *Knight's Gambit*—or even

2. See below, Stevens Genealogy, p. 449.

of *Light in August*, if his reading was not very careful—could dispose him toward this view. But if he makes this mistake, he is very likely to miss the tone and even the basic meaning of the novel. For if any one thing about this novel soon becomes clear, it is that Gavin, and not for the first time in Faulkner's fiction, is treated as a figure of fun—almost as the butt of the author's jokes.

Gavin has dedicated himself to the fight against the Snopeses. We need not take too seriously some of his confidential comments to Ratliff on the strategy of the warfare. In these communications, Gavin shows a saving sense of humor, though he evidently takes his war against Snopesism seriously. He is far from victorious; he is indeed a sort of Don Quixote. Naturally, his much younger nephew looks up to him with a boy's admiration. Naturally, his twin sister, Maggie Mallison, loves him and, as he is well aware, would like to mother him and protect him from some of his follies. His companion-in-arms, Ratliff, has a genuine fondness for him and stands in a certain awe of his book learning. Nevertheless, Gavin again and again in the novel is made to play the fool. As a Snopes killer, he is not impressive, and in much of this novel we are invited to smile at his follies.

Early in the novel, Gavin falls under the sway of the incomparable Eula. At the Cotillion Ball he sees her dancing with Manfred de Spain, steps up, and jerks Manfred away from his partner. A few moments later, in the alley behind the ballroom, he gets his face well bloodied for his pains. His nephew, writing long after the event, explains Gavin's action in this way: "What he was doing was simply defending forever with his blood the principle that chastity and virtue in women shall be defended whether they exist or not" (p. 76). The gesture is gallant and even touching, but where chastity and virtue do not exist, it is idle, not to say officious, to defend them; and when there is a husband, as there is in this case, a husband who chooses not to see the liberties being taken with his wife, an outsider's attempt to defend them is compounded folly.

The reader may want to dismiss the rivalry between Gavin and Manfred de Spain as trivial. Manfred's derisively speeding past the Stevens house with his automobile's cutout open is boyishly silly, and so is Gavin's retaliation by planting tacks and, later, a sharpened rake in the street. Such matters may not answer to the requirements of a serious novel. But we should not make assumptions about the seriousness of *The Town* before we have read it through. Faulkner evidently means for us to be aware of the silliness and to laugh at the comedy, some of it Rabelaisian, as he exposes his hero's follies.

The exposure is still more withering when Gavin, a few years later, now twenty-three years old and city attorney, draws up a suit against Mayor de Spain's bonding company because brass fittings have been stolen from the town power plant. Nobody in the town, except perhaps Gavin himself, is deceived as to what his motive is. Old Judge Dukinfield, for example, remarks: "I dont believe either plaintiff or defendant will need more counsel than are represented tonight but they are welcome to bring juniors if they like—or should we say seconds?" (p. 87). And when Gavin persists in his ridiculous suit, Judge Dukinfield recuses himself so that Gavin's father, Judge Stevens, can preside. (This is legally irregular, but Judge Dukinfield knows that to call in Gavin's father is, in this situation, the way to get some common sense into the matter, for the romantic Gavin needs someone here who can exert a father's authority.)

Because of Eula's visit to him the night before the hearing, Gavin withdraws the suit, and now Manfred de Spain stands before Judge Stevens with his face, as Ratliff describes it, "still full of that laughing." When the Judge asks: "Manfred, do you want to resign?" De Spain answers cheerfully: "I'll be glad to. But not for the city: for Gavin. I want to do it for Gavin. All he's got to do is say Please" (p. 98). When Gavin, his face "paper-colored," remains silent, Manfred laughs and walks out of the room. Judge Stevens then speaks to Gavin as father rather than as judge: "So you dont want him not to be mayor. Then what is it you do want? For him not to be alive? Is that it?" To which Gavin replies: "What must I do now, Papa? Papa, what can I do now?" (p. 99). His collapse into a child's almost tearful bewilderment is complete.

On the night before this incident, Eula had come to Gavin's office, but not, as he first thought, to intercede with him for her lover Manfred and not to intervene with him for the sake of her husband, Flem Snopes. She has another motive in offering her body to him. As she explains to him, she does so "because you are unhappy. I dont like unhappy people. They're a nuisance" (p. 93). Gavin, crushed at what he has heard, protests: "So you came just from compassion, pity. . . . Does it mean that little to you? . . . Dont tell me next that this is why Manfred sent you: to abate a nuisance!"

Eula's behavior here is so direct as to seem brutal. It shocks Gavin, as it might anyone. But Gavin is peculiarly vulnerable to the stunning effect of her action and her explanation of it, for Gavin has idealized her, and like the true romantic that he is, has surrounded her with all sorts of virtues as well as fascinations. He wants not merely sex but love. It is probable that he does not really want her body at all, for there is almost a note of hysteria when she moves toward him. "Dont touch me!" he calls out. A few moments later she tells Gavin to lock the door. "I've already drawn the shade," she says. "Stop being afraid of things. Why are you afraid?" Gavin cries out "No," and pours out his feelings thus: "I might—would—have struck her with my out-flung arm, but there was room: out of the trap now and even around her until I could reach the door knob and open it" (p. 95).

Gavin's conduct seems so strange that some commentators have concluded that he is impotent; but his behavior throughout the novel is not that of an impotent man. He does, in fact, eventually marry—another woman, Melisandre Backus Harriss—as we learn from *Knight's Gambit* and from *The Mansion*. His almost terrified revulsion from Eula comes not from impotence but rather from a romanticism rooted in idealism and strongly tempered by Puritanism. Gavin is a countrified descendant of Sir Tristan.

This tradition of romantic love, which dates far back into the Middle Ages, has been described by Denis de Rougemont in *Love in the Western World*.[3] The conception of a passionate and thrilling love, so irresistible that those possessed by it count mere happiness well lost, dominates the stories of the Arthurian cycle; modified and in a different key, it runs through the fiction of the

3. New York, Anchor Books, 1957. First published in 1939; Eng. trans. 1940.

eighteenth and nineteenth centuries; in vulgarized forms it still constitutes the staple of tin-pan alley lyrics and Hollywood movies. Romantic love is so familiar that it may seem hardly worth commenting on here. Yet because of the particular attention Faulkner gives to it, especially as it overwhelms characters like Gavin Stevens and Horace Benbow, this attitude toward woman and love is worth tracing to its ultimate roots.

Rougemont observes that "happy love has no history—*in European literature*" (p. 43). In other literatures, yes. But something happened to Europe in the twelfth century which has affected ever since the rhetoric of love poetry and the very conception of love in Western culture. According to Rougemont's account, the troubadors of Provence were infected with the heresies of the Cathars, a group whose doctrines had much in common with Manichaeanism and Gnosticism. The love which they sang does not look forward to the possession of the loved one, but is a transcendent love —love for a lady who is an ideal or a dream vision rather than a woman of flesh and blood. Because the Cathars frowned upon the flesh as evil, the love they celebrated could not be consummated in this world but only in the world to come, when death has freed the soul from its bondage to the body. The courtly lover, as Rougemont argues, is really in love with death: the passion that possesses him is a dark passion. It is incapable of any real satisfaction in the flesh, and indeed one could say of it, in a kind of heretical parody of Christianity, "My kingdom is not of this world."

Rougemont takes the story of Tristan and Iseult as typical of this conception of love. Iseult actually hates Tristan, and is willing to accept his companionship only because his mission is to bring her as a bride to his uncle King Mark. But when by mistake Tristan and Iseult drink the love potion, they are fatally attracted to each other. The attraction, as Rougemont points out, has its curious aspects, and their conduct shows some inconsistencies. Though Tristan desires Iseult so much that he cannot live without her, her attraction seems to be in direct ratio to the fact that she is denied him. Thus when the lovers, alone in the forest, might possess each other, Tristan lays a naked sword between them, and this is how King Mark finds them asleep. What the lovers really want is not fleshly union in a world of created forms but a release from consuming passion through death. They have listened to the song of darkness into which all forms and beings will be ultimately dissolved and in which the released spirit is finally reunited with the world spirit from which it came.

Once one has stated the conception in its purity, one is forced to add that it would be very difficult to follow in practice a so rigorously Puritanical notion of love. This difficulty has helped disguise the fact that the Western tradition of romantic love has its source in a life-denying idealism, with strong Manichaean overtones. The denial of marriage made by the cult of romantic love came, very early, to mean not abstention from sexual intercourse but a justification of adultery. But despite the distortions and final vulgarization of the cult, the essential linkage of irresistible passion with the death wish has, Rougemont maintains, never been completely broken. So late as the nineteenth century, for example, Wagner in his *Tristan und Isolde* was able to reassert, unmistakably, the pristine character of the myth. The love-death which Tristan and Isolde desire is actually a release from desire, a yearning for the "blessed twilit glory of the spirit after it has been rescued at the price of a fatal wound inflicted on the body" (p. 235).

Rougemont's analysis has received criticism on several counts. His psychology is oversimple: he attributes to "courtly" love elements that are found to some degree in all sexual love. Moreover, his history of ideas is oversimple: his assertion that courtly love owes its origin to a "Gnostic Eros" is much too sweeping. In his *Mind and Heart of Love* [4] Father M. C. D'Arcy points out that "Gnosticism seems to have been one of those unfortunate forms of thought for which human beings have a chronic appetite" (p. 57). Yet Father D'Arcy goes on to say that there "is no reason . . . to reject de Rougemont's main thesis, even though it be an oversimplification and pressed too far as an explanation of the history of European civilization. It is enough if we accept his view that romance did contain a special doctrine of love. When the

4. New York, Meridian Books, 1956.

Provençal romance united with Celtic myths and dreams, the characteristic traits of that doctrine become unmistakable. Love is a rapture, a divine transport; it desires union wth the infinite, and from that union there is no return" (p. 226) .

It is interesting to apply Rougemont's thesis to some of Faulkner's romantic lovers. Gavin Stevens, of course, does not think of himself as listening to the seductive voices of night and would be shocked to be told why he feels revulsion from actual physical contact with Eula. But he has clearly turned her into a goddess. He never tires of referring to her as a Helen or a Lilith or even an Isolde, and her divinity depends upon the fact that his love for her has to remain unrequited. When Eula, therefore, in an almost business-like way, begins to pull down the shades in his office and obviously in another moment will start pulling off her clothes, he suffers panic.

Gavin, of course, is something more than a belated Tristan. His motivation is complicated. It includes a fierce resentment of Eula, a resentment which comes out quite clearly when he insults her by suggesting that "you really ought to be in bed this minute with your husband, or is this one of Manfred's nights?" (p. 92). It also includes hurt pride, for he is stung by the fact that Eula is offering herself to him in pity—"because you are unhappy." Gavin furiously resents the condescension, but, as Rougemont would suggest, he may unconsciously be hugging to himself his unhappiness. For Gavin is thoroughly orthodox in insisting that love—at least the passionate, bewildering, romantic love that he craves—is necessarily unhappy. Later, he is to predict that Eula's daughter Linda "is doomed to anguish and to bear it, doomed to one passion and one anguish and all the rest of her life to bear it, as some people are doomed from birth to be robbed or betrayed or murdered" (p. 351).

In his encounter with Eula at his office, Gavin only partly understands his motives, but he is at other times rather perceptive about himself. Gavin once says of his speculations as to Eula's relations to Flem and to Manfred: "So you see how much effort a man will make and trouble he will invent to guard and defend himself from the boredom of peace of mind" (p. 135). Gavin sees his in-

dulgence in such cogitations as resembling the pervert "who deliberately infests himself with lice."

Gavin's sister Maggie understands the essential nature of her
brother's attitude toward romantic love. When Gavin is going
through his troubles with Eula, Maggie says: "You don't marry
Semiramis . . . you just commit some form of suicide for her."
Maggie's statement might come literally out of Rougemont's book,
but she knows that Gavin will not commit suicide for his Semiramis
and predicts that he will in fact marry a widow with grown children, a prophecy which is later fulfilled.

One of the section headings of Rougemont's book is entitled
"Marrying Iseult?" Marriage with Iseult is inconceivable, for to
marry her is to have her "dwindle into a wife," as Congreve's Mil-
lamant phrased it. Or as Rougemont puts it: "In countless nauseating novels there is now depicted the kind of husband who fears
the flatness and the same old jog-trot of married life in which his
wife loses her 'allure' because no obstructions come between them"
(p. 295).

Flem can remain married to Eula, since there is no question of
passion: he is impotent. Manfred can carry on his affair with Eula
for eighteen years, not because their adulterous relation keeps her
perennially interesting, but simply because he has no romantic
illusion that he has to protect. Manfred is the rather cheerful,
fleshly lover who enjoys his affair with Eula but feels no need
to bring the soul into it. But Gavin cannot contemplate marrying
his Iseult; when, much later, he does marry Melisandre, his marriage involves friendship and even affection, but presumably not
much passion.

After the night on which Eula offered Gavin her body, Gavin
sees very little of her, though he does see a good deal of her daughter Linda. What he tells himself is that he is trying to save the
child from Snopesism. He chats with her in the best elderly-uncle
fashion, buys her ice cream sodas, advises her about her reading,
presents her with books of poetry, and in general occupies himself,
as his sister Maggie somewhat sardonically puts it, with "forming
her mind." In this activity many aspects of Gavin's character come
into play: a real generosity, a love of the role of cultural cicerone,

and a vicarious fulfillment of himself in toying with the idea that since Linda is the child of his inamorata, she is his child spiritually. But even in his little tête-à-tête with Linda, Gavin continues to play one of the variations of the Tristan role. Linda's youth, in this instance, acts as the obstacle which renders impossible his physical possession of her and therefore allows her to be a romantic object. In a recent book entitled *Comme Toi-même: essais sur les mythes de l'amour*,[5] Rougemont concerns himself with impuberty as a romantic obstacle and cites instances from such people as Novalis, Edgar Allan Poe, and Lewis Carroll. As he puts it, *Alice in Wonderland* "was born of the love of 'nymphets,' repressed by the pure conscience of the clergyman but avowed in certain of his poems and revealed by the often ferocious pleasantries of his letters to his little girls" (p. 56). (Rougemont, by the way, takes over the word "nymphets" for his French text. Indeed, he points out that in the twentieth century impuberty is one of the few taboos which remain available for courtly love, and remarks that in the twelfth century the romance of Tristan was at least as shocking as *Lolita* is today.)

Nowhere is Gavin more the dream-smitten romantic than in his aspirations for Linda. He wants to get her out of Jefferson not merely to save her from Snopesism but to give her an opportunity to fulfill the romantic dream. His notion of the setting in which to fulfill it is, of all places, Greenwich Village. To Ratliff's question, put with a countryman's innocence, as to just what Greenwich Village is, Gavin gives a fancy answer. It is "a place with a few unimportant boundaries but no limitations where young people of any age go to seek dreams." With robust common sense, Ratliff remarks that he had always "thought that-ere was a varmint you hunted anywhere" (p. 350). A moment later he teases Gavin by suggesting that any "good God-fearing upright embattled Christian . . . Yoknapatawphas" overhearing Gavin at this moment would think he was preparing "a deliberate incitement and pandering to the Devil his-self." But Gavin is too far gone in his dream to laugh. He is dead serious about the whole matter.

5. Paris, Albin Michel, 1961.

For Gavin, Linda is an important person because, as he believes, she has the capacity for passion, the passion he associates with anguish. If Ratliff had cared to pursue his point, he might have suggested to Gavin that by his whole attempt to form Linda's mind, he had pushed her toward this conception of romantic passion, and that in predicting for her a romantic doom, he was not merely reading her palm but had, in fact, already acted as inciter and panderer.

The unromantic and practical Ratliff believes that if Gavin is so much concerned about Linda's future woes, he might at least try to protect her. He says to Gavin: "Marry her. Naturally you never thought of that" (p. 351). But Gavin has already thought of that and rejected it. The reason he gives Ratliff seems to concern itself with his own welfare rather than Linda's. He says: "That's my fate: just to miss marriage." And when Ratliff suggests that what he really means is to "escape" marriage, Gavin says: "I never escape it. Marriage is constantly in my life. My fate is constantly to just miss it or it to, safely again, once more safe, just miss me." This is the statement of a man who likes to believe in irresistible passions and dooms and things fated. Gavin does so in the best style of romantic love, though his word-play with "safely again" and "once more safe" hints that he is to some extent aware of the kind of game he is playing with himself. At any rate, it is clear to Ratliff that his intellectual friend does not really want to be married to anybody.

In *The Mansion* Linda does indeed suffer the doom which Gavin had predicted for her. She falls in love with a young Jewish sculptor, but so sharply does she feel the antithesis between romantic love and marriage that she refuses to go through any marriage ceremony with him until just before they go to take part in the Spanish Civil War. When, after his death, she returns to Jefferson, there would seem to be no impediment to her marriage with Gavin. He is one of the few people whom she sincerely trusts, and presumably he feels her fascination as a person and as a woman. But now it is the memory of her dead young husband that will lie between them like a sword. Gavin, as an idealist, respects the passionate attachment which Linda has felt for her husband, and he is scrupulous in feeling that as an older man he should not take advantage of Linda's loneliness or sense of gratitude. But Gavin is still playing Tristan. When he refuses to marry her, Linda offers her body to him, using the blunt, sexual word. In doing so, she startles Gavin almost as much as her mother had on the night in Gavin's office thirty years before. Gavin, the romantic idealist, refuses Linda's offer, as he had refused her mother's. Later, they are to establish a kind of special Platonic relationship; and Linda rather proudly repeats Gavin's remark that they are the two in all the world who do not need the act of sex in order to trust and love each other. This, too, is the kind of transcendence that finds its place in the neo-Platonic-Gnostic-Puritan tradition. Their relationship achieves an almost precise symbolical representation in *The Mansion* when they arrange to have adjoining rooms in the hotel, so that each will be conscious that the other is, though physically separated, close by, and each can rap on the wall to remind the other Platonic lover of their spiritual union.

It is touching that Linda should covet for Gavin the kind of passionate sexual love which she herself has experienced. But why she thinks he will be able to achieve it in marriage—since she seems to think that it is something outside marriage—is not easy to say. Perhaps had she known that Gavin would eventually marry Melisandre Backus she would not have expected it. For Gavin, as we learn in *The Mansion,* had also formed Melisandre's mind when she was twelve, thirteen, and fourteen, much as he had Linda's. But "pretty soon Melisandre committed the irrevocable error of getting a year older" (p. 194), and the relationship was broken off. When, many years later, Gavin marries her, she is a widow with grown children, and there is in the marriage none of the anguished passion that Gavin associates with his Helens and Iseults. It may well have been a happy marriage, but the very fact of happiness would for the gun-shy Gavin have removed the possibility of a romance in the grand manner.

Though it is interesting to refer the notions of Gavin Stevens (and his young nephew Charles Mallison) to the Tristan myth as set forth by Rougemont, it is not in the least necessary to suppose that Faulkner ever read Rougemont. As Rougemont makes abundantly clear, the myth of passionate love has diffused itself throughout the literature of the West and is a part of the culture in which we live. Faulkner might have derived the myth from almost anywhere—from Wagner or Balzac or Flaubert—or, to mention less exalted sources, from the movies of the twenties. What is interesting is that Gavin's view of romantic love should refer itself so clearly to the archetypal pattern as described by Rougemont.

It is the easier to account for this fact if one remembers that Jefferson represents what is still an essentially traditional society. There is a sense of community: no one entertains any doubt as to what the prescribed values are. The townspeople are human enough to enjoy scandal, to glory in the daring of those who will flaunt community opinion, and to applaud and perhaps envy De Spain's cuckolding of Flem Snopes; but there is no haziness about what is good and what is bad, what is proper and what is improper, and the sanctions against those who defy the community mores are still powerful enough to render respectability something above mere conformity.

Moreover, the community is still deeply tinged with Puritanism. It is this narrow-minded and rigid Puritanism that provokes some of the sharpest thrusts made by Gavin and by Charles Mallison. Charles, for example, in looking back upon the episode in which Eula dances with such splendid "unshame" with De Spain, talks about "the little puny people" who had fallen "back speechless and aghast in a shocked circle around them," and he refers to "the other little doomed mean cowardly married and unmarried husbands looking aghast" (p. 75). In contrast to these people, Charles sees his Uncle Gavin as "brave and unlucky" and Manfred de Spain as "brave and lucky" (p. 74). Yet even the unlucky Gavin is better off than the "little cautious men" who did not fall under Eula's spell. The pressure of small-town respectability and a Puritan ethic sharpens for Charles, and perhaps for many others, the sense of Eula's romantic desirability. It may even be true that the aura of divinity that surrounds Eula requires precisely these taboos, obstacles, and hindrances. Lacking them, the romantic nimbus about her might disappear entirely.

The stories and novels of Faulkner are filled with characters who are smitten with romantic love. The young ascetic school-teacher Labove in *The Hamlet* is an example, though a rather special one. His "love" for Eula obviously contains a desperate kind of hatred as well as a passionate attraction toward her. He does not want to marry her: he simply wants to possess her once. But for three years she obsesses him—perhaps because of the very impossibility of his possessing her. When he grasps Eula in his arms, he says to her: "Fight it. Fight it. That's what it is: a man and woman fighting each other" (p. 122).

Bayard Sartoris in *The Unvanquished* may represent another variant of the courtly lover. We are never told whether or not he was really in love with his Drusilla, but there is certainly an attraction of a kind and, as his stepmother, Drusilla is effectually and "romantically" barred from him. Drusilla herself is a perfect instance of the true devotee of romantic love. When she gives the pistols to Bayard, she exclaims: "How beautiful you are. . . . young, to be permitted to kill . . . to be permitted . . . to take into your bare hands the fire of heaven that cast down Lucifer" (p. 274). But her ecstatic tribute to the beauty of his young man-hood derives half its passion from his standing already in the shadow of death. Perhaps the most extreme devotee of the Tristan myth turns out to be Quentin in *The Sound and the Fury,* whose love is barred by the most powerful obstacle in Western culture, that of incest. (*The Wild Palms,* Faulkner's version of "the world well lost for love," I shall treat in a later volume.)

I am tempted to round out this partial list of Faulkner's courtly lovers with one more extreme instance of such love, one in which the love madness has moved across the line into actual insanity. In the story entitled "A Rose for Emily," Miss Emily Grierson poisons the lover who was about to desert her and keeps his body in one of the upstairs bedrooms of the house in which she lives alone. Many years later it is found by the townspeople when, at her death, they break into the closed bedroom. With Miss Emily, the romantic love which Rougemont insists is actually a love of death has fulfilled itself literally.

The prominence Faulkner has given to his romantically obsessed lovers has upset some of his readers. They object that he has no place in his consciousness for mature sexual love. Maxwell Geismar and Leslie Fiedler [6] have remarked that Faulkner fears and hates women. A milder charge, and one more generally made, is that Faulkner writes about love between men and women as an adolescent might, one who had never got beyond the youthful dream and therefore knew nothing about mature sexual relationships. The truth may well be that Faulkner the man was so good a romantic and so thoroughly immersed in the tradition of courtly love as to share in this most stubborn illusion of our culture. But his strength as an artist is that he has been able to portray the illusion so honestly and to relate it to so large a context of reality that we can see it for what it is even though it is presented with full dramatic sympathy. In any case, it is absurd to say that one cannot find in the body of Faulkner's work plenty of examples of mature sexual love.

To begin with a humble but telling case, there are the furniture dealer and his wife who appear at the end of *Light in August*. The furniture dealer loves his wife and he finds Byron Bunch as lover very funny. Though he has never heard of Tristan, he recognizes for what it is the sword that lies between Byron and Lena when they retire for the night. Then there is Jack Houston in *The Hamlet,* who for years resisted marrying his childhood sweetheart, but whose marriage, when it comes about, is apparently completely fulfilling and happy, so much so that the sudden death of the young wife leaves the husband utterly desolate. There is also the marriage of the Mallisons, the brother-in-law and sister of Gavin Stevens. Their marriage is the quiet background for much that goes on in *The Town* and in *Intruder in the Dust*. The Mallisons' relationship is not made unreal by hints of idyllic tenderness or of transcendent rapture. There is bantering and even bickering between husband and wife, but there is the sense of stability, full trust, and complete acceptance of each by the other.

But are the Mallisons really in love? Has their passion—if it ever existed—not burned down into mere amiability? This is not so much to ask a question as to beg the question, and the tacit

6. See below, Notes, p. 410.

assumption that begs the question was not invented by Faulkner. As Rougemont has observed, for a long, long time Western culture has found frustrated love or adultery much more "interesting" than marriage. In his novels Faulkner has found his special interest in the failures of love—love violated, or love betrayed, or love perverted, but he knows the fact of love fulfilled, and the failures of love as he treats them actually point by implication to the positive case.

Would Jack Houston's fulfilled love have remained, however, true love? Had he lived with his wife for twenty-five years rather than the few months accorded to him, would the radiance of passion which apparently still suffuses him at the time of his wife's early death have persisted? One might ask the same question with reference to the young Negro in the story "Pantaloon in Black," whose anguish at the death of his young wife is so touchingly related in that story.

Ernest Hemingway, whose romantic lovers are of the true breed, was aware of the problem. It is significant that he always managed to separate his rapturous true lovers after a few months, as with the death in childbed of Catherine in *Farewell to Arms,* or after three days, as with the death of Robert Jordan in *For Whom the Bell Tolls.* Hemingway might very well have taken his motto from the German romantic poet Novalis: "All passions end like a tragedy. Whatever is finite ends in death."

There are traces of this sentiment in Faulkner, since he is a man of our disordered and difficult times, but he did have a traditional society behind him as Hemingway did not; and for all the violence and disorder in Yoknapatawpha, the county still represents a stable and relatively unified society. This fact allows Faulkner to put some of the problems of modern man and modern romantic love as sharply and significantly as he does. Rougemont, in commenting on the latter-day profanation of the Tristan myth, writes that the *"claim to passion* put forward by the romantics . . . becomes a vague yearning after affluent surroundings and exotic adventures, such as a low grade of melodramatic novel can satisfy symbolically. . . . Purpose and key have been lost and forgotten; and passion, although the need of it still disturbs us, is now a mere sickness of instinct, seldom fatal, usually poisonous and depressing" (p. 241). In Faulkner's world, however, the myth still carries lethal power. Passion still costs something and can on occasion lead to death. This is true because, to use Rougemont's words, "the degradation of the external 'obstacle' " has not occurred in Yoknapatawpha. Marriage is still a stable institution and the community mores cannot be flaunted with impunity.

All of this obviously bears upon Faulkner's conception of woman—especially of woman as the nonromantic and "practical" creature around whom the romantic builds his dreams and who never really participates in those dreams—that is, is never really taken in by the dream. Such seems to be the conception in his earlier novels. Does the conduct of Eula in *The Town* suggest a revision of this conception? Specifically, why does Eula not elope with her lover De Spain or divorce Flem and marry De Spain or at least get out of Flem's house and set up her own establishment? It has scarcely been noticed that Gavin, at the end of their meeting in his office, asks her to leave Flem. He says to her: "You told me not to expect: why dont you try it yourself? We've all bought Snopeses here, whether we wanted to or not; you of all people should certainly know that. I dont know why we bought them. I mean, why we had to: what coin and when and where we so recklessly and improvidently spent that we had to have Snopeses too. But we do. But nothing can hurt you if you refuse it, not even a brass-stealing Snopes" (p. 95).

But Eula does not leave Flem. She lives in his house as his wife and puts up with the presence of a man whom she obviously detests, though one assumes that it is not a question of mere inertia or cowardice, for later she proves herself capable of taking her own life when she decides that something really important is at stake. But even this drastic action does not, as we shall see, make her a romantic idealist.

The two or three meetings of Eula and Gavin that occur in *The Town* afford Faulkner opportunities to push further the differences between men and women—differences already dramatized in the earlier novels. On the one occasion when Gavin calls upon Eula at her own house, she tries to tell him a few home truths about himself and about herself, but she puts the matter in terms of the difference between men and women. She tells Gavin that he doesn't know very much about women, remarking (p. 226) that "women aren't interested in poets' dreams. They are interested in facts. It doesn't even matter whether the facts are true or not, as long as they match the other facts without leaving a rough seam." And this is the bitter wisdom that Gavin is to chew on again and again in the course of the novel. Later on, however, Eula tells Gavin that perhaps she was "completely wrong that morning when I said how women are only interested in facts." Men too, she concedes, are interested in facts. The difference is this: "women dont care whether they are facts or not just so they fit, and men dont care whether they fit or not just so they are facts" (p. 330). This statement is not very illuminating, but the illustration that she adds does shed some light on what she must mean: if you are a man, she says, you can't meekly submit to having someone take your pocketbook even if resistance means getting your face bloodied and some teeth knocked out. It's not a matter of saving your cash but saving your honor. If you submit without a fight, "even though you might face the friends who love you afterward you never can face the strangers that never heard of you before" (p. 331). A man has to defend his honor. A woman does not feel the pinch of honor.

Yet, a few hours after telling this to Gavin, Eula will commit suicide to protect the good name of her daughter. The point is that Eula does not see herself as dying for honor—not at least in the man's sense of the term. Her act is practical; it shows a concern with facts, or at least with the way in which facts fit together. Her suicide is based on what Eula regards as the realities of human nature and particularly of feminine nature.

Eula is apparently not interested in respectability—only in a special and limited way. She doubtless is aware that most of the town knows about her relationship with Manfred de Spain. She may even suspect that a great many people think that Flem Snopes is not actually the father of her child. Even so, Linda still has a name and social position which are not jeopardized by people's knowing these things. On the other hand, Linda will clearly suffer if the fact of her mother's adultery is proclaimed and the public forced to take cognizance of it.

Faulkner apparently intends us to regard Eula's action as heroic. Charles Mallison tells of seeing the funeral wreath hanging upon the door of the Snopes bank, and says that he came to realize years later, that it was "not the myrtle of grief . . . [but] the laurel of victory" (p. 337). But Faulkner has made it clear that Eula does not think of her act as romantic. Like all true women, Eula is a realist. Her death is not a quixotic gesture: it rather resembles the female panther's protecting her young. In this struggle she is not fighting with wraiths and phantoms: her opponent is real. She knows what she is doing.

Gavin, on the other hand, will not quite see this motive or else will so far forget it that when Ratliff suggests that perhaps in this humdrum small town Eula killed herself because she was bored, Gavin seizes enthusiastically upon the explanation: " 'She loved, had a capacity to love, for love, to give and accept love. Only she tried twice and failed twice to find somebody not just strong enough to deserve, earn it, match it, but even brave enough to accept it. Yes,' he said, sitting there crying, not even trying to hide his face from us, 'of course she was bored' " (p. 359).

The double role that woman plays, the role that is so baffling to the romantic Gavin, may be illustrated somewhat more simply from Gavin's sister Maggie. Maggie would agree with Eula that "women aren't interested in poets' dreams. They are interested in facts." If Maggie does not say precisely this to her brother, she does say to him (p. 48) that "women are not interested in morals. They aren't even interested in unmorals. The ladies of Jefferson dont care what [Mrs. Snopes] does. What they will never forgive is the way she looks. No: the way the Jefferson gentlemen look at her."

Maggie has no special liking for Eula Snopes, but she understands her and she regards with concern and apprehension her brother's chivalrous folly. When Maggie is not too much concerned, she can even look upon his folly with amusement and affectionate exasperation. After Gavin's disastrous fight in the alley with Manfred, his sister berates him, but at the same time she is furious that Eula did not make some acknowledgment of his gallantry: Maggie thinks she might at least have sent him a flower.

Maggie sees through the conventions of society. As a loving wife and sister, secure in her love, she is not afraid on occasion to flaunt those conventions. To help her brother, she will even call upon Mrs. Snopes. Yet paradoxically, it is the Maggie Mallisons of the world who are the backbone of society. They are the reason for its necessarily clumsy conventions, and without their support those conventions could not be maintained. This point is made by Gavin himself in something he says to his sister. When Maggie, in spite of her amusement at Gavin's attempt to form Linda's mind, invites Linda to lunch, Gavin in his gratitude says: "bless you" and praises Maggie for having tried "always to deny that damned female instinct for uxorious and rigid respectability which is the backbone of any culture not yet decadent, which remains strong and undecadent only so long as it still produces an incorrigible unreconstructible with the temerity to assail and affront and deny it—like you—" (p. 182). The statement of the case is somewhat tangled, as Gavin's speeches in *The Town* are apt to be, but it is not too hard to unravel. Gavin is saying that any healthy culture has to embody the female instinct for respectability, and yet the proof that a culture is healthy is that the most "respectable" women are so secure in their respectability that they can afford, when they please, to deny it. If there is a contradiction here, the women will not be bothered by it, for it is Gavin's devoted belief that women "dont need minds at all, except for conversation. . . . And I have known some who had charm and tact without minds even then. Because when they deal with men . . . all they need is instinct . . . the infinite capacity for devotion untroubled and unconfused by cold moralities and colder facts" (p. 192).

Though Eula's suicide does not represent an alteration in Faulkner's notion of feminine psychology, this is not to say that the reader may not have some difficulty in accepting it. He may feel that he simply does not know enough about what has gone on in Eula's mind. He sees her almost entirely from the outside and thus has to infer her motives. Indeed, it may be that Faulkner, in his anxiety to have Eula's behavior baffle and shock Gavin

Stevens, has succeeded only too well and produced a character whose behavior baffles and shocks the reader too.

One further point ought to be added. Eula may be the divinely beautiful woman with a fine healthy body and no romantic nonsense about her that Faulkner means to portray, but she is also (though Gavin, under the spell of her divinity, could never say so even to himself) a little underbred. Certainly her practicality is almost too unsqueamish. For practical she is. Why, though she loathes Flem, should she bother to leave him? He is impotent. Eula apparently is satisfied with her long-term sexual relationship with Manfred de Spain, and Flem, presumably, raises no objection and sets up no inconvenient hindrances.

One significant reflection of Eula's sensibility and of her relationship to Manfred comes out in a remark she makes to Gavin on the night on which she offered her body to him in his law office. When Gavin refuses her invitation, she finally tells him "you're a gentleman and I never knew one before." The implication is that Manfred de Spain is, however adequate as a lover, not a gentleman. Though her remark seems to carry no trace of irony, his bitter reply discounts the compliment: evidently Gavin fears that a gentleman is something less than a man, his power and vigor enfeebled by refinement.

The structure of *The Town,* like that of so many of Faulkner's novels, is loose and episodic, and some of the best incidental comedy of the novel is to be found in episodes which seem to have no close connection with the main plot. One thinks of the brass-stealing episode with which the novel begins, the doings at Montgomery Ward Snopes' "atelier," Mrs. Hait's encounter with the mule in her yard, and the descent upon Jefferson of the four little half-Indian Snopeses, the progeny of Byron Snopes. None of these episodes is tied very tightly to the story of Gavin's obsession with Eula or to his attempt to educate Linda. Their linkage is rather with the course of Flem's education in the ways of the town. In his first years in Jefferson, Flem learns painfully, by trial and error, to distinguish between what you can steal profitably and what you cannot.

In Frenchman's Bend, Flem had seemed to be a man never at a loss: he conducted his activities with all the sure instinct of a weasel or a ferret. But in *The Town* he is represented as a curious, quiet, somewhat shy and sometimes baffled young man. In trying to steal the brass fittings from the machinery at the power house, he makes a serious mistake, but he fares better as he becomes experienced in town ways. Though he is finally successful in his attempt to become the vice-president of the Sartoris bank, Flem has to learn about banks and banking, and begins by cautiously depositing his money in the other bank, because—at least in Ratliff's interpretation—he is quite certain that the bank of which he is an officer is vulnerable. His reasoning here is that of the naïve countryman: he knows that only a few years before, Byron Snopes was able to steal from this bank and get away with it.

Though Gavin Stevens has difficulty in accounting for some of Flem's actions, and even attributes certain of them to such perfectly natural and human vices as a resentment at being cuckolded, Ratliff early discerns that the real key to Flem's conduct is his yearning for respectability. Ratliff proves to be quite right. It is Flem's need for respectability that causes him to take a hand in closing down Montgomery Ward Snopes' dirty-picture exhibition and in getting Montgomery Ward completely out of Jefferson. One is not to suppose that Flem has become virtuous—merely respectable. The public image that he now affects might be tarnished by a kinsman's disgrace. The same motive accounts for Flem's actions in the mule-in-the-yard episode, an episode that ends with his "eliminating" I. O. Snopes—as Ratliff puts it—out of Jefferson.

Insofar as Flem's career is a satire on the money-power in society, his assumption of the cloak of respectability is relevant: this is what finance-capitalism has always done. Faulkner evidently means Flem to become, in our eyes, more contemptible but also more formidable. Ratliff (p. 259) makes a very shrewd comment upon the perniciousness of respectability: "When its jest money and power a man wants, there is usually some place where he will stop; there's always one thing at least that ever—every man wont do for jest money. But when its respectability he finds out he wants and has got to have, there aint nothing he wont do to get it and then keep it."

Faulkner pays a certain price, however, for making Flem respectable. As long as Flem represented pure acquisitiveness—as long as he loved money and power as sheer abstractions—he could count in the novel almost as an elemental force. Doubtless, the respectability that Flem comes to relish is sheer abstraction too, but this later failing of Flem's brings him closer to the breed of human beings that we know and are. In spite of Ratliff's remark on respectability as an irresistible passion, Flem will seem to us less portentous. He becomes more despicable but more vulnerable as he begins to pay attention to what people may think of him. He must acquire a certain kind of house with certain kinds of furnishings, not because he wants them or cares for them, but because he believes they are what is expected of him.

Finally, in order to win his great prize, the presidency of the bank, Flem plays upon the affections of his supposed daughter Linda. He makes the gesture which she can interpret only as meaning that he really loves her. When Flem succeeds in making Linda press her face against his collar, crying "Daddy! Daddy! Daddy! Daddy!" he has become humanly wicked. His acts of villainy in *The Hamlet* were more like the motions of a black snake or a weasel. What he does to Linda is different, and may be thought to be of a piece with the general trimming down to human size that all the characters of *The Hamlet* suffer when they are brought into the town.

Along with making Flem humanly wicked goes an invitation to the reader to accord Flem a measure of human pity. Eula tells Gavin that Flem is impotent and adds: "You've got to be careful or you'll have to pity him" (p. 331). She follows up this warning with a suggestion that Flem is after all a man, with something like a man's sense of honor. The reason that one must not pity Flem is that "he couldn't bear being pitied. . . . he can live with his impotence, but you mustn't have the chance to help him with pity." But a Flem who can be pitied or who, because he has a man's pride, must not be allowed to suspect that he is being pitied, is a Flem who demands a greater revelation of his inner life than we are ever given in *The Hamlet* or *The Town*. This suggestion of possible humanity, introduced so late in the novel, is bound to be disturbing. If we knew more about Eula's inner life, we might know how seriously to take her observations on Flem. As it is, this tantalizing hint of a human soul within the monster has to be put down as a failure in tone.

Another problem in tone is the episode involving the four little Byron Snopeses. Because they are children, we may be the more shocked by their sheer devilishness. They are decribed as not looking dangerous or threatening "in the same sense that four shut pocket knives dont look threatening. They look like four shut pocket knives but they dont look lethal." But the children are lethal—as lethal as the switch knife with a six-inch blade that one of them carries. The way in which they dispose of the Pekinese dog to whose collar, with its gold nameplate, they have taken a fancy, or their attempt to burn Doris Snopes at the stake, indicates how seriously lethal they are. There is humor here, but of a blood-thirsty sort that may produce a shudder rather than a smile.

Most of all, the reader may be troubled by Faulkner's having chosen to conclude the novel with this particular episode. The appearance of the little half-Indian Snopeses is introduced almost casually. It is as a kind of afterthought that Charles Mallison, who is relating this part of the novel, brings in the account of Byron's children. Charles has been describing his uncle's weeping over the death of Eula, when suddenly, à propos of nothing, he says: "And one more thing. One morning—it was summer again now, July—the northbound train from New Orleans stopped. . . . Then four things got off. I mean, they were children" (p. 359).

The connection of the episode with the main plot is certainly tenuous. Something can be said for its value as an element of symbolic contrast: the little half-Indian Snopeses point up how far gone in respectability Flem now is. When the children get off the train at Jefferson, Charles tells us that Flem Snopes wasn't there because he "was busy being a banker now and a deacon in the Baptist church" (p. 359). But if respectability has turned his wickedness into devious channels, the old Snopes drive nevertheless remains a force, as the behavior of Flem's little relatives testifies. They are for direct action. In them the basic Snopes nature, "red in tooth and claw," carries on unabashed and uninhibited. Snopes depravity has here been grafted onto fresh primitive stock—the Jicarilla Indian squaw who is their mother. The now highly respectable Flem Snopes is compelled to send them away, and, as Ratliff remarks, the exploits of the children represented the "last and final end of Snopes out-and-out unvarnished behavior in Jefferson." Henceforth, Flem has decided, Snopes behavior must wear a decent coat of varnish.

The Town, as the middle part of the trilogy, will seem to some readers a rather frail and limber board placed across two firmly based stools. It constantly threatens to drop the reader between the splendidly conceived *Hamlet* on the one side and the excellent, though very different, *Mansion* on the other. Since Faulkner indulges in so much recapitulation in *The Mansion,* one is tempted to advise the reader simply to omit reading *The Town* and to move from *The Hamlet* directly to *The Mansion.* In thus avoiding the central novel of the trilogy, one would lose nothing very essential, though he would forego some incidental comedy that is interesting on its own account.

Some of the comedy in *The Town* is almost macabre; some of it is of a cartoon-like exaggeration, especially in the episodes told by Ratliff; some of it is a variety of social comedy, dealing as it does with the social ambitions, jealousies, rivalries, and discomfitures that one finds in the life of a closely knit small town. Indeed a special requisite for reading this novel is an ability to appreciate the different kinds of comedy in their relation to one another, not mistaking this or that comic element as "the serious" matter which the other comic elements serve as foils. Thus the reader will be mistaken if he assumes that since the antics of Mrs. Hait and Tom Tom are funny, Gavin Stevens' sophomoric posturings and high-minded silliness must *not* be funny.

A related problem of tone has to do with the author's attitude toward his characters and their actions. Most readers are prepared to believe that an author's view of things is not necessarily to be identified with that of any of his characters, but in reading *The Town* something more is required: the reader must be especially sensitive to the minds and personalities of the three narrators if he is to be able to make the proper discounts and corrections as he listens to them describe and interpret events. The narrators often differ in their interpretations of characters and events. Sometimes they even differ as to the facts. Moreover, they speak at various times in different moods and in different tones of voice.

Gavin and his nephew Charles see things through a romantic blur. Chafing at the more irritating aspects of small-town respectability, Gavin is determined to regard Eula as a kind of Mississippi Madame Bovary. But Eula, healthy, earthy, and strong-minded, is the least romantic person in town. The numinous haze that she wears, the special aura that witnesses to her divinity, resides in the eye of the beholder. Throughout her life she confounds Gavin by not behaving as he expects the heroine of a romantic novel to behave: she is dispassionate and practical. And at the end, she confounds him once more by killing herself: the dispassionate woman is capable of the heroic act, though Gavin persists in interpreting her act in terms of his romantic dream. He prefers a romantic to an heroic Eula: she killed herself because she was bored, the demi-goddess condemned to live among dull shopkeepers.

As *Sartoris* and *Sanctuary* tell how Horace Benbow learned about the nature of women and reality and evil, so *The Town* outlines Gavin's education in the nature of women and reality. Gavin's course of instruction is the theme of *The Town*, insofar as it has a theme. (How much of the character of Horace has been fed into that of Gavin is marked by the fact that in *Sartoris* it was Horace who took Montgomery Ward Snopes with him to France to serve in the wartime YMCA. In *The Town* it is Gavin who takes him.)

Ratliff is the most nearly trustworthy observer in the novel. He lacks Gavin's book learning, but he also lacks (and this may be an advantage in a witness) Gavin's romantic imagination. Ratliff is shrewd and hard-headed. He was born in Frenchman's Bend and has something of the funded wisdom of the folk society out of which he came. It is Ratliff who is the spokesman for the traditional society, though he is no narrow advocate of the morals and manners of Jefferson and his is certainly no mere echo of Jefferson

opinion. He sees through its pretensions, and he also sees through
—if affectionately—the pretensions and sillinesses of his friend
Gavin Stevens. But Ratliff loves to embroider a tale, and he sometimes magnifies and distorts events in his exuberant telling. He
acknowledges the trait in the third volume of this trilogy, *The
Mansion* (p. 119), in the disarming remark: "I dont think I prefer
it to happened that way." Unless the reader is prepared to see that
the narrators of *The Town* are sometimes consciously (like Ratliff) or unconsciously (like Gavin) "preferring" to see matters as
having happened in certain ways, he will probably miss not only
the jests but even the facts of the novel.

11

Faulkner's Revenger's Tragedy

(THE MANSION)

WITH *The Mansion*, the third novel in Faulkner's trilogy, we change atmosphere once more, not so radically as in moving from *The Hamlet* to *The Town*, yet the shift in mood and tone is sufficiently sharp. In the middle section of *The Mansion* we are, to be sure, back in the small-town atmosphere of Jefferson, listening to Gavin Stevens talk, or hearing the chatter of his nephew Charles Mallison, now a Harvard graduate, who has some of the pertness of a young cynic and who, in spite of his affection for his uncle, sees him more and more as a lovable old fuddy-duddy.

Much of *The Mansion*, however, occupies itself with a very different world, with the world of the sharecropper Mink Snopes in Frenchman's Bend, and later on, with his life in the Mississippi State Penitentiary at Parchman. The whole last third of the novel is dominated by Mink. In those last chapters even the scenes laid in Jefferson are keyed to the somber, intensely personal world of Mink, who, undaunted by every kind of difficulty and handicap, makes his way from Parchman to Memphis to Jefferson and on into Flem Snopes' sitting room, where he puts a bullet into Flem's brain.

One might say that in this novel the function of the relaxed small town is to provide a contrasting background to the drama of crime and revenge. Jefferson is shaken by forces that lie outside it and beneath it. So also one can say of Gavin Stevens, the optimist, the romanticist, the believer in the more tidy decencies of life, that his function in this novel is to be shaken by forces which he always manages to underestimate and to misunderstand.

The atmosphere of *The Mansion* is not at all that of *The Hamlet,* though like *The Hamlet,* it is far removed from the coziness of *The Town.* In *The Mansion* we have left the world of *The Hamlet,* the half-mythological world that basks in the heat of the long hot summer, the world of robust pastoral, the dusty and remote Mississippi Arcadia that witnessed the auction of the spotted horses. Yet the world in which Mink moves is also removed from actual life. In certain respects it is a heroic world, and, in this last novel of the trilogy, Mink becomes a hero.

The novel is concerned even more than most Faulkner novels with the notion of honor. Mink kills not for gain nor out of fear but for the sake of honor—for the first time when he shoots Jack Houston and in consequence will spend the next thirty-eight years in the penitentiary, and later, only five days out of the penitentiary, when he shoots again to avenge himself for the betrayal of clan loyalty by his kinsman. Mink may not seem to be a very promising hero or a very convincing example of the man of honor. He shoots Jack Houston from ambush. Gavin Stevens remembers the incident as "a cowardly and savage murder," and V. K. Ratliff calls Mink "the only out-and-out mean Snopes we ever experienced" (*The Town,* p. 79). More than once Mink Snopes is compared to a poisonous snake, either a rattlesnake or a viper or (something out of Faulkner's reading in Kipling) a "krait" (p. 45).

In preparing Mink for his heroic role, Faulkner does not try to purify him or whitewash him. He is presented as unfeeling toward his wife and his two young daughters. He treats them brutally in the first sections of *The Mansion,* and once he is in the penitentiary he puts them out of his mind altogether. One of the ironies of the novel is that in 1946, thirty-eight years after Mink had seen his family for the last time, he is unaware that he is standing only a few feet away from his younger daughter. He is outside a dingy house on a Memphis street. Inside the house, which is a brothel, is his daughter, the madam. Mink has lost complete touch with his family. But the near juxtaposition of father and daughter tells its own story of Mink's indifference and his family's squalor.

Mink has, too, all the prejudices of people of his breeding and education. He is suspicious of Negroes and townsfolk. He is in no way presented as an exemplar of the downtrodden proletarian, the hardworking and oppressed laboring man, or a put-upon peasant. Faulkner has not made it easy for us to see Mink in a heroic light and yet, as we shall see, he manages to do just this.

Ratliff, in characterizing Mink as "the only out-and-out mean Snopes we ever experienced," perhaps unwittingly calls attention to something else which makes Mink unique among the Snopeses. He is the only Snopes with a sense of honor—the only Snopes, that is, who can feel resentment and lash out against it, imprudently and to his own hurt.

Wallstreet Snopes and his brother Admiral Dewey Snopes do have a sense of honor, but Montgomery Ward Snopes, the intellectual and artistic member of the family, denies that they are true Snopeses. As Montgomery Ward puts it: "I dont count Wallstreet and Admiral Dewey and their father Eck, because they dont belong to us: they are only our shame" (p. 83). Montgomery Ward —who later on is to end up with a lucrative job on the fringes of the movie industry in Hollywood—ruminates slyly on his family: "They call the best of lawyers, lawyers' lawyers and the best of actors an actor's actor and the best of athletes a ballplayer's ballplayer. All right, that's what we'll do: every Snopes will make it his private and personal aim to have the whole world recognize him as THE son of a bitch's son of a bitch" (p. 87). But Eck, Montgomery suspects, escaped inheriting the Snopes blood through his mother's taking "some extracurricular night work nine months before he was born."

Perhaps one ought also to make an exception of Ab Snopes, Flem's father, remembering his horse-trading rivalry with Pat Stamper, as recounted in *The Hamlet*—a foolhardy quixotic gesture done for the honor of Yoknapatawpha County—and remembering also his fierce resentments which ended in barn-burning episodes. Ab showed vestiges of a kind of "honor" together with something of the downright meanness which Ratliff attributes to Mink.

The insidious horror of Snopesism is its lack of any kind of integrity—its pliability, its parasitic vitality as of some low-grade, thoroughly stubborn organism—and its almost selfless ability to keep up pressure as if it were a kind of elemental force. These are Flem's special qualities. The difficulty of fighting Flem and Snopesism in general is that it is like fighting a kind of gangrene or some sort of loathsome mold. The quality of honor—even a mean and rancorous "honor"—would immediately make it vulnerable not merely by acting as a brake upon its purely predatory impulses but by tempting it to fight back occasionally against odds that would ensure its defeat. It is because he lacks honor that Flem is really invulnerable. In *The Hamlet* the law could not touch him. Like finance-capitalism itself, Flem works inside the law. The law is actually on his side. It will therefore be only the madman, the outlaw, or the passionate man who can strike him down. And this is of course exactly what happens.

In mentioning finance-capitalism, one risks making the Snopes trilogy a kind of allegory in which finance-capitalism invades and destroys the old order of the South. That would be a mistake, for the trilogy is not so systematic as to deserve to be called an allegory. Moreover, one sees that Snopesism is the enemy not only of the old aristocratic order but also of the old folk society. As a corollary to this statement we may say that just as honor is an important ingredient in the aristocratic code, so it is in the folk society. As we have seen, the yeoman farmer and even the poor white trash possess, in their own terms of course, as keen a sense of honor as any member of the plantation order. As Faulkner's old hunting companion, John Cullen, has remarked: "Faulkner's treatment of Mink Snopes in *The Mansion* proves again that he understands and in many ways admires what some people call the poor white. No group of people on earth has more of that kind of fierce independence than the poor backwoods, uneducated people of Mississippi. Mink's good qualities exist all over the South among the pure Anglo-Saxon stock who pioneered it and who have had little contact with the outside world. They will die for what they believe to be right."[1] Mink is a man who has been brought up to believe in the clan and who possesses the clan virtues. When Flem refuses to respond to his "blood cry for help from kin to kin," he has violated one of the few bonds for which Mink has any respect, and Mink dedicates the rest of his life to destroying him.

The Mink Snopes we meet in *The Town* and *The Mansion* is, to be sure, in many ways quite different from the Mink Snopes we see for the first time in *The Hamlet*. Faulkner had either forgotten some of the details of Mink's story as he told it there—there is some specific evidence to indicate that he had forgotten—or else in the later volumes he conceived of Mink's character in rather different terms.[2] Characters do look different when seen from altered perspectives. In *The Hamlet* the character of Mink is seen either through Ratliff's eyes or the eyes of the author writing as impersonal observer. In *The Mansion,* however, there is a definite attempt to follow the play of Mink's own thought, even in some of the sections that are told in the third person. Faulkner has not only altered perspective but added details calculated to allow us to see the situation from Mink's point of view: that of a deprived man, conscious of his weakness, conscious of his poverty, and fiercely resenting any insult to his dignity. In *The Hamlet* Mink shoots Houston because he has got into a quarrel with him over a heifer. This is substantially the story told in *The Mansion,* but in *The Mansion* it is told more circumstantially and with more dramatic sympathy.

In both novels Mink Snopes tries the typically Snopesian trick of arranging to have the more prosperous farmer feed his starved beast through the winter and then reclaim her in the spring. In *The Mansion,* when his plan backfires and Mink finds himself working out the price of the cow's keep, he stoically endures weeks of backbreaking work until the price set by the law has been met. But the addition of a one-dollar pound fee is a culminating insult

1. John B. Cullen, with Floyd C. Watkins, *Old Times in the Faulkner Country* (Chapel Hill, University of North Carolina Press, 1961), pp. 126–27.

2. See below, Notes, p. 412.

that Mink's pride cannot brook. Mink, having discharged his gun at Houston, says to the dead or dying man: "I aint shooting you because of them thirty-seven and a half four-bit days. That's all right; I done long ago forgot and forgive that. . . . I killed you because of that-ere extry one-dollar pound fee" (p. 39).

One of the real difficulties with this novel is the character of Linda Snopes. Linda leaves Jefferson in 1927, after her mother's death, and does not return until August 1937, as a young widow whose husband has died fighting for the Spanish Loyalists and who, in the same conflict, has had her ear drums burst. She does not have her mother's beauty, but she is a strange and troubling figure in this little town and continues to exert a tremendous fascination over Gavin Stevens.

The general nature of the relationship which exists between Gavin and Linda has been discussed in the preceding chapter. But Linda's behavior in this novel raises some special problems. The reader may wonder that Linda would come back to Jefferson at all or that she would urge Gavin to be married—to someone else— or that she would be willing to live again in the same house with Flem Snopes. What kind of woman is Linda? What are her basic values and her motivations? She is an almost clinically pure example of a woman who is restless, alienated, and disturbed. Faulkner makes no such comment on her in the course of the novel, nor does he allow Charles or Gavin or Ratliff to say any such thing. But the facts of the novel speak for themselves.

In forming Linda's mind, Gavin may have wrought better than he knew. For if Linda's mother had no romantic nonsense about her at all, it is evident that Linda has. She is as suspicious of marriage as is Gavin himself. She yearns for love, but apparently believes that it involves agony and anguish, and must involve them if it is really love. This notion need not have come merely out of the volume of John Donne's poems that Gavin gave her. What she saw in her own home as a little girl surely had its effect. Ratliff makes the perfectly sound point that there was never anything that she could have observed in that nineteen years of her mother's marriage which could have given her any feeling for the worth of marriage as an institution.

In *The Town* there are plenty of hints about Linda's troubled and confused feelings toward her mother as well as toward her supposed father. Linda, for example, desperately wants a father, and so hungry is she for this relation that when the wretched Flem Snopes, in order to try to get her inheritance from her grandfather, seems to express a love and need for her, Linda responds with "Daddy! Daddy! Daddy! Daddy!" Later (p. 346), after her mother's death, Linda cannot weep and gives as her reason: "[Flem's] not my father." Gavin, lying manfully, swears that Flem is, and momentarily believing the generous lie, Linda can find relief in tears, saying: "When I thought he wasn't my father, I hated [my mother] and Manfred both. Oh yes, I knew about Manfred: I have . . . seen them look at each other. . . . But now that I know he is my father, it's all right. I'm glad. I want her to have loved, to have been happy.—I can cry now" (p. 346).

Now, after some eight or nine years in New York, Linda returns to Jefferson as a young woman who has experienced a great passionate love and suffered bereavement and injury for a lost cause. She returns to a countrified provincial town from which she has become thoroughly alienated. The reader may feel that Linda's alienation from her native state was a very good thing. But it leaves her at loose ends, with abundant energy and high ideals and a great urgency to carry them out in a community which is thoroughly suspicious of everything for which she stands. Linda represents a type of woman that we have encountered in earlier novels: the woman who is not anchored by family and children and who, therefore, like Miss Burden or Drusilla Sartoris, must give herself to a cause. Yet Linda is treated with great dramatic sympathy. Gavin regards her as a person of matchless devotion and ardor. Charles, if he sometimes leers a bit with his sophomoric Freudianism, admires and is attracted to her. Even Ratliff, though he warns Gavin about Linda's potentialities, regards her with friendliness.

Linda returns to Jefferson as the essential Utopian, the indefatigable do-gooder. She will not renounce the Communist Party. She will not let Gavin have her Party card. She will make common cause with Jefferson's two socialists, the idealistic Finnish brothers, and she will not be bullied out of her schemes for helping out at the Negro school. Gavin stands up for her against the inquiries of the FBI (though presumably his notions about what can be done for the betterment of race relations in Jefferson accord less with Linda's than with those of the Negro principal of the school, who thanks Linda but asks that she let the school alone). Gavin defends Linda's right to do whatever her idealism demands that she should do. The Second World War gives her an outlet for her energies. She becomes a riveter—in the Pascagoula shipyards, because Gavin thinks that as long as she is within the bounds of the state, he may be able to protect her should her Communist record be used against her.

Linda's lack of feminine softness—we are told that she got out of the South too young to "have formed the Southern female habit-rite of a cavalier's unflagging constancy" (p. 358)—her quacking tone-deaf voice, her frankness and directness—all give her a manner that could make her seem grotesque, but Faulkner does not treat her so. She has force and dignity; she never becomes the shrill and frenetic embodiment of a cause.

When the war is over, it seems to Charles that there is "nothing for Linda to tilt against now in Jefferson" (p. 351), but she does return, to live in "that Snopes-colonial mausoleum with that old son of a bitch" Flem, a man who "needed a daughter or anybody else about as much as he needed a spare bow tie or another hat." Her motive is puzzling. She now knows that Flem is not her father. She has every good reason to hate him. If she has close friends in the town besides Gavin Stevens, we do not hear of them.

At first the town thought (p. 356) that it was "jealousy and rage" at Gavin's having married Melisandre Backus that kept Linda in Jefferson. But Linda, of course, has urged Gavin to marry, and Charles describes Linda's look of satisfaction at Gavin's establishment at Rose Hill as if she herself "had actually invented the whole business" (p. 357). He watches her sitting there with Melisandre, "eating like a man," not "eating grossly: just soundly, heartily, and looking . . . yes, by God, that was exactly the word: happy. Happy, satisfied, like when you have accomplished something, produced, created, made something." But the reason for Linda's living on with Flem Snopes continues to puzzle her friends. Ratliff rather darkly hints that something is afoot because, as he says, Linda does not have enough in Jefferson to keep her busy and satisfied: no ships to rivet, and now "she's done run out of colored folks too for the time being" (p. 361).

Linda has in fact come back to see justice executed on Flem. In this novel she becomes a sort of Medea, an implacable avenging spirit, biding her own time, giving no hint of what she actually means to do, making use of Gavin Stevens, and, as part of her scheme, willing to live in the same household with the hated Flem Snopes as she coolly plans his execution.

Why does she hate him so much and what is the special quality of her hate? Linda as a young girl had craved his love and approval and had—as she knows now—been deliberately tricked into feeling a kind of gratitude and affection for him. Her realization of this betrayal and her knowledge of the coldly despicable motivation which allowed him to use a child's affection in this manner provide two reasons for her feelings toward her supposed father. She knows too that he pitilessly used her mother and was at least indirectly responsible for her death. She knows that he has obtained possession of her Communist Party card and would not hesitate to use it against her. But if Linda's vengeance is in a sense inspired by a personal passion, it seems to be also abstract and almost disinterested. She is perfectly aware that Flem is a soulless banker, a man who forecloses on poor farmers and robs widows and orphans. Flem indeed is the perfect incarnation of all that Linda has been taught to hate in the system of finance-capitalism. Even if Linda were not an ideological Communist—and she probably is not—and even if her allegiance to the Party were founded simply on pity for the poor and hatred for the grasping money-lenders and exploiters of labor, Flem would be peculiarly abhorrent to her. Gavin Stevens seems to interpret Linda's Communism as simply a fervently held idealistic liberalism—as his interview with the FBI agent would suggest. But Faulkner has apparently meant us to take it more seriously: at least he makes her a person who believes sufficiently in direct action to liquidate an enemy.

Is it really credible, however, that Linda would plan Flem's murder? Are we convinced? For the reader who finds it difficult to accept her action, Faulkner has provided company in Gavin Stevens. The knowledge of what Linda has done, once Gavin has reluctantly accepted it, almost crumples him up. But I see no special reason to doubt that Linda would do precisely what she did. Her motivation has been carefully prepared, and though we are not made privy to Linda's thoughts as she plans Flem's death, such reticence is a favorite technique of Faulkner's. With very few of his characters are we taken into the decision chamber of their souls to watch the process by which they come to act. Gavin certainly suspected nothing of Linda's plans and is never more fatuous than in some of his attempts to keep Linda from knowing the risk in getting Mink out of the penitentiary or, later, from knowing that her act had proved deadly. Right up to the end, he is telling Ratliff that nobody "is going to tell [Linda] that her act of pity and compassion and simple generosity murdered the man who passes as her father" (p. 391). He completely underestimates Linda as a woman or as a committed human being. Ratliff, however, is not taken by surprise, and, looking back, one can find that he has dropped a good many hints to Charles and Gavin of something in the wind.

Does Flem have enough force of character to serve as the villain upon whom punishment is executed? Is his calm under the threat of assassination credible? And if credible, does it not confer upon him a certain dignity? Anthony West, reviewing *The Mansion* in *The New Yorker,* could actually write that Flem is "a finely conceived tragic figure in the true sense of the word"—surely one of the most inept misreadings of Faulkner ever recorded.[3] Flem is a kind of monster who has betrayed everyone, first in his lust for pure money-power, and later in what Faulkner regards as a more loathsome lust, a desire for respectability. It is just because

3. Dec. 5, 1959, p. 236. "As a simple child of nature," West writes, Linda "might be excused for feeling cheerful about having got somebody nasty rubbed out without having to do anything actively horrid about it herself."

Faulkner has made him so purely monstrous that he finds it so difficult to give him a human vocation.

This general problem has come up again and again in modern Southern fiction. One thinks of Robert Penn Warren's Bogan Murdock in the novel *At Heaven's Gate,* or of Allen Tate's George Posey in *The Fathers.* People who really are set upon power, who are loveless and incapable of loving, who are not bound by the ordinary bonds and ties that hold men to family, clan, and community—how is one to describe them? It is the problem of describing the vacuum which is at the eye of the hurricane—the center of the force that generates destruction, but which is itself pure negativity.

Thomas Sutpen, because he is a less pure case than Flem or Popeye, and because, in his innocence, he holds certain passionate convictions, challenges the role of a tragic hero. Jason Compson, despicable as he is in his petty meannesses, is at least recognizably human. But what can be done to render Flem a human being when he comes in from the purlieus of Frenchman's Bend and settles down in the small-town atmosphere and becomes successful and powerful? What human role can he fulfill?

Faulkner has probably done as well as can be done. The man with no lusts, no real appetites except for power and respectability, sits in his mansion with his hat on, his feet propped on the neat little board which he has had a carpenter screw onto the elaborate mantelpiece. Flem's footrest is momentarily touching in revealing a kind of furtive humanity, but it is also characteristic of the business man. It shows prudence: one doesn't scar the mantelpiece and destroy its value by putting one's feet on it. It is nicely practical: the wooden footrest attached to the mantel can be removed if Flem should ever want to sell the house. But there is also a sneaking indulgence: the man without appetites will pleasure himself to this extent, to sit with his feet propped up comfortably as he might have sat in Varner's store out at Frenchman's Bend.

As for Flem's meeting his end with dignity: the same problem emerges with the death of Popeye. Popeye uttered no terrified cry and made no frantic effort to escape. He runs out his string in lethargy and inertia, and one can claim dignity for his exit about as plausibly as one can claim it for Flem's. In both cases I see not so much fortitude as a kind of reptilian coldbloodedness or even the torpor of the bloated leech.

Flem, except as he has been reflected and magnified against the clouds of the imaginations of people like Gavin and Ratliff, is finally a negative quantity. He is the shadow cast by an interest rate or an animated mortgage, with hands and feet, who can walk around and, of necessity, has to take a little food from time to time. He is the hollow man indeed, a ghost, and though a good raconteur like Ratliff can give a hair-raising description of a ghost, the photograph of a ghost is always bound to be disappointing.

Mink Snopes, on the contrary, is entirely believable. He was so in *The Hamlet* and he grows in stature as *The Mansion* develops. He possesses only two things of value: his identity and the savage pride with which he defends that identity. He is mean, cruel, and callous to human claims of any sort; he is selfish and self-centered, as witness his treatment of his wife and daughters. But because he owns nothing but himself, he must protect the honor of that self with passionate ardor.

Mink is filled with fury when his self-appointed lawyer broaches the idea that he may want to plead insanity and thus escape the penitentiary, for insanity is an imputation which Mink rejects on every count: he has the illiterate rustic's horror of being called "crazy," and moreover he has no wish to repudiate his responsibility for the act of vengeance. His killing of Houston was not an irresponsible or compelled act: it was an act for which he insists on taking responsibility.

Later, in the penitentiary, when Montgomery Ward Snopes has been bribed by Flem to incite Mink to escape and, by providing women's clothes for his disguise, to ensure that the escape will be a failure, Mink's pathetic heroism is such that even Montgomery Ward—the only world-weary Snopes, the only detached aesthete of all the Snopeses—is moved to pride. He had had difficulty in persuading Mink to put on a "petticoat and a woman's sunbonnet," since Mink had felt that "a man should be permitted to run at his fate . . . in the decency and dignity of pants" (p. 85). Montgomery describes the way in which Mink, so dressed, moved across the empty penitentiary compound, seeming, in this environment, as alien "as a paperdoll blowing across a rolling mill." Montgomery says: "I was proud, not just to be kin to him but belonging to what Reba called all of us poor sons of bitches. Because it took five of them striking and slashing at his head with pistol barrels and even then it finally took the blackjack to stop him, knock him out" (p. 85).

Curiously, Mink does not hold the betrayal against Montgomery Ward. Montgomery Ward was only Flem's instrument, and Mink will not expend his vengeance on anyone short of Flem himself. He tells Montgomery: "I reckon you'll see Flem before I will now. . . . Tell him he hadn't ought to used that dress. But it dont matter. If I had made it out then, maybe I would a changed. But I reckon I wont now. I reckon I'll jest wait" (p. 86). The resolution expressed here is utterly unshakable. One can feel the gray steel in it. It will carry Mink through the next twenty-three years.

Mink is in a profound sense a religious man. He thinks that he has repudiated religion and at the beginning of the novel says that he doesn't believe in Old Moster. Instead he believes in something more impersonal—in what he calls "They" or "It." [4] He has not gone to church since he was fifteen and he has a contempt for preachers. But later on, during his penitentiary career, apparently he does come to believe in Old Moster after all. What he comes to say over and over again is: "Old Moster jest punishes; He dont play jokes" (p. 407). Indeed, once his abortive attempt to escape is past, Mink's faith that there is some kind of justice never wavers —though he doesn't call it justice, merely "fairness"—a justice that will see to it that he will have his innings against Flem.

The warden at the penitentiary notices Mink's confidence and is puzzled though powerfully impressed by it. Mink, for example, is completely certain that an enemy named Stillwell, who threatens his life if he ever leaves the penitentiary, will be taken care of in due time. When the warden tries to find from Mink the source

4. See below, Notes, p. 412.

of his belief, Mink answers him: "I didn't need no church. . . . I done it in confidence" (p. 100). And by "in confidence" Mink means in trust, in complete faith.

Mink is one of Faulkner's many "Calvinists," who do not believe in a God of love or mercy, but do believe that there is a final justice. Old Moster will see to it that Mink gets out of the penitentiary while Flem is still alive, and He will see to it that Mink, with a weapon in his hand, will some day stand face to face with Flem. There are provisos, to be sure, but they are provisos that any Calvinist would honor. God helps those who help themselves: Mink must be prepared to endure to the limit and to dare to the utmost. But most of all, Mink must never waver in his trust in Old Moster's "fairness."

There is nowhere else in Faulkner a more complete and devoted trust. Mink does all that the human being can do and a little more. When he is robbed, he refuses to despair. In one of the funniest and at the same time most pathetic scenes, he fights off the temptation—after thirty-eight years in the penitentiary—to spend his tiny hoard of money riotously on soda water, the weakness of his boyhood. He allows nothing to alter his purpose or, even for a moment, to shake his faith that he can put a bullet into Flem Snopes and settle their account.

This conception of honor, so hair-raising in its single-minded purpose, is something literally out of this world—certainly out of the world of the twentieth century. Mink's desire for revenge is almost as selfless and detached as that of a character in an Elizabethan revenge play. The law whose infraction Mink would avenge is that of the clan, something which might still have made sense in the Highlands of eighteenth-century Scotland but which seems to have very little to do with the America of the 1940s.

Faulkner has dramatized most vividly the primitive nature of Mink's values by stressing how strange and alien Mink finds the twentieth-century world when he comes out of prison. In thirty-eight years the world has changed so much that it has become bewildering and would be frightening to anyone less resolute than Mink. He does not know how to read—that is, he cannot "read writing," though he can interpret figures. Highway signs such as those denoting Route 61 or Route 90 did not exist when Mink had entered the penitentiary. When he encounters these numbers on the highway, he reasons that they are not mileposts, since the figures do not decrease or increase; yet if they are not mileposts, they remain a mystery to him. When Mink comes to the city of Memphis, which he has not seen for over forty years, the traffic light at the street intersection is staggeringly strange and makes no sense at all. But Mink refuses to be bewildered by it, studies the eddying tides of pedestrian traffic, and speedily adjusts himself to them. Part of the adjustment is a willingness to accept anything. A kind policeman takes pity on Mink and hands him a half-dollar. Mink, bowing to the new custom of the country, asks the next officer whom he sees for "the half a dollar" and nearly gets arrested. Most people would collapse after a few hours of exposure to such Alice-in-Wonderland experiences, but Mink keeps his nerve; he does not even spend much time in speculation over the new wonders, and certainly he never deviates for a moment from his purpose.

Mink's bargaining about a gun and ammunition is superbly done. The wretched proprietors of the unlicensed pawnshop handle him with the most cynical salesmanship. When they find that he has only ten dollars, they offer him a "snub-nosed, short-barrelled" pistol, so "swollen of cylinder and rusted over, with its curved butt and flat reptilian hammer" (p. 291) that it resembles a terrapin. (Mink's comment when he first sees it is: "Hit looks like a cooter.") The salesman dismisses any notion of that sort: "That's a genuine bulldog detective special forty-one, the best protection a man could have. That's what you want, aint it—protection?" Mink agrees that he doesn't want to shoot anybody, it's just protection that he wants, but protests that the pistol is dirty inside. The proprietor has a rhetoric equal to the occasion: "You can see through it, cant you? . . . Do you think a forty-one-caliber bullet cant go through any hole you can see through?" And finally they dole out to Mink, for a little more money, three bullets. After all, "What does he want with a whole box, just for protection?" (p. 292).

Mink has to try one of the precious bullets in order to see

whether the miserable rusty weapon will fire at all. This necessity tests Mink severely. He says to himself: "It's got to shoot. . . . It's jest got to. There aint nothing else for hit to do. Old Moster jest punishes; He dont play jokes" (p. 398). At his first try there is only a "faint vacant click," but when he pulls the trigger once more, the second cartridge does fire and so startles Mink that he has to spring in one "frantic convulsion to catch his hand back before it cocked and fired the pistol on the last remaining cartridge by simple reflex" (p. 406).

When Mink makes his way finally into Flem's room and faces his enemy, the pistol does fail to fire. Mink has "raised the toad-shaped iron-rust-colored weapon in both hands and cocked and steadied it, thinking *Hit's got to hit his face:* not *I've got to* but *It's got to* and pulled the trigger and rather felt than heard the dull foolish almost inattentive click" (p. 415). But Mink does not lose his nerve or his faith. Flem sees "Mink's grimed shaking child-sized hands like the hands of a pet coon as one of them lifted the hammer enough for the other to roll the cylinder back one notch so that the shell would come again under the hammer," for Mink's only recourse is to try once more to fire the last and apparently defective cartridge. But Mink tells himself: *"Hit's all right. . . . Hit'll go this time: Old Moster dont play jokes* and cocked and steadied the pistol again in both hands" (p. 416), and this time the gun roars and Flem's body is on the floor.

The Mansion is, like *The Town,* a work of episodic structure: chapters 13 and 14 are especially loose in their attachment. Chapter 14 has to do with the Meadowfill episode and the way in which Gavin Stevens, with a piece of clever detective work, prevents a murder and manages to win something away from Flem Snopes. It is a fairly clear-cut victory, though Gavin deprecates its size and importance, and at the end says: "It's hopeless. Even when you get rid of one Snopes, there's already another one behind you even before you can turn around" (p. 349).

Chapter 13 has to do with the way in which Ratliff manages to eliminate Clarence Snopes by getting old Will Varner, upon whose support Clarence's political career rests, to force Clarence to retire from politics. The story is told in the best Ratliff manner. It has to do with the ruse by which the dogs of the community were deceived into wetting on Clarence's trouser legs as if they were the dogs' regular sniffing posts. This indignity is too much for Will Varner, who refuses to support a candidate whom even the mongrels of the community seem to despise.

Several commentators have been puzzled by the story: they would like to believe in the triumph of good over evil, but they balk at taking it literally, and do not know how to interpret the story otherwise. Apparently, it does not occur to them to allow for the broad embellishings of a tale which Ratliff devised and got circulating through the community and which was so good a story that it caught on, and by turning Clarence into a laughing stock made old Will Varner withdraw his support.

The moral of the story is simple enough: a certain kind of wickedness is better fought by being rendered ridiculous than by being exposed for what it is. As for the political effectiveness of Ratliff's account of Clarence and the dogs: those who enjoyed Ratliff's telling of it knew enough about Ratliff and enough about dogs not to have been worried about its literal truth. Even city-bred critics ought to have been kept from literal acceptance by noting the broadness of Ratliff's account, in which, at the climax, "frustrated dogs" are seen "circling round and round the automobile [into which Clarence has escaped] like the spotted horses and swan boats on the flying jenny, except the dogs was traveling on three legs, being already loaded and cocked and aimed you might say" (p. 317).

The reader could omit chapters 13 and 14, skipping from page 293 to page 350, without losing any matter of real consequence for the story proper. But these chapters, by recounting minor victories in the war against Snopesism, may be said to lead up to the major victory with which the novel ends.

That victory involves very different strategies from those employed by Gavin and Ratliff. Mink Snopes, aided by Linda, who has learned direct action on the battlefields of Spain, strikes directly at the brain-center of Snopesism. But the death of Flem is not the result of a violent and impulsive act. It is premeditated: Mink has spent at least twenty-three years in his contemplation of the crime, and Linda's part has been planned for at least a year. As the novel is written, however, we are not allowed to see her involvement until we come right up to the shooting. Indeed, Mink has all along been worried about what to do with Linda. He has heard that she lives in the house with her supposed father. He has also been told that she is stone deaf, but Mink has learned to trust no one and he wonders whether this story of Linda's deafness may not turn out to be a trick. He had even used a subterfuge to bring himself before the penitentiary physician in order to question him as an expert about how much a deaf person can hear, including the concussion of a gun. On the night of the murder, therefore, when Mink sees that Linda is actually in Flem's house but not in the room where he might have expected to find her, he reflects that since he has only one bullet, he must find "a stick of stovewood or a piece of ahrn somewhere" so that he can deal with her after he has shot Flem. Indeed, after Mink's gun has finally roared, and he discovers Linda behind him, speaking to him, he hurls the pistol at her and rushes for the door. But Linda, the priestess of vengeance, is as calm as Mink is frantic: she catches the pistol and the astonished Mink hears her say "in that quacking duck's voice that deaf people use: "Here. Come and take it. That door is a closet. You'll have to come back this way to get out'" (p. 416).

Mink's surprise at having his weapon handed back to him and being politely shown out of the house is as nothing compared to the shock that comes to Gavin Stevens when he learns at last why Linda concerned herself with Mink's pardon. Perhaps his resistance to any such notion springs from the probability that one side of his mind has all along been stirred to uneasiness by hints, speedily suppressed, which point to Linda's guilt. Her guilt, if admitted to himself, would of course involve his own guilt as an accessory before the fact.

Faulkner has handled the whole sequence of events most skillfully—so skillfully that the way in which he has disposed his narration is worthy of review.[5] The first section of the novel (chapters 1–5) takes us from Mink's quarrel with Houston in 1907 to his

5. See below, Table of Events, p. 413.

release from the penitentiary on September 26, 1946. By the end of this section we know that his petition for pardon has been signed by Linda Snopes and we know of Mink's resolution to kill Flem, but we have been told nothing about Linda's motivation, nor does Mink know why certain people have taken pity on him.

The second section (chapters 6–11) follows the fortunes of Linda after a brief recapitulation of her early life, from her return to Jefferson in August 1937 on up to Gavin's marriage to Melisandre Backus in 1942. It has very little to say about Mink Snopes, but a great deal to say about Linda's relations to Gavin and her life in the Snopes mansion where, unaccountably, she lives with the reptilian Flem. But this section ends with a hint of what is to come. For when Charles Mallison says to Ratliff that Gavin can't marry Linda now since he has already got a wife, Ratliff replies "That's right. . . . She aint going to marry him. It's going to be worse than that" (p. 256).

The third section of the book works out what that "worse" will be, but in its own terms and with its own system of suspense and delayed revelation. The section begins—it is now September 1946 —with a return to the fortunes of Mink (chapter 12), who has just been released from the penitentiary. We find him trying to cope with his strange and bewildering world, as he makes his way to Memphis, secures his gun, and starts toward Jefferson: "He was all right now. All he had to do now was to get to Jefferson, and that wasn't but eighty miles."

Then Mink, for a time, drops completely out of sight. We are presented with chapter 13, which tells how Ratliff, a year earlier, in the summer of 1945, eliminated Clarence Snopes. Chapter 14 tells of the way in which Gavin saves Mr. Meadowfill's life and discomforts Orestes Snopes. (The happenings run from 1943 to 1946.) Chapter 15, like chapters 13 and 14, treats of events in the fall and winter of 1945: we learn that Linda has returned to Jefferson from her welding job in Pascagoula. With chapter 16 we have come to June 1946. We learn of Linda's persuading Gavin to arrange for Mink's release from the penitentiary and of the precautions that Gavin took to ensure Flem's safety. By providing an income for Mink but tying it to Mink's promise to leave the state at once and never to come back, Gavin hopes to make all safe. Gavin probably hoped that the illiterate Mink would conclude that his pardon too was linked to the acceptance of the money. If so, he was mistaken. Mink will not accept the money, since he cannot give the promise, but he finds a way to make the warden of the penitentiary think that he has accepted it and the warden lets him go free.

Thus on the afternoon of September 26, Gavin learns by long-distance telephone that Mink, almost without money but uncommitted by any promise, has left the penitentiary. The five days that follow are filled for Gavin with frantic attempts to locate Mink, to have him detained in Memphis, to warn Flem, and most of all to keep Linda from knowing what her generous act may have precipitated. On October 2, Gavin's friend in Memphis reports that Mink had bought a ten-dollar pistol and explains why the police had at first missed the place where he bought it; but he is able to assure Gavin that there is no need to worry, since "the pistol was only technically still a pistol" and probably won't function. But Gavin, who had received the news of the murder the evening before, drily replies that "the pistol was here last night. It functioned" (p. 395).

Faulkner is thus not playing for gross suspense as to the event. We learn here in chapter 16 that Mink was successful. But precisely what Mink did during the last days of his journey from Memphis to Jefferson and how he got into Flem's house and how, finally, mission accomplished, under Linda's cool direction he made his way out of the door to freedom—for an account of all this we must wait until chapter 17. But there are advantages in the sequence that Faulkner uses. Since we already know that he has succeeded, we are left free to concentrate on Mink's hopes, fears, and actions as he fulfills his own life by ending Flem's.

At the end of chapter 17 the reader learns for the first time about Linda's part in the vengeance. He finds that Linda has been aiding Mink all along and that her concern to have Mink released was that he might execute judgment upon Flem. But Gavin Stevens does not learn all this until later, in the course of chapter 18. When Ratliff asks him whether he reckons that Linda "really never knowed what that durn little rattlesnake was going to do the minute they turned him loose," Stevens answers a little too quickly: "Certainly not" (p. 419). But later, when Gavin finds that, over two months before, Linda had ordered the car in which she will leave Jefferson, and that the Memphis dealer has had it ready for some two weeks past, he cannot conceal from himself any further Linda's premeditation of Flem's murder. By this time, Linda knows that Gavin knows, but she makes no apology to him. She kisses him good-bye, and as Gavin looks into her eyes he sees that "they were not secret: intent enough yes, but not secret; some-day perhaps he would remember that they had never been really tender even" (p. 424). And Gavin reflects that Linda had deliber-ately "let him discover the [circumstances of the purchase of the new car] and what it implied in the circumstances of her so-called father's death" (p. 425).

So Gavin's education in the nature of women is taken one stage further. He is not so much angry at Linda as completely shaken about himself, to the point that, after Linda's departure, he tells Ratliff, "I'm not safe." And when Ratliff does not understand, Gavin goes on to explain: "I mean, you're not safe. Nobody is, around me. I'm dangerous. Cant you understand I've just com-mitted murder?" (p. 427).

But there is one more matter that has to be carried out before the episode can be called finished. Gavin feels that he must find Mink—not as an officer of the court and not even as a law-abiding citizen to make an arrest, but in order to hand Mink money to enable him to get away. Thus, though Gavin's earlier self-accusa-tions are a bit rhetorical, in the end he does become an accessory after the fact, and quite deliberately.

As Gavin and Ratliff set out to find Mink, Ratliff sums up the story of Flem. Linda, as Flem's heiress, has declared that she is giving the Snopes mansion back to the last of the de Spains, the Major's sister and her spinster daughter. All of Flem's "ram-shacking and foreclosing and grabbing and snatching" have thus ended in the possession of the Snopes mansion by "a bedrode old lady and her retired old-maid schoolteacher daughter that would a lived happily ever after in sunny golden California" (p. 429).

Ratliff observes that "maybe there's even a moral in [this story] somewhere, if you jest knowed where to look." But Gavin, who has had the moral stuffings knocked out of him, comments: "There aren't any morals. . . . People just do the best they can." Ratliff's comment is: "The pore sons of bitches," and Stevens echoes him: "The poor sons of bitches" (p. 429).

But the novel itself, though it may not have a "moral," does imply a commentary on humankind, a commentary which is less despairing than the observation that Ratliff and Gavin make and one that assigns to mankind a less passive and more heroic role. In fact, Ratliff, after having made a few shrewd inferences from the evidence, offers a theory which attributes to Mink and Linda heroic resolution and commitment. Having examined the pistol and the nicks made by the firing pin in the cartridges, Ratliff reconstructs the murder: Mink must have "stood there in front of Flem and snapped" the pistol "at him and then turned the cylinder back to try again since that was all he had left. . . . and this time one of them went off" (p. 430). Ratliff even tries to imagine what must have gone on in Flem's mind. He says to Gavin: "What do you reckon Flem's reason was for setting there in that chair letting Mink snap them two shells at him until one of them went off and killed him?" And when Gavin says harshly "I dont know," Ratliff teases him a little by saying: "Maybe he was jest bored too," remembering Gavin's eager acceptance of the notion that Eula had committed suicide because she was just bored.

Then, more seriously, Ratliff does offer his theory. There is, he tells Gavin, a boy's game called "gimme lief," in which one boy strikes another one and then stands ready to take whatever retaliation the other boy can offer. Honor is at stake. Having said "gimme lief" and hit your opponent with a switch or stick, or thrown once at him with a green apple or a rock, then "you would stand still and he would take the same switch or stick or apple or rock or anyways another one just like it, and take one cut or throw at you. That was the rule" (p. 430). Perhaps Flem obeyed the rule. If he did, he revealed that he had an elemental sense of honor after all; but perhaps Flem waited in sheer resignation, sensing that when Linda came back, she was going to see to it, one way or another, that her mother was avenged. As for Linda, Ratliff believes that she felt a responsibility to act. Else "she could a waited two more years and God His-self couldn't a kept Mink in Parchman without He killed him, and saved herself not jest the bother and worry but the moral responsibility too. . . . Only she didn't" (p. 431).

This is a code of action—and perhaps a code of honor—which Gavin cannot accept and which he pushes aside almost in terror. He shouts to Ratliff: "I wont believe it! . . . I wont! I cant believe it. . . . Dont you see I cannot?" (p. 431). There is nothing in Gavin's conception of things that will allow room for it: it contradicts not only Christianity but any rationalistic humanism. It is stark and implacable and cruel, and that Mink and especially Linda could honor such a code is a supposition hard for Gavin to face.

The reader may share Gavin's difficulties, but whether or not he is convinced by Linda's actions, he will almost certainly be convinced by Mink's. It is Mink who dominates the end of the novel, and by focusing upon Mink, Faulkner provides a handsome conclusion to the work.

Since he is a countryman, raised in Frenchman's Bend, Ratliff can guess where Mink will be hiding, and he and Gavin do find Mink where Ratliff expected to find him, crouching in the cellar of what was once Mink's home. The flame of a cigarette lighter reveals him where he "half-squatted half-knelt, blinking up at them like a child interrupted at its bedside prayers" (p. 432). Gavin persuades Mink to take the two hundred and fifty dollars, but only after explaining that this time there are no strings attached.

How badly Gavin has been shaken by the whole experience is implied by Ratliff's actions. We are told that gentle and tender as a woman, Ratliff opened the car door for Stevens to get in. " 'You all right now?' he said." To which Gavin's reply is "Yes I tell you, goddammit." He and Ratliff, "two old men themselves, approaching their sixties" (p. 434), get into the car to go back to Jefferson, but Ratliff, as he puts the car in gear, cannot resist one more bit of teasing. He expresses the hope that Linda does not have a daughter "stashed" out somewhere to bring back to Jefferson. For, as he tells

Gavin, "You done already been through two Eula Varners and I don't think you can stand another one."

With their departure the scene is left to Mink, who does not lie down again but "just continue[s] to kneel on the crude platform of old boards he had gathered together to defend himself from the ground in case he dropped off to sleep." Mink has the countryman's fear of catching cold by sleeping on the ground. On his journey to Jefferson he had had difficulties in avoiding sleeping on the ground, but he could not risk becoming ill. The fear of contracting an illness, of course, masks a deeper fear of the earth; but it is more than fear: it is a feeling that even has an attractiveness: "the ground itself never let a man forget it was there waiting, pulling gently and without no hurry at him between every step, saying, Come on, lay down; I aint going to hurt you. Jest lay down" (p. 434).

Mink steps outside into the night and starts walking west, walking now as a free man, having achieved his aim, completely fulfilled. He is so completely fulfilled that, in his weariness, he feels that perhaps he can now afford to risk lying down, for a little while, on the ground itself, and "to show how much he dared risk it, he even would close his eyes, give [the ground] all the chance it wanted; whereupon as if believing he really was asleep, it gradually went to work a little harder, easy of course, not to really disturb him: just harder, increasing" (p. 435).

In the discussion of *Light in August* the observation was made that all the men in that novel strained to hold themselves up in a kind of rigid agony above the relaxed female earth. So, in some sense, do all Faulkner's male characters. But Mink, having won his battle, at last can come to terms with the earth, and now, as fully spent as any salmon that has fought its way up over the falls and back into its native stream, Mink lies at lease—lies on the earth itself, content to see what the earth will do with him. As he is lulled toward the beginnings of sleep, he can feel "the Mink Snopes that had had to spend so much of his life just having unnecessary bother and trouble" begin to seep away, "easy as sleeping" into the ground—"down and down into the ground," which was already "full of the folks that had the trouble but were free now, so that it was just the ground and the dirt that had to bother and worry and anguish with the passions and hopes and skeers, the justice and the injustice and the griefs, leaving the folks themselves easy now." But as Mink feels himself slipping gently away into this last engulfment, he still holds on to his pride—in fact, he can accept the flowing back into the undifferentiated earth only because he knows himself "equal to any, good as any, brave as any, being inextricable from, anonymous with all of them" (p. 435).

Faulkner ends the passage with a final flourish of rhetoric in which he flashes names that Mink could never have heard of. Those with whom Mink is now "anonymous" include "Helen and the bishops, the kings and the unhomed angels, the scornful and graceless seraphim" (p. 436). But if Faulkner is putting words into Mink's dying mouth, it is easy to forgive him in this instance. For he is simply embellishing with literary terms an experience which is substantially Mink's own. Even the "unhomed angels" are not an extravagance in this context, for Mink, had it ever been possible for him to hear, was equipped by temperament and experience to understand what the greatest of the scornful and graceless seraphim meant when he proclaimed:

> All is not lost, the unconquerable Will,
> And study of revenge, immortal hate,
> And courage never to submit or yield. . . .

12

The Story of the McCaslins

Go Down, Moses has a great deal more over-all unity than a superficial glance might suggest. A more useful, though more prosaic, title would be *The McCaslins,* for the book has to do with the varying fortunes of that family and only one story, "Pantaloon in Black," does not deal with it directly.

For most readers "The Bear" overshadows everything else in the book. This, in a way, is unfortunate, for splendid as "The Bear" is as a long story—and it is perhaps Faulkner's masterpiece —there are other worthy stories here: "The Fire and the Hearth," very rich and splendid, is only less fine than "The Bear." Faulkner himself regarded *Go Down, Moses* not as a collection of stories but as a novel. Whether or not the reader thinks it deserves that name, there is no question that the connections between the various narratives are important, and not the least loss in isolating "The Bear," as many readers do, is to deprive it of the richness of background which it needs and which it gains from the rest of the book.

One might even say that to achieve full coherence "The Bear" needs to be kept in the context in which its author placed it. This is particularly true if we consider the story not in the shortened form in which it appears in *Big Woods,* but as it is printed in *Go Down, Moses,* with the long and puzzling section 4. In *Faulkner in the University* (p. 273), Faulkner tells us that section 4 is part of "the novel [*Go Down, Moses*] but not part of the story ["The Bear" as printed in *Big Woods*]. This section [4] doesn't belong with the short story. The way to read that ["The Bear" as a separate story] is to skip that [section 4] when you come to it." [1] "Delta Autumn" also suffers considerably when read in isolation or relative isolation from the rest of *Go Down, Moses*.

The story of the McCaslins has its somber elements, particularly the episode of old Carothers McCaslin's incest and of the suicide of his Negro mistress when she finds that her daughter by old Carothers is to bear a child begotten by Carothers himself. There is in the account of the McCaslins a deeply religious element in Isaac's attempt at expiation for the family's guilt and his vow of renunciation, the keeping of which entails the sacrifice of his home and his hope for a son. But the story has its elements of comedy, and the function of the comedy here, as so often with Faulkner, is not to provide "relief"—not, that is, to lighten our hearts and assuage our feelings when they have been oppressed by dark and tragic doings, but rather to give perspective to the various events, to present a total view in which the values of the story—using the term *values* in something of the painter's sense—can be established and defined.

The first part of *Go Down, Moses,* the story entitled "Was," provides a good illustration of this comic function. "Was" begins with a brief introductory section that has nothing to do with the story proper, but frankly looks forward to the greater stories embedded in the novel and particularly to "The Bear." This introductory section opens with a name followed by a series of appositives: "Isaac McCaslin, 'Uncle Ike,' past seventy and nearer eighty than he ever corroborated any more, a widower now and uncle to half a county and father to no one" (p. 3). But Uncle Ike does not even appear in the story that "Was" tells; indeed, Isaac McCaslin had not even been born in 1859, the year in which the events of "Was" take place. Faulkner is here anticipating with a vengeance. The first sentence of "Was" (which is not really a sentence: it has neither verb nor terminal punctuation) is followed

1. See below, Notes, p. 414.

by a page-long sentence that begins, with a lower-case letter, as follows: "this was not something participated in or even seen by himself, but by his elder cousin, McCaslin Edmonds, grandson of Isaac's father's sister." The word "this" does refer to the happenings to be narrated in "Was," but the rest of this brief section 1 reverts to further talk about old Ike and looks ahead to what will be told about him later in the book. It is only with section 2 of "Was" that we begin the story proper. We abruptly plunge *in medias res:* "When he and Uncle Buck ran back to the house . . ." etc. "He," as the reader has just been told, is Isaac McCaslin's cousin, McCaslin Edmonds, and Uncle Buck is the man destined to become the idealistic Isaac McCaslin's father. The story "Was," then, tells us something about Isaac's father and the kind of man he was, and something about the boyhood of Isaac's elder cousin with whom he holds his long and passionate colloquy, pages later, in "The Bear."

The first sentence of section 2 says that he and Uncle Buck were running, and we quickly find out why. Tomey's Turl, one of the slaves, has fled from the plantation. We are to witness a man hunt —later on there will be hounds following the trail of a human being; but this is no Uncle-Tom's-Cabin-style pursuit of an Eliza trying to escape over the ice. Uncle Buck has to wait to find a necktie, for the chase is going to lead to Mr. Hubert Beauchamp's place, where Mr. Hubert lives with his maiden sister, Miss Sophonsiba, and Uncle Buck will need a necktie: this particular man hunt merges into something like a social call. (The chase has had to be made several times before: it is a ritual rather than a practical act.) The preparations for it involve rescuing the pet fox from the dogs that have broken into the house, and in getting a quick breakfast, for Uncle Buck has no intention of starting the chase on an empty stomach, and since he knows whom he is chasing, there is no need for it. The old bachelor of sixty and the nine-year-old boy finally get started on their pursuit of Tomey's Turl, a young man, three-quarters white, in love with Tennie Beauchamp, a slave girl on the next plantation, and who slips away to visit her about twice a year.

In the chase as described in "Was," all the usual values are reversed: it is Tomey's Turl who controls the situation from beginning to end. When the dogs are set upon him, he lets them catch up with him, and since they all know him perfectly well, the boy sees them "trying to jump up and lick him in the face until even Tomey's Turl slowed down and he and the dogs all went into the woods together, walking, like they were going home from a rabbit hunt" (p. 14). Later it is discovered that Tomey's Turl has shut the dogs up in a cotton house and gone on about his proper business, which is to call upon his sweetheart, Tennie. It is Tomey's Turl who precipitates the poker game that almost turns out to be disastrous for Uncle Buck. Finally, it is Tomey's Turl, coming upon the scene as a kind of *deus ex machina,* who produces the denouement. Uncle Buck, the pursuer, on the other hand, risks his freedom on this expedition and it is he who is barely rescued from the particular slavery that he dreads.

There has been very little comment upon this story. For many critics "Was" has evidently proved more difficult than rewarding, and of those who have made their way through it few have found it particularly amusing, though surely some of the scenes in it are among the funniest that Faulkner has ever written. There are, for example, the humors of Miss Sophonsiba, with her faded coquetry, her pretensions to gentility, and her attempts to persuade her brother to call the plantation "Warwick," since Mr. Hubert is, if Miss Sophonsiba's suppositions are correct, the true and deprived Earl of Warwick. The painting here is done with comic strokes almost as broad as those of Smollett.

Broadly humorous—almost farcical—is the matter of making Uncle Buck's salvation from marriage to Miss Sophonsiba depend upon the turning of a card. But there is subtlety too, and for those who know something of poker, the account of the game between Mr. Hubert and Uncle Buddy is delightful. But my present concern is not to obtain wider enjoyment for a story which will probably always be for the general run of readers somewhat special. It is rather to suggest some of the relationships of this curious story to the rest of the book. Tomey's Turl is something of the picaresque hero, never at a loss, in full command of his little world. But though he is a comic character, he is accorded full dignity, and in the complete context of *Go Down, Moses* he has to be seen in other than a comic light. He is the child of incestuous loins.[2] It is because of his impending birth that his grandmother had drowned herself in despair. Later on, when Isaac McCaslin will learn the facts of Turl's birth, this knowledge will change the course of Isaac's life.

In "Was," Uncle Buck and Uncle Buddy are almost "humors" characters. They are bachelors of the comic stereotype, desperately holding on to their bachelorhood; but in the full context of the novel their lives have a serious significance. They are singularly undoctrinaire abolitionists, who have worked out a kind of practical accommodation between themselves and their slaves. For Ike they will come to represent an ideal and a promise. Does the author, then, place these homespun idealists in a comic light in order to undercut Isaac's act of dedication to the ideal? Does he treat the chase after Tomey's Turl humorously in order to suggest that slave-hunting in the South was not really cruel and had its lighter moments? Hardly. The judgment passed upon slavery generally in *Go Down, Moses* is a withering one. What Faulkner is doing is giving human depth to what is too often treated as melodramatic abstraction, and this process points two ways: if, by "humanizing" slavery, he seems to make it more tolerable, the same process makes it the more terrible and anguishing. In general, Faulkner is providing the perspective in which we shall have to view Uncle Ike's act of renunciation and in which perspective the complexity of his motives will be revealed. Only as viewed in such perspective can the final value of his action be made.

"Was" is followed by "The Fire and the Hearth," a long story that is surely one of Faulkner's finest, though one which seems to have been noticed by few readers. The time of this story is 1941; the physical setting is the plantation founded by old Carothers McCaslin, that which his grandson, Ike McCaslin, has renounced, and which is now in the hands of the great-great-grandson of the daughter of old Carothers. Like "Was," "The Fire and the Hearth" is basically comic. Lucas Beauchamp, the son of Tomey's Turl, now himself an old man, is attending to his moonshine still near one of the old Indian mounds on the plantation. Part of the

2. See below, McCaslin Genealogy, p. 448.

mound sloughs away and he finds in the disturbed earth a solitary gold coin. The story tells how he goes about hunting the rest of the buried treasure, how he bamboozles the city slicker out of the gold-finding machine, and how he proves more than a match for the plantation owner, Roth Edmonds. At a superficial glance, the staple of "The Fire and the Hearth" would seem to be the old-fashioned comedy built around an old Negro's victory over the dominant white community—Brer Rabbit outwitting Brer Fox and Brer Bear. But the comedy in this story is thoroughly grounded in human nature, not in some patronizing idea of the Negro character. Moreover, it is a comedy that trenches hard upon pathos.

Consider the ending of the story. Molly, Lucas' wife, prepares to divorce her husband of forty-five years. She tells Edmonds that Lucas is staying up every night all night long "hunting that buried money. He dont even take care of his own stock right no more. I feeds the mare and the hogs and milks, tries to. But that's all right. I can do that. I'm glad to do that when he is sick in the body. But he's sick in the mind now. Bad sick" (p. 101).

Molly tells Edmonds that she is afraid, and when he asks "Afraid of what?" she answers "I'm afraid he's going to find it" (p. 102). Molly feels that her husband is not only "bad sick" but too old to recover and in danger of infecting his son-in-law with the same sickness. But Lucas refuses to knuckle under to his wife's demands that he give up the gold-finding machine. When Edmonds tries to intercede, Lucas says quietly but firmly, "I'm going to be the man in this house" (p. 121). Lucas lets the divorce proceeding go right up to the final pronouncing of the decree before he yields and tells the judge: "We dont want no voce. Roth Edmonds knows what I mean" (p. 128). And when Lucas yields, he yields without grudging. On their way home in Edmonds' car, he buys old Molly a little sack of the stick candy that she loves and gives it to her as a peace offering. The next day he brings the money-finding machine to Roth Edmonds and asks him to get rid of it. Edmonds, impressed by the strength of the old man's mania to find the treasure and touched by his decision to remain with the wife of his youth, in an access of good feeling suggests putting away the machine for Lucas and letting Lucas use it occasionally on the sly: "Look here. You dont have to do that. Aunt Molly's old, and she's got some curious notions. But what she dont know—." But Lucas will not have it that way. His reply has dignity and wisdom, and because of that it carries a special pathos. He asks Edmonds to get rid of the machine: "I dont want to never see it again. Man has got three score and ten years on this earth, the Book says. He can want a heap in that time and a heap of what he can want is due to come to him, if he just starts in soon enough. I done waited too late to start." He has not lost his faith that the gold is buried somewhere on the plantation; he has seen the hole where the two white men, as the plantation legend goes, dug some out, and the churn in which it was buried. But he concludes: "I am near to the end of my three score and ten, and I reckon to find that money aint for me" (p. 131).

Yet if the story proper has to do with Lucas' quiet later years and if it is keyed generally to the comic, there is within it an episode, told in terms of a long flashback, which is hair-raising in its excitement. It reveals to us a young man of passion and violence, the Lucas of many years ago, who skirted the edge of tragedy. This story within the larger story is one of the most moving that Faulkner ever wrote. When Zack Edmonds' young wife is dying in childbirth, Lucas, one of his tenants, then a young man, swims the flooded creek in a desperate attempt to summon a doctor. He succeeds in getting through, but by the time the doctor arrives, the young woman is already dead. That night Lucas' wife moves into the big house with her own infant to suckle and care for the little white child.

After nearly six months of his wife's living in the Edmonds' house, Lucas goes to Zack Edmonds and tells him: "I wants my wife. I needs her at home." Lucas has spent too many nights keeping alive the fire on the hearth of his cabin while Molly is away, and now suddenly and almost unaccountably he is overcome with a wracking fury. It is much more than an aching hunger for his old life with her in their own cabin. He feels that his honor has in some terrible way been infringed. For when Molly comes back that night and sits by the hearth, suckling the child as she waits for supper to cook, Lucas notices that it is the white one "nuzzling into the dark swell of her breast," and shouts out to her: "Whar's ourn? Whar's mine?" Molly calmly tells him: "Right yonder on the bed, sleeping! Go and look at him! . . . I couldn't leave him [the white child]! You know I couldn't! I had to bring him!" (p. 50). But Molly's calm good sense and the white man's indifference to the fact that his child is spending the night in the cabin act to infuriate Lucas. He is now certain that he has been cuckolded, but he will not be a tame cuckold. He will assert his honor even if it means being lynched afterward.

The psychology of Lucas is very brilliantly rendered. He will not come under cover of darkness into the house of the man whom he intends to kill. We are told that he "could not have said why" (p. 52), but the reason will be obvious to the reader: it is a question of honor. He waits for daylight before he walks into the room in which Edmonds is asleep. In the contest that follows, the white man keeps his nerve. He senses Lucas' desperation but he understands Lucas well enough to know that his only hope lies in what appeal he can make to Lucas' sense of honor through maintaining his own courage. Lucas throws away his razor, "the naked blade whirling almost blood-colored into the first copper ray of the sun before it vanished," with the remark, "I dont need no razor. My nekkid hands will do. Now get the pistol under your pillow" (p. 53). The pistol is actually in the bureau drawer. Edmonds gets it and tosses it onto the bed where both men will have an equal chance to seize it.

Lucas knows very well what the white man's real weapon is, and he tells him: "I know you aint [going to run] . . . Because you know that's all I needs, all I wants, is for you to try to run, to turn your back on me and run" (p. 54). Lucas, well aware that his hardest struggle will be with his own sense of honor, the kind of *noblesse oblige* which he associates with their common ancestor, old Carothers McCaslin, calls out to the white man: "For the last time. Take your pistol. I'm coming."

Edmonds then almost overplays his hand. He says to Lucas: "Come on then. Do you think I'm any less a McCaslin just because I was what you call woman-made to it? Or maybe you aint even

a woman-made McCaslin but just a nigger that's got out of hand?"
With this taunt, Lucas is beside the bed, and both are "kneeling,
their hands gripped, facing across the bed." What adds poignancy
to the situation (but also heightens the rivalry) is that the two
men had lived almost like brothers until they were both grown.
"They had fished and hunted together, they had learned to swim
in the same water, they had eaten at the same table in the white
boy's kitchen and in the cabin of the negro's mother; they had slept
under the same blanket before a fire in the woods" (p. 55).

" 'For the last time,' Lucas said. 'I tell you—' Then he cried, and
not to the white man and the white man knew it. . . . 'I tell you!
Dont ask too much of me.' " Edmonds finds his hands locked tight
in Lucas' grip, and staring at the "spent and frantic face opposite
his," hears Lucas say: "I give you your chance. . . . Then you laid
here asleep with your door unlocked and give me mine. Then I
throwed the razor away and give it back. And then you throwed
it back at me. That's right, aint it?" (p. 55). And when the white
man says "Yes," Lucas prepares to kill him. He flings the white
man away from the bed, coming up in the same motion with the
pistol. But Lucas is still not quite ready to fire. As the white man
gathers himself to leap, it seems to him that Lucas does not even
seem to notice, and Edmonds says to himself: "He cant even see
me right now." But Lucas can talk to him and does: "You knowed
I could beat you, so you thought to beat me with old Carothers,
like Cass Edmonds done Isaac: used old Carothers to make Isaac
give up the land . . . All I got to give up is McCaslin blood
that rightfully aint even mine . . . And if this is what that Mc-
Caslin blood has brought me, I dont want it neither" (p. 57).

When Edmonds suddenly leaps to seize the pistol, Lucas jams
it against Edmonds' side and pulls the trigger. But Edmonds is
saved by a misfire. Later that day Lucas gets the defective cartridge
out of his pocket and looks at it, musing that the cartridge contained two lives, because, as he reflects (p. 58), *"I would have paid.
I would have waited for the rope, even the coal oil. I would have
paid. So I reckon I aint got old Carothers' blood for nothing, after
all. Old Carothers,* he thought. *I needed him and he come and
spoke for me."*

Later that day, all passion spent, Lucas accepts with a kind of peace his wife's tending the two children. He is still not completely certain that his wife has not been unfaithful with Edmonds. He says to himself: "I wont never know." But he goes on to say to himself: "I dont want to." He lives out his life on the place, preserving his independence and his dignity and his sense of honor. Now, forty-odd years later, the owner of the plantation, from whom he means to get the money to buy the money-finding machine, is Roth Edmonds, the little white child whom Molly nursed and who grew up with Lucas' own son.

Lucas has a real lust for power much like that of such Faulkner characters as Thomas Sutpen and old Carothers. There is nothing in particular that he wants to buy with the treasure that he hopes to find; he wants the money as a symbol of power. Lucas is obviously a lonely man and values power as an adjunct of his independence.

What is Lucas' general world view? Since he is a part of an old-fashioned society, we can put the question more normally by asking, "What is his religion?" Lucas, it is plain, has no special piety aside from a kind of ancestor worship for his old progenitor Carothers McCaslin. Lucas' ethics takes the form of a strict code of honor. One is tempted to call him a kind of old-fashioned Calvinist. In his moving speech of renunciation he can tell us that "Man has got three score and ten years on this earth, the Book says." But for him, as for so many of the older Calvinists on this continent, the sense of a prevailing determinism does not depress, but acts as a spur to the will. One remembers that Lucas told Roth Edmonds not only that a man "can want a heap" in his three score and ten years but, significantly, that "a heap of what he can want is due to come to him, if he just starts in soon enough." Lucas is convinced that he simply has waited too late to start.

One of the very important functions in this novel of Lucas and his story is to provide a contrast to the character of Isaac McCaslin, whose story will be presented at length in "The Bear." The two men are by far the most important figures in *Go Down, Moses*. Each is admirable in his own way, but the virtues of the two men are rather different and even stand in contradiction. I think that the reader is very likely to disguise from himself how much these characters assume contradictory attitudes toward the world. The fact that Lucas is a Negro who stands up with such pride and integrity for his own rights, unwilling to scrape and truckle before the whites, conceals what might otherwise be regarded as a kind of hardness and selfishness. (Many readers, as a matter of fact, know Lucas only through *Intruder in the Dust*.) Roth Edmonds sees old Lucas as "more like old Carothers [McCaslin] than all the rest of us put together" and considers Lucas as "contemptuous, as old Carothers must have been, of all blood black white yellow or red, including his own" (p. 118). On the other hand, Isaac's own sense of the guilt incurred by his family and by his whole community in the matter of black chattel slavery recommends to the same reader a man who, on other counts, might possibly be regarded as weak and impractically idealistic. We shall do well, therefore, to see what these characters think of each other and in general to avail ourselves of the many-sided view of them afforded by Faulkner's placing them in the total context of the novel.

There is no doubt as to what Lucas thinks of Uncle Ike: Lucas sees Ike's compassion as tinged with weakness. In his violent colloquy with Edmonds in "The Fire and the Hearth" Lucas makes it very plain that he believes that Cass Edmonds played upon Isaac's sympathies in order to get him to hand over his inheritance: that Isaac was made to feel that "old Carothers would have told [him] to give in to the woman-kin that couldn't fend for herself" (p. 56). Now this is patently absurd, as we shall see when we come to read the relevant account in "The Bear," but that Lucas could have believed it does indicate how powerfully the concept of old Carothers affects his notion of things. Isaac himself is well aware of what Lucas thinks of his action: "That I reneged, cried calf-rope, sold my birthright, betrayed my blood, for what he too calls not peace but obliteration, and a little food" (p. 109). Because of the way in which this passage is fitted into its context, there is even a hint that Isaac himself may agree with Lucas' interpretation of his action. But we shall return to this later in the chapter.

The next part of *Go Down, Moses,* "Pantaloon in Black," may be described as a kind of "Wordsworthian" story—that is to say, the story of a simple and primitive man who displays a capacity for grief and an intensity of emotion that put to shame the man of cultivated sensibility. If the adjective "Wordsworthian" seems forced, we could say instead that "Pantaloon in Black" is a "Hemingway" story: the inarticulate man of action, tough and apparently hardboiled, exhibits a depth of suffering that goes far past the conventional and sophisticated gestures of the literate man of feeling.

The hero is a two-hundred-pound young Negro whose wife of a few months has just died. His grief is anguished, but he can express himself only in violent activity. Whiskey does no good. When he seeks the excitement of a dice game, he gets into a fight with the cheating white man who is running the game and ends up by cutting the man's throat. Though he does not try to escape from the law, he literally cannot contain himself, and when, after begging the jailer not to lock him up, he finds himself in a cell, he rips the steel barred door out of the wall, "bricks hinges and all, and walks out of the cell toting the door over his head like it was a gauze window-screen" (p. 158), but trying to reassure the jailer by calling out: "It's awright. It's awright. Ah aint trying to git away." After he has been subdued by the other inmates of the jail and is lying on the floor, "laughing, with tears big as glass marbles running across his face," he keeps saying: "Hit look lack Ah just cant quit thinking. Look lack Ah just cant quit."

All the latter part of the action is related by the deputy sheriff, who is frankly baffled, quite unable to understand the man's motives. As he tells his wife: "His wife dies on him. All right. But does he grieve? He's the biggest and busiest man at the funeral. Grabs a shovel before they even got the box into the grave they tell me, and starts throwing dirt onto her faster than a slip scraper could have done it" (p. 155). And so the sheriff goes on to recount the rest of what is to him an incredible tale. He is honestly puzzled by what has happened and he is also—this is just after the Negro has been lynched—a "little hysterical." The reader, however, can understand if he will, though if he becomes preoccupied with the sheriff's apparent heartlessness and lack of sympathy with a Negro murderer, he may miss the story too. For the deputy sheriff's function is not to call attention to himself or even to what he represents, but to provide a means for our understanding.

The "wawkin" episode in the story is particularly poignant, and it is rendered with full conviction and authority. The funeral is over. The bereft man refuses his aunt's attempt to keep him away from his darkened house and later refuses too a friend's well-meant offer of a jug. The friend tells him: "You dont wants ter go back dar. She be wawkin yit." He insists upon returning to the empty cabin and prepares to feed his dog and to sit down to his own meal. Then the dog, which had not wanted to enter the house with him, slips out again. He hears it stop and begin to howl (p. 140), "and then he saw her too. She was standing in the kitchen door, looking at him." The man remains motionless, neither breathing nor speaking until he is sure that his voice will be all right and—here is the stroke of genius—"his face fixed too not to alarm her. 'Mannie,' he said. 'Hit's awright. Ah aint afraid.' " The living man is not afraid of the dead revenant; he is so caught up in the wonder of seeing her again that his only fear is that he will frighten her away. But as he takes a step toward her, allowing himself to breathe once more, she has already begun to fade. "She was fading, going. 'Wait,' he said, talking as sweet as he had ever heard his voice speak to a woman: 'Den lemme go wid you, honey.' "

Even when the apparition has vanished, he will not give up. He takes two plates from the table and draws up two chairs and sits down waiting again "until he knew his voice would be what he wanted it to be. 'Come on hyar, now,' he said roughly. 'Come on hyar and eat yo supper. Ah aint gonter have no—' " But the simulated gruffness of the familiar command will not work either, nor will the imitative magic of his own attempt to eat. She will not join him, and raising "the cold and glutinous peas to his mouth," he feels in the act of touching them the shock of the inert and lumpish world of mortality: "The congealed and lifeless mass seemed to bounce on contact with his lips. Not even warmed from mouth-heat, peas and spoon spattered and rang upon the plate; his chair crashed backward" (p. 141).

"Pantaloon in Black" is tied to the story of the McCaslins merely by the fact that the hero rents his cabin from Carothers Edmonds and by the fact that Rider, too, on his wedding night, builds a fire on the hearth just as Uncle Lucas Beauchamp, Edmonds' oldest tenant, had done. Thus "Pantaloon in Black" may be said to provide a kind of counterpoint to the story of the older couple, Lucas and Molly, and to suggest that the primitive world, to which Lucas reaches back in time, has, in this community, survived into the 1940s. Since "Pantaloon in Black" is not a necessary part of the chronicle of the McCaslin's, it may be that Faulkner decided to include it in this book only because it reveals one more aspect of the world in which "The Bear" take place.

The next story, "The Old People," is more closely related to "The Bear." The boy who, in this story, is initiated into the life of the hunter by having his forehead marked with the blood of his first buck, is Isaac McCaslin, the hero of "The Bear." The plot element here is slight, so slight that one is tempted to regard "The Old People" not so much a story as merely a lovingly elaborated character sketch of the old hunter Sam Fathers, part Negro and part Chickasaw Indian, who becomes Isaac's mentor. The day after Isaac has gone through his rite of initiation, he has the experience already alluded to in chapter 3, his vision of the great antlered animal "coming down the ridge, as if it were walking out of the very sound of the horn which related its death" (p. 184). Here the experience of the supernatural—we are at liberty to explain it, if we like, in terms of the psychology of the excited young boy—matches in its skillfulness and conviction the impingement of the supernatural in "Pantaloon in Black." The descant on the inexhaustible life of nature with which "The Old People" closes is picked up in "The Bear" and there rises to full diapason.

The first three sections of "The Bear" make a magnificent hunting story. Since they provide no special difficulty and since the story has been so widely celebrated and so much written about, it is appropriate here simply to point to a few of the great scenes.

Old Ben is a prodigious bear who is hunted yearly though without any real hope that he can be taken. Isaac, at the age of ten, begins to go with the men on the yearly hunt, but it is not until he is sixteen that the hunters are successful. Faulkner has underlined the lack of any real expectation of victory in the hunt and calls it the "yearly pageant-rite of the old bear's furious immortality" (p. 194). It *is* a rite and Isaac's participation in the hunt is frankly called a "novitiate": the boy is trying to learn how to become a man. On first being taken to the hunt, "it seemed to him that . . . he was witnessing his own birth" (p. 195). The priest who presides over this initiation is Sam Fathers, and, following Sam's directions, Isaac ranges the woods, but fails to see the bear, and Sam tells him:

> "I reckon that was all right. Likely he's been watching you. You never saw his foot?"
> "I . . ." the boy said. "I didn't . . . I never thought . . ."
> "It's the gun," Sam said. He stood beside the fence, motionless, the old man, son of a negro slave and a Chickasaw chief, in the battered and faded overalls and the frayed five-cent straw hat which had been the badge of the negro's slavery and was now the regalia of his freedom. The camp—the clearing, the house, the barn and its tiny lot with which Major de Spain in his turn had scratched punily and evanescently at the wilderness—faded in the dusk, back into the immemorial darkness of the woods. *The gun,* the boy thought. *The gun.* "You will have to choose," Sam said. [p. 206]

And so the boy tries again, this time leaving the gun aside, putting away even his compass and watch, and he does see the bear:

> It rushed, soundless, and solidified—the tree, the bush, the compass and the watch glinting where a ray of sunlight touched them. Then he saw the bear. It did not emerge, appear: it was just there, immobile, fixed in the green and windless noon's hot dappling, not as big as he had dreamed it but as big as he had expected, bigger, dimensionless against the dappled obscurity, looking at him. Then it moved. It crossed the glade without haste, walking for an instant into the sun's full glare and out of it, and stopped again and looked back at him across one shoulder. Then it was gone. It didn't walk into the woods. It faded, sank back into the

wilderness without motion as he had watched a fish, a huge old bass, sink back into the dark depths of its pool and vanish without even any movement of its fins.   [p. 209]

Later, Isaac learns the wilderness so well that he can find Old Ben's crooked footprints whenever he wishes, and once, armed with a gun and with a pack of hounds that includes a little fyce dog, a mongrel terrier, he surprises Old Ben. The dogs are so close that the bear is forced to turn at bay, but the fyce rushes on at Old Ben and Ike suddenly realizes that the fyce is not going to stop. "He flung the gun down and ran. When he overtook and grasped the shrill, frantically pinwheeling little dog, it seemed to him that he was directly under the bear. He could smell it, strong and hot and rank. Sprawling, he looked up where it loomed and towered over him like a thunderclap. It was quite familiar, until he remembered: this was the way he had used to dream about it" (p. 211).

Sam Fathers remarks afterward to the little dog: " 'You's almost the one we wants. . . . You just aint big enough. We aint got that one yet. He will need to be just a little bigger than smart, and a little braver than either.' He withdrew his hand from the fyce's head and stood looking into the woods where the bear and the hounds had vanished. 'Somebody is going to, some day.' 'I know it,' the boy said. 'That's why it must be one of us. So it wont be until the last day. When even he [Old Ben] dont want it to last any longer' " (p. 212).

Sometime later Sam does find his dog, an immense mongrel, which is trapped by Sam and gradually and patiently broken to command. The first hunt with Lion, however, is not successful. Though Lion does turn the bear, Boon Hogganbeck—the poor white who is also part Indian and a notoriously bad shot—fails to score a hit. But Major de Spain encourages them for having drawn blood and promises that the next year they will succeed. So Isaac should have hated and feared Lion, for his presence signified that the annual hunt for Old Ben would end. Yet the boy does not hate the dog: "It seemed to him that there was a fatality in it. It seemed to him that something, he didn't know what, was beginning; had already begun. It was like the last act on a set stage. It was the beginning of the end of something, he didn't know what except that he would not grieve. He would be humble and proud that he had been found worthy to be a part of it too or even just to see it too" (p. 226).

Isaac had earlier refused an opportunity to shoot Old Ben, and when his kinsman asked him why he did not shoot, he found it difficult to say what his reason was. If the reader here ascribes Ike's reluctance to humanitarian motives, he will have missed the point completely. The reference to the stage gives the clue: one does not want a great drama to end, and yet one is eager for the end; the great process must work itself out to its culmination. The stage reference is also the clue to the meaning of his statement that he knew that he would not grieve at the ending. For a great drama has its catharsis; we leave it, to use Milton's lines, with "calm of mind, all passion spent." So Isaac is certain he "would be humble and proud that he had been found worthy to be a part of it."

Section 3 recounts the last hunt. Old Ben is finally brought to bay; Lion, though Old Ben rakes his stomach with his claws, holds him by the throat; and Boon Hogganbeck, this time not trusting to any gun, leaps upon Old Ben's back and finally manages to reach his heart with a knife. But section 3 does not end with the actual killing of the bear. It finds its climax in the deaths of the dog Lion and old Sam Fathers. At the culmination of the hunt, Sam Fathers had collapsed, his will to live having simply given out. The hunters bring the old man back to the lodge, and Boon Hogganbeck carries in his arms the half-disemboweled but still living dog. The men go into town for a doctor, leaving Isaac and Boon Hogganbeck to watch over the old man and the dog. When they return the next day, they find Boon and Ike squatting beside Lion's grave and the Indian-style grave of Sam Fathers: "the platform of freshly cut saplings bound between four posts and the blanket-wrapped bundle upon the platform" (p. 252).

Cass Edmonds suspects that Sam Fathers has asked Boon to kill him and then bury him in the old fashion. He walks steadily up to the distraught man, and "quickly yet still not fast," takes hold of Boon's gun, saying to him quietly, "Turn it loose, Boon" (p.

253). But the frantic man keeps his hold on the gun and continues his frenzied protest: "This is the way he wanted it. He told us. He told us exactly how to do it. And by God you aint going to move him. So we did it like he said, and I been sitting here ever since to keep the damn wildcats and varmints away from him and by God—" But Cass suddenly takes possession of the gun, empties its magazine of shells, and asks once more: "Did you kill him, Boon?" Boon moves then like a drunken man or a man who is blind. With one hand out, he blunders toward the big tree, and to the boy's horrified gaze he "seemed to stop walking before he reached the tree so that he plunged, fell toward it, flinging up both hands and catching himself against the tree and turning until his back was against it, backing with the tree's trunk his wild spent scoriated face and the tremendous heave and collapse of his chest." When Cass persists in trying to force an admission from the hard-pressed man, it is too much for the boy Isaac. He springs between them, facing McCaslin, weeping. "The water felt as if it had burst and sprung not from his eyes alone but from his whole face, like sweat. 'Leave him alone!' he cried. 'Goddamn it! Leave him alone!' " (p. 254).

The story of the boy's initiation might end just here, with this magnificent scene. But Faulkner had in mind a bigger story, and so added the long and difficult section 4 and the somewhat enigmatic section 5. With section 4, we are five years further on. Isaac has now come of age and we are allowed to overhear his long conversation with his elder cousin, McCaslin Edmonds, over his decision to give up the plantation which he has inherited from his father. It is a tangled argument, and Isaac confesses, as he tries to make his kinsman understand why he has to repudiate his inheritance, that he does not fully understand how he has come to his decision. Indeed, he is evidently thrashing about for rationalizations and justifications. The course of his argument takes him into family history, the history of America, the history of the South and the meaning of its participation in the Civil War, the relation of the Negro to the white and of man to nature.

Two experiences we find, as the argument unfolds, have a special bearing upon his decision. One of them has to do with what he learned about the wilderness from Sam Fathers, especially in the hunt for Old Ben. The other experience also occurred in the year Isaac was sixteen. Reading in the old plantation ledgers, he had discovered the crime of incest committed by his grandfather, old Carothers McCaslin. The knowledge of such depravity in his own family pierces deep into a spirit which had learned from Sam Fathers a conception of nature that amounts to the sacramental.

As we might expect, the young man's argument is far from coherent; he repeatedly shifts ground and changes the basis for the argument. This kind of wobbling has irritated readers who wanted a straightforward and eloquent reason for his act of repudiation and have little patience with his troubled confusion. Isaac begins by arguing that he does not actually own the land for the good reason that his father did not own the land to transmit to him. If one goes back through the chain of reputed owners, he finally comes to the old Chickasaw Indian chief who first sold the land and finds there the title flawed, for in the very act of selling it, the Indian forfeited his claim. When he first viewed the land as something that could be sold, it immediately ceased to be his and therefore he could convey no valid title. But Isaac is quite aware that this is a kind of logic-chopping that does not touch the real reasons, which have compulsive meaning for him. These exist in an experience which transcends legalism and logic itself. Indeed, a little later Isaac gives up this line of argument altogether and concedes that his grandfather did have title to the land.

He does so in the course of rejecting his cousin's view that God is perverse or impotent or blind. On the contrary, Isaac affirms the fact of Providence. God not only knew that Carothers McCaslin owned the land; He Himself made it possible, for he saw that the land, before any white man ever set foot upon it, was accursed. So God brought the white man to the land, bringing in one evil to destroy another evil "as doctors use fever to burn up fever, poison to slay poison" (p. 259). God knew that old Carothers McCaslin would not serve his purpose, but He knew that he would have children, the children who were Isaac's father and uncle, men who refused to live in a house built by slave labor, leaving the big house for the Negro slaves and building themselves a log cabin, men who attempted in their own way to give the slaves they inherited a portion of freedom.

Edmonds protests that there were very few men in the South like Buck and Buddy McCaslin, and as for Providence, how account for the events of 1861–65? Ike agrees that God saw that there would not be enough Bucks and Buddies to free even "some of His lowly people" and that a stronger medicine was required. So God brought about the Civil War. For Ike, God's hand in the war is obvious. It was, he argues, a miracle that it was fought at all. What people except his own would have accepted such odds, and how would the broad-acred Midwest and the mercantile East, with their diverse interests and sympathies have been forced to unite their power and fight except as provoked by such audacity? For Ike, God's hand also shows in the fact that the South came so close to winning—in the sheer mischances that lost battles, such as Lee's orders found by a Yankee intelligence officer on the floor of a saloon, or in the moment of victory, Jackson's being shot out of his saddle by a patrol of his own men in the darkness. When Edmonds asks Ike how, in view of such happenings as these, he can say that God turned "His face to" the South, Ike argues in effect that God loved the South enough to ensure that it would lose. For God had found that the people of "the land which He still intended to save" could "learn nothing save through suffering" (p. 286).

It is a curious and perhaps fanciful interpretation of history. The reader is at liberty to dismiss it as such, but he should accept what it can tell us—what it is meant to tell us—about the nature of Isaac McCaslin. In accepting the defeat of the South as providential, Isaac refuses to disown his people and their valorous defense of their homeland. He makes it plain, too, that he distrusts abstract solutions of all kinds. He has great respect for old John Brown; little respect for what he bitterly describes as "the bellowing of politicians, the mellifluous choiring of self-styled men of God" (p. 287). Against these noisy idealisms, Ike sets up not only John Brown's commitment to action but the little concrete acts of kindness of Southern women to the slaves. These, he is quick to say, were "not enough," though at least they were deeds, not wordy vaporings. But suffering was required for a people who could apparently learn only in that way and who could "remember nothing save when underlined in blood" (p. 286). The war, then, was necessary and was even ordained by Providence. But what was the South's conscious motive for fighting? Isaac thinks that the people of the South fought "not because they were opposed to freedom as freedom but for the old reasons for which man (not the generals and politicians but man) has always fought and died in wars: to preserve a status quo or to establish a better future one to endure for his children" (p. 290).

After this long digression on the war, the speakers return to the problem of the Negroes' future, the prime hope for which Isaac finds in the virtues of the Negro people. When Edmonds cites their promiscuity and violence and instability and lack of control, Ike replies with praise of their endurance and "pity and tolerance and forbearance and fidelity and love of children. . . . whether their own or not, or black or not" (p. 295). The virtues of the Negro, Ike says, derive from "the old free fathers a longer time free than us," and this mention of freedom brings back to his mind Sam Fathers, who for Ike is the free man par excellence. It is thus not by logic so much as by a stream-of-consciousness association that the conversation moves around from a discussion of slavery and the Civil War to what Sam Fathers had taught Isaac about the wilderness. Yet clearly the experience with Sam Fathers in the wilderness relates to Isaac's renunciation of his heritage. For Isaac wants to be free; he feels that Sam Fathers has shown him the way to freedom; and though he never quite formulates this for himself, his divesting himself of his patrimony is an attempt to gain this cherished freedom.

The mention of the "old free fathers" brings to Isaac's mind the memory of a conversation with Edmonds that had occurred seven years before, when Ike was fourteen. Sam Fathers had told Edmonds about Isaac's rescue of the little dog from the bear, and Edmonds was curious to know why Isaac had not used his gun. When the boy, honestly baffled, had said that he didn't know, Edmonds had tried to help his young kinsman understand himself. He had got down from the shelf Keats' poems and had read his

"Ode on a Grecian Urn," rereading the third stanza, and repeating, as he put the book down: "She cannot fade, though thou hast not thy bliss, / Forever wilt thou love and she be fair" (p. 297).

Perhaps Edmonds was right in his divination. Perhaps Ike unconsciously had forborne to put an end to the hunt, preferring the quest itself to the success that would end it in the very process of crowning it. But Isaac had been puzzled by the poem and had remarked, "He's talking about a girl," to which the older man had replied, "He was talking about truth." The boy had thought to himself, in his honesty, "Somehow it had seemed simpler than that" (p. 297). But he was willing to let the matter drop as he heard his kinsman go on to give his definition of truth. Edmonds' mind had evidently moved on from "Forever wilt thou love" to the end of the poem, "Beauty is truth, truth beauty." At any rate, he had told Ike that Keats was writing about the nature of truth, the truth that "covers all things which touch the heart" (p. 297). Edmonds might actually have been remembering—though it is improbable that he was—Keats' famous statement to his friend Bailey: "I am certain of nothing but the holiness of the Heart's affections and the truth of Imagination—What the imagination seizes as Beauty must be truth" [3]—or even less probably Edmonds might be remembering Wordsworth's statement that the object of poetry is truth, "not individual and local, but general, and operative; not standing upon external testimony, but carried alive into the heart by passion: truth which is its own testimony, which gives competence and confidence to the tribunal to which it appeals, and receives them from the same tribunal." [4] Whether or not we presuppose on Edmonds' part so intimate a knowledge of the Romantic poets, he evidently knew what those poets were talking about and he believed that Isaac had been motivated by a like insight.

The mention of "the old free fathers" had, however, set up still

3. M. B. Forman, ed., *Letters of John Keats* (London, Oxford University Press, 1947), p. 67.

4. Thomas Hutchinson, ed., rev. ed., E. de Selincourt, *Poetical Works* (London, Oxford University Press, 1956), p. 737

another train of thought: Edmonds evidently believes that their land is not free of guilt but is "indubitably . . . cursed" (p. 298). Isaac repeats the word "cursed," but goes on to disagree with his cousin: the curse is not on the land but on "us." When Edmonds argues that the patrimony, curse and all, devolves upon Isaac, Isaac interrupts him with the statement: "I am free"—free of the succession and, presumably, of the curse.

Edmonds then recurs to the matter of Providence, saying in effect: If you were chosen by Providence, as you say your father and uncle were, and if in order to free you of the curse, God required "a bear and an old man" (p. 299), and fourteen years to ready you and Old Ben for the experience and perhaps seventy years to prepare Sam Fathers for it—all this "just for you"—how long will it take for the curse to be lifted? To which Ike answers that it will take a long time; he has never thought otherwise.

But Edmonds recurs once more to Isaac's earlier argument: if on the instant that the Indian chief "realised that he could sell the land to [Carothers McCaslin], it ceased forever to have been his" (p. 300), then upon whom did it devolve? Upon whom, if not upon Sam Fathers, his son, from whom Isaac had learned the nature of freedom? "And who inherited from Sam Fathers, if not you?" So according to him, Isaac was, even in terms of his own fantastic argument, the true inheritor of the land. But by making this argument, Edmonds—quite consciously—is conceding Isaac's basic point. And Isaac acknowledges the concession with his reply, a curious non sequitur which in the context makes complete sense. "Yes. [I am the true heir of Sam Fathers.] Sam Fathers set me free" (p. 300).

Though section 4 of "The Bear" is dominated by the conversation between Isaac and Edmonds, there are in it several long and important passages that throw a great deal of light upon Isaac's decision. First, there is that which describes Isaac's reading in the plantation ledgers the comedy and the tragedy of plantation life, including the cryptic account of the drowning of the slave Eunice and the birth of Tomey's Turl. Second, there is the account of Isaac's attempt, as a boy of nineteen, to track down Fonsiba, one of Tomey's Turl's children, who had left the plantation. He has followed her along the muddy roads of December to a forlorn spot in Arkansas, where her husband had been given a farm by the United States government. Isaac's mission is to make sure that she received her share of the inheritance left by old Carothers McCaslin to her father, Tomey's Turl. The episode has an important bearing on Isaac's development. The alienation of the Negro from the white now comes home to him. When he sees Fonsiba, she turns out to be "no one he had ever known" (p. 276). He feels a sense of guilt almost amounting to despair. To Fonsiba's husband, wearing his lensless gold-framed spectacles, so obviously impractical as he sits "in the midst of that desolation, that muddy waste fenceless and even pathless," Isaac exclaims: "the whole South is cursed, and all of us who derive from it, whom it ever suckled, white and black" (p. 278). When Fonsiba's husband replies that the "curse you whites brought into this land has been lifted" and that a new era dedicated to freedom has come, Ike, feeling that the orators have deluded the Negro with their rhetoric, bitterly asks: "Freedom from what? From work? Canaan?" (p. 279). But as we have seen, two years later Isaac, not without some trace of the same delusion, will be telling his kinsman that "Sam Fathers set me free."

Section 4 also contains a fine episode having to do with Ike's inheritance from his mother's brother, Hubert Beauchamp, who at his nephew's birth filled a silver cup with gold pieces against his coming of age. But his feckless uncle, through the years, borrowed back the gold pieces, leaving IOU's in their place, and finally had substituted for the silver cup itself a tin coffee pot. So when Isaac, at twenty-one, opens the package, he finds that the fabulous inheritance, so carefully preserved, temptingly shaken so many times in the past that his child's ear might hear the jingle, has dwindled into a cheap piece of tin filled with worthless paper. It is a nice commentary on inheritances and one that would not be lost on this particular inheritor, already preparing to renounce his patrimony.

Ike, having made his renunciation, has bought carpenter's tools and means to live by his own hands, but he has not reckoned with the needs and desires of his wife. In taking the vow of poverty, he has not had the forethought to take also the vow of chastity. Isaac's wife is not at all prepared to renounce the plantation and cannot understand why her husband should want to give it up. Section 4 closes with a powerful scene in which, throwing aside her modesty, she locks the door of their rented room and calls him to her bed, using her body to extort from him the promise that he will reassume possession of the plantation. He says to himself: "She is lost. She was born lost. We were all born lost" (p. 314). And this is a far cry from his earlier statement, "Sam Fathers set me free." Few human beings—and especially few women, so Isaac thinks—are capable of making the renunciation of material things that is the door to freedom.

Many years after the publication of *Go Down, Moses*, Faulkner, answering questions at the University of Virginia, made some rather harsh comments on Isaac's wife. He called her ethics those of a prostitute.[5] Andrew Lytle, on the other hand, has written a very sympathetic account of the wife. Lytle says that she acts as she does "for the sake of a communion of real marriage" and that her offering her naked body with its renunciation of her modesty is "the measure of her desperation." He goes on to observe that marriage as an institution is certainly strengthened by the physical location in property, as the personal communion is "fixed in the sensible joining of flesh." Here I believe that of the two, Lytle is closer to the truth, for later in *Go Down, Moses* we are told (as perhaps Faulkner had forgotten) that Isaac had lost his wife "but lost her, because she loved him. But women hope for so much. They never live too long to still believe that anything within the scope of their passionate wanting is likewise within the range of their passionate hope" (p. 352).

To sum up, section 4 related Isaac's novitiate to all the problems of manhood and citizenship. The danger is that the reader, confronted with so many episodes and passages of self-examination, may lose the line of the story and thus may feel that the whole account ravels out into a series of separate memories and happenings. How bring so rich a manifold into focus? How provide a suitable ending for such a story as this? Faulkner has succeeded

5. See below, Notes, p. 416.

brilliantly. Daringly, in section 5, he takes us back to a point in time three years before Isaac's act of renunciation. It is now two years after the deaths of Old Ben and Sam Fathers, and Isaac is revisiting the scene of the hunt. The land has been sold to a lumber company; a narrow-gauge railroad has been driven through it; and the wilderness is visibly disappearing. But the plot of land on which Lion and Sam Fathers lie buried is still untouched: "After two winters' blanketings of leaves and the flood-waters of two springs, there was no trace of the two graves anymore at all. But those who would have come this far to find them would not need headstones but would have found them as Sam Fathers himself had taught him to find such: by bearings on trees: and did, almost the first thrust of the hunting knife finding (but only to see if it was still there) the round tin box manufactured for axle-grease and containing now Old Ben's dried mutilated paw, resting above Lion's bones" (pp. 327–28).

On this day Isaac feels the wilderness alive—alive with

the myriad life which printed the dark mold of these secret and sunless places with delicate fairy tracks, which, breathing and biding and immobile, watched him from beyond every twig and leaf until he moved, moving again, walking on; he had not stopped, he had only paused, quitting the knoll which was no abode of the dead because there was no death, not Lion and not Sam: not held fast in earth but free in earth and not in earth but of earth, myriad yet undiffused of every myriad part, leaf and twig and particle, air and sun and rain and dew and night, acorn oak and leaf and acorn again, dark and dawn and dark and dawn again in their immutable progression and, being myriad, one: and Old Ben too, Old Ben too; they would give him his paw back even, certainly they would give him his paw back: then the long challenge and the long chase, no heart to be driven and outraged, no flesh to be mauled and bled—

The basic symbolism of the story is clear. Old Ben obviously represents the wilderness itself, nature, against which man must pit his strength. Nature is awesome, powerful, terrible, and yet must be respected and finally loved. One can "possess" the wilderness only by respecting and loving the wilderness, not by filing legal title and turning its trees into so many board feet of lumber, or even more abstractly, into so many shares on the stock exchange. But though the basic symbolism is clear, the story is anything but a mechanical allegory. One cannot force it into that form, and some otherwise astute readers have got into trouble because they have found that Old Ben or Lion as symbols would not mesh cleanly and smoothly with the other elements of an over-all symbolic system.

What Isaac learns from his experience with Old Ben is something that is quite universal: it has to do with a perennial problem and with a problem made more and not less relevant in these days of man's conquest of nature. Man's attitude toward nature is a function of the health of his own nature. His necessary conflict with it provides the discipline out of which qualities such as humility and courage come. Man has to contend with nature and to prey upon it; only thus can he sustain life. In symbolic terms it is thus proper that Old Ben should be an awesome and dangerous force and that he should have to be hunted.[6] But when man loses his awe of nature through a purely efficient utilization of it, or when he ceases to love it and to carry on his contention with it in terms of some sort of code, then he not only risks destroying nature but risks bestializing his own nature.

In the last section of the story Isaac's sacramental view of nature is most movingly presented. Yet the way in which section 5 is made to end has confused a number of readers. Isaac, as he moves on from the graves of Sam Fathers and Lion, is attracted by a strange noise, a hammering sound "loud and heavy and not rapid yet with something frenzied about it, as [if] the hammerer were not only a strong man and an earnest one but a little hysterical too" (p. 330). As Isaac gets closer to the source of the noise, he sees Boon Hogganbeck sitting under a solitary tree, the branches of which are literally swarming with frantic squirrels. Boon is "hammering the disjointed barrel [of his gun] against the gun-breech" like a

6. See below, Notes, p. 416.

madman. He doesn't even look up to see who is approaching. He simply screams "Get out of here! Dont touch them! . . . They're mine!" (p. 331).

Some readers have been troubled by the fact that the mood of Isaac's elegiac meditation upon the destruction of the wilderness should be noisily broken into by what seems to be an example of pure greed. When Faulkner was asked about this incident, he answered by saying that Boon's ineptness with a gun underlines "the heroic tragedy of the bear and the dog" by showing us "the last survivor being reduced to the sort of petty comedy of someone trying to patch up a gun in order to shoot a squirrel." [7] Poor Boon was never handy with a gun, and this incident, to be sure, does emphasize the disappearance of the heroic world of the bear hunt. But something further, I think, needs to be said, particularly with reference to Boon's screaming out "Don't touch them! . . . They're mine!" One notices that he doesn't even look up to see that it is his friend Isaac. He is quite beside himself, almost hysterical, his voice "hoarse" and "strangled." Why? Evidently because he too has been hard hit by what he has seen that morning, though Boon is responding in his own way to the destruction of the wilderness. He lacks Isaac's lettered sensibility and spiritual resources, but Boon, too, senses that the old world has been lost, and in a kind of desperation he would hold on to—would frantically fend others away from—the tree full of squirrels which represents something of the abundance and freedom of the old wilderness.

The part of the novel that follows "The Bear" is entitled "Delta Autumn." In this story Faulkner gives us one last view of Isaac McCaslin. It is the year 1940 and Isaac, now over seventy years old, has once more gone out on the annual hunt, though by this time the wilderness has retreated so far from Jefferson that the hunters must drive a night and a day in order to reach it. One of the hunters, Roth Edmonds, is the owner of the plantation on which Lucas Beauchamp hunted buried treasure (in "The Fire and the Hearth"). But Roth has something on his mind, and the

7. *Faulkner in the University,* p. 60.

troubling fact shows itself in "the sullen, handsome, brooding face which appeared now darker and more sullen still in the light of the smoky lantern" (p. 345). His bitterness is revealed in his cynical remarks about men's lacking a sense of honor; he says that a man behaves properly simply because "a man in a blue coat, with a badge on it [is] watching him" (p. 346). The talk shifts to some teasing remarks addressed to Roth about hunting does and yet having the same doe to hunt again the next season.

What the jesting allusion refers to becomes clear on the next day, when Roth leaves an envelope with Isaac to be handed to someone who perhaps will come into camp looking for him. The person turns out to be a woman, and as her conversation with Isaac—she calls him "Uncle Isaac"—soon reveals, she is a grand-daughter of James Beauchamp (Tennie's Jim). She has her baby with her, a child whose father is Roth Edmonds. But Roth has left no message for her—as she finds when she opens the envelope —simply more money; but he had given her money before. The evil in the family past has reappeared, and though the woman tells Isaac that Roth does not know who she is, Isaac knows that once more a descendant of old Carothers McCaslin's slave Eunice has been injured by a descendant of old Carothers. Isaac is over-come with "amazement, pity, and outrage" (p. 361). He makes the one family acknowledgment that he can make. He gets down the silver hunting horn that General Compson had given him long ago and gives it to the woman for her son. But he has no advice for her except to "go back North. Marry: a man in your own race. That's the only salvation for you—for a while yet, maybe a long while yet" (p. 363). To this the woman, who has been blazing silently down at him, replies: "Old man, have you lived so long and forgotten so much that you dont remember anything you ever knew or felt or even heard about love?"

She slips out of the tent and leaves Isaac shaken with despair at what has happened here in the wilderness, in which he thought he had learned about truth and courage and honor. "No wonder the ruined woods I used to know dont cry for retribution!" he thought. "The people who have destroyed it will accomplish its revenge."

A number of readers have expressed themselves as less than

satisfied with Isaac McCaslin's behavior. One commentator speaks
of his "compromises with segregation." [8] But this is to read the
story as a tract, to misinterpret Isaac's character as developed
through the whole novel, and to ignore the dramatic context.
After all, the incidents that "Delta Autumn" portrays are supposed to have happened in Mississippi some twenty years ago, and
the character who is censured was born in 1867. It is true that
Isaac makes only a personal response to the girl's plight and that
he can give only a symbolic acknowledgment—the one treasured
possession that is his. But the fact that his power and influence
are limited is perhaps directly related to the renunciation that he
had made many years before. In divesting himself of his legacy—
for the best of motives, let us say—he has thereby reduced his
power to act.

One can, if he likes, make a sharper indictment of Isaac Mc-
Caslin while appealing only to elements within the dramatic context of the story. The girl herself, Roth's paramour and the mother
of his child, makes upon Uncle Isaac her own judgment, one that
may or may not be just and which is certainly filled with her own
bitterness. She tells him that she could have made a man of Roth.
He is not a man yet, and the reason that she gives is this: "You
spoiled him. You, and Uncle Lucas and Aunt Mollie. But mostly
you." Isaac is astonished at this indictment, but she goes on to
give her reasons: "When you gave to his grandfather that land
which didn't belong to him, not even half of it by will or even
law." If Ike's renunciation was a kind of vicarious atonement, an
act of sacrifice and expiation, as perhaps in some sense it was, the
act can also be viewed as a dodging of responsibility, and the girl,
in her bitterness, regards it as such. As we have already seen, her
"Uncle Lucas" too had criticized it in something like these terms,
believing that Isaac had acted out of weakness. And General
Compson long ago had hinted at such an explanation, though he
denied that he believed that it was the true one. He had told
Isaac: "I dont believe you just quit. It looks like you just quit but
I have watched you in the woods too much and I dont believe
you just quit even if it does look damn like it" (p. 309).

Against Isaac's apologia as presented in section 4 of "The Bear,"

8. See below, Notes, p. 417.

the reader must weigh these other interpretations of his motives and criticisms of his actions. Whatever the reader makes of these, the fact that they have a place in *Go Down, Moses* effectively undercuts any notion that Faulkner is asking the reader to accept Isaac's action as the ideal solution of the race problem or even to regard his motivation as obviously saintlike. Faulkner has not aimed at a tract on civil rights. Instead, he has done the much more exciting and valuable thing of creating, to use Andrew Lytle's words, "a believable individual, of a certain heritage, in a certain time and place, acting among individuals who perform out of the mores of a society."

The girl's question to Isaac—her asking whether the old man knows anything about love—goes sharply home. For there, whether or not through his own fault, Isaac is a failure. Though he is "uncle to half a county," he does not have the son for whom he had yearned. If, as the author tells us, the woods are his mistress and wife, they are the only mistress and wife that he has— one almost says that he has truly ever had. In Isaac there is a definite streak of asceticism, and his sacrifice of patrimony and his insistence upon earning his living by the work of his own hands are related to this asceticism and in part accounted for by it. To say this is not at all to rob Issac of his dignity and pathos. He remains one of Faulkner's most interesting and touching characters. But Faulkner has not set him up as a model, nor does Isaac set himself up as such. He never says even to his own cousin, "Do thou likewise."

Something further ought to be said about Roth Edmonds, the obvious villain of "Delta Autumn." He has begotten a child upon a woman whom he will not marry. He comes off very badly in the eyes of Isaac McCaslin and in the eyes of the reader. In "The Fire and the Hearth," on the other hand, he comes off rather well in his dealings with the aged Lucas and his wife Molly. (Both stories, by the way, are of the same period: Malcolm Cowley dates "Delta Autumn" 1940; I make out the date for "The Fire and the Hearth" to be 1941). In "The Fire and the Hearth" Roth shows a genuine piety toward Molly, his old foster mother; he is not unsympathetic with Lucas. He is, as men go, "indifferent honest." Yet such decencies make him a more humanly interesting villain and thereby, in a sense, darken his treachery. Something is wrong with Roth and something that need not be referred to "the old furious McCaslin blood." Perhaps Roth's growing up without the presence of a mother has something to do with it; perhaps, as the girl says, he was "spoiled." At any rate, at forty-three he is still unmarried and very probably will remain so. (I think it doubtful that he would have married the woman who bore him a child, even if she had had no trace of Negro blood.) But this deficiency of character is not a matter which Faulkner was committed to account for, either in this story or elsewhere. Roth is no more a model villain than Uncle Ike is a model saint. He is a complicated mixture of good and evil and thoroughly credible.

It might be thought that the ending of "Delta Autumn," with Isaac McCaslin's final sense of outrage and despair, provides the proper ending for *Go Down, Moses*. Most authors would have been content to end the novel here, and perhaps Faulkner would have been well advised to do so. Instead, however, he elected to end with a short section, the title section of the novel ("Go Down, Moses"), which constitutes a sort of coda to the work as a whole. The plot of this concluding story is quite simple.

The eldest daughter of Lucas and Molly Beauchamp has a son who has gone North and has killed a Chicago policeman. He has been caught, tried, and convicted, and is about to be executed. His grandmother appeals for help to Gavin Stevens, since he is county attorney. Molly is joined in her appeal by Miss Worsham (in *Intruder in the Dust* she will be known as Miss Habersham). Molly's brother, Hamp Worsham, is a descendant of one of Miss Worsham's father's slaves, and Hamp and his wife work for her.

Stevens tries to reason with Miss Worsham that murder is a serious crime, that Samuel (Butch) Beauchamp is the bad son of a bad father—the father had deserted Butch's mother and later killed a man—and that in any case his execution cannot be prevented. Miss Worsham does not even try to counter these perfectly sound observations. She simply points out that the murderer "is the only child of [Molly's] oldest daughter, her own dead first child," and insists that he "must come home" (p. 376).

Gavin finds this view of the matter quite unanswerable; so he

275

and the newspaper editor (whom he calls in for help) arrange to have the young Negro's body brought home. To this end, Gavin takes up a collection around the town square. With this collection, plus Gavin's and the editor's more substantial contributions and the twenty-five dollars in "frayed bills and coins" pushed upon Gavin by Miss Worsham, they do arrange for the body to be sent back from Chicago in a decent casket, with flowers, and to be driven out in proper state to the country graveyard.

After her talk with Gavin, Miss Worsham goes home to break the news to Molly that her grandson is already dead and that his body is being sent home. That evening, Gavin calls on Miss Worsham. Molly is there and as Gavin approaches, he hears her intoning "Roth Edmonds sold him. Sold my Benjamin. . . . Sold him in Egypt." [9] What Roth Edmonds had done was to catch Butch breaking into his commissary store and to order him off the place. Butch had come on into Jefferson then and had spent a year in and out of the local jail and finally had moved out of the county.

When Gavin hears Molly chanting "Sold him in Egypt," he tries to reason with her. " 'No he didn't, Aunt Mollie. It wasn't Mr Edmond. Mr Edmonds didn't—' *But she cant hear me,* he thought. She was not even looking at him" (p. 380). For Aunt Molly, Roth Edmonds, the man who sent her grandson out of the small familiar world, obviously bears the responsibility for his death.

Miss Worsham understands and sympathizes with Molly. It is significant that she prefers not to appeal to Roth Edmonds and evidently she counts on no help from Molly's husband, Lucas Beauchamp. She had produced her own small store of bills and coins to take care of what, in her innocence, she thought would be sufficient for "the immediate expenses."

Arthur Mizener has written by far the best account of this story. He is concerned primarily with the plight of the American intellectual, typified in this instance by Gavin Stevens, in his relation to the small town community to which he does and does not belong. With some of these observations, interesting as they are, I am not presently concerned. But I am very much concerned with the way in which this last section of the book establishes power-

9. See below, Notes, p. 420.

fully the sense of the community, and this matter Mizener has put for us very well. The story, he writes, "shows us the grandeur and pathos, the innocence and the incongruity of the community's solidarity which makes Miss Worsham speak quite unconsciously of the grief, which is primarily her Negro sister Mollie's, as 'our grief'; it shows us the essentially irrelevant bad taste of the casket and flowers and the wonderfully incongruous bishoplike purr of the hearse" [10] as it carries the body around the little town square before it turns out into the country to take Molly's grandson home.

It is important that, at the end of this account of the McCaslins, we receive this powerful reminder of the fact of the community. Gavin Stevens must respond to its claims as does the newspaper editor and, indeed, as do "the merchants and clerks and barbers and professional men who had given Stevens the dollars and half-dollars and quarters." These and even the ones who did not give may be said to take part in a kind of ritual action as they quietly watch the hearse "with [its] unctuous . . . almost bishoplike purr" move into the "square, crossing it, circling the Confederate monument and the courthouse," and finally swing on out into the country toward the Edmonds plantation.

Stevens and the editor do not follow the hearse into the country. As they turn back into town, the editor confides to Stevens that Aunt Molly had asked whether a notice of the funeral was going to be put in the paper. She wants it in the paper. She will not be able to read it, but "Miss Belle will show me whar to look and I can look at hit."

We shall miss the point if we take this as a kind of comic note on which Faulkner would have his novel end. It is comic only in the sense that life seen in a long perspective always tends to be comic. Gavin Stevens, who does not always understand matters, does understand here: "Since it had to be and [his grandmother] couldn't stop it, and now that it's all over and done and finished, she doesn't care how he died. She just wanted him home, but she wanted him to come home right" (p. 383). Molly represents the

10. "The Thin, Intelligent Face of American Fiction," *Kenyon Review, 17* (1955), 517.

basic virtues of all Faulkner's women, the virtues that Faulkner feels are the bedrock of any civilization. It may seem odd to have this book close on an episode in which Molly and her white counterpart, Miss Worsham, dominate the action, especially when one remembers how much of the book has to do with Lucas' striving with his fate and with Isaac McCaslin's initiation, self-discipline, and attempted expiation. But the actions of Lucas and Ike are unthinkable except against the background of such a community, and it is the women who most typically embody and express its claims.

13

The Community in Action

(INTRUDER IN THE DUST)

Intruder in the Dust represents a very curious mixture of literary excellence and faults. But its essential faults are not those that in the past have come in for rough handling by the critics. These latter tend to disappear, once the reader has put aside a few misconceptions. Such objections center around the character of Gavin Stevens and some of his talk on the race problem. It led Edmund Wilson, in his review of the book in *The New Yorker*, to treat the novel as "a kind of counter blast to the anti-lynching bill and to the civil rights plank of the Democratic platform," and other reviewers made much the same point.

Most readers find it impossible not to condescend to Gavin Stevens. They can scarcely be blamed, and in itself the condescension does no harm to the novel. What is of damaging consequence, however, is that many readers are quite certain that Faulkner admires Gavin Stevens, regards him as a kind of projected image of himself, and means to use him as his mouthpiece. But as the earlier chapters of this book should have made plain, Gavin Stevens occupies no privileged position in Faulkner's novels: sometimes he talks sense and sometimes he talks nonsense. Doubtless, what he says often represents what many Southerners think and what Faulkner himself—at one time or another—has thought. But Gavin is not presented as the sage and wise counselor of the community. His notions have to take their chances along with those of less "intellectual" characters.

A more cogent objection to this novel is the incoherence of the plot. *Intruder in the Dust* is another of Faulkner's flirtations with the detective novel. This is not to be held against it, of course; but the plot of a good detective story must justify its complications, and that of *Intruder* scarcely does so. When the excellent movie was made of the novel, the director very sensibly simplified the plot by reducing the number of times that Vinson Gowrie's grave was reopened.

Worse than the extravagances of the plot, however, is the incoherence of motivation and action. The murderer's motive for putting into the grave of his first victim, Vinson Gowrie, the body of Jake Montgomery, whom he has just killed, does not make entire sense. If the purpose was to remove the body of Vinson because it would not show the right kind of bullet hole, what is gained by substituting a body which will show no bullet hole at all, and one which is not even supposed to be in this grave? It would have made more sense to put Vinson back in his grave, and cart away the body of Jake. Was Crawford desperate and therefore foolish in doing what he did? Or was the action imposed upon Crawford by the author himself simply to complicate the plot?

When Crawford, from his hiding place, sees Miss Habersham, Charles Mallison, and Aleck dig up Jake's body and rebury it, and is therefore forced to dig up the body once more, this time he does leave the coffin empty. But why does he give Jake's body a hasty and therefore necessarily shallow burial elsewhere? Why doesn't he simply put the body of Jake Montgomery in the quicksand along with his brother Vinson's? That would have been quicker and easier, and apparently he was near enough to the quicksand portion of the creek to have done so.

Strangely enough, difficulties of this sort seem not to have troubled most readers of the novel; their objections lie, as I have said above, with Gavin Stevens. They feel that he talks too much and, worse than that, they cannot stomach what he says. This kind of reader comes to the novel with certain expectations and certain hostilities and irritabilities. In the charged atmosphere of today (and of 1948, when the novel appeared) such bias is to be expected. It becomes necessary, then, to remind the reader that *Intruder in the Dust* is a novel and not, in spite of Edmund Wilson's comments,[1] a tract.

The surcharged atmosphere in which the novel has been read played all sorts of tricks on its reviewers. Elizabeth Hardwick, writing in the *Partisan Review*,[2] said that "the bare situation of the novel is brilliant," and went on to specify why: "an old Negro, Lucas Beauchamp, a man apart, 'not arrogant, not scornful, just intractable and composed,' *pretends* to be a murderer, wants to be innocently lynched, to add his own blood to the South's dishonor, as his last act of contempt for his oppressors." But Lucas Beauchamp does not pretend to be a murderer, and he has not the least desire to be lynched. He sends for a lawyer and tries to get a private detective. Though the situation looks black, he does not give up his case. To depend upon a boy's ability—not to mention his willingness—to check up on the bullet wound in a body now buried in an out-of-the-way cemetery is to rely on a forlorn hope, but Lucas does not dismiss it contemptuously. He plays it for what it is worth, and when the opportunity offers, he makes his appeal to the boy.

Other readers have not gone so far as to say that Lucas wants to be lynched, but they are so certain of his victimization that they are led to say that the community was determined to lynch him, whether or no. Irving Malin assumes that Lucas is to be lynched because he is "discovered one day standing next to the body of a white man. It does not matter," he says, "whether he is innocent or guilty." [3] But Mr. Malin is too eager to find against the community; even in New York City or Cleveland or Detroit, the presence of a man with a pistol that has just been fired, standing above the still-warm body of a man who has just been shot, affords a strong presumption of guilt. As for its not mattering to the community whether Lucas is innocent or guilty, that conclusion is contra-

1. "Faulkner's Reply to the Civil Rights Program," *New Yorker*, 24 (1948), 106, 109–12.

2. "Faulkner and the South Today," *Partisan Review*, 15 (1948), 1130–35.

3. *William Faulkner: an Interpretation* (Stanford University, Stanford University Press, 1957), p. 7.

dicted by the events. Late in the novel Charles Mallison notes with scorn the speed with which the people in the crowded square slip away, once they find out that Lucas is not guilty. He observes bitterly: "They ran. . . . there was nothing left for them to do but admit that they were wrong. So they ran home" (p. 197).

How did Lucas manage to get himself in the embarrassing position in which he stands, pistol in hand, over a still-warm corpse? Because, as we are to learn, Crawford Gowrie had concocted an elaborate plot to kill his brother Vinson and uses Lucas as a scapegoat. Lucas invariably carries his pistol with him every Saturday, just as he wears his good suit and hat; it is part of his holiday dress. Crawford Gowrie knows this and builds his scheme upon it. He sends a message asking Lucas to meet him near the store on this Saturday morning; and when they meet, he bets Lucas that he can't hit a stump fifteen feet away. Lucas fires his pistol, wins the bet, and is now holding a "hot" pistol. Crawford then asks Lucas to wait at this spot for a few minutes until Crawford can return with Workitt's receipt for the material that Lucas believes Crawford has stolen from Workitt. (Lucas had apparently threatened to report the theft to Workitt unless Crawford could prove that he had really paid for the material.) After Crawford has left Lucas, his brother Vinson comes up to Lucas (evidently having been sent by Crawford—this would have to be part of Crawford's plot). As Vinson stands beside Lucas, he is shot from a distance by Crawford. Hence it is that Lucas is discovered standing over the body of the slain man, holding a pistol from which a bullet has been recently fired.

Now we have every right to protest that such a plot is much too tricky and that a would-be murderer, less imaginative than Faulkner but more practical in the ways of crime, would have concocted some other way to stop the mouths of Vinson and Lucas, both of whom know that Crawford has been stealing lumber. But if the reader is going to accept the elaborate arrangement that will place Lucas apparently red-handed at the scene of the crime, he has little right to object if people in the community assume, as most people elsewhere would assume under the circumstances, that Lucas is the murderer. In any case, it is essential to our understanding of the novel for us to realize that when Gavin Stevens tells Lucas that he will take his case, he does so in spite of a presumption of Lucas' guilt that amounts almost to certainty. We must realize too that Charles Mallison, at the beginning, assumes that Lucas is guilty of murder.

At this point the figure of Lucas Beauchamp calls for a more careful look. We may be tempted to see in Lucas a champion of Negro rights. In one important regard he is such a champion, but hardly in a programmatic sense. Lucas is basically a strong-minded individual with pride in himself, but his loyalty is not so much to his race as to his family. He is obviously very proud of being a McCaslin and he imitates very carefully the stance of his white ancestor, old Carothers McCaslin. Lucas, after all, is the same man whom we met in "The Fire and the Hearth." He is no would-be martyr; he is no crusader for civil rights; he is the tough and fearless old aristocrat who makes no concessions, who manages to keep his courage and his dignity under the most difficult of situations, and whose enforced passivity as prisoner is by no means to be confused with the courting of unjust punishment nor even the merely Stoical endurance of undeserved punishment. Lucas is an old man hustled into jail, an old man who has an incredible tale to tell and who is wise enough to know that it will be difficult to get anybody to listen to him, let alone believe him. This is the character that Faulkner renders so convincingly that even in his passivity he counts as a positive force throughout the novel.

Faulkner does emphasize the fact that many of Lucas' problems stem from the fact that he refuses to behave as the white community expects a Negro to. The author reconstructs for us what has gone on in the minds of the typical white men in this community: "We got to make him be a nigger first. He's got to admit he's a nigger. Then maybe we will accept him as he seems to intend to be accepted" (p. 18). It is interesting to see how Lucas handles himself in the face of this kind of truculence, especially when it becomes belligerently hostile.

One such incident occurs when Lucas, at the country store, encounters three young white men, the crew of a "nearby sawmill, all a little drunk." One of them says to Lucas: "You goddamn

biggity stiffnecked stinking burrheaded Edmonds sonofabitch."
Lucas replies: "I aint a Edmonds. I dont belong to these new
folks. I belongs to the old lot. I'm a McCaslin" (p. 19). This is not
precisely the soft answer that turneth away wrath, and it is not
meant to be. The young ruffian at once threatens Lucas because
of "that look" on his face, to which Lucas retorts: "Yes, I heard
that idea before, and I notices that the folks that brings it up aint
even Edmondses" (p. 19). The young white man snatches a club
to bash in Lucas' head and is barely restrained by the proprietor's
son. But Lucas refuses to run. He finally moves toward the door
"without haste," and goes out calmly eating his gingersnaps. The
terms of Lucas' retort are significant: they suppose his dignity not
as a Negro but as a McCaslin; they involve not his race but his
family. (They probably are, as such, the more infuriating to the
underbred drunken white man. But we are concerned here with
Lucas' conception of himself, not with that aspect of the matter.)
Lucas is not consciously fighting for a cause. He is being himself,
though in daring to be himself he undoubtedly promotes the
cause.

Not the least important ingredient in Lucas is his patience, a
patience which is tinged with philosophy and humor. A nice
example occurs in the passage that closes chapter 3. Charles Mallison, having been fixed by the eye of this ancient mariner, is now
getting ready to launch out on his insane quest to check the bullet
hole in the buried body. He tries to get the last details about the
cemetery from Lucas and then he explains to Lucas, almost frantically, that he can't possibly get back to town before midnight or
one o'clock. Lucas quietly answers: "I'll try to wait."

The comment cannot be taken as merely "straight"—a declara-
tion of Stoic submissiveness. Lucas is quite conscious of the grim
humor of his statement. But it is no pert sarcasm either. Lucas'
reply might very well qualify as one of Mr. William Empson's
famous seven types of ambiguity. It can, and in the whole context
must, mean several things: since all I can do is wait, I will try to
shape my mind to that; my task (of waiting) will require more
effort even than yours; I know that yours isn't going to be easy

for you, but my waiting isn't going to be exactly easy for me either. We ought to be well enough acquainted with Lucas Beauchamp at this point to credit him with all of the possible meanings.

The way in which Charles Mallison incurred his obligation to Lucas is told in the opening chapter, with the account of the rabbit hunt and of the boy's falling into the icy creek, and the scene in Lucas' cabin in which the old man quietly exercises his authority, though with the courtesy of an old friend of the family. When Charles makes his *gaffe* of trying to pay Lucas for the meal that Molly has served him, Lucas disposes of the matter firmly but with calm and unruffled civility.

There follows the very sensitive handling of the white boy's sense of embarrassment at his faux pas, the sudden shift from shame to anger as he hears the rejected coins ring on the cabin floor, and then, as the weeks pass, the boy's bafflement and resentful frustration at the way in which the old man parries his every attempt to discharge the obligation. By countering each present sent by the boy with a present of his own, Lucas manages to keep the boy in his debt. Typical of Faulkner's sure touch is the way in which he handles the boy's sense of relief when one day Lucas meets him on the street and looks straight at him without recognition, seeming to have forgotten him completely. But later the boy learns that Lucas' wife has died not long before this encounter, and thinks with a kind of amazement: "He was grieving. You dont have to not be a nigger in order to grieve" (p. 25). So the boy has to make another test, and this time, when Lucas again passes him without a sign of recognition, the boy says to himself: "He didn't even fail to remember me this time. He didn't even know me," and experiences a sort of peace in believing that "it's over" and that he is now free of any debt to the old man, since Lucas has not "even bothered to forget me." But when the shocking news of Lucas' arrest for murder reaches him, the boy finds that Lucas has not forgotten him and that he is not at all free. His first impulse had been to evade responsibility by getting out of town, but he cannot really do this, and finally, in fascinated horror, he finds himself in the crowd watching Lucas being taken into the jail.

He then realizes that Lucas is looking at him and addressing him directly: "You, young man. Tell your uncle I wants to see him" (p. 45).

Charles Mallison would, of course, have been unable to perform his mission without the aid of Miss Habersham. He had to have—though he did not then know it—her pickup truck, but he needs even more than that her counsel and her moral backing. For reason and prudence are thoroughly on the side of his uncle, Gavin Stevens, who simply wants Lucas to get a fair trial and only such punishment as the law will properly mete out. The boy's former experiences with Lucas—and perhaps his present instincts—tell him that Lucas, in spite of his wildly improbable story, is innocent. But he is only sixteen, and too much is being asked of him; and so, without Miss Habersham's help, he could hardly have succeeded. In any case, he badly needs the confidence which an older person can instill. Miss Habersham herself is not at all at a loss. She can tell Charles: "Naturally [Lucas] wouldn't tell your uncle. He's a Negro and your uncle's a man" (p. 89). And again: "Lucas knew it would take a child—or an old woman like me: someone not concerned with probability, with evidence. Men like your uncle and Mr Hampton have had to be men too long, busy too long" (p. 89).

Charles would probably not have been able to carry out his mission successfully except for one other factor—a turn of events he could not have foreseen. The discovery that the body in Vinson Gowrie's grave was not that of Vinson at once disposed of difficulties that might well have wrecked Charles' attempt to rescue Lucas: the problem of getting the corpse into town and of bringing from the big city—in time to save Lucas—an expert capable of proving that the bullet that had killed Vinson could not have come from Lucas' gun. The discovery that the body of Jake Montgomery was lying in Vinson's grave immediately puts Lucas in the clear: there is to be no slow and perhaps difficult task of proving to the sheriff that Lucas is innocent. In this instance, Faulkner's having given a complicating twist to the plot makes for ultimate simplification of the story.

Once Charles has conveyed this surprising information to his uncle, his job is basically done, but not so with Miss Habersham's. For it turns out that Gavin, in spite of his earlier confidence that Lucas will be safe in the jail and that there will be no lynching, now, perhaps because he is at last conscious of the fact that Lucas is innocent, finds that he is not nearly so confident that there will not be a jail delivery. Accordingly, he makes his strange request of Miss Habersham. Deputies guarding the jail are "just men with guns. . . . But if a woman, a lady, a white lady . . ." Miss Habersham understands him and agrees, though she puts a little barb into the lawyer as she does so: "So I'm to sit there on that stair-case with my skirts spread or maybe better with my back against the balustrade and one foot propped against the wall of Mrs. Tubbs' kitchen while you men who never had time yesterday to ask that old nigger a few questions and so all he had last night was a boy, a child—" (p. 118). But Miss Habersham does not push her advantage further. She is eminently practical: she asks him to drive her home first so she can get her mending. If she is going to have to sit there at the jail all morning, she wants something to do with her hands. Otherwise, she points out, Mrs. Tubbs, the jailer's wife, "will think she has to talk to me" (p. 118).

Gavin Stevens is plainly puzzled at the turn of events. He is willing to admit his own moral bankruptcy: "it took an old woman and two children . . . to believe truth for no other reason than that it was truth, told by an old man in a fix deserving pity and be-lief, to someone capable of the pity even when none of them really believed him" (p. 126). Then bewilderment takes over, for he asks his nephew: "When did you really begin to believe him? . . . I want to know, you see. Maybe I'm not too old to learn either." But the boy tells him honestly, "I don't know."

Up to this point in the novel, the poor whites and the yeoman whites who live in Beat Four have been depicted as pitiless and vindictive. They constitute the basic threat to Lucas and to the law. When the sheriff and Gavin and Charles drive to the little country graveyard and prepare, now by daylight, to open the grave once more, old Mr. Gowie, the father of the dead man, comes out to challenge them. He answers fully to our expectation of what the head of the Gowie clan should look like and how he

should act. Consequently it is a brilliant stroke on Faulkner's part
to reveal to us—through the revelation to Charles—that old Mr.
Gowrie is wracked with deeply human grief. Charles, watching
the old man's face, "thought suddenly with amazement: *Why, he's
grieving:* thinking how he had seen grief twice now in two years
where he had not expected it or anyway anticipated it, where in
a sense a heart capable of breaking had no business being: once
in an old nigger who had just happened to outlive his old nigger
wife and now in a violent foulmouthed godless old man who had
happened to lose one of the six lazy idle violent more or less lawless . . . sons" (p. 161). The enlargement of the boy's sympathies
thus works in two directions to include the chief of the lynchers-
to-be as well as the man in danger of being lynched.

Because this novel has to do essentially with a young boy's growing up into manhood, and because, in any case, Lucas, by his
situation, is prevented from taking very much action, much of the
novel properly occupies itself with what is going on inside Charles
Mallison's head—with his conflicts and discoveries and dubieties
and decisions. The general parallel between this novel and *The
Unvanquished* or "The Bear" is rather close. The tension in both
cases is between a boy's ties with his community—his almost fierce
identification with it—and his revulsion from what the community seems committed to do. Thus, from the very nature of the
book, Charles Mallison's conflict of loyalties and his relation to
his own community must come in for a prominent part. This is
one of the justifications for the occurrence in this novel of the
long tirades by his uncle, Gavin Stevens.

Gavin is the person who would naturally talk to the boy about
the problems that are disturbing him, and the adult's notions
about the community, the Negro, and the nature of the law and
justice represent for the boy at once a resource and an impediment. It is against these that his own developing notions must
contend and it is these views which he must accept, repudiate, or
transcend. As for the merits of Gavin Stevens' theories as such, the
reader who is interested in them may consult the discussion of
them to be found in the Notes, page 420. But as far as the novel
itself is concerned, they are subordinate to the main matter:

Charles Mallison's development toward wider sympathies and a sharper ethical conscience.

The boy's attitude toward his homeland and toward the North, therefore, is of the first importance. The cosmopolitan reader may be surprised—and even appalled—at the notion that this Southern boy could see in his mind's eye the Northerners as consisting of "countless row on row of faces which resembled his face and spoke the same language he spoke and at times even answered to the same names he bore yet between whom and him and his there was no longer any real kinship and soon there would not even be any contact . . . because they would be too far asunder even to hear one another" (p. 152). But this vision is not an argument put forward by the author. It is simply a fact, part of a cultural situation that has to be taken into account.

So also with the observation that "every Southern boy fourteen years old" is capable of reliving the moment just before Pickett's charge at Gettysburg as if the issue had not been decided and its success were still a live possibility: "the guns are laid and ready in the woods and the furled flags are already loosened to break out and Pickett himself . . . [is] waiting for Longstreet to give the word and it's all in the balance" (p. 194). To call this passage "literary, flamboyant, historically ridiculous in terms of America today" is simply beside the point. As a matter of fact there were plenty of Southern boys in the 1940s who felt this way—and there are still some in the Mississippi of 1963. But in any case, to deny this belief to Charles Mallison is to remove one of the poles of his inner conflict and thus to misconceive the precise quality of his action. For it is just because the boy loves his native land and exults in its history that the threat of the lynching becomes for him something terrible: he sees the mob turning into one horrible face, "the composite Face of his native kind his native land, his people his blood his own with whom it had been his joy and pride and hope to be found worthy to present one united unbreakable front to the dark abyss" (p. 194).

It is because of his fierce patriotism and his resentment of the outlanders' eagerness to believe the worst that he feels so thoroughly betrayed by the action of his own people. They have been willing to believe Lucas a murderer, and now when they have found out that he is innocent, they rush home for fear that they may have to buy him "a package of tobacco" as a peace offering. Such is his bitter observation. But the bitterness is a function of his close tie to his people. Indeed, the whole experience, in which the boy meets a test of courage and experiences a deepening of his moral sensitivity, is conditioned by this tie. The particular experience that Faulkner describes is, apart from this tie, incomprehensible.

Much of the material that bears upon Charles' lover's quarrel with his community occurs in the tangled and difficult chapter 9. It is a lover's quarrel: this is how one has to describe Charles' jealous anxiety with regard to Jefferson. We are told of his "fierce desire that [his people] should be perfect because they were his and he was theirs, that furious intolerance of any one single jot or tittle less than absolute perfection—that furious almost instinctive leap and spring to defend them from anyone anywhere so that he might excoriate them himself without mercy since they were his own and he wanted no more save to stand with them unalterable and impregnable" (p. 209).

At the beginning of chapter 9, Charles and his uncle have just returned from the cemetery in Beat Four where the sheriff has opened the grave and confirmed the fact that Vinson Gowrie is not buried in it. Charles has now gone twenty-four hours without sleep, and the suspense about Lucas and the intolerable excitement of the night's foray are beginning to tell upon the boy. He feels "something hot and gritty inside his eyelids like a dust of ground glass" (p. 180). There is a tremendous compulsion to let go and slip off into forgetfulness, and yet he is too keyed up to be able to go to sleep. For one thing, he is very much concerned with how the town is going to take the discovery that they have made about Vinson Gowrie's murder.

Charles' thoughts, therefore, as they dominate chapter 9, are those of a person lightheaded from fatigue and lack of sleep, and the play of his thoughts occasionally takes on the quality of hallucination. Indeed, some of his reveries—for example, those on the spectacle of the crowd sweeping into the square and then later suddenly surging away from the jail and out of town—are tinged with more than a touch of hysteria. At one point Charles hears himself laughing and then discovers that the tears are pouring down his face. It is in this context that he has his vision of the Face, and later on, when he ruminates bitterly on the fact that the crowd seems to him to have fled, afraid to face the fact that they were wrong about Lucas, Charles has another vision, not of the Face but of "the back of a head, the composite one back of one Head one fragile mushfilled bulb indefensible as an egg yet terrible in its concorded unanimity rushing not at him but away" (p. 192).

Charles is appalled at the apparent unanimity with which the citizenry have acted, first in coming into the town to witness—he fears—a lynching, and then, with an equal unanimity, suddenly jumping into their cars and pouring out of the town square and into the roads leading to the country. The air of hallucination which this exodus takes on arises from the boy's fatigue and sleeplessness, but Charles' obsession with images of composite Faces and Heads reflects his basic concern: the notion of a community is dear to him. He does not think of himself as a member of a mere collection of people who happen to live in a place called Jefferson. Instead, he belongs to an organic society that shares basic assumptions. The proof of its organic unity is that its members can, without thinking or prior consultation, suddenly move together in a concordant action.

The tinge of hysteria comes out quite clearly when the tired boy, impatient to get home, is amused in spite of himself at the inability of his uncle to ease the family car into the solid stream of traffic flowing around the town square. Charles turns his thoughts to the plight of Miss Habersham and envisions her, now at the wheel of her light truck, trying to make her way to her house, not half a mile away, so that she can feed the chickens. He imagines Miss Habersham, since she is a practical woman, finally deciding to drive along *with* the traffic in the hope of finding a gap to turn through it, but, mile after mile, still carried along with it, until hours later she halts on a country backroad "among the crickets and treefrogs and lightningbugs and owls . . . and

. . . at last a man in his nightshirt and unlaced shoes, carrying a lantern" (p. 189) answers her questions about how to get back to Jefferson.

Such flights of fancy mingle in this chapter with the more serious issues that lurk just below Charles' immediate consciousness. The serious concerns emerge quite clearly when the boy talks to his uncle about why the crowd poured back out of Jefferson as soon as it learned what had been found in the Beat Four cemetery. Charles insists that the members of the crowd ran to avoid admitting they had been wrong, but his uncle finds this a little too simple and proceeds to give his own explanation of the meaning of their unanimous flight. Gavin sees the crowd as something quite other than a mob: his shrewd surmise is that, in the first place, there were *too many* of them to constitute a lynching mob. Gavin evidently finds in the unanimity of the community something of hope rather than menace.

As an account of the importance of the community, this whole section of *Intruder in the Dust* ought to be compared with *Light in August*. The tone is different and the focus is different. Whereas in *Light in August* the community constitutes the necessary background of much of the action and gives that action its significance but is itself almost invisible, in *Intruder in the Dust* the meaning of the community is uppermost in the minds of Gavin and Charles and constitutes the chief topic of their speculation and dialogue. Whatever we may feel about Gavin's disquisition on the subject, the boy's sense of identity with his people and his desire to protect them from themselves is in itself eloquent.

Because *Intruder in the Dust* concerns Charles' coming of age morally, it is the boy who acts and makes the moral decisions. But Lucas, though limited to a passive role, is at the center of the process. He looms powerfully at the beginning of the novel, and at the end Faulkner has managed a fine exit for him. Charles and his uncle watch Lucas walking up the street on his way to the law office, and when Charles says: "He's coming up here," his uncle says: "Yes. . . . To gloat" (p. 240). He says it good-humoredly, however, and he hastens to add that since Lucas is a gentleman, "he wont remind me to my face that I was wrong; he's just going to ask me how much he owes me as his lawyer." This turns out to be a sound prediction, but there is more to the confrontation than this. Lucas leaves with the honors of the field, and he is allowed the last word.

After Gavin has suggested to Lucas that he owes a debt to Miss Habersham and should take her some flowers, Lucas delivers the flowers and returns to the law office. Once more, he broaches the question: "I believe you got a little bill against me" (p. 244). But Gavin denies that Lucas owes him anything, and when Lucas proposes then to pay something to Charles, Gavin threatens to "have [them] both arrested, [Lucas] for corrupting a minor and [Charles] for practising law without a license." This is a bargaining maneuver which Lucas can appreciate and relish, and he more than rises to the occasion. There must have been at any rate some expenses; he will at least pay the expenses. "Name your expenses," Lucas says, "at anything within reason and let's get this thing settled" (p. 245). So Gavin tells him about breaking his fountain pen while writing down some information given him by Lucas. It cost Gavin two dollars "to have a new point put in [the fountain pen]. You owe me two dollars." So Lucas opens his coin purse and carefully counts out two dollars, the last fifty cents in pennies, explaining: "I was aiming to take them to the bank but you can save me the trip. You want to count um?" (p. 246). Gavin says that he does indeed want them counted, but that since Lucas is doing the paying, he will have to do the counting. Lucas assures the lawyer that "it's fifty of them," but Gavin insists on the counting with: "This is business," and watches while Lucas puts the pennies on the desk and makes his tally. After shoving the fifty pennies across the desk, however, Lucas keeps his seat, and Gavin is forced to say, "Now what? What are you waiting for now?" And Lucas has, indeed, the last word: "My receipt" (p. 247).

The movie, "Intruder in the Dust," omitted this bargaining and money-counting scene. In place of it, the final shot showed Lucas moving away down the street as Gavin and his nephew watched from a window in the office. As they watched him, they talked about him, and their conversation made obvious their admiration for him as a man and their indebtedness to him for having given them a lesson in the need for keeping the moral conscience sensitive and alert. But it will be a very obtuse reader who fails to see the meaning as presented in the novel. The comedy of the bargaining, the insistence on treating the issue involved strictly as a matter of business, the counting out of every jot and tittle of the small payment, and, at the end, the business-like demand for a receipt —these are ways of avoiding any sentimental awkwardness. Lucas is well aware of what he owes to Gavin Stevens and what he owes to the boy. No one knows better than Lucas himself that what the boy has done cannot be repaid with money. It was Lucas, after all, who taught the boy that there are some things that one must not try to settle with a money payment. But the token payment in this instance, meticulously counted out, not for services rendered but "for expenses," is appropriate and even tactful. The handful of coins that, years before, dropped from Charles' hand onto the floor of Lucas' cabin, has at last been accepted by Lucas. And Lucas, in his turn now, puts on the office table his own handful of coins in token of a debt beyond payment. The comic mode turns out to be just the right solution of the problem. People who understand and feel affection for each other can turn the most serious matter into a joke, and may prefer the affectionate joke for expressing, without embarrassing sentimentality, the deepest kind of understanding.

14

History and the Sense of the Tragic

(ABSALOM, ABSALOM!)

Absalom, Absalom!, in my opinion the greatest of Faulkner's novels, is probably the least well understood of all his books. The property of a great work, as T. S. Eliot remarked long ago, is to communicate before it is understood; and *Absalom, Absalom!* passes this test triumphantly. It has meant something very powerful and important to all sorts of people, and who is to say that, under the circumstances, this something was not the thing to be said to that particular reader? To the young Frenchman who had served in the *maquis,* to the young writer in New York interested in problems of technique, a little weary from having given his days and nights to the prose of Henry James, to the Shrevelin McCannons all over Canada and the United States with their myths of the South compounded out of *Uncle Tom's Cabin* and *Strange Fruit*—to all these *Absalom, Absalom!* had something to give. That is important, and I do not mean to disparage it. Yet the book has its own rights, as it were, and in proportion as we admire it, we shall want to see not merely what we can make of it but what it makes of itself. In any case, the book is more than a bottle of Gothic sauce to be used to spice up our own preconceptions about the history of American society.

Harvey Breit's sympathetic introduction to the Modern Library edition provides a useful—because it is not an extreme—instance of the typical misreading that I have in mind. Mr. Breit writes:

> It is a terrible Gothic sequence of events, a brooding tragic fable. . . . Was it the "design" that had devoured Sutpen and prevented him from avowing the very thing that would have saved the design? Was it something in the South itself, in its social, political, moral, economic origins that was responsible for Sutpen and for all the subsequent tragedy? Quentin can make no judgment: Sutpen himself had possessed courage and innocence, and the same land had nourished men and women who had delicacy of feeling and capacity for love and gifts for life.

These are questions which the typical reader asks. Shreve, the outsider, implies them. But it is significant that Quentin does not ask them. The questions are begged by the very way in which they are asked, for, put in this way, the questions undercut the problem of tragedy (which is the problem that obsesses Quentin). They imply that there is a social "solution." And they misread Sutpen's character in relation to his society and in relation to himself.

It is the quality of Sutpen's innocence that we must understand if we are to understand the meaning of his tragedy, and if we confuse it with innocence as we ordinarily use the term or with even the typical American "innocence" possessed by, say, one of Henry James' young heiresses as she goes to confront the corruption of Europe, we shall remain in the dark. Sutpen will be for us, as he was for Miss Rosa, simply the "demon"—or since we lack the justification of Miss Rosa's experience of personal horror, we shall simply appropriate the term from her as Shreve, in his half-awed, half-amused fashion, does.

Faulkner has been very careful to define Sutpen's innocence for us. "Sutpen's trouble," as Quentin's grandfather observed, "was innocence" (p. 220). And some pages later, Mr. Compson elaborates the point: "He believed that all that was necessary was courage and shrewdness and the one he knew he had and the other he believed he could learn if it were to be taught" (p. 244). It is this innocence about the nature of reality that persists, for Sutpen "believed that the ingredients of morality were like the ingredients of pie or cake and once you had measured them and balanced them and mixed them and put them into the oven it was all finished and nothing but pie or cake could come out" (p. 263). That is why Sutpen can ask Quentin's grandfather, in his innocence, not "Where did I do wrong" but "Where did I make the mistake . . . what did I do or misdo . . . whom or what injure by it to the extent which this would indicate? I had a design. To accomplish it I should require money, a house, a plantation, slaves, a family—incidentally of course, a wife. I set out to acquire these, asking no favor of any man" (p. 263).

This is an "innocence" with which most of us today ought to be acquainted. It is par excellence the innocence of modern man, though it has not, to be sure, been confined to modern times. One can find more than a trace of it in Sophocles' Oedipus, and it has its analogies with the rather brittle rationalism of Macbeth, though Macbeth tried to learn this innocence by an act of the will and proved to be a less than satisfactory pupil. But innocence of this sort can properly be claimed as a special characteristic of modern man, and one can claim further that it flourishes particularly in a secularized society.

The society into which Sutpen rides in 1833 is not a secularized society. That is not to say that the people are necessarily "good." They have their selfishness and cruelty and their snobbery, as men have always had them. Once Sutpen has acquired enough wealth and displayed enough force, the people of the community are willing to accept him. But they do not live by his code, nor do they share his innocent disregard of accepted values. Indeed, from the beginning they regard him with deep suspicion and some consternation. These suspicions are gradually mollified; there is a kind of acceptance; but as Quentin tells Shreve, Sutpen had only one friend, Quentin's grandfather, General Compson, and this in spite of the fact that the society of the lower South in the nineteenth century was rather fluid and that class lines were flexible. Men did rise in one generation from log cabins to great landed estates. But the past was important, blood was important, and Southern society thought of itself as traditional.

That Sutpen does remain outside the community comes out in

all sorts of little ways. Mr. Compson describes his "florid, swaggering gesture" with the parenthetical remark: "yes, he was underbred. It showed like this always, your grandfather said, in all his formal contacts with people" (p. 46). And Mr. Compson goes on to say that it was as if John L. Sullivan "having taught himself painfully and tediously to do the schottische, having drilled himself and drilled himself in secret . . . now believed it no longer necessary to count the music's beat, say." Yet though Sutpen's manners have been learned painfully, Sutpen has complete confidence in them. "He may have believed that your grandfather or Judge Benbow might have done it a little more effortlessly than he, but he would not have believed that anyone could have beat him in knowing when to do it and how" (p. 46).

Mr. Compson is not overrating the possession of mere manners. More is involved than Miss Rosa's opinion that Sutpen was no gentleman. For Sutpen's manners indicate his abstract approach to the whole matter of living. Sutpen would seize upon "the traditional" as a pure abstraction—which, of course, is to deny its very meaning. For him the tradition is not a way of life "handed down" or "transmitted" from the community, past and present, to the individual nurtured by it. It is an assortment of things to be possessed, not a manner of living that embodies certain values and determines men's conduct. The fetish objects are to be gained by sheer ruthless efficiency. (Sutpen even refers to "my schedule.") Thorstein Veblen would have understood Sutpen's relation to traditional culture. Sutpen is on all fours with the robber baron of the Gilded Age building a fake Renaissance palace on the banks of the Hudson. The New York robber baron's acquiring a box at the opera did not usually spring from a love of music, and one is tempted to say that Sutpen's unwillingness to acknowledge Charles Bon as his son does not spring from any particular racial feeling. Indeed, Sutpen's whole attitude toward the Negro has to be reinspected if we are to understand his relation to the Southern community into which he comes.

It would seem that the prevailing relation between the races in Jefferson is simply one more of the culture traits which Sutpen takes from the plantation community into which he has come as a boy out of the mountains of western Virginia. Sutpen takes over the color bar almost without personal feeling. His attitude toward the Negro is further clarified by his attitude toward his other part-Negro child, Clytie.[1] Mr. Compson once casually lets fall the remark that Sutpen's other children "Henry and Judith had grown up with a negro half sister of their own" (p. 109). The context of Mr. Compson's remarks makes it perfectly plain that Henry and Judith were well aware that Clytie was indeed their half-sister, and that Clytie was allowed to grow up in the house with them. This fact in itself suggests a lack of the usual Southern feeling about Negroes. Miss Rosa is much more typically Southern when she tells Quentin, with evident distaste, that Clytie and Judith sometimes slept in the same bed.

After Sutpen has returned from the war, Clytie sits in the same room with Judith and Rosa and Sutpen and listens each evening to the sound of Sutpen's voice. When Sutpen proposes to Rosa, he begins, " 'Judith, you and Clytie—' and ceased, still entering, then said, 'No, never mind. Rosa will not mind if you both hear it too, since we are short for time' " (p. 164.) Clytie is accepted naturally as part of the "we." She can be so accepted because acceptance on this level does not imperil Sutpen's "design." But acceptance of Charles Bon, in Sutpen's opinion, would. For Sutpen the matter is really as simple as that. He does not hate his first wife or feel repugnance for her child. He does not hate just as he does not love. His passion is totally committed to the design. Not even his own flesh and blood are allowed to distract him from that.

As for slavery, Sutpen does not confine himself to black chattel slavery. He ruthlessly bends anyone that he can to his will. The white French architect whom he brings into Yoknapatawpha County to build his house is as much a slave as any of his black servants: Sutpen hunts him down with dogs when he tries to escape.

The trait that most decisively sets Sutpen apart from his neighbors in this matter of race is his fighting with his slaves. Sutpen is accustomed to stripping to the waist and fighting it out with one

1. For the Sutpen Genealogy see below, p. 451.

of his slaves, not with rancor, one supposes, and not at all to punish the slave but simply to keep fit—to prove to himself and incidentally to his slaves that he is the better man. Some of Sutpen's white neighbors come to watch the fights as they might come to watch a cockfight. But it is significant that they come as to something extraordinary, a show, an odd spectacle; they would not think of fighting with their own slaves. To Miss Rosa, Sutpen's sister-in-law, the ultimate horror is that Sutpen not only arranges the show but that he enters the ring himself and fights with no holds barred—not even eye-gouging.[2]

Sutpen is not without morality or a certain code of honor. He is, according to his own lights, a just man. As he told Quentin's grandfather with reference to his rejection of his first wife: "suffice that I . . . accepted [my wife] in good faith, with no reservations about myself, and I expected as much from [her parents]. I did not [demand credentials], as one of my obscure origin might have been expected to do. . . . I accepted them at their own valuation while insisting on my part upon explaining fully about myself and my progenitors: yet they deliberately withheld from me one fact which I have reason to know they were aware would have caused me to decline the entire matter" (p. 264). But Sutpen, as he tells General Compson, "made no attempt to keep . . . that [property] which I might consider myself to have earned at the risk of my life . . . but on the contrary I declined and resigned all right and claim to this in order that I might repair whatever injustice I might be considered to have done [in abandoning my wife and child] by so providing for" them.[3]

Moreover, Sutpen is careful to say nothing in disparagement of his first wife. Quentin's grandfather comments upon "that morality which would not permit him to malign or traduce the memory of his first wife, or at least the memory of the marriage even though he felt that he had been tricked by it" (p. 272). It is Sutpen's innocence to think that justice is enough—that there is no claim that cannot be satisfied by sufficient money payment. Quentin imagines his grandfather exclaiming to Sutpen: "What kind of

2. See below, Notes, p. 426.
3. See below, Notes, p. 428.

abysmal and purblind innocence would that have been which someone told you to call virginity? what conscience to trade with which would have warranted you in the belief that you could have bought immunity from her for no other coin but justice?" (p. 265).

Sutpen thinks of himself as strictly just and he submits all of his faculties almost selflessly to the achievement of his design. His attitude toward his second wife conforms perfectly to this. Why does he choose her? For choose he does: he is not chosen—that is, involved with her through passion. The choice is calculated quite coldbloodedly (if, to our minds, naïvely and innocently). Ellen Coldfield is not the daughter of a planter. She does not possess great social prestige or beauty and she does not inherit wealth. But as the daughter of a steward in the Methodist church, she possesses in high degree the thing that Sutpen most obviously lacks —respectability. Mr. Compson sees the point very clearly. He describes Mr. Coldfield as "a man with a name for absolute and undeviating and even Puritan uprightness in a country and time of lawless opportunity, who neither drank nor gambled nor even hunted" (p. 43). For Sutpen, respectability is an abstraction like morality: you measure out so many cups of concentrated respectability to sweeten so many measures of disrespectability—"like the ingredients of pie or cake."

The choice of a father-in-law is in fact just as symbolically right: the two men resemble each other, for all the appearance of antithetical differences. Mr. Coldfield is as definitely set off from the community as is Sutpen. With the coming of the Civil War, this rift widens to an absolute break. Mr. Coldfield denounces secession, closes his store, and finally nails himself up in the attic of his house, where he spends the last three years of his life. No more than Sutpen is he a coward: like Sutpen, too, his scheme of human conduct is abstract and mechanical. "Doubtless the only pleasure which he had ever had . . . was in [his money's] representation of a balance in whatever spiritual counting-house he believed would some day pay his sight drafts on self-denial and fortitude" (p. 84).

This last is Mr. Compson's surmise; but I see no reason to question it or to quarrel with the motive that Mr. Compson assigns for Coldfield's objection to the Civil War: "not so much to the idea of pouring out human blood and life, but at the idea of waste: of wearing out and eating up and shooting away material in any cause whatever" (p. 83). Mr. Coldfield is glad when he sees the country that he hates obviously drifting into a fatal war, for he regards the inevitable defeat of the South as the price it will pay for having erected its economic edifice "not on the rock of stern morality but on the shifting sands of opportunism and moral brigandage" (p. 260).

Some critics have been so unwary as to assume that this view of the Civil War is one that the author would enjoin upon the reader, but William Faulkner is neither so much of a Puritan nor so much of a materialist as is Mr. Coldfield. The truth of the matter is that Mr. Coldfield's morality is simply Sutpen's turned inside out. Faulkner may or may not have read Tawney's *Religion and the Rise of Capitalism;* but on the evidence of *Absalom, Absalom!* he would certainly have understood it.

Sutpen is further defined by his son, Charles Bon. Bon is a mirror image, a reversed shadow of his father. Like his father, he suddenly appears out of nowhere as a man of mystery: "a personage who in the remote Mississippi of that time must have appeared almost phoenix-like, fullsprung from no childhood, born of no woman and impervious to time" (p. 74). Like his father, Bon has an octoroon "wife," whom he is prepared to repudiate along with his child by her. Like his father, he stands beyond good and evil. But Bon is Byronic, rather than the go-getter; spent, rather than full of pushing vitality; sophisticated, rather than confidently naïve.

Sutpen is the secularized Puritan; Bon is the lapsed Roman Catholic. Whereas Sutpen is filled with a fresh and powerful energy, Bon is world-weary and tired. Bon is a fatalist, but Sutpen believes in sheer will: "anyone could look at him and say, *Given the occasion and the need, this man can and will do anything*" (p. 46). Bon possesses too much knowledge; Sutpen on the other hand is "innocent." The one has gone beyond the distinction between good and evil; the other has scarcely arrived at that distinction.

The father and the son define the extremes of the human world: one aberration corresponds to—and eventually destroys—the other. The reader is inclined to view Bon with sympathy as a person gravely wronged, and he probably agrees with Quentin's interpretation of Bon's character: that Bon finally put aside all ideas of revenge and asked for nothing more than a single hint of recognition of his sonship. Faulkner has certainly treated Bon with full dramatic sympathy, as he has Sutpen, for that matter. But our sympathy ought not to obscure for us Bon's resemblances to his father, or the complexity of his character. Unless we care to go beyond Quentin and Shreve in speculation, Charles Bon displays toward his octoroon mistress and their son something of the cool aloofness that his father displays toward him. If he is the instrument by which Sutpen's design is wrecked, his own irresponsibility (or at the least, his lack of concern for his own child) wrecks his child's life. We shall have to look to Judith to find responsible action and a real counter to Sutpen's ruthlessness.

These other children of Sutpen—Judith and Henry—reflect further light upon the character of Sutpen—upon his virtues and upon his prime defect. They represent a mixture of the qualities of Sutpen and Coldfield. Judith, it is made plain, has more of the confidence and boldness of her father; Henry, more of the conventionality and the scruples of his maternal grandfather. It is the boy Henry who vomits at the sight of his father, stripped to the waist in the ring with the black slave. Judith watches calmly. And it is Judith who urges the coachman to race the coach on the way to church.

Henry is, of the two, the more vulnerable. After Sutpen has forbidden marriage between Bon and Judith and during the long period in which Henry remains self-exiled with his friend Bon, he is the one tested to the limit by his father's puzzling silence and by his friend's fatalistic passivity. But he has some of his father's courage, and he has what his father does not have: love. At the last moment he kills, though he kills what he loves and apparently for love. It is the truly tragic dilemma. Faulkner has not chosen to put Henry's story in the forefront of the novel, but he has not needed to do so. For the sensitive reader the various baffles through which that act of decision reaches us do not muffle but, through their resonance, magnify the decisive act.

Henry's later course is, again, only implied. We know that in the end—his last four years—he reverted to the course of action of his grandfather Coldfield, and shut himself up in the house. But there is a difference. This is no act of abstract defiance and hate. Henry has assumed responsibility, has acted, has been willing to abide the consequences of that action, and now, forty years later, has come home to die.

If it is too much to call Henry's course of action renunciation and expiation, there is full justification for calling Judith's action just that. Judith has much of her father in her, but she is a woman, and she also has love. As Mr. Compson conjectures: "And Judith: how else to explain her but this way? Surely Bon could not have corrupted her to fatalism in twelve days. . . . No: anything but a fatalist, who was the Sutpen with the ruthless Sutpen code of taking what it wanted provided it were strong enough. . . . [Judith said] *I love, I will accept no substitute; something has happened between him and my father; if my father was right, I will never see him again, if wrong he will come or send for me; if happy I can be I will, if suffer I must I can*" (p. 121). It is Judith who invites Charles Bon's octoroon mistress to visit Bon's grave. It is Judith who, on his mother's death, sends to New Orleans for Bon's son and tries to rear him. Some years later she also tries to free him (as Quentin conjectures) by promising to take care of his Negro wife and child if he will go to the North to pass as white, and Quentin imagines her saying to him: "Call me Aunt Judith, Charles" (p. 208). But Quentin's conjectures aside, we know that Judith did take him into the house when he was stricken with yellow fever, and that she died nursing him. The acknowledgment of blood kinship is made; Sutpen's design is repudiated; the boy, even though he has the "taint" of Negro blood, is not turned away from the door.

Both Henry's action, the violent turning away from the door with a bullet, and Judith's, the holding open the door not merely to Bon, her fiancé, but literally to his part-Negro son, are human actions, as Sutpen's actions are not. Both involve renunciation, and both are motivated by love. The suffering of Henry and Judith is not meaningless, and their very capacity for suffering marks them as having transcended their father's radical and disabling defect.

Faulkner has not put the contrast between the children and their father explicitly nor with quite this emphasis. In the first place, it is Sutpen's story that he is telling (or rather it is Sutpen's story that Quentin and Shreve are trying to recreate). The stories of Judith and, particularly, Henry are dealt with only obliquely. But the Judith, who, in the hard and poverty-stricken years after the war, learns to plough like a man and who collects the dimes and quarters in the rusty can to pay for the headstone for Charles Bon's grave and who asks Bon's son to call her Aunt Judith is a very different person from the dreamy and willful girl to whom Henry introduced Bon at Sutpen's Hundred. And on the night when Quentin and Miss Rosa break into the decaying mansion and find Henry, who has come home to die, what looks out from Henry's eyes is not "innocence." Faulkner does not name it, but he does dramatize for us Quentin's reaction to it. At the least, it is knowledge, a fearful knowledge bought with heroic suffering.

One must not alter the focus of the novel by making wisdom won through suffering the issue. But the consequences entailed upon Judith and Henry have to be mentioned if only to discourage a glib Gothicizing of the novel or forcing its meaning into an overshallow sociological interpretation.

Miss Rosa feels that the Coldfields are all cursed; and certainly the impact of Sutpen upon her personally is damning: she remains rigid with horror and hate for forty-three years. But it is Miss Rosa only who is damned. Judith is not damned; nor am I sure that Henry is. Judith and Henry are not caught in an uncomprehending stasis. There is development: they grow and learn at however terrible a price. Uncle Ike in "The Bear" also inherits a curse: an ancestral crime that, for him at least, involves the necessity for renunciation and expiation. I cannot see that the "curse" inherited by Judith and Henry is essentially different in nature or that the general moral pattern in *Absalom, Absalom!* differs radically from that in "The Bear."

Sutpen, as has been pointed out, never learns anything; he remains innocent to the end. As Quentin sees the character: when Charles Bon first comes to his door, Sutpen does not call it "retribution, no sins of the father come home to roost; not even calling it bad luck, but just a mistake . . . just an old mistake in fact which a man of courage and shrewdness . . . could still combat if he could only find out what the mistake had been" (p. 267). I have remarked that Sutpen's innocence is peculiarly the innocence of modern man. For like modern man, Sutpen does not believe in Jehovah. He does not believe in the goddess Tyche. He is not the victim of bad luck. He has simply made a "mistake." He "had been too successful," Mr. Compson tells Quentin; his "was that solitude of contempt and distrust which success brings to him who gained it because he was strong instead of merely lucky" (p. 103).

Marshall McLuhan has somewhere pointed out that the more special feats of James Fenimore Cooper's woodsmen are always attributed to their skill, but those of William Gilmore Simms' woodsmen, to their luck. On this perhaps whimsical test of the sectional character, Sutpen turns out to be a Yankee, not a Southerner at all. At any rate, Sutpen resembles the modern American, whose character, as Arthur M. Schlesinger has put it, "is bottomed on the profound conviction that nothing in the world is beyond [his] power to accomplish." [4] Sutpen is a "planner" who works by blueprint and on a schedule. He is rationalistic and scientific, not traditional, not religious, not even superstitious.

We must be prepared to take such traits into account if we attempt to read the story of Sutpen's fall as a myth of the fall of the Old South. Unless we are content with some rather rough and ready analogies, the story of the fall of the house of Sutpen may prove less than parallel. The fall of the house of Compson as depicted in *The Sound and the Fury* is also sometimes regarded as a kind of exemplum of the fall of the old aristocratic order in the South, and perhaps in some sense it is. But the breakup of these two families comes from very different causes, and if we wish to use them to point a moral or illustrate a bit of social

4. "What Then is the American, This New Man," *American Historical Review*, 48 (1943), 244.

history, surely they point to different morals and illustrate different histories. Mr. Compson, whose father, General Compson, regarded Sutpen as a "little underbred," has failed through a kind of overrefinement. He has lost his grip on himself; he has ceased finally to believe in the values of the inherited tradition. He is a fatalist and something of an easy cynic. His vices are diametrically opposed to those of Thomas Sutpen, and so are his virtues.

One could even argue that Faulkner's most pertinent account of the fall of the Old South is set forth in his story of the rise of the Snopes clan. The latter-day Compsons and Sartorises and Benbows lack the requisite resolution and toughness to cope with the conditions of the modern world. The Snopeses, therefore, because they recognize no values but self-interest and have unlimited vitality, threaten to take over the modern South. But the story of Flem Snopes is a kind of success story, not a tragedy; and if Snopesism is destroying the older aristocracy, it is not Snopesism that destroys Sutpen. Indeed, Sutpen is at some points more nearly allied to Flem than he is to the Compsons and the Sartorises. Like Flem, he is a new man with no concern for the past and has a boundless energy with which to carry out his aggressive plans.

Yet to couple Sutpen with Flem calls for an immediate qualification. Granting that both men subsist outside the community and in one way or another prey upon the community, Sutpen is by contrast a heroic and tragic figure. He achieves a kind of grandeur. Even the obsessed Miss Rosa sees him as great, not as petty and sordid. His innocence resembles that of Oedipus (who, like him, had been corrupted by success and who put his confidence in his own shrewdness). His courage resembles that of Macbeth, and like Macbeth he is "resolute to try the last." Perhaps the most praiseworthy aspect of Faulkner is his ability to create a character of heroic proportions and to invest his downfall with something like tragic dignity. The feat is, in our times, sufficiently rare.

Faulkner's concern with innocence runs through all the novels. One of General Compson's impressions of Sutpen is that he spoke "with that frank innocence which we call 'of a child' except that a human child is the only living creature that is never either frank or innocent" (p. 246). Nor, as we have seen, are Faulkner's women innocent. The only people in Faulkner who are "innocent" are adult males; and their innocence amounts finally to a trust in rationality—an overweening confidence that plans work out, that life is simpler than it is.[5]

But though Faulkner criticizes rationalism, he never glorifies irrationality. Even Uncle Isaac in "The Bear" does not merely accept nature, content to contemplate its richness and perennial vitality. He does not argue that because the spoliation of the wilderness is a rape that brings its own curse, man ought to cut no trees. He does not believe that it is possible for man to go back to Adam's existence in the happy Garden. Uncle Isaac acts; he helps kill the bear; he goes on the hunt to the end of his days. But he knows that efficiency as an end in itself is self-defeating. It is man's fate to struggle against nature; yet it is wisdom to learn that the fight cannot finally be won, and that the contest has to be conducted with love and humility and in accordance with a code of honor. Man realizes himself in the struggle; but the ultimate to be gained in the struggle is wisdom. Sutpen never really acquires wisdom, for he never loses his innocence. He will never learn. The figure of Time with his scythe never received a more grim embodiment than it does in the grizzled Wash Jones raising his rusty implement to strike Sutpen down.

Sutpen belongs to the company of Conrad's Kurtz (though perhaps Kurtz did learn something at the very end; Marlow thinks that he did). But it is not difficult to find his compeers closer to home. I have already suggested that we might search for them with good hope of success among the brownstone mansions of post-Civil-War New York. But it is easy to locate them in recent fiction. As was remarked in an earlier chapter, the Southern novelists of our time have been fascinated by this kind of character, perhaps because for them he still has some aura of the monstrous, and is still not quite to be taken for granted.

Up to this point we have been concerned with the character of Thomas Sutpen, especially in his relation to the claims of the family and the community. We have treated him as if he were a historical figure, but of course he is not. More than most charac-

5. See below, Notes, p. 429.

ters in literature, Thomas Sutpen is an imaginative construct, a set of inferences—an hypothesis put forward to account for several peculiar events. For the novel *Absalom, Absalom!* does not merely tell the story of Thomas Sutpen, but dramatizes the process by which two young men of the twentieth century construct the character Thomas Sutpen. Fascinated by the few known events of his life and death, they try, through inference and conjecture and guesswork, to ascertain what manner of man he was. The novel then has to do not merely with the meaning of Sutpen's career but with the nature of historical truth and with the problem of how we can "know" the past. The importance of this latter theme determines the very special way in which the story of Sutpen is mediated to us through a series of partial disclosures, informed guesses, and constantly revised deductions and hypotheses.

Young Quentin Compson, just on the eve of leaving Mississippi for his first year at Harvard, is summoned by Miss Rosa Coldfield and made to listen to the story of her wicked brother-in-law, Thomas Sutpen. Sutpen had been a friend of Quentin's grandfather, General Compson, and as Quentin waits to drive Miss Rosa out to Sutpen's Hundred after dark, as she has requested, Quentin's father tells him what he knows about the Sutpen story.

Nobody had really understood the strange events that had occurred at Sutpen's Hundred—the quarrel between Thomas Sutpen and Henry, the disappearance of Henry with his friend Charles Bon, the forbidding of the marriage between Judith and Bon, and later, and most sensational of all, Henry's shooting of his friend Charles Bon at the very gates of Sutpen's Hundred in 1865. Mr. Compson makes a valiant effort to account for what happened. What evidently sticks in his mind is the fact that Charles Bon had an octoroon mistress in New Orleans. Presumably Judith had told General Compson or his wife about finding the octoroon's picture on Charles Bon's dead body. But in any case the visit, at Judith's invitation, of the woman to Charles Bon's grave would have impressed the whole relationship upon General Compson and upon his son, Mr. Compson. Mr. Compson thinks that it was the fact of the mistress that made Thomas Sutpen oppose Bon's marriage to his daughter, but that Henry was so deeply committed to his friend that he refused to believe what his father told him about Bon's mistress, chose to go away with Charles, and only at the very end, when Charles Bon was actually standing before his father's house, used the gun to prevent the match.

It is not a very plausible theory. For though it could account for Sutpen's opposition to Bon, it hardly explains Henry's violent action, taken so late in the day. Mr. Compson does the best that he can with this aspect of the story and says (p. 97): "[Henry] loved grieved and killed, still grieving and, I believe, still loving Bon, the man to whom he gave four years of probation, four years in which to renounce and dissolve the other marriage, knowing that the four years of hoping and waiting would be in vain." But Mr. Compson has to concede that, after all, "it's just incredible. It just does not explain. . . . something is missing" (p. 100).

Quentin's other informant about the Sutpens is Miss Rosa Coldfield, Sutpen's sister-in-law. Miss Rosa clearly does not understand what happened. She exclaims that "Judith's marriage [was] forbidden without rhyme or reason" (p. 18), and her only theory for accounting for the murder is that Sutpen was a demon, and as a demon, dowered his children with a curse which made them destroy themselves. Even Judith evidently did not know why her marriage was forbidden nor did she know why her brother killed Charles Bon. After the murder and Henry's flight, Judith tells Mrs. Compson, the General's wife, that the war will soon be over now because "they [the Confederate soldiers] have begun to shoot one another" (p. 128). The remark indicates her bafflement as well as her despair.

By the time we have reached the end of section 5—that is, half way through the book—we have been given most of the basic facts of the Sutpen story but no satisfactory interpretation of it. We know the story of Sutpen's life in the Mississippi community pretty much as the community itself knew it, but the events do not make sense. The second half of the book may be called an attempt at interpretation. When section 6 opens, we are in Quentin's room at Harvard and Quentin is reading a letter from his father telling about the death of Miss Rosa Coldfield. From this time on until past midnight, Quentin and Shreve discuss the story of Sutpen and make their own conjectures as to what actually happened. In this second half of the book there are, to be sure, further disclosures about Sutpen, especially with reference to his early life before he came to Mississippi. Sutpen, it turns out, had once told the story of his early life to General Compson, and his information had been passed on to Quentin through Mr. Compson. As Shreve and Quentin talk, Quentin feeds into the conversation from time to time more material from his father's and grandfather's memory of events, and one very brilliant scene which he himself remembers: how, hunting quail on a gray autumn day, he and his father came upon the graves in the Sutpen family graveyard and his father told him the touching story of Judith's later life. But as the last four sections of the book make plain, we are dealing with an intricate imaginative reconstruction of events leading up to the murder of Charles Bon—a plausible account of what may have happened, not what necessarily did happen.

If the reader reminds himself how little hard fact there is to go on—how much of the most important information about the motivation of the central characters comes late and is, at best, vague and ambiguous—he will appreciate how much of the story of Sutpen and especially of Sutpen's children has been spun out of the imaginations of Quentin and Shreve.[6]

Absalom, Absalom! is indeed from one point of view a wonderful detective story—by far the best of Faulkner's several flirtations with this particular genre. It may also be considered to yield a nice instance of how the novelist works, for Shreve and Quentin both show a good deal of the insights of the novelist and his imaginative capacity for constructing plausible motivations around a few given facts. This theme would obviously be one dear to Faulkner's heart. Most important of all, however, *Absalom, Absalom!* is a persuasive commentary upon the thesis that much of "history" is really a kind of imaginative construction. The past always remains at some level a mystery, but if we are to hope to understand it in any wise, we must enter into it and project ourselves imaginatively into the attitudes and emotions of the histori-

6. See below, Notes, p. 429.

cal figures. Both of the boys make this sort of projection, though one would expect it to be easy for Quentin and difficult for Shreve. Actually, it does not work out in this way, for Shreve enters into the reconstruction of the past with ardor. He finds it, in his lack of any serious emotional commitment, a fascinating game—in fact, he consistently treats it as a game, saying "Let me play now." The novelty of fitting actual human beings into roles that he had earlier connected only with the stage intrigues him. At one point he teases Quentin by saying "Jesus, the South is fine, isn't it. It's better than the theatre, isn't it. It's better than Ben Hur, isn't it" (p. 217). Quentin, on the other hand, is too much involved—too fully committed to the problems and the issue—actually to enjoy the reconstruction. He feels a compulsion to do so, of course, the same compulsion that had caused him, against his better judgment, to go up into the bedroom at Sutpen's Hundred and look upon the wasted face of Henry Sutpen.

To note that the account of the Sutpens which Shreve and Quentin concoct is largely an imaginative construct is not to maintain that it is necessarily untrue. Their version of events is plausible, and the author himself—for whatever that may be worth—suggests that some of the scenes which they palpably invented were probably true: e.g. "the slight dowdy woman . . . whom Shreve and Quentin had . . . invented" and who was probably "true enough" (p. 335). But it is worth remarking that we do not "know," apart from the Quentin-Shreve semifictional process, many events which a casual reader assumes actually happened.

To provide some illustrations: Charles Bon's telling Henry "So it's the miscegenation, not the incest, which you cant bear" (p. 356) is a remark that rests upon no known fact. It is a conjecture, though a plausible one. Again, Bon's agonized waiting for his father to give him the merest hint of a father's recognition and Bon's comment that this was all that Sutpen needed to do to stop his courtship of Judith are both surmises made by Quentin and Shreve. So too is the scene in which the boys imagine the visit of Bon and Henry to New Orleans and hear Bon's mother's bitter question, "So she [Judith] has fallen in love with him" (p. 335), and listen to her harsh laughter as she looks at Henry. The wonderfully touching scene in which Judith asks Charles Bon's son to call her "Aunt Judith" is presumably an imaginative construction made by Quentin.

One ought to observe in passing that in allowing the boys to make their guesses about what went on, Faulkner plays perfectly fair. Some of their guesses have the clear ring of truth. They are obviously right. On the other hand, some are justified by the flimsiest possible reasoning. For example, notice Shreve's argument (p. 344) that it was Henry, not Bon, who was wounded at the battle of Shiloh.

One of the most important devices used in the novel is the placing of Shreve in it as a kind of sounding board and mouthpiece. By doing so, Faulkner has in effect acknowledged the attitude of the modern "liberal," twentieth-century reader, who is basically rational, skeptical, without any special concern for history, and pretty well emancipated from the ties of family, race, or section. In fact, Shreve sounds very much like certain literary critics who have written on Faulkner. It was a stroke of genius on Faulkner's part to put such a mentality squarely inside the novel, for this is a way of facing criticism from that quarter and putting it into its proper perspective.

Shreve teases Quentin playfully and even affectionately, but it is not mere teasing. When Shreve strikes a pose and in his best theatrical manner assigns a dramatic speech to Wash, Faulkner, in one of his few intrusions as author, observes: "This was not flippancy. . . . It too was just that protective coloring of levity behind which the youthful shame of being moved hid itself." The author remarks on Quentin's "sullen bemusement" but also on the "flipness, the strained clowning" (p. 280) on the part of both.

It is curious that Shreve, all of whose facts have been given him by or through Quentin, is allowed in the latter chapters to do most of the imaginative work—far more, I should say, than is allowed to Quentin. This is the more interesting since Quentin has met three of the participants in the tragedy face to face and is filled with vivid impressions of the scene. Perhaps the fact that Quentin is so involved makes it difficult or distasteful for him to talk. At any rate, it is the "outsider" who does most of the imaginative reconstruction. Quentin's role at times becomes merely that of a check or brake upon Shreve's fertile imagination.

The last sections of the novel tell us a great deal about Shreve's and Quentin's differing attitudes toward history and of their own relation to history. Shreve has been genuinely moved by the story of Sutpen. For all of his teasing, he is concerned to understand, and late in the evening he says to Quentin: "Listen. I'm not trying to be funny, smart. I just want to understand it if I can and I dont know how to say it better. Because it's something my people haven't got" (p. 361). And though he cannot suppress his bantering tone in alluding to the Southern heritage—it is "a kind of entailed birthright . . . of never forgiving General Sherman, so that forevermore as long as your childrens' children produce children you wont be anything but a descendant of a long line of colonels killed in Pickett's charge"—Shreve's question is seriously put. What is it that Quentin as a Southerner has that Shreve does not have? It is a sense of the presence of the past, and with it, and through it, a personal access to a tragic vision. For the South has experienced defeat and guilt, and has an ingrained sense of the stubbornness of human error and of the complexity of history. The matter has been recently put very well in C. Vann Woodward's *The Burden of Southern History:* "The experience of evil and the experience of tragedy," he writes, "are parts of the Southern heritage that are as difficult to reconcile with the American legend of innocence and social felicity as the experience of poverty and defeat are to reconcile with the legends of abundance and success." [7]

In remarking on how little of hard fact one has to go on, we should bear in mind particularly the question of Bon's Negro blood and of his kinship to Henry. Quentin says flatly (p. 269) that "nobody ever did know if Bon ever knew Sutpen was his father or not." Did anyone ever know whether Bon knew that he was part Negro? In their reconstruction of the story, Shreve and Quentin assume (p. 356) that Bon was aware that he was Henry's part-Negro half-brother (though on page 327 Quentin and Shreve

7. Baton Rouge, Louisiana State University Press, 1960, p. 21.

assume that Bon did not know that he had Negro blood). If in fact Bon did have Negro blood, how did Shreve and Quentin come by that knowledge? As we have seen, neither Judith nor Miss Rosa had any inkling of it. Nor did Mr. Compson. Early in the novel he refers to Bon's "sixteenth part negro son." Since Bon's mistress was an octoroon, his son could be one-sixteenth Negro only on the assumption that Charles Bon was of pure white blood—and this is evidently what Mr. Compson does assume. Mr. Compson, furthermore, knows nothing about Bon's kinship to Henry.

The conjectures made by Shreve and Quentin—even if taken merely as conjectures—render the story of Sutpen plausible. They make much more convincing sense of the story than Mr. Compson's notions were able to make. And that very fact suggests their probable truth. But are they more than plausible theories? Is there any real evidence to support the view that Bon was Sutpen's son by a part-Negro wife? There is, and the way in which this evidence is discovered constitutes another, and the most decisive, justification for regarding *Absalom, Absalom!* as a magnificent detective story. Precisely what was revealed and how it was revealed are worth a rather careful review.

In the course of his conversation with Quentin, Shreve objects that Mr. Compson "seems to have got an awful lot of delayed information awful quick, after having waited forty-five years" (p. 266). Quentin confirms the fact that his father *had* got delayed information—had got it from Quentin himself—had got it indeed the day after "we" (that is, Quentin and Miss Rosa) had gone out to Sutpen's Hundred. A little later (p. 274), when Quentin tells Shreve of Sutpen's long conversation with General Compson about his "design" and about the "mistake" that Sutpen had made in trying to carry it out, Shreve asks Quentin whether General Compson had then really known what Sutpen was talking about. Quentin answers that General Compson had not known; and Shreve, pressing the point, makes Quentin admit that he himself "wouldn't have known what anybody was talking about" if he "hadn't been out there and seen Clytie." The secret of Bon's birth, then, was revealed to Quentin on that particular visit.[8] Shreve's

8. See below, Notes, p. 436.

way of phrasing it implies that it was from Clytie that Quentin had got his information, but, as we shall see, it is unlikely that Clytie was Quentin's informant. In any case, when Shreve puts his question about seeing Clytie, he did not know that another person besides Clytie and her nephew was living at Sutpen's Hundred.

Miss Rosa has sensed that "something"—she does not say *someone*—was "living hidden in that house." When she and Quentin visit Sutpen's Hundred, her intuition is confirmed. The hidden something turns out to be Henry Sutpen, now come home to die. Presumably, it was from Henry Sutpen that Quentin learned the crucial facts. Or did he? Here again Faulkner may seem to the reader either teasingly reticent or, upon reflection, brilliantly skillful.

We know from the last section of the book that after Miss Rosa had come down from the upstairs room with her "eyes wide and unseeing like a sleepwalker's" (p. 370), Quentin felt compelled to go up to that room and see what was there. He does go, though Faulkner does not take us with him into the room. He descends the stairs, walks out of the house, overtakes Miss Rosa, and drives her home. Later that night, however, after he has returned to his own home and is lying sleepless, he cannot—even by clenching his eyelids—shut out his vision of the bed with its yellowed sheets and its yellowed pillow and the wasted yellow face lying upon it, a face with closed "almost transparent eyelids" (p. 373). As Quentin tosses, unable to erase the picture from his eyes, we are vouchsafed one tiny scrap of his conversation with Henry, a conversation that amounts to no more than Quentin's question "And you are—?" and Henry's answer that he is indeed Henry Sutpen, that he has been there four years, and that he has come home to die. How extended was the conversation? How long did it last? Would Henry Sutpen have volunteered to a stranger his reason for having killed Charles Bon? Or would Quentin Compson, awed and aghast at what he saw, put such questions as these to the wasted figure upon the bed? We do not know and Faulkner —probably wisely—has not undertaken to reconstruct this interview for us. (It is possible, of course, that Henry did tell Miss Rosa why he had killed Bon and that Miss Rosa told Quentin in the course of their long ride back to Jefferson.) [9]

At all events, the whole logic of *Absalom, Absalom!* argues that *only* through the presence of Henry in the house was it possible for Quentin—and through Quentin his father and Shreve and those of us who read the book—to be made privy to the dark secret that underlay the Sutpen tragedy.

At the end of the novel Shreve is able to shrug off the tragic implications and resume the tone of easy banter. His last comment abounds with the usual semisociological clichés: the Negroes "will bleach out again like the rabbits and the birds. . . . In a few thousand years, I who regard you will also have sprung from the loins of African kings" (p. 378). Though the spell of the story has been powerful enough to fire his imagination and involve all his sympathies, he is not personally committed, and we can see him drawing back from the tragic problem and becoming again the cheery, cynical, common-sense man of the present day. In the long perspective of history, how few issues really matter! The long perspective is antihistorical: make it long enough and any "sense of history" evaporates. Lengthen it further still and the human dimension itself evaporates.

From his stance of detachment, Shreve suddenly, and apropos of nothing, puts to Quentin the question "Why do you hate the South?" And Quentin's passionate denial that he hates it tells its own story of personal involvement and distress. The more naïve reader may insist on having an answer: "Well, does he hate it?" And the response would have to be, I suppose, another question: "Does Stephen Daedalus hate Dublin?" Or, addressing the question to Stephen's creator, "Did James Joyce hate Ireland?" The answer here would surely have to be yes and no. In any case, Joyce was so obsessed with Ireland and so deeply involved in it that he spent his life writing about it.

At this point, however, it may be more profitable to put a different question. What did the story of Sutpen mean to Quentin? Did it mean to him what it has apparently meant to most of the

---

9. For a time scheme of the night visit to Sutpen's Hundred see below, p. 440.

critics who have written on this novel—the story of the curse of slavery and how it involved Sutpen and his children in ruin? Surely this is to fit the story to a neat, oversimple formula. Slavery was an evil. But other slaveholders avoided Sutpen's kind of defeat and were exempt from his special kind of moral blindness.[10]

What ought to be plain, in any event, is that it is Henry's part in the tragic tale that affects Quentin the most. Quentin had seen Henry with his own eyes and Henry's involvement in slavery was only indirect. Even Henry's dread of miscegenation was fearfully complicated with other issues, including the problem of incest. In view of what we learn of Quentin in *The Sound and the Fury,* the problem of incest would have fascinated him and made him peculiarly sensitive to Henry's torment. Aside from his personal problem, however, Sutpen's story had for Quentin a special meaning that it did not have for Shreve.

The story embodied the problem of evil and of the irrational: Henry was beset by conflicting claims; he was forced to make intolerably hard choices—between opposed goods or between conflicting evils. Had Henry cared much less for Bon, or else much less for Judith, he might have promoted the happiness of one without feeling that he was sacrificing that of the other. Or had he cared much less for either and much more for himself, he might have won a cool and rational detachment, a coign of vantage from which even objections to miscegenation and incest would appear to be irrational prejudices, and honor itself a quaint affectation whose saving was never worth the price of a bullet. Had Henry been not necessarily wiser but simply more cynical or more gross or more selfish, there would have been no tragedy.

To say that Quentin was peculiarly susceptible to this meaning of Henry's story is not to make of Shreve a monster of inhumanly cool irrationality. But Shreve is measurably closer to the skepticism and detachment that allow modern man to dismiss the irrational claims from which Quentin cannot free himself and which he honors to his own cost.

The reader of *Absalom, Absalom!* might well follow Quentin's example. If he must find in the story of the House of Sutpen some-

10. See below, Notes, p. 441.

thing that has special pertinence to the tragic dilemmas of the South, the aspect of the story to stress is not the downfall of Thomas Sutpen, a man who is finally optimistic, rationalistic, and afflicted with elephantiasis of the will. Instead, he ought to attend to the story of Sutpen's children.

The story of Judith, though muted and played down in terms of the whole novel, is one of the most moving that Faulkner has ever written. She has in her the best of her father's traits. She is the stout-hearted little girl who witnesses without flinching scenes which force poor Henry to grow sick and vomit. She is the young woman who falls in love with a fascinating stranger, the friend of her brother, who means to marry him in spite of her father's silent opposition, and who matches her father's strength of will with a quiet strength of her own. She endures the horror of her fiancé's murder and buries his body. She refuses to commit suicide; she keeps the place going for her father's return. Years later it is Judith who sees to it that Bon's mistress has an opportunity to visit his grave, who brings Bon's child to live with her after his mother's death and, at least in Quentin's reconstruction of events, tries to get the little boy to recognize her as his aunt and to set him free, pushing him on past the barriers of color.[11] When she fails to do so, she still tries to protect him. She nurses him when he sickens of yellow fever, and she dies with him in the epidemic. She is one of Faulkner's finest characters of endurance—and not merely through numb, bleak Stoicism but also through compassion and love. Judith is doomed by misfortunes not of her making, but she is not warped and twisted by them. Her humanity survives them.

Because Henry knew what presumably Judith did not know, the secret of Bon's birth, his struggle—granted the circumstances of his breeding, education, and environment—was more difficult than Judith's. He had not merely to endure but to act, and yet any action that he could take would be cruelly painful. He was compelled to an agonizing decision. One element that rendered tragic any choice he might make is revealed in Henry's last action, his coming home to die. One might have thought that after

11. See below, Notes, p. 442.

some forty years, Henry would have stayed in Mexico or California or New York or wherever he was, but the claims of locality and family are too strong and he returns to Sutpen's Hundred.

Absalom, Absalom! is the most memorable of Faulkner's novels —and memorable in a very special way. Though even the intelligent reader may feel at times some frustration with the powerful but darkly involved story, with its patches of murkiness and its almost willful complications of plot, he will find himself haunted by individual scenes and episodes, rendered with almost compulsive force. He will probably remember vividly such a scene as Henry's confrontation of his sister Judith after four years of absence at war—the boy in his "patched and faded gray tunic," crashing into the room in which his sister stands clutching against her partially clothed nakedness the yellowed wedding dress, and shouting to her: "Now you cant marry him . . . because he's dead . . . I killed him" (p. 172). Or there is Miss Rosa's recollection of the burial of Charles Bon. As she talks to Quentin she relives the scene: the "slow, maddening rasp, rasp, rasp, of the saw" and "the flat deliberate hammer blows" as Wash and another white man work at the coffin through the "slow and sunny afternoon," with Judith in her faded dress and "faded gingham sunbonnet . . . giving them directions about making it." Miss Rosa, who has never seen Bon alive and for whom he is therefore a fabulous creature, a mere dream, recalls that she "tried to take the full weight of the coffin" as they carried it down the stairs in order "to prove to myself that he was really in it" (p. 151).

There is the wonderful scene of Thomas Sutpen's return to Sutpen's Hundred, the iron man dismounting from his "gaunt and jaded horse," saying to Judith, "Well, daughter," and touching his bearded lips to her forehead. There follows an exchange that is as laconically resonant as any in Greek tragedy: " 'Henry's not—?' 'No. He's not here.'—'Ah. And—?' 'Yes. Henry killed him' " (p. 159). With the last sentence Judith bursts into tears, but it is the only outburst of which Judith is ever guilty.

The reader will remember also the scenes of Sutpen's boyhood and young manhood—perhaps most vivid of all of them, that in which the puzzled boy is turned away from the plantation door by the liveried servant. Sometimes the haunting passage is one of mere physical description: the desolate Sutpen burial ground with the "flat slabs . . . cracked across the middle by their own weight (and vanishing into the hole where the brick coping of one vault had fallen in was a smooth faint path worn by some small animal—possum probably—by generations of some small animal since there could have been nothing to eat in the grave for a long time) though the lettering was quite legible: *Ellen Cold-field Sutpen. Born October 9, 1817. Died January 23, 1863*" (p. 188). One remembers also the account of something that had taken place earlier in this same graveyard, when Bon's octoroon mistress, a "magnolia-faced woman a little plumper now, a woman created of by and for darkness whom the artist Beardsley might have dressed, in a soft flowing gown designed not to infer bereavement or widowhood . . . knelt beside the grave and arranged her skirts and wept," while beside her stood her "thin delicate child" with its "smooth ivory sexless face" (p. 193).

There is, too, the ride out to Sutpen's Hundred in the "furnace-breathed" Mississippi night in which Quentin shares his buggy with the frail and fanatical Miss Rosa, and smells her "fusty cam-phor-reeking shawl" and even her "airless black cotton umbrella." On this journey, as Miss Rosa clutches to her a flashlight and a hatchet, the implements of her search, it seems to Quentin that he can hear "the single profound suspiration of the parched earth's agony rising toward the imponderable and aloof stars" (p. 362). Most vivid of all is the great concluding scene in which Clytie, seeing the ambulance approaching to bear Henry away, fires "the monstrous tinder-dry rotten shell" (p. 375) of a house, and from an upper window defies the intruders, her "tragic gnome's face be-neath the clean headrag, against a red background of fire, seen for a moment between two swirls of smoke, looking down at them, perhaps not even now with triumph and no more of despair than it had ever worn, possibly even serene above the melting clap-boards" (p. 376).

These brilliantly realized scenes reward the reader and sustain him as he struggles with the novel; but it ought to be remembered that they are given their power by the way in which the novel is

structured and thus constitute a justification of that peculiar structure. For example, consider Henry's confrontation of Judith with
the word that he has killed her lover. The incident is alluded to
in remarks made to Quentin by Miss Rosa (section 1), and later by
Mr. Compson as he talks to Quentin on the porch of their home
in the fading daylight (section 2). But the first major preparation
for this scene does not occur until the end of section 3 with Wash's
riding up to Miss Rosa's house on a saddleless mule and shouting
"Hello, hello" at intervals until she comes to the door. Whereupon, "he lowered his voice somewhat, though not much.
'Air you Rosie Coldfield?' he said" (p. 133). But what he had
to tell her is not stated. The reader may very well guess what
it was, but if he wants to hear the rest of Wash's speech, he must
read on all the way through section 4 to find, at the very end:
" 'Air you Rosie Coldfield? Then you better come on out yon.
Henry has done shot that durn French feller. Kilt him dead as a
beef.' " But the postponement of what Wash had to impart is, of
course, no mere teasing of the reader. Because of what we learn
in section 4, the episode becomes invested with tremendously in-
creased power. The repetition with added and altered detail functions somewhat like the folk-ballad device of incremental repetition.

The conclusion of section 5 brings us up to the confrontation
scene itself. For this scene, the sequel to the murder so tersely reported by Wash, is now visualized for us through Quentin's
imagination: our own imaginations have been prepared for the
presentation, and we are likely to hear the brother and sister, as
Quentin does, speaking to one another in "brief staccato sentences
like slaps, as if they stood breast to breast striking one another in
turn neither making any attempt to guard against the blows" (p.
172).

The ending of section 5, however, does something more than
bring to climactic focus the meeting of Henry and Judith: it generates a new line of suspense. For Quentin is jerked out of his
abstracted reverie by suddenly apprehending the significance of
something Miss Rosa has been saying. He asks her to repeat, and
section 5 closes with her words: "There's something in that house.

. . . Something living in it. Hidden in it. It has been out there for four years, living hidden in that house" (p. 172).

Section 6 resumes other narrative lines of the story and describes the decaying mansion at Sutpen's Hundred as Quentin had seen it a few years earlier on a hunt. But at the end of the section Shreve recurs to the possibility of something hidden at Sutpen's Hundred and of the journey that Quentin made with Rosa to test her intuition that this was so. The section ends with Shreve's excited query: "and so you went out there, drove the twelve miles at night in a buggy and you found Clytie and Jim Bond both in it and you said You see? and she (the Aunt Rosa) still said No and so you went on: and there was?" "Yes." "Wait then. . . . For God's sake wait" (p. 216).

Shreve is here the proper surrogate for the reader. The reader too wants to know the secret, but he does not want (or ought not to want) to know too quickly. Shreve, who is in some sense the perfect audience, yearns to know the secret, but only at the proper time when the revelation can come with full significance. Scattered through sections 7 and 8 there are a number of references to what Quentin's journey to Sutpen's Hundred revealed, though each of these sections ends with another and less important disclosure. The account of Quentin's journey is reserved for the last pages of the book. Indeed, though Quentin must have at some point during the evening told Shreve what he found at Sutpen's Hundred, his recounting it to Shreve is in fact never presented in this book. Instead, there is a compulsive re-enactment of the episode as Quentin lies in his bed, unable to sleep, feeling, even with the "chill pure weight of the snow-breathed New England air on his face" the dust of that "breathless . . . Mississippi September night" (p. 362).

Absalom, Absalom! is in many respects the most brilliantly written of all Faulkner's novels, whether one considers its writing line by line and paragraph by paragraph, or its structure, in which we are moved up from one suspended note to a higher suspended note and on up further still to an almost intolerable climax. The intensity of the book is a function of the structure. The deferred and suspended resolutions are necessary if the great scenes are to have their full vigor and significance. Admittedly, the novel is a difficult one, but the difficulty is not forced and factitious. It is the price that has to be paid by the reader for the novel's power and significance. There are actually few instances in modern fiction of a more perfect adaptation of form to matter and of an intricacy that justifies itself at every point through the significance and intensity which it makes possible.

15

Man, Time, and Eternity

(THE SOUND AND THE FURY)

The Sound and the Fury proved to be Faulkner's first great novel, and in the opinion of many qualified judges it remains his best. It has attracted, more than any other of his books, a mass of detailed exegesis and commentary, some of it beside the point, some of it illuminating indeed. Yet there are things that remain to be said about this brilliant but curious and difficult novel, particularly in the matter of disposition of themes and the relative emphasis that Faulkner accords them.

The salient technical feature of *The Sound and the Fury* is the use of four different points of view in the presentation of the breakup of the Compson family. This special technique was obviously of great personal consequence to Faulkner, as evidenced by his several references to it in the last few years. The story is told through one obsessed consciousness after another, as we pass from Benjy's near-mindlessness to the obsessed mind of Quentin and then to the very differently obsessed mind of Jason. The first three sections are all examples of the stream-of-consciousness method, and yet, as Lawrence Bowling[1] has well observed, how different they are in movement, mood, and effect!

The reader's movement through the book is a progression from murkiness to increasing enlightenment, and this is natural, since

1. "Technique of *The Sound and the Fury*," *Kenyon Review, 10* (1948), 552–66.

we start with the mind of an idiot, go on next through the memories and reveries of the Hamlet-like Quentin, and come finally to the observations of the brittle, would-be rationalist Jason. Part of the sense of enlightenment comes simply from the fact that we are traversing the same territory in circling movements, and the cumulative effect of names and characterizations begins to dramatize for us with compelling urgency a situation we have come to accept almost as our own.

Readers of this novel some thirty years ago were shocked at what seemed an almost willful obscurity, and the difficulties entailed by Faulkner's method are not to be minimized. Some passages in Quentin's section, for example, seem to me so private as to be almost incomprehensible. But a generation of sensitive readers has testified to the almost palpable atmosphere of the first sections of the book. We do learn what it is like to live in such a family through being forced to share the minds of the three brothers in their special kinds of obsession. The sense of frustration and "entrapment" is overpowering. Benjy is obviously a victim in the sense in which an animal is, but Quentin is hardly less so, and even the horribly "sane" Jason feels victimized, as he shows in his compulsive talk. There is, therefore, as we move toward the end of the book, the sense of coming out into an objective world, a world in which objects take on firmness of outline and density and weight, in which objective truth, and not mere obsessional impressions, exists. Though the fourth section is not passed through Dilsey's mind, it is dominated by Dilsey; and the world in which Dilsey moves is an objective world, not simply the projection of a distempered spirit.

The states of consciousness of the three brothers provide three quite different modes of interpretation. Consider them, for a moment, under the rubric of poetry. Benjy's section is filled with a kind of primitive poetry, a poetry of the senses, rendered with great immediacy, in which the world—for Benjy a kind of confused, blooming buzz—registers with great sensory impact but with minimal intelligibility. Quentin's section is filled with poetry too, though his is essentially decadent: sensitive but neurotic and hopeless, as it rings sadly through a series of dying falls. Entering

Jason's section, we have no poetry at all, since Jason, the "sane" man, has consciously purged his mind of every trace of this perilous and impractical stuff. (One might claim, to be sure, that Jason's section does in fact attain to poetry, since perfect expression is in itself a kind of poetry. Jason's brilliant, if unconscious, parade of his vulgarity and his relentless exposure of his essential viciousness do carry prose—though ordinary and unpretentious—to the very brink of poetry.) With the last section we again encounter poetry, but of a more usual kind, especially in those passages which reveal Dilsey's reaction to the Easter service; and here it is neither primitive nor decadent, but whole, complex, and mature.

We can look at the four sections in quite another way, noticing what different conceptions of love they imply. Benjy represents love in its most simple and childlike form. His love for Caddy is intense and unreflective. To him Caddy smells like trees. The syllables of her name—when he hears the golfers call out *caddy*— cause him to break out into hopeless crying, but his love is necessarily inarticulate and therefore almost formless.

Quentin's love for Caddy is self-conscious, formal, even abstract. Quentin believes that he is so much in love with his sister that he would gladly die in order to pull her away from the noise of the loud world and find in some corner of hell a quiet refuge for himself and her. He begs his father to believe that they have committed incest; but Quentin is not really in love with his sister's body, only in love with a notion of virginity that he associates with her. Though he thinks he is committing suicide because Caddy has given herself to various men and then has been forced into a loveless marriage, Quentin is really, as his sister knows, in love with death itself.

In contrast with this incestuously Platonic lover, Jason has no love for Caddy at all, and no love for anyone else. His notion of the proper amatory relationship is to provide himself with a "good honest whore" (p. 251). The relationship he desires is a commercial one: you know where you stand; there is no romantic nonsense about it. Jason, if he could, would reduce all relationships to commercial transactions.

Another way in which to contrast the first three sections is to

observe the different notions of time held by the Compson brothers. Perrin Lowrey finds that each of the brothers has a defective
sense of time.[2] Benjy, of course, is unconscious of time. Past and
present jumble together in his mind, and so in the first section of
the book the reader moves from one event to another, sometimes,
without warning, across a gap of years, since for Benjy events are
related only through some casual and accidental association. In
contrast, Quentin is obsessed with time. In the long stream-of-
consciousness meditation which occupies his section of the book,
his obsession comes out in dozens of ways, including his avoidance
of looking at clocks. Jason, too, is harried by time, but in a very
different way: far from wishing to obliterate it, he would like to
catch up with it. Throughout his section Jason is always racing
the clock and is usually late because he always thinks of time, as
Lowrey says, in a "mechanical and minute-to-minute sense." It is
only in the fourth section of the book, the one dominated by Dilsey, that we enter into a proper notion of time. Dilsey knows how
to interpret her backward and defective kitchen clock. When it
strikes five times she automatically corrects the error and announces that it is eight o'clock. Her ability to make sense of the
clock is simply one aspect of her ability to make sense of past,
present, and future. All are aspects of eternity, and Dilsey, in her
simple religious faith, believes in an order that is grounded in
eternity.

Jean-Paul Sartre has argued, in an essay that has proved most
influential, that Faulkner's characters, because they are committed
to the past, are helpless. The Faulknerian character's point of
view, as Sartre described it in a graphic metaphor, is that of a
passenger looking backward from a speeding car, who sees, flowing
away from him, the landscape he is traversing. For him the future
is not in view, the present is too blurred to make out, and he can see
clearly only the past as it streams away before his obsessed and
backward-looking gaze.[3] Sartre's account of the matter does apply
in good measure to Quentin, but it does not apply to many of

2. "Concepts of Time in *The Sound and the Fury*," R. S. Downer, ed., *English
Institute Essays* (New York, Columbia University Press, 1952), pp. 57–82.

3. "A Propos de *Le Bruit et la fureur*," *La Nouvelle Revue française*, 52 (1939);
Eng. trans. in *William Faulkner: Three Decades of Criticism*, Frederick J. Hoffman
and Olga W. Vickery, eds. (Michigan State University Press, 1960), pp. 225–32.

Faulkner's characters and it is certainly not to be attributed to Faulkner himself. Perhaps a more accurate way of stating the truth that inheres in Sartre's view is to say: man's very freedom is bound up with his sense of having some kind of future. Unless he can look ahead to the future, he is not free. The relation that the three Compson brothers bear to the future and to time in general has everything to do, therefore, with their status as human beings.

Benjy, as we have seen, is locked almost completely into a timeless present. He has not much more sense of time than an animal has, and therefore he possesses not much more freedom than an animal does. Rollo May, in his book *Existence: A New Dimension in Psychiatry and Psychology*,[4] has some interesting comments to make upon this matter of an animal's ability to take account of time—its ability, for example, to anticipate punishment. May says that experiments indicate that sheep can maintain such an anticipation for perhaps fifteen minutes, and dogs, for about half an hour. A human being, of course, can project himself into the future not for hours or weeks but for years and decades.

Quentin's obsession with the past is in fact a repudiation of the future. It amounts to the sense of having no future. May comments: "Severe anxiety and depression blot out time, annihilate the future. . . . the most painful aspect of the sufferer's predicament is that he is unable to imagine a future moment in time when he will be out of the anxiety" (p. 68). This would seem to be almost precisely Quentin's case: he has no future. Caddy's betrayal of her honor and the fact that she is cut off forever from Quentin mean that he possesses no future he is willing to contemplate. Thus, with relation to the future—any future—Quentin is listless and apathetic. He would like to do away with time, locking himself into some past from which there would be no development and no progression. Hence the dream that appeals to Quentin: time congealed into a changeless moment; he and Caddy in some cozy private niche in hell, enclosed in the clean flame, isolated from everything else. Quentin's wish to do away with time finds a symbolic expression in his twisting the hands from his watch. Again, a quotation from May's *Existence* is apposite: "For certain

4. New York, Basic Books, 1958.

neurotics who are psychopathic personalities, time is boredom; one must 'kill time' (which is perhaps a way of killing oneself)." Quentin's dismembering his watch on the morning of his suicide can be viewed as an attempt to kill time and therefore a preliminary act to killing himself.

Joe Christmas is another Faulkner character who is trapped in the past and who, because he has no future, has no true freedom. Seven days after he has murdered Joanna Burden, it occurs to him that during his whole lifetime he has been running in a circle, and he says to himself (*Light in August,* p. 296): "I have been farther in these seven days than in all the thirty years. But I have never got outside that circle. I have never broken out of the ring of what I have already done and cannot ever undo."

As for the remaining Compson brother, if the lack of a future entails a lack of freedom for both Benjy, who is little more than an animal, and for Quentin, who cannot look at the future, Jason at least, with his rejection of the past and his constant gaze into the future, ought, one might suppose, to have complete freedom. But Jason, by insisting on seeing time only with regard to something to be done, is incapable of any real living. Like the frenetic businessman, Jason is always preparing to live, not living—or in Alexander Pope's words, "Never blessed, but always to be blessed." The Negro called old man Job hits off Jason's situation very aptly (p. 267). He tells Jason: "You's too smart fer me. Aint a man in dis town kin keep up wid you fer smartness. You fools a man whut so smart he cant even keep up wid hisself." When Jason asks who that smart man might be, old man Job's prompt answer is "Dat's Mr Jason Compson." Jason is so committed to preparation for the future that he is almost as enslaved as are his brothers.

I have said that to Dilsey neither the past nor the future nor the present is oppressive, because to her they are all aspects of eternity, and her ultimate commitment is to eternity. It may be useful therefore to notice how the plight of each of the brothers constitutes a false interpretation of eternity. Benjy lives in a specious eternity: his present does not include all in timelessness—past, present, and future gathered together in a total pattern—but is a purely negative eternity, since it contains no past and no future.

Quentin, we may say, wants to take eternity by storm—to reach it by a sort of shortcut, which in effect means freezing into permanence one fleeting moment of the past. Eternity is thus for Quentin not something which fulfills and enfolds all time, but simply a particular segment of time, like one note of music infinitely sustained. Jason is committed neither to a timeless present nor to a frozen past but to a making ready for the truly happy state. Jason's eternity is the empty mirage of an oasis toward which he is constantly flogging his tired camel and his tired self.

Though these patternings [5] do emerge from a contemplation of the first three sections, and though they are important for an understanding of the novel, they do not show on the surface. The reader's impression of *The Sound and the Fury* is not of an elaborately formal abstract structure but quite the reverse. Rarely has a novel appeared so completely disordered and unconnected and accidental in its concreteness. Benjy's section has notoriously seemed a clutter of facts and memories, hard particularities and irrational concretions, a cluster that illustrates nothing and points nowhere.[6] Quentin's section is only less difficult than Benjy's, though certainly quite as rich in conveying the sounds, smells, and shapes of a particular world. It is the apparent formlessness of so much of the book that has tempted the commentators to insist upon the underlying patterns. The patterns are there, but the knowledge that they are there is bought too dearly if it results in turning the three brothers into abstractions, mere stages in a dialectic. Quentin, for example, is a human being who, in spite of his anguished speculations upon the nature of time, is related to a culture; he is not a monstrous abstraction but a young man who has received a grievous psychic wound.

A way of seeing Quentin in a different, and perhaps a fuller, perspective is to note that he is another of Faulkner's many Puritans. (Faulkner makes Quentin's Puritanism plain in the appendix on the Compsons that he drew up for the Modern Library edition.) Quentin reveals his Puritanism most obviously in his alarm at the breakdown of sexual morality. When the standards of sex-

5. See below, Notes, p. 443.
6. See below, Notes, p. 444.

ual morals are challenged, a common reaction and one quite natural to Puritanism is to try to define some point beyond which surely no one would venture to transgress—to find at least one act so horrible that everyone would be repelled by it.

All of this can be said in a slightly different way, one that will relate Quentin to what has been said earlier in this book about courtly love. Quentin is, almost in the very terms used by Denis de Rougemont, a classical instance of the courtly lover. When Faulkner writes that Quentin "loved not his sister's body but some concept of Compson honor," he might be quoting from Rougemont, though in all likelihood he never read *Love in the Western World*. Again it might be Rougemont speaking when Faulkner observes that Quentin "loved death above all . . . loved and lived in a deliberate and almost perverted anticipation of death as a lover loves and deliberately refrains from the waiting willing friendly tender incredible body of his beloved, until he can no longer bear not the refraining but the restraint and so flings, hurls himself, relinquishing, drowning" (p. 9). In the end it is not the body of his sister but the river of death to which Quentin gives himself.[7]

It might be objected that the passage just quoted represents an afterthought on Faulkner's part, since it is from the appendix and not the novel proper, but the novel has many passages that clearly exhibit Quentin in the guise of Rougemont's Tristan. The union Quentin desires with his sister is not to be accomplished physically but rather by having it thought that he had done so in order that the world "would have to flee [them] of necessity" (p. 195). When Quentin's father asks him whether he had actually tried to make Caddy commit incest with him, Quentin gives the surprising answer: "I was afraid to." Then, in a burst of honesty that shows how his "love" parallels the Puritanism of the Cathars and their fear of the flesh, Quentin confesses that he was afraid to ask Caddy for fear that she might say yes.

Mr. Compson is very shrewd in his understanding of his son, even though he is mistaken in his prediction that Quentin will not commit suicide. He tells him: "you will not do that until you

7. See below, Notes, p. 444.

come to believe that even she was not quite worth despair perhaps." Evidently, Mr. Compson doubts that Quentin will ever come to such a point, and Quentin himself in this conversation with his father insists that he "will never do that" (p. 196). But as the weeks passed after Caddy's marriage, perhaps Quentin did suspect that his anguish was diminishing and might finally become tolerable. Perhaps he killed himself for fear that if he waited longer, the staunchless wound would heal. Perhaps Quentin was really in love with his despair.

To say that Quentin is an almost classic instance of the romantic lover is not, of course, to say all that is important about him. It is merely to define his prime aberration, not to account for the ultimate result or to indicate how he received his major psychic wound. With regard to this, there are several hints embedded in the Quentin section. For example, there is a reference to a fight Quentin had in school. Though he told his father that it was because of some trick that one of the boys played on the teacher, one wonders whether this was so. Was the fight really occasioned by someone's having made a disparaging remark about Caddy's conduct? There is an interesting and tantalizing evocation of unhappiness during Quentin's school days (p. 107): an afternoon in the schoolroom in which a dreamy and unhappy boy is unable to keep his mind on his work, is mildly humiliated by the teacher, and reveals himself to be deeply troubled in some obscure way. There is also the painful memory of his leg's having been broken in a fall from a horse, and the sick feeling at hearing that the bone had not been properly set and had to be rebroken.

Whatever the special causes of Quentin's spiritual malaise, the general conditioning cause is quite evident. The curse upon Quentin and the rest of the Compsons is the presence of their hypochondriac, whining mother. Again and again on his last day of life he says to himself, "If I only had a mother," and he remembers associating his mother with a scene pictured in one of the books in the family library. There was portrayed "a dark place into which a single weak ray of light came slanting upon two faces lifted out of the shadow" (p. 191). In Quentin's troubled memory the pictured faces become those of his mother and father. He remembers that he would feel a compulsion to turn back to the picture until "the dungeon was Mother herself she and Father upward into weak light holding hands and us lost somewhere below even them without even a ray of light." Remembering his mother on the day of his death, Quentin says to himself: "Done in Mother's mind though. Finished. Finished. Then we were all poisoned" (p. 121).

The Sound and the Fury has on occasion been read as another Faulknerian document describing the fall of the Old South. Perhaps it is, but what it most clearly records is the downfall of a particular family, and the case seems rather special. The basic cause of the breakup of the Compson family—let the more general cultural causes be what they may—is the cold and self-centered mother who is sensitive about the social status of her own family, the Bascombs, who feels the birth of an idiot son as a kind of personal affront, who spoils and corrupts her favorite son, and who withholds any real love and affection from her other children and her husband. Caroline Compson is not so much an actively wicked and evil person as a cold weight of negativity which paralyzes the normal family relationships. She is certainly at the root of Quentin's lack of confidence in himself and his inverted pride. She is at least the immediate cause of her husband's breakdown into alcoholic cynicism, and doubtless she is ultimately responsible for Caddy's promiscuity.[8] There is some evidence that Caddy's conduct was obsessive and compulsive, a flight from her family. She tells her brother Quentin: "There was something terrible in me sometimes at night I could see it grinning at me I could see it through [my lovers] grinning at me through their faces" (p. 131).

In Faulkner's story "That Evening Sun," the events of which apparently occur in 1898, the earlier family relationships of the Compsons are revealingly portrayed. When Nancy, their Negro servant, is terrified of going home because she fears that her common-law husband is coming there to cut her throat, Mr. Compson is sympathetic and tries to be helpful. He obviously finds it difficult to take with full seriousness Nancy's irrational conviction that her man is lurking about ready to kill her, but

8. See below, Notes, p. 445.

Mr. Compson does take with great seriousness her abject terror, and he tries to find some solution that will calm her—having her stay with a friend, or putting the case before the police. But his wife, in notable contrast, is far too self-centered to view Nancy's plight with any sympathy. Nancy's terror is to Mrs. Compson simply a nuisance, and the sooner Nancy is got out of the house the better.

In that story the Compson children have already assumed the personality patterns that we shall find later. Though they are too young to comprehend fully Nancy's desperation, Caddy and Quentin at least respond to the Negro woman's terror with concerned curiosity and, insofar as they are capable, sympathy. Jason is already a wretched little complainer, interested neither in Nancy nor in his brother and sister except as he may get his way by constantly threatening to "tell on" them.

Mr. Compson by 1910 was a defeated man. Perhaps he had always been a weak man, not endowed with the fighting spirit necessary to save his family. But there are plenty of indications that he was a man possessed of love and compassion. Benjy remembers a scene in which Caddy and Father and Jason were in Mother's chair. Jason had been crying, and his father was evidently comforting him. Caddy's head, Benjy remembers, was on Father's shoulder. And when Benjy himself went over to the chair, "Father lifted me into the chair too, and Caddy held me" (p. 91). Long after Mr. Compson's death, Dilsey remembers him as a force for order in the household and reproaches Jason with the words: "if Mr Jason was still here hit ud be different" (p. 225). And when Caddy pleads with her cold-hearted brother to be allowed to see her baby, she says to him: "You have Father's name: do you think I'd have to ask him twice? once, even?" (p. 227). The attentive reader will have noticed that even in his drinking, Mr. Compson has evidently gone from better to worse. Caddy tells Quentin: "Father will be dead in a year they say if he doesnt stop drinking and he wont stop he cant stop since I since last summer" (p. 143). Evidently, the knowledge of his daughter's wantonness had hit Mr. Compson hard, and his parade of cynicism about women and virginity, so much of which Quentin recalls on the day of his death, must have been in part an attempt to soften the blow for Quentin and perhaps for himself. We miss the point badly if we take it that Mr. Compson, comfortable in his cynicism, simply didn't care what his daughter did.

Quentin was apparently very close to his father and the influence of his father on him was obviously very powerful. The whole of the Quentin section is saturated with what "Father said" and with references to comparisons that Father used and observations about life that Father made. Though his father seems to have counseled acquiescence in the meaninglessness of existence, it is plain that it was from him that Quentin derived his high notion of the claims of honor. Quentin has not the slightest doubt as to what he ought to do: he ought to drive Caddy's seducer out of town, and if the seducer refuses to go, he ought to shoot him. But Quentin is not up to the heroic role. He tries, but he cannot even hurt Ames, much less kill him. Caddy sees Quentin as simply meddling in her affairs, the quixotic little brother who is to be pitied but not feared or respected.

Since *Absalom, Absalom!* was written years after *The Sound and the Fury,* we must exercise caution in using the Quentin of the later novel to throw light upon the Quentin of the earlier. But Faulkner, in choosing the character Quentin for service in *Absalom, Absalom!,* must have deemed the choice a sound one. He must have felt that the experience that Quentin was to undergo in talking with his father about the Sutpens and on his journey out to Sutpen's Hundred would be compatible with, and relevant to, what he had Quentin undergo in *The Sound and the Fury.* The Quentin of *The Sound and the Fury* would indeed have been terribly impressed by Henry Sutpen's acceptance of the heroic and tragic role thrust upon him by circumstance, and the more humiliated to have to acknowledge his own pitiful inadequacy when it became necessary to protect his own sister's honor. (Presumably Quentin's encounter with Dalton Ames occurred in the summer before he saw Henry Sutpen—that is, just before he went off to Harvard in September—rather than after he saw Henry. But the two experiences could not have been widely separated in time, and the sight of Henry, who had assumed the heroic role and wrecked his life for it, would have deepened Quentin's sense of failure with Caddy's seducer, Ames.)

Quentin is emotionally committed to the code of honor, but for him the code has lost its connection with reality: it is abstract, rigidified, even "literary." Quentin's suicide results from the fact that he can neither repudiate nor fulfill the claims of the code. The idiot Benjy, of course, has no code at all. His is an inarticulate love, a love that is as direct and wordless as an odor ("Caddy smelled like trees"). Nevertheless, Benjy's love is recognizably human in that it asks something of the loved one. Benjy can sense Caddy's betrayal of honor: he screams in horror when he smells the perfume that she has worn for her lover, and is not appeased until she has washed it off.

The third brother, Jason, has repudiated the code of honor. He has adopted for himself a purely practical formula for conduct. Money is what counts. He wants none of Quentin's nonsense nor of the other kinds of nonsense in which people believe—or in which they pretend to believe. But though Jason's ostensible code is purely practical, reducing every action to its cash value, his conduct has in fact its nonpractical aspect. For Jason harbors a great deal of nonpractical and irrational bitterness, even sadism. When, in order to see the disappointment upon Luster's face, Jason deliberately drops the passes to the minstrel show into the fire, he is satisfying his perverted emotion even though he pretends to be merely throwing away what cannot be sold. His stealing systematically the money that Caddy is sending for the benefit of her daughter answers to his mercantilism, but Jason is not content to steal Quentin's allowance. He also wants the enjoyment of teasing and hurting the girl.

In his appendix on the Compsons, Faulkner declares that Jason was "the first sane Compson since before Culloden" (p. 16). In view of the quixotic Compsons, with their zest for spending themselves on foolish enterprises and their impossible notions of honor, one sees the ironic justification of the term *sane* as applied to Jason. But sanity as Jason exemplifies it is something inhuman. Jason does not love even his mother, Faulkner tells us, for he is "a sane man always," and love always involves a contradiction of such sanity. Benjy's idiocy and Quentin's quixotic madness are finally less inhuman than Jason's sanity. To be truly human one must transcend one's mere intellect with some overflow of generosity and love. Faulkner tells us that Jason is able to compete with, and even hold his own with, the Snopeses. This is the highest accolade that Faulkner can bestow on Jason, and of course, the worst damnation that he can utter. When a Compson turns Snopes, then the family has indeed run out, and the end of an order has come.

The section devoted to Jason has in it some of the most brilliant writing that Faulkner ever did. Jason is a brutal and cold-hearted man, but he does have a certain wit and a brittle logic which allows him to cap any remark made to him by his defiant niece or his ailing mother or one of his business associates. Jason is rarely at a loss, and he is so self-righteous in his bitterness that many of his comments carry a kind of nasty conviction. For example, here is Jason feeling sorry for himself: "Well, Jason likes work. I says no I never had university advantages because at Harvard they teach you how to go for a swim at night without knowing how to swim and at Sewanee they dont even teach you what water is. I says you might send me to the state University; maybe I'll learn how to stop my clock with a nose spray and then you can send Ben to the Navy I says or to the cavalry anyway, they use geldings in the cavalry" (p. 213).

Jason is typically sardonic in his description of his father's funeral. His ineffective and sycophantic Uncle Maury has braced himself for the ordeal with a few drinks and has tried to disguise the fact by chewing cloves. The tell-tale smell, however, gives him away to Jason, who observes: "I reckon [Uncle Maury] thought that the least he could do at Father's funeral [was to take a drink] or maybe the sideboard thought it was still Father and tripped him up when he passed. Like I say, if [Father] had to sell something to send Quentin to Harvard we'd all been a damn sight better off if he'd sold that sideboard and bought himself a one-armed straight jacket with part of the money" (p. 215).

Jason's usual mode is a rather ponderous sarcasm. The opening paragraph of his section of the novel is typical: "Once a bitch always a bitch, what I say. I says you're lucky if her playing out of school is all that worries you. I says she ought to be down there in that kitchen right now, instead of up there in her room, gobbing paint on her face and waiting for six niggers that cant even stand up out of a chair unless they've got a pan full of bread and meat to balance them, to fix breakfast for her" (p. 198).

For some eighty pages, in a coldly furious monologue, Jason pitilessly exposes himself. Indeed, Faulkner does more in these eighty pages to indict the shabby small-town businessman's view of life than Sinclair Lewis was able to achieve in several novels on the subject. Jason takes his place as one of the half-dozen of Faulkner's most accomplished villains. Faulkner's resourcefulness and his imaginative power keep his villains from conforming to a stereotype. Anse, Flem, Popeye, Thomas Sutpen, Percy Grimm, and Jason Compson—how different they are in personality and appearance and manner! All but Jason come largely of poor-white stock, but they have to yield nothing in meanness to this déclassé aristocrat—or is Jason's mother right in regarding him as pure Bascomb? Jason has more vitality than Anse Bundren, less maniacal fury than Percy Grimm, and far less staying power than one finds in Flem Snopes' cold rapacity. Jason does not match either the courage or the quality of perverse magnificence that attaches itself to Thomas Sutpen. Even so, in this company of prime villains Jason is among his peers, and Jason's treatment of his sister, his idiot brother, and his niece shows studied cruelty that is unmatched by any of Faulkner's other villains.

A common trait in Faulkner's villains is the lack of any capacity for love. Their lack of love shows itself in two ways, two ways that come eventually to the same thing: their attitudes toward nature and toward women. They do not respond to nature—they may very well violate nature. In quite the same way, they have no interest in women, or use them as means to their own ends. They are impotent like Flem and Popeye, or they are strong-willed abstemious men like Thomas Sutpen. Jason Compson, with no interest in nature, or in women except as objects to be manipulated, is of this breed.

The disintegration that took place in the Compson family after

Jason became its head is revealed most clearly and terribly in the character of Candace's daughter, Quentin. The child is nearly everything that Jason bitterly accuses her of being: she is a cheap little wanton, offering herself to almost any man who puts in an appearance, and in her wantonness she resembles her mother. But the daughter lacks certain virtues that her mother possessed: graciousness, pity, and disinterested love. Quentin despises Benjy, the unfortunate to whom Caddy gave her love, and this is not hard to understand, remembering that she has always seen Benjy as an adult-sized all-but-mindless being and never as the little brother—the relationship in which her mother knew him. But it still is hard to forgive the callousness she shows to Dilsey. Though at times she has to appeal to Dilsey for protection from her cruel uncle, and though Dilsey always tries to mother her, Quentin shows her little love or consideration. When Dilsey remonstrates with Jason and goes on to reassure Quentin with the words "Now, now, I aint gwine let him tech you," and puts her hand on Quentin, Quentin knocks it down, blurting out: "You damn old nigger" (p. 203).

What has happened to the girl Quentin is what might have been expected. Reared in a loveless home, lacking even what her mother had had in the way of family companionship, she shows the effect of the pressures that have been exerted upon her all her life. She is cheap and thoughtless, and she has absorbed from her uncle something of his cruelty. It is very difficult for people to be good when they are frustrated and dreadfully unhappy, and Quentin is indeed dreadfully unhappy. She exclaims: "I don't see why I was ever born," and when Jason reproaches her for her loss of reputation in the town, she answers him by saying: "I dont care. I'm bad and I'm going to hell, and I dont care. I'd rather be in hell than anywhere where you are" (p. 207).

In a way the girl senses what has misshaped her. At one point she appeals, in her desperation, to Mrs. Compson, saying: "Why does [Jason] treat me like this, Grandmother? I never hurt him" (p. 276). And when her grandmother tells her that Jason "is the nearest thing to a father you've ever had. It's his bread you and I eat. It's only right that he should expect obedience from you," the girl jumps up and says to Jason: "Whatever I do, it's your fault. If I'm bad, it's because I had to be. You made me. I wish I was dead. I wish we were all dead" (p. 277).

The girl's plight is very much that of Joe Christmas, who was warped by his feeling that the fanatic old Doc Hines was always watching him with hatred. Faulkner, to be sure, does not sentimentalize Quentin. He does not minimize her shortcomings or imply that she was the mere victim of her environment, but his bitterest judgment upon Jason and what Jason's cruelty entailed is in his presentation of what Jason has caused Caddy's baby to become.

The downfall of the house of Compson is the kind of degeneration which can occur, and has occurred, anywhere at any time. William Butler Yeats' play *Purgatory* is a moving dramatization of the end of a great house in Ireland. The play ends with the last member of the family, a murderous-minded old tinker, standing outside the ruins of the ancestral house; but the burning of that house and the decay of the family have no special connection with the troubles of Ireland. According to the author, the disaster resulted from a bad marriage! The real significance of the Southern setting in *The Sound and the Fury* resides, as so often elsewhere in Faulkner, in the fact that the breakdown of a family can be exhibited more poignantly and significantly in a society which is old-fashioned and in which the family is still at the center. The dissolution of the family as an institution has probably gone further in the suburban areas of California and Connecticut than it has in the small towns of Mississippi. For that very reason, what happens to the Compsons might make less noise and cause less comment, and even bring less pain to the individuals concerned, if the Compsons lived in a more progressive and liberal environment. Because the Compsons have been committed to old-fashioned ideals—close family loyalty, home care for defective children, and the virginity of unmarried daughters—the breakup of the family registers with greater impact.

The decay of the Compsons can be viewed, however, not merely with reference to the Southern past but to the contemporary American scene. It is tempting to read it as a parable of the disintegration of modern man. Individuals no longer sustained by familial and cultural unity are alienated and lost in private worlds. One thinks here not merely of Caddy, homeless, the sexual adventuress adrift in the world, or of Quentin, out of touch with reality and moving inevitably to his death, but also and even primarily of Jason, for whom the breakup of the family means an active rejection of claims and responsibilities and, with it, a sense of liberation. Jason resolves to be himself and to be self-sufficient. He says: "Besides, like I say I guess I dont need any man's help to get along I can stand on my own feet like I always have" (p. 224). Jason prides himself in managing matters by himself and— since this is the other side of the same coin—refuses to heed the claims of anyone but himself. In his appendix Faulkner says that Jason thinks "nothing whatever of God one way or the other" but simply tries to keep clear of "the police" and fears and respects "only the Negro woman" (p. 16), Dilsey. Jason is done with religion in every way, including its etymological sense as a "binding back." Jason is bound back to nothing. He repudiates any traditional tie. He means to be on his own and he rejects every community. The fact shows plainly in the way he conducts himself not only in his own household but also in the town of Jefferson.

The one member of the Compson household who represents a unifying and sustaining force is the Negro servant Dilsey. She tries to take care of Benjy and to give the girl Quentin the mothering she needs. In contrast to Mrs. Compson's vanity and whining self-pity, Dilsey exhibits charity and rugged good sense. She is warned by her daughter Frony that taking Benjy to church with her will provoke comments from the neighbors. "Folks talkin," Frony says; to which Dilsey answers: "Whut folks? . . . And I know whut kind of folks. Trash white folks. Dat's who it is. Thinks he aint good enough fer white church, but nigger church aint good enough fer him" (p. 306). Frony remarks that folks talk just the same, but Dilsey has her answer: "Den you send um to me. Tell um de good Lawd dont keer whether he smart er not. Dont nobody but white trash keer dat." All of which amounts to sound manners and to sound theology as well.

Faulkner does not present Dilsey as a black fairy-godmother or as a kind of middle-aged Pollyanna full of the spirit of cheerful optimism. Even his physical description of her looks in another direction. We are told that she had once been a big woman, but now the unpadded skin is loosely draped upon "the indomitable skeleton" which is left "rising like a ruin or a landmark above the somnolent and impervious guts, and above that the collapsed face that gave the impression of the bones themselves being outside the flesh, lifted into the driving day with an expression at once fatalistic and of a child's astonished disappointment" (p. 282). What the expression means is best interpreted by what she says and does in the novel, but the description clearly points to something other than mindless cheeriness. Dilsey's essential hopefulness has not been obliterated; she is not an embittered woman, but her optimism has been chastened by hurt and disappointment.

Faulkner does not make the mistake of accounting for Dilsey's virtues through some mystique of race in which good primitive black folk stand over against corrupt wicked white folk. Dilsey herself has no such notions. When her son Luster remarks of the Compson household: "Dese is funny folks. Glad I aint none of em," she says: "Lemme tell you somethin, nigger boy, you got jes es much Compson devilment in you es any of em" (p. 292). She believes in something like original sin: men are not "naturally" good but require discipline and grace.

Dilsey, then, is no noble savage and no *schöne Seele*. Her view of the world and mankind is thoroughly Christian, simple and limited as her theological expression of her faith would have to be. On the other hand, Dilsey is no plaster saint. She is not easy on her own children. ("Dont stand dar in de rain, fool," she tells Luster.) She does not always offer the soft answer that turneth away wrath. She rebukes Mrs. Compson with "I dont see how you expect anybody to sleep, wid you standin in de hall, holl in at folks fum de crack of dawn," and she refuses Mrs. Compson's hypocritical offer to fix breakfast, saying: "En who gwine eat yo messin? Tell me dat" (p. 287). Dilsey's goodness is no mere goodness by, and of, nature, if one means by this a goodness that justifies a faith in man as man. Dilsey does not believe in man; she believes in God.

Dilsey's poverty and her status as a member of a deprived race do not, then, assure her nobility, but they may have had something to do with her remaining close to a concrete world of values so that she is less perverted by abstraction and more honest than are most white people in recognizing what is essential and basic. In general, Faulkner's Negro characters show less false pride, less false idealism, and more seasoned discipline in human relationships. Dilsey's race has also had something to do with keeping her close to a world still informed by religion. These matters are important: just how important they are is revealed by the emphasis Faulkner gives to the Easter service that Dilsey attends.

The Compson family—whatever may be true of the white community at large in the Jefferson of 1910—has lost its religion. Quentin's sad reveries are filled with references to Jesus and Saint Francis, but it is plain that he has retreated into some kind of Stoicism, a version which is reflected in his father's advice to him: "We must just stay awake and see evil done for a little. Quentin's reply is that "it doesn't have to be even that long for a man of courage" (p. 195), and the act of courage in the Roman style takes Quentin into the river. Mrs. Compson, when she finds that the girl Quentin has eloped, asks Dilsey to bring her the Bible, but obviously Mrs. Compson knows nothing about either sin or redemption. Her deepest concern is with gentility and social position. And Jason, as we have seen, worships only the almighty dollar.

The first three sections of the book do little to carry forward the story of what happened at the Compsons' on the Easter weekend. Benjy's section obviously does not do so, and it is only in the light of a reading of the rest of the book and a careful rereading of his section that the references to the present occasion emerge. Quentin's section dates from eighteen years before, and though what passes through Quentin's agonized spirit on the 2d of June, 1910, has its ultimate bearing on the events that occur in the Compson household on Easter day, 1928, the connection is not direct. Even the third section, that narrated by Jason, is not very directly related to the hectic events of Easter Sunday. For one

thing, Jason's is set back one day earlier than Benjy's section: that
is, Jason's tirade on the subject of bitches and of what is happening to the Compsons is uttered on Good Friday, whereas Benjy's
section gives us the events of Holy Saturday. In a general way Jason's
section does prepare us for what the girl Quentin is going to do,
but much of it is simply typical of almost any day in the Compson
household for the last year. All three sections, then, bend the bow
or coil the spring for an action that will discharge itself only in
the last section of the novel. None of the three—not even the
third—has much narrative drive, and the first two, in general
structure, resemble mood pieces, even mood poems, rather than
narrative transactions. This is not, to be sure, said by way of
disparagement: such action as occurs in *The Sound and the Fury*
is quite sufficient for the purposes of a powerful novel.

Easter Sunday breaks bleak and chill and gray. It begins ap-
propriately with Mrs. Compson's complaining and Dilsey's getting
the fire started and the household tasks going, but once it is discovered that Quentin is not in her room, events accelerate. All of
Jason's frenetic activity comes to a head when he makes the horrified discovery that his victim has found out where he has hidden
the money that he has stolen from her and has escaped with it.
But we do not immediately follow Jason on his frantic pursuit
of his niece. Instead, once Jason is out of the house on his way
to the sheriff's, we follow Dilsey and Benjy to church for the Easter
service, and this service, in which Dilsey finds her exaltation, is
counterpointed against Jason's attempt to find his niece and retrieve the money.

The eloquent sermon to which Dilsey listens sitting "bolt upright" and with tears sliding "down her fallen cheeks" (p. 311)
describes Mary's sorrow and the crucifixion of Jesus, but ends with
the promise of resurrection and of ultimate glory in which all the
arisen dead "whut got de blood en de ricklickshun of de Lamb"
(p. 313) shall participate. It is a vision of eternity which gives
meaning to time and will wipe away all tears in a final vindication
of goodness and in a full consolation of those who mourn. Beside
Dilsey, Benjy sits, "rapt in his sweet blue gaze," as if he, too, understood. As Dilsey continues to weep on her way home, her

345

daughter Frony tries to make her stop crying, pointing out that people are looking and that they will be passing white folks soon. But Dilsey does not care what people think and, caught up in her own vision, says to Frony: "I've seed de first en de last." And when Frony asks "First en last whut?" Dilsey tells her: "Never you mind. I seed de beginnin, en now I sees de endin" (p. 313). With the girl Quentin's departure, the sad story of the Compson family is now at an end. All are dead or departed except the whining hypochondriac Mrs. Compson, the cold and sterile bachelor Jason, and the uncomprehending Benjy.

Easter morning brings to Dilsey a vision that gives meaning to human events, but the Mrs. Compson to whom she returns is still full of uncomprehending reproaches. Mrs. Compson cannot understand why this latest disaster has befallen her. "It cant be simply to hurt and flout me. Whoever God is, He would not permit that. I'm a lady. You might not believe that from my offspring, but I am" (p. 315). In the meantime, Jason is off on his vain pursuit.

Jason's conversation with the sheriff reveals that the sheriff has a very clear idea of what has been going on and how Jason has mistreated his niece. The sheriff understands that the girl's act of "stealing" the money from Jason is essentially a recovery of her own property and that a rough kind of justice has been done. He tells Jason, "You drove that girl into running off" (p. 320). He refuses to act in any way to help Jason recover the money, and Jason goes away in a cold fury to pursue Quentin himself. Too wrought up even to drive his car properly, Jason heads for Mottstown, where the show is playing and where Jason expects to find Quentin and the young showman with whom she has eloped.

We are told that Jason did not think at all of his niece or of "the arbitrary valuation of the money" that she had taken. "Neither of them had had entity or individuality for him for ten years; together they merely symbolized the job in the bank of which he had been deprived before he ever got it" (p. 321). So the man who has become a kind of personified yearning for money sets out to recover not an errant girl and an actual sum of money but an abstract symbol.

Jason, who had boasted that he could get along without anyone, gets no help from anyone in his pursuit of Quentin. When he tries to make his way into the railway car belonging to the show people, he nearly gets himself killed. In his frenzy to get an answer out of the little man he finds in the car, he strikes him on the head, and the little man, in retaliating, almost succeeds in sinking a rusty hatchet in his head before someone comes to pull him off. Finally, with his raging headache—for Jason cannot stand the smell of gasoline—he is reduced to crazy-headed impotence and forced to hire a Negro man to drive him back to Jefferson. He is quite incapable of driving himself. At the end the cold-hearted Jason sits marooned on his rock of self-sufficiency.

Faulkner's titles are often whimsical, containing some meaning private to himself which never becomes completely clear in the novel. The title of *The Sound and the Fury,* however, provides a true key, for the novel has to do with the discovery that life has no meaning. Shakespeare's lines from *Macbeth,* "[Life] is a tale/ Told by an idiot, full of sound and fury,/Signifying nothing," quite aptly apply to the first section of the novel. Benjy's section, a tale told by an idiot, is not a tale told at all, but a kind of fuguelike arrangement and rearrangement of sights, smells, sounds, and actions, many of them meaningless in themselves, but tied together by some crisscross of association.

Quentin's section, too, echoes the title. Quentin has learned all too well his father's despairing philosophy, which sees human beings as merely dolls filled with sawdust. What spills from the side of such a doll can never be the healing blood of a Savior, with its promise of redemption. Quentin's own phrasing is: "dolls stuffed with sawdust swept up from the trash heaps where all previous dolls had been thrown away the sawdust flowing from what wound in what side that not for me died not" (p. 194).

Jason hopes to find meaning in life by discarding all idealisms, illusions, and emotional ties, and reducing life to its inexorable brass tacks. He manages to come out with a meaning of a sort, but it is a very thin and impoverished one. At the end of the novel he has scarcely made good his boast that he is a free man able to stand on his own feet with no help from anybody. He has indeed

347

finally succeeded, with his brittle rationalism, in outsmarting himself.

For Dilsey life does have meaning, though many of her betters would dismiss what she takes to be its meaning as illusion, the opium dispensed to a poor and illiterate people. Faulkner makes no claim for Dilsey's version of Christianity one way or the other. His presentation of it is moving and credible, but moving and credible as an aspect of Dilsey's own mental and emotional life. At any rate, it does not avail for those who will not avail themselves of it. Mrs. Compson is much too tightly locked up in her own egotism and self-pity to derive any help from it, and Jason has consciously disavowed it long ago.

Faulkner closes his novel with a final confrontation of the two remaining Compson brothers, the one who believes he can live by pure reason alone and the other who is bereft of reason, neither of whom is, therefore, fully human. Meaning for Benjy is succession in due order, driving around the courthouse square to the right of the monument rather than the left. When Luster, bored and mischievous, whips up the mare and swings her to the left of the monument, Benjy finds himself confronted by nightmare and screams his outrage—the store fronts and buildings of Jefferson are all moving in insane reverse from the order in which he knows he ought to find them.[9] Hearing Benjy's outcry, the maddened Jason, now back from the fruitless chase after his niece, snatches the reins and, cursing, turns the old horse into the accustomed route. Whereupon Benjy ceases his bellowing as his world moves again into accustomed order, "as cornice and façade flowed smoothly once more from left to right; post and tree, window and doorway, and signboard, each in its ordered place" (p. 336). This is about as much meaning as experience can have for Benjy. For his frenzied "sane" brother, experience has hardly this much.

9. See below, Notes, p. 445.

16

The World of William Faulkner

(THE REIVERS)

THE EVENTS THAT make up the story told in *The Reivers* take place in 1905. The world of mechanization comes into the dozing little county seat of Jefferson in its most romantic form—as the improbable and exciting early automobile. Faulkner has not always smiled upon the offerings of the twentieth century, with its neon lights, jerry-built ranch houses, and the various other gauds and cheap devices of a plastic or chromium civilization, but in *The Reivers* he enters into the spirit of such expansive souls as those of Mr. Buffaloe, the town's mechanical genius, and of Boon Hogganbeck, the happy-go-lucky, illiterate sportsman. The early motor-car was a challenge, a challenge not to be resisted by the eleven-year-old Lucius Priest,[1] who is innocent, nor by Boon Hogganbeck, who in his own way is innocent too, nor by Ned Mc-Caslin, who is not innocent at all.

Temptation comes when Lucius' father, mother, and grandfather are called out of town to attend a funeral. The car keys are already in Boon's possession and the fact that the road to Memphis runs through the all-but-impassable Hell Creek bottom is itself an incitement. The adventure takes them into the big city, where Boon casually puts them up at Miss Reba's brothel, and later out to Parsham, where there is some very extraordinary horse-racing

1. For the Priest Genealogy see below, p. 448.

at a private track. The stakes in the betting are high, amounting to nothing less than the recovery of the family automobile that Ned McCaslin has managed to barter away.

The adventures that befall Lucius are exciting and for him sufficiently perilous, but the outcome is not dire. Lucius eventually enjoys a reasonable triumph, though he experiences some anguish because of his sense of guilt, his somber apprehensions of a deserved punishment, and the homesickness that occasionally attacks a little boy who is tired, hungry, and much too far away from his mother. The Lucius who tells the story is now, in 1961, a man in his late sixties, but though the passage of time has softened and blurred the pain, his account conveys the sense of immediate experience. It may verge on the improbable and some readers will think it fantastic, but it never becomes, in the telling, soft-headed or irresponsibly soft-hearted. The world that the boy encounters is our world of good and evil, and the boy learns how thoroughly intermingled good and evil are.

The Reivers is thus essentially the story of a boy's initiation into manhood, a theme which obviously has a large place in Faulkner's fiction. One remembers such extended treatments as those given in *The Unvanquished,* "The Bear," and *Intruder in the Dust.* *The Reivers* is by no means the least interesting or least moving of these initiation stories. In any case, it has its own character and quality, one of its distinctions being that it is the only one of the four that is consistently comic in spirit.

Other Faulknerian themes and situations are to be found in *The Reivers.* There is the heroic journey, as in *As I Lay Dying,* though the ordeal of getting the motor car through the mudholes of Hell Creek bottom can be keyed—even if we see Boon striving "like a demon, titanic, ramming his pole beneath the automobile" (p. 87)—to a very different kind of comedy than that invoked to form an amalgam with the terrible and the heroic in Faulkner's account of the Bundrens' crossing of the flooded Yoknapatawpha. There is also the complicated wager, such as that found in the story "Was," and the elaborate bargaining, as is carried out by Ratliff in *The Hamlet.*

Typically Faulknerian confrontations and contrasts abound in

The Reivers. The way in which a man's psychology differs from a woman's comes in for elaborate though often humorous treatment. Much is made of the contrast between the quiet dignity, resilience, and wisdom of the Negro, and the bluster of the rough-hewn poor white. In the deputy sheriff Butch the bluster is crude and cruel; in Boon Hogganbeck there is something boyish and even high-hearted in it. But Boon, with all his occasional heroic virtue, is clearly not a gentleman, whereas Uncle Parsham Hood, the Negro farmer, is every inch one.

In view of the recurrence of so much familiar material—theme, situation, technique—one could make the mistake of dismissing *The Reivers* as simply warmed-over fare. But there is nothing tired or mechanically repetitive in Faulkner's last novel. Some of his basic convictions about human nature receive their happiest and most skillfully dramatic treatment here. Moreover, Faulkner has been extremely successful in his handling of the tone of this novel, casting over Yoknapatawpha County and its inhabitants a kind of golden retrospective atmosphere. The county of 1905, seen as Lucius Priest remembers it, takes on something of the attraction of a country in romance: there were giants in those days and there were worthy giant killers.

Even a casual reading of *The Reivers* will suggest that in this novel the definition of a gentleman receives more than usual attention. In *The Unvanquished* Bayard Sartoris wondered whether he could prove himself a man, and in "The Bear" Isaac McCaslin hoped to be found worthy of the heroic enterprise he was going to be allowed to witness. But for Lucius Priest the matter to the fore is whether this thing or that is what a gentleman would do. Remembering what the Elizabethans called books that undertook to set forth the proper virtues necessary to the fashioning of a gentleman, we might say that *The Reivers* is a sort of latter-day "courtesy book."

Eleven-year-old Lucius is, to be sure, concerned to prove himself a man, to keep from crying, although he is bewildered, homesick, and forced to see and do too much. But the focus of the novel is upon the boy's attempt to preserve a code which is constantly being violated by his elders. Lucius knows that you don't say

certain things about a woman, and when Otis does so, Lucius attacks him even though it means taking a cut across his hand from
an open knife. Since Lucius knows that a man does not strike a
woman, he is genuinely shocked when he hears that Boon has actually hit Everbe, and, bawling and crying, stretches as high as he
can in order to strike at Boon's face.

But Lucius can sometimes approve of Boon. He does so when he
hears of Boon's attacking Butch as soon as the two are released
from their jail cells. "He had to do that," Lucius says, for Butch
has made disparaging remarks about the woman Boon loves, and
Lucius knows that this is not to be tolerated. One must avenge
the insult even if it means being put right back in the jail cell
from which one has just been released.

Most important of all, Lucius knows that one must not lie or
break a solemnly given promise. When he has been brought home
after his adventure to face the music, what shames him most is his
consciousness that he broke his word. It is not the fact that he
risked his grandfather's automobile, or even the worry he caused
his parents, for which he expresses contrition. Perhaps it is because
breaking his word entailed these other offences that Lucius puts
it first. At any rate, the heinous fault that he ultimately feels the
need to confess is breaking his promise to help Aunt Callie look
after the other children. He says: "I lied."

The story of Lucius' initiation into manhood comes to a proper
close with the confrontation with his father and the matter of his
acceptance of his punishment. The boy and his father go down
into the cellar, the father carrying the razor strop and the mother,
though tearful, making no motion to intervene. But when the
father and son are alone, they find themselves at an impasse. The
boy is willing to accept his punishment; in a sense he craves punishment as necessary to atone for the serious betrayal that he
knows he has made. Yet both father and son sense that a whipping will not suffice. Lucius thinks: "if after all the lying and de-
ceiving and disobeying and conniving I had done, all [Father]
could do about it was to whip me, then Father was not good
enough for me. And if all that I had done was balanced by no
more than that shaving strop, then both of us were debased" (p.

301). Lucius is aware that his fault is no mere boyish prank, and that an extra big whipping will not be enough to square accounts. In the experience of the last four days Lucius has stepped across the boundary from boyhood into manhood, and what might conceivably be accounted part of the discipline of a boy is now obviously quite inadequate. Lucius' grandfather breaks the impasse by coming into the cellar, dismissing Mr. Priest, and taking over the office of judgment and punishment. When Lucius' father protests that the razor strop "is what you would have done to me twenty years ago," his father answers: "Maybe I have more sense now" (p. 301).

Alone with his grandfather, Lucius finds that the punishment is to consist in his living with and redeeming what he has done and in assimilating what he has learned through the doing. When the boy protests that he can't live with the burden of his guilt the rest of his life, his grandfather answers: "Yes you can. You will. A gentleman always does. A gentleman can live through anything. He faces anything. A gentleman accepts the responsibility of his actions and bears the burden of their consequences, even when he did not himself instigate them but only acquiesced to them, didn't say No though he knew he should" (p. 302). With this final comment the theme of the gentleman and what being a gentleman entails comes to a firm conclusion.

Faulkner has provided plenty of examples for the aspiring young Lucius. There are, of course, his father and his grandfather ("Boss"); but he meets many others on his travels. There are Colonel Linscomb, at whose home in Parsham the adventure ends, and Mr. Van Tosch, the real owner of the horse that Lucius rides in the race at Parsham. Mr. Van Tosch, though a "foreigner" and a man unacquainted with some of the local customs, shows himself to be a man not only of integrity but of courtesy and honor. Uncle Parsham, patriarch and pillar of the church, is also a gentleman, very plainly so. He has a fine sympathy and understanding for the white child, and he shows a perfect social tact in dealing with his young guest.

Ned McCaslin is also a gentleman, though his virtues point to rather different aspects of this somewhat ambiguous concept. Ned

353

is a man of the world. He has the right touch with the ladies and the right touch in dealing with certain financial problems. Ned is not the stalwart prop of any community but the picaresque hero. This is not to say that he lacks moral fastidiousness. He rightly values the niceties and scorns the little dirtinesses that smudge and stain life. He tries to prevent Lucius' hearing obscenities and tries to shut up the foul-mouthed little Otis, whom he regards with contemptuous distaste.

Ned's financial ethics are pretty much those of Robin Hood: he has no compunction in taking from the rich—by way of a rigged horse-race, for example—and providing for the poor and needy. He is genuinely touched on hearing Bobo Beauchamp's account of the predicament into which he has got himself, and risks a good deal—most of it other people's property, to be sure—in order to rescue him. Ned shows no twinge of conscience in allowing Grandfather Priest to lose the $495 bet, and the explanation that he gives to Lucius, who quite properly wonders about the morality involved, shows an engaging if somewhat original discrimination between points of honor: "Do you want Boss to insult me, or do you want me to insult Boss, or do you want both?" (p. 304). When Lucius asks what he means by this, Ned answers: "When I offers to pay his gambling debt, aint I telling him to his face he aint got enough sense to bet on horses? And when I tells him where the money come from I'm gonter pay it with, aint I proving it?" Lucius can find his way through this parade of logic and can understand why the offer to return the money to his grandfather might conceivably be regarded as a disparagement of his grandfather's knowledge of horses, but he tells Ned that he still doesn't see "where the insult to you comes in." Ned is pat with his answer: "He might take it" (p. 304). Ned's sexual ethics are of a piece with his financial ethics. He is perfectly prepared to take his fun where he can find it, as his encounters with the cook at Parsham, his attempts to bed Minnie, and his references to his wife make clear.

One of the finest gentlemen in the story, whose virtues are not lost upon Lucius, is Mr. Poleymus, the constable at Parsham. Mr. Poleymus comes of sturdy yeoman stock and makes no pretensions to refinement, but he manifests an integrity, a kindliness, and an essential courtesy that entitles him to the status of gentleman in all the best senses of the term. Though quite without bluster, he is entirely capable of putting Butch in his place. As Ned describes the episode, Mr. Poleymus "walked up to Butch and snatched that pistol outen his hands and reached up and ripped that [deputy-sheriff's] badge and half his shirt off too." Ned's summarizing comment is that he "may be little, and he may be old; but he's a man." We find his courage matched by tenderness for his invalid wife: it is he who now cooks, keeps house, and lifts "her in and outen the bed day and night" (p. 257).

Mr. Poleymus' virtues include sensitivity and imagination: he is not handcuffed by conventional notions. When he finds that Lucius is staying with Uncle Parsham, his first impulse is to take the boy to his own house. He says: "I dont think I like that—a white boy staying with a family of niggers." Lucius refuses to go, but the constable, though keeping his voice "still really kind," insists. At this point Ned says to Mr. Poleymus: "There's somewhere you stops. . . . There's somewhere the Law stops and just people starts" (p. 243). Mr. Poleymus replies: "You're right," and asking Lucius once more if this is really his choice, sends him off with "old Possum."

Claiming a modest place at the bottom of this list of gentlemanly exemplars is the seedy little brothel manager, Mr. Binford. In his own corrupt way he essays the role of gentleman too. He presides over Miss Reba's establishment with some sense of decorum. A certain formality at table and some tone of domestic respectability lent by his presence are his contributions. He is perhaps oversensitive at being the only drone in this hive of worker bees, and his sense of personal honor is therefore a shade too nice: woe to the person who casts aspersions on him. Even Miss Reba has to be careful or he will walk out on her, as he has more than once done in the past.

There may be some doubt as to the status of the kindly and helpful railway conductor, but there can be none about the classification of Butch, the brassy deputy-sheriff, the wretched little Otis, or honest Boon Hogganbeck. They are not gentlemen. This is not to say that Boon is irredeemable. Though he never will learn to be a gentleman, he presumably does learn to be a loyal husband and a good father. To be a gentleman is not everything, as Lucius is well aware. He feels very close to Boon; but Boon is not his ideal.

The Negro characters in *The Reivers* are interesting and are handled with great vivacity, conviction, and dramatic sympathy. The generalization fully applies to Minnie, who is not turned into a caricature, as well as to Ned McCaslin and Uncle Parsham. Ned and Uncle Parsham between them pretty well exemplify all the virtues that Faulkner is inclined to attribute to his Negro characters. As we have already suggested, Ned is the wily Odysseus, the concoctor of schemes, the amatory tomcat. Uncle Parsham is the natural aristocrat, the devout churchman, the man of high ethical sense and of the deep insight that comes from purity of heart and range of sympathy.

In the long conversation that Ike McCaslin and McCaslin Edmonds hold in section 4 of "The Bear," Isaac gives his statement of the typical virtues of the Negro, and Gavin Stevens, in *Intruder in the Dust,* gives similar testimony: the Negro has kindliness, warmth, a love of children, and a power to endure. Faulkner celebrates these virtues again and again, and they are the virtues manifested by Uncle Parsham in his treatment of Lucius Priest. But they are fundamentally "private" virtues. With regard to the world at large, Faulkner's Negro characters face problems unknown to the white characters. What particularly distinguishes men like Ned and Uncle Parsham—and, we might add, men like Lucas Beauchamp—is their ability to carry the special burden imposed on them by a caste society. They succeed in maintaining their dignity though they are denied the usual resources of pride and the ordinary protections that men use to guard their self-respect. To hold on to good humor and good sense and yet avoid cringing and truckling servility calls for sanity, imagination, and moral courage.

In earlier chapters we have seen what risks Lucas Beauchamp occasionally had to take in order to hold up his head in a world that was prepared to knock it off because he was "uppity." Even

Dilsey has to cope with this problem. She forces Jason Compson to fear and respect her though she is armed with little more than a dedication so evident that Jason, almost in spite of himself, is overawed. To maintain his dignity, Ned McCaslin depends primarily upon wit and a certain coolness of address. When the brash deputy-sheriff makes a remark about not taking to "strange niggers around here" and inquires for Ned's name, Ned gives it in full: "Ned William McCaslin Jefferson Missippi." Butch tells him: "You got too much name. You want something quick and simple to answer to around here until you can raise a white mushtash and goat whisker like old Possum there, and earn it. We dont care where you come from neither; all you'll need here is just somewhere to go back to. But you'll likely do all right; at least you got sense enough to recognize Law when you see it" (p. 173). Ned's answer is somewhere between impertinence and respect, between sarcastic humor and a certain disarming jocularity. He answers: "Yes sir. I'm acquainted with Law. We got it back in Jefferson too" (p. 173). One might observe in passing that Butch's remarks pay a grudging tribute to the respect in which Uncle Parsham is held. His bearing, his serenity, his very appearance with white mustache and goatee accord with a dignity that Butch concedes has been "earned."

If some of his Negro characters are forced to assume a pose or play a role, Faulkner acknowledges it. Ned, in talking with white men, Lucius notices, sometimes becomes "Uncle Remus"; and in "The Fire and the Hearth" we witness the transformation by which "without effort or even design Lucas became not Negro but nigger, not secret so much as impenetrable, not servile and not effacing, but enveloping himself in an aura of timeless and stupid impassivity" (p. 60). The reaction is that of a cuttlefish enveloping himself in inky fluid, and the motive is the same: the whiskey still has been discovered and Lucas means to disclaim responsibility. Faulkner is a realist, depicting the world that he knows, in which even a Lucas Beauchamp is sometimes forced into subterfuge. But Faulkner never forgets that there is a real man, sometimes a man of great integrity and essential dignity, behind the mask or beneath the cloak of impassivity. He is aware of the problem and sympathizes with the man who has to wrestle with it, whether it be Lucas in a moment of open defiance, as in *Intruder in the Dust*, or Uncle Parsham, who has earned genuine respect from a grudging world by a lifetime of sanity, moral strength, and dignity.

Faulkner's management of the tone of this novel and the special kind of comedy he achieves is nicely exemplified by his portrayal of Everbe's reformation. One might suppose that it was foolhardy to attempt to tell once more the old story of the honest whore, the prostitute with heart of gold, who manages to reform and become again a "good woman." But it is plain that Faulkner has calculated the risks rather well. He has been careful to key the whole episode to comedy and to avoid any note of the sentimental. Everbe, to be sure, has her pathos: she is a big girl, without coquetry, too honest to conceal her feelings, too obvious a target for the two rambunctious men after her favors, and Faulkner does not try to prettify her. Lucius, after fifty-six years, remembers her as "a big girl that stillness looked well on; grief too. . . . Or maybe not grief so much as shame" (p. 202). But his memories are not sentimental and do not screen out the comedy involved in Everbe's awkward subterfuges as she tries to fend off her suitors, or in Boon Hogganbeck's outrage and exasperation that she should decide to "quit" now just when he has made the long trip from Jefferson to see her.

Faulkner has been careful to let us know that Everbe did not have very much of a chance, that she was forced into prostitution, and that she has apparently not yet become hardened by her life in Miss Reba's establishment. At least she still responds to the innocence of children and tries to protect them from the viciousness of the world. She does the best she can to keep Lucius from seeing and hearing things that ought to be kept from a child, and she even tries to do something for her young relative, the dreadful little Otis.

In seeking to protect Lucius and Otis, Everbe is helped by Miss Reba, but the two women work under difficulties. Mr. Binford rather understandably finds it odd, under the circumstances, that

Lucius should refuse a drink of beer, and he finds incomprehensible the reason that Lucius gives for the refusal. (Lucius explains
that he has promised his mother never to take a drink at any time
unless his father or grandfather specifically invite him to do so.)
The answer prompts an ironic comment: "I see. You just
promised her you wouldn't drink with Boon. You didn't promise
not to go whore-hopping with him" (p. 108). Miss Reba shouts:
"You son of a bitch," and Mr. Binford tries to quiet her with
"That'll do," but Miss Reba is not easily suppressed. She has been
stung both in her pride and her sense of propriety. "Like hell,"
she tells Mr. Binford. "I can throw you out too. Dont think I
wont. What the hell kind of language is that." Everbe tries to
hush both of them: "And you too!" she says to Miss Reba. "You're
just as bad! Right in front of them—" Everbe, in saying "them,"
is still naïvely thinking that Otis needs protection.

It is Lucius, of course, who accomplishes Everbe's reform. In
his innocence he cannot believe that certain things can be true of
a woman or, in any case, true of Everbe. It is Lucius' loyalty
to his idea of her and his attempt to defend her good name that
enable her to break with the life of prostitution. Boon and Everbe,
hearing a noise, stop a fight between Lucius and Otis. Lucius, who
scorns tattling, refuses to say why they were fighting. But Everbe
forces the truth from Otis, and when she returns to Lucius she
says: "You fought because of me. I've had people—drunks—fighting over me, but you're the first one ever fought for me. I aint
used to it, you see. That's why I dont know what to do about it.
Except one thing. I can do that. I want to make you a promise.
Back there in Arkansas it was my fault. But it wont be my fault
any more" (p. 159). This is the moment of Everbe's decision to reform.

In the days that follow, Lucius becomes Everbe's refuge and
protector against the amorous advances of both Boon and Butch.
Lucius may not be fully aware of how he is being used as a shield,
but others are. Uncle Parsham says to Ned McCaslin: "He's stood
everything else you folks got him into since you brought him here.
. . . Didn't he have to watch it too, right here in my yard and my
house, and down yonder in my pasture both, not to mention what

he might have seen in town since—that man horsing and studding at that gal, and her trying to get away from him, and not nobody but this eleven-year-old boy to run to? not Boon Hogganbeck and not the Law and not the grown white folks to count on and hope for, but just him?" (p. 255).

The other factor in Everbe's reformation is that she is deeply attracted to Boon Hogganbeck, the bumbling, appealing, foolishly naïve man who is so passionately interested in her. Later she is to tell Boon that the reason she is refusing herself to him, and to anyone else, is that she is in love with him. With her country up-bringing and the substratum of Protestant Puritan attitudes, Everbe will make a great distinction between love and sex. She is now emotionally stirred by a man, and looks beyond any casual week-end encounter. Boon Hogganbeck, in his passionate and fool-ish impatience, wants her body here and now without any thought of what is to come later. But in line with Faulkner's conception of the relation of men and women, once Everbe has made up her mind, it will be she who will dictate the terms.

In his treatment of the story of Everbe, Faulkner would seem to have compounded folly by grafting onto the improbable story of the reformation of a whore the equally improbable story of a good woman who makes the great sacrifice of her virtue for the sake of someone she loves. Yet in the upshot, instead of canceling each other out, it may be that the twin improbabilities act to support each other. Everbe's temporary lapse, her prudent selling of her-self once more, serves to reduce the sense of strained falsetto shrill-ness. We may find it easier to believe in the sincerity of Everbe's attempt to trudge along the strait and narrow path back to virtue just because she is willing to abandon it temporarily in order to detour around a particularly nasty mudhole.

When the horse upon whom the fortunes of all of them depend has been confiscated by Butch, the "stallion deputy sheriff," Everbe decides that the great sacrifice is called for. To save the man she loves and little Lucius and all the rest of them, the horse must be returned in time to run the race, and the only quick means for getting it back, she recognizes, is for her to give in to the importunate solicitations of Butch. She does recover the horse and saves the fortunes of her party, the Boon-Lucius-Ned coalition, but it is a near risk that she takes. Boon, in his fury at her having given in to Butch, strikes her, and Lucius, after first shutting his ears in horror against the news that Everbe has succumbed once more, finally believes it and hardens his heart against her. His feelings have been badly hurt and, like the little idealist that he is, he tends to be implacable and unforgiving. Finally, the hard-boiled Miss Reba pleads Everbe's cause. She says, speaking of Lucius: "Watch him. Jesus, you men. And here's another one that aint but eleven years old. What the hell does one more matter? aint she been proving ever since Sunday she's quit? If you'd been sawing logs as long as she has, what the hell does one more log matter when you've already cancelled the lease and even took down the sign?" (p. 280).

Lucius is touched and walks around to the other side of the car to proffer his forgiveness and understanding to Everbe, who sits there, her eye blackened, "too big to shrink even, shamed . . . her mouth puffed a little." When Lucius tells her that it's all right, she replies: "I thought I had to. I didn't know no other way." Miss Reba now comments upon the ease of granting forgiveness, her comment deriving not so much from the terms of Christian charity as out of her whoremistress' wisdom: "You see? How easy it is? That's all you need to tell us; we'll believe you. There aint the lousiest puniest bastard one of you, providing he's less than seventy years old, that cant make any woman believe there wasn't no other way" (p. 280).

In Miss Reba's comment we hear another variation on Faulkner's familiar theme of the difference between men and women. There are further developments of the theme: if Everbe acts in character in making the sacrifice for her man, so does Boon act perfectly in character in making his lunge at Butch in the jail. Miss Reba observes: "You got to admire him for it," and Lucius agrees. As he puts it, "He had to do that" (p. 277). On this point the code is inflexible, and Lucius is already sufficiently initiated to know it.

As measured by the code of the gentleman, Boon's striking Everbe is insupportable; but in another code, that which governs the relations of men and women, there is something to be said in extenuation—at least Ned McCaslin, who fancies himself an expert in these matters, tries to convince Lucius that this is so. He tells Lucius: "Hitting a woman dont hurt her because a woman dont shove back at a lick like a man do; she just gives to it and then when your back is turned, reaches for the flatiron or the butcher knife. That's why hitting them dont break nothing; all it does is just black her eye or cut her mouf a little. And that aint nothing to a woman. Because why? Because what better sign than a black eye or a cut mouf can a woman want from a man that he got her on his mind?" (p. 263). This may be wisdom of a sort, though Lucius will obviously have great difficulty in fitting it into his paradigm of a gentleman's conduct. But Boon is no gentleman and perhaps Everbe does not expect or want him to be. Ned may be closer than Lucius to a correct reading of Everbe's reaction to a blow struck frantically by a loved one out of an agony of love betrayed.

Lucius, in trying to learn to be a gentleman, has also been learning what it takes to be a man. As he rides in the buggy on the way to Uncle Parsham's, he suddenly starts crying, because he is homesick and because he hadn't any dinner "but a piece of cornbread." Uncle Parsham understands and lets him weep, but finally tells him: "Now you can quit. We're almost home; you'll have just time to wash your face at the trough before we go in the house. You dont want womenfolks to see it like that" (p. 247).

Not least among the pieces of wisdom dispensed to Lucius is what Uncle Parsham tells him about the contrasting natures of mules and horses. The difference between the mule and the horse is the difference between sagacity and mere ardor, between wisdom and folly. The folly is on occasion heroic folly, but it is folly just the same. Uncle Parsham tells the boy that "when a horse gets a wrong notion in his head, all you got to do is swap him another one for it," but that a mule "can hold two notions at the same time and the way to change one of them is to act like you believe he thought of changing it first. He'll know different, because mules have got sense. But a mule is a gentleman too, and when you act courteous and respectful at him without trying to buy him or scare him, he'll act courteous and respectful back at you—as long as you dont overstep him. That's why you dont pet a mule like you do a horse: he knows you dont love him: you're just trying to fool him into doing something he already dont aim to do, and it insults him" (p. 245).

Many of Faulkner's characters exalt the horse and chivalry, the code of values developed by knightly horsemen to which the horse has given his name. Faulkner has a weakness for such blindly ardent devotees who recklessly spend themselves for an idea or on an impulse—whether they be Miss Jenny Du Pre's brother Bayard, who charged the Federal army in order to pick up some anchovies, or Joe Christmas, who always put himself at the highest fence, and who once, in disgust at the fecund-mellow voices of Negro women, sought the smell of horses as something uncompromisingly masculine, even "a mare horse [being] a kind of man." But Faulkner, as early as *Sartoris,* pays his respect to the homely mule, and it is no accident that some of the characters he most admires understand the mule and partake of his intelligence, his common sense, and his stubborn patience.

What Uncle Parsham told Lucius on this occasion about mules apparently stayed with him. Half a century later, when Lucius Priest rates the animals in terms of intelligence, he puts the rat first, the mule second, cats third, and dogs and horses last. His reasons for putting the rat and the cat so high are rather chilling: the rat is able to make use of man so as to take superb care of itself. The cat uses man too, for it is incapable of loving him and would not lift a paw to help him. Dogs, because they are "courageous" and "faithful," and horses, since they can be tricked and cajoled by a child into breaking their limbs or hearts "in running too far too fast or jumping things too wide or hard or high," (p. 122) cannot be regarded as very intelligent. A mule, "unlike a horse . . . is far too intelligent to break its heart for glory running around the rim of a mile-long saucer" (p. 121). This is a rating of sheer intelligence, one reminds oneself, and not of generally admirable qualities. The fact that the rat can win first place on such a scale suggests the inadequacy of mere intelligence. Lucius Priest, it is plain, loves dogs and horses, and does not love rats. He loves dogs and horses in part for their weakness, that disabling and irrational loyalty. But he admires the mule too. The mule is, as Uncle Parsham maintained, a "gentleman," possessed of certain decencies and courtesies even if he also possesses realism and sagacity. Intelligence is a virtue and is to be valued, and it can be valued the more when it does not eat up the other virtues.

There is, I suppose, a kind of parable here. Some kind of mean must exist between the ratlike intelligence of a Flem Snopes or a Jason Compson, on the one hand, and on the other, the too-generous ardor of a Quentin Compson, the riderless horse breaking his neck by attempting the hurdle much too high. Faulkner values fervor and courage but he also values intelligence, and if he seems at times to associate some of his more admirable Negro characters with the mule, the association is meant as a compliment. But the association is not fixed and the equation is not so simple as this—mules: Negroes:: horses: white men. The Negro Lucas Beauchamp on at least two occasions takes the chivalrous action and is saved from breaking his neck not by his own sagacity but by luck; on the other hand, the character who exhibits most consistently the virtues that Faulkner attributes to the mule is a white man, V. K. Ratliff. In general, Faulkner does not make the mistake of conceiving that fiction should present some golden mean—some happy balance struck between coldblooded intelligence and quixotic, self-abandoning ardor. In his novels he gives us both extremes and the whole range of mixtures that lie between them.

It may be useful to contrast *Light in August,* the first novel discussed in this book, with *The Reivers.* There can be no doubt as to which is the greater novel: *The Reivers* has neither the amplitude nor the intensity of *Light in August.* It does not plumb the depths of the human spirit as *Light in August* does. Yet there are patterns of thought and action common to the two books, and therefore comparable though the author has lighted them in different ways. Byron Bunch's pursuit of Lena, who is not a prostitute but who is certainly a Magdalen of a kind and who has just borne a bastard child, corresponds at least in a general way to Boon Hogganbeck's pursuit of Everbe Corinthia. In both novels there is a great deal of comedy, but neither the comedy involving Boon or Byron nor that involving Everbe or Lena is bitter and corrosive. Byron is the quiet, methodical little Puritan; Boon, the relatively uninhibited son of nature. Lena and Everbe are both "very women." They are products of the same rural culture, and possessed of inner resources that make them almost formidable in their simplicity. But we see Everbe closer up: she is a warmer creature than Lena, less sure of herself, and clearly in love with the man who will eventually claim her.

In *The Reivers* there is no real equivalent to Hightower and his agonies, or to the lonely Miss Burden, or to the painfully distraught modern Ishmael, Joe Christmas. The tense and obsessed Percy Grimm has been gentled, in *The Reivers,* into the noisy Butch Lovemaiden, with his bluster and his small tyrannies, but without the deadly concentration of Grimm. Mr. Poleymus is of the same breed as Byron Bunch. He has folk wisdom, an unshakable grasp on the basic human decencies, and a business-like courage that carries him right on through what he has to do.

In *Light in August* the Negro and the aristocrat have little part in the action. The reader is always aware that Jefferson, like any other town in the deep South, has a large Negro population, and an oblique reference to Colonel Sartoris reminds him that some of the old county families still survive, but apart from the declassed Hightower and the few Negroes that move for a moment into camera focus in an occasional scene, the characters in *Light in August* are all poor whites or whites of yeoman stock.

In *The Reivers,* on the other hand, the full spectrum of Faulkner's social world is exhibited. Lucius Priest's family come of planter stock, though the Priests now live in town and Lucius' grandfather is a banker. We have glimpses of the Priest household before Lucius starts out on his adventure, and Lucius returns to the world of the gentry in the scene at Colonel Linscomb's great house at Parsham, where he meets the Colonel and Mr. Van Tosch and confronts his grandfather. In spite of his sense of guilt and some sense of awe at Colonel Linscomb's establishment, it is a world to which Lucius is relieved to be able to return. He can now throw off his responsibility—for Boon, for Everbe, for the horserace—and be a child again.

The Reivers is crowded with Negro characters—Negroes of all degrees and kinds, a variety that includes Aunt Callie, the fat cook at Parsham, and Miss Reba's servant Minnie, with her resplendent gold tooth; young Negro boys like Lycurgus or Colonel Linscomb's jockey McWillie; and men to be reckoned with, men so impressive as Ned McCaslin and Uncle Parsham Hood.

It is appropriate that Faulkner's last novel should exhibit—whether by conscious design is immaterial—the full range of the classes and kinds of people who live in his famous county. The fact that some of them live forty miles away across the Tennessee line does not matter, for these are the proper neighbors of their Mississippi counterparts, and the west Tennessee county in which Faulkner's Parsham [2] is located is no more fabulous and no less real than Yoknapatawpha itself.

As the reviews of *The Reivers* indicate, some readers have been tempted to attribute the absence of characters like Joe Christmas or Joanna Burden to the author's revulsion from violence and strife, and to a general mellowing of his views of human nature. It may be so, though in *The Mansion,* the novel written just before *The Reivers,* there is no discernible abatement of violence. As for Faulkner's view of human nature, *The Reivers* itself shows that Faulkner has not radically modified his notion that most human beings are cross-grained and cantankerous. The fact that the spirit of *The Reivers* is comic and that most of its characters are good and kindly people is scarcely evidence of a late mellowing. Conversely, in a novel as generally dark and violent as *Sanctuary* there is a lively sense of the comic aspect of human life, and even in *The Sound and the Fury* Faulkner acknowledges a deep respect for the human being's power of endurance and his capacity for kindness and goodness. The truth of the matter is that Faulkner's world has always had room in it for a wide range of experience and that Faulkner has never offered his world as proof of any special thesis about human nature other than the marvelous capacity human beings have for goodness and evil. If we do feel, however, that there is a hint of the reminiscent and the valedictory in what might be considered the aging novelist's more tranquil glance back at his familiar county, the change is

2. See below, Notes, p. 446.

merely a matter of lighting. There is no real alteration of the landscape and, even if the light is softened, no relaxation of the artistry. Here an important distinction should be made between *The Reivers* and works such as *Requiem for a Nun* or *A Fable*. In *Requiem for a Nun* the attempt to make an honest woman of Temple Drake led to some strained oversimplifications. In *A Fable* the attempt to make a case for certain human values led to allegorical abstractions, which again involve oversimplifications.

The Reivers, in spite of its improbable yarn, does not oversimplify. Though Faulkner expects us to believe that Everbe does become a good woman and that she and Boon Hogganbeck are going to live happily ever after, the ups and downs of their marital happiness are clearly foreshadowed. Boon will not, to be sure, torture himself with memories of his wife's earlier life, as Temple Drake's husband did in *Requiem for a Nun,* and Everbe is not likely, even if she could afford it, to employ Minnie as a house servant so as to have someone to talk to about the good old days in the brothel. Everbe and Boon will be protected from such pickings at the moral scab by their unself-consciousness, their earthiness, and in short, their level of culture. Their typical difficulties, one predicts, will be somewhat different: Boon once in a while will come home drunk, and Everbe will sometimes adopt a shrewish tone in insisting that the improvident Boon make plans for the proper rearing and education of their children.

If the future of Boon and Everbe is presented as hopeful, it is not really much more hopeful than the future of Byron and Lena at the conclusion of *Light in August*. The basis of hope for both couples is essentially the same. The difference between *The Reivers* and *Light in August* lies not in Faulkner's having repudiated the world of his earlier novels for a different and more hopeful world but simply in his having limited himself to one segment of that earlier world. This chosen segment is already clearly visible in *Light in August*—and even in such novels as *The Hamlet* and *Sartoris*. *The Reivers* does not reveal the depths of Faulkner's world—the violence, isolation, and agony to be found in *Light in August, The Sound and the Fury,* or *Absalom, Absalom!*—but it does, as we have suggested, show the full range of the human types to be found in that world. All the classes and kind are here—the total social structure.

Taken together, the Yoknapatawpha novels and stories create for us an amazingly rich and intricate world, and one that embodies its own principles of order. The human society there depicted shows the influence of the physical land and the climate. Even the town dwellers of Jefferson have not broken their ties with the land. Moreover, the society of Jefferson and Yoknapatawpha has its location in time as well as space. It bears a special and significant relation to history. It has a sort of collective memory. Because it does, it can see itself in a dramatic role. It embodies a style of life. Most of all, this society is bound together by unspoken assumptions—that is to say, it is a true community. Its members are related to each other not merely by function but by common loves, hates, and fears. The fact that it is provincial does not prevent its serving as an excellent mirror of the perennial triumphs and defeats of the human spirit. Nor does that fact insulate it from the great world outside. The special problems of modern man, on occasion, make their appearance within it, and their modernity is the more sharply defined by being set off against the concrete particularity of its old-fashioned order.

Like any other world truly wrought of the imagination, Faulkner's is a realm of the spirit. In spite of the harsh realism and the much-advertised violence of Faulkner's work, his "facts" are important only as they exhibit purpose and value. Even lack of purpose and value take on special meaning when brought into Faulkner's world, for its very disorders are eloquent of the possibilities of order: Joe Christmas' alienation points to the necessity for a true community, and the author's dramatically sympathetic delineation of Joe's plight may be said to point to the possibility of that true community. It is difficult to think of an author whose basic assumptions are farther from the currently fashionable world of the absurd. For Faulkner's work speaks ultimately of the possibilities and capacities of the human spirit for finding and embodying meaning.

Notes

2. THE PLAIN PEOPLE

Charles Mallison as Faulkner's Mouthpiece

The passage (*Town*, p. 307) figures prominently in Steven Marcus'
"Faulkner's Town," *Partisan Review*, 24 (1957), 432–41; reprinted in
William Faulkner: Three Decades of Criticism, Frederick J. Hoffman
and Olga W. Vickery, eds., (Michigan State University Press, 1960),
pp. 382–99. Mr. Marcus remarks that Charles Mallison expresses here
"one of the most explicit and critical statements Faulkner has made
about his culture. It is a negative judgment, a judgment of failure
upon a culture being devastated from within by its own values—values
it has always had, even in its palmiest days when there were giants in
the Southern earth." He says that the tyranny established by the "incorrigible and unreconstructible Baptists and Methodists" generates
"both the fatal, desperate passions of the Eulas and de Spains, and
the meanness of spirit against which they batter themselves and which
finally, meanly, extirpates them as it tends to extirpate most impulses
toward sensibility, vitality and style. It is utterly appropriate that a
Snopes should come to power in this culture; he is no harbinger of
something new and alien, something out of the North, or part of the
'coastal spew of Europe,' but the fulfillment of a tradition, its native,
purified, stripped-down product."

There is a certain neatness in being able to damn the culture you
dislike with words out of Faulkner's own mouth. But if we can be
certain that Charles is speaking for Faulkner here, how can we be
sure that he is not speaking for him when he utters very different
sentiments a few pages further on? Charles remarks of Linda (p. 340)

that "she had the whole town on her side now, the town and the county and everybody who ever heard of her and Mr. de Spain or knew or even suspected or just guessed anything about the eighteen years. . . . Because I know now that people really are kind, they really are . . . even the most Methodist and Baptist of the Baptists and Methodists." Eula Snopes (speaking for the author?) makes the same point on page 329: "Because people are really kind, you know. All the people in Yoknapatawpha County that might have made sure Mama knew about us, for her own good, so she could tell Papa for his own good."

The novels of Faulkner can tell us a good deal about the quality of Southern culture, but the way to read them is not to seize upon remarks made by the characters to support our own conceptions or preconceptions. We compound the folly involved in this kind of reading when we decide hastily that this or that remark made by a character bears the stamp of Faulkner's personal approval.

As for Faulkner's attitude toward Southern culture, it is a mixture of deep affection and furious disapproval, of abiding loyalties and sharp specific disagreements. The complications of his attitude doubtless reveal themselves through the speeches and actions of his characters, but we must not expect to find Faulkner's judgment neatly summed up in a diatribe.

Books that Deal with Southern Rural Folk

A useful (and interesting) book to read for the light it throws on the plain people of the Yoknapatawpha novels is *Old Times in the Faulkner Country* by John B. Cullen, with Floyd C. Watkins (Chapel Hill, 1961). Though this book provides general information about the customs, manners, and habits of the people, as well as the geographical detail of Lafayette County, and has to do with the various classes of society who live there, it will prove helpful in giving the reader some special insights into the life of the plain people. John Cullen was one of Faulkner's old hunting companions, and Mr. Watkins has been very skillful in developing the book so that we have not only Cullen's ideas about Faulkner's world but the sense of listening to Cullen talk about them. (*Old Times in the Faulkner Country* also suggests possible originals for some of Faulkner's characters and sources of some of the incidents in his novels.)

Another very useful book with reference to the rural folk of the

South is Thomas D. Clark's *Pills, Petticoats, and Plows* (Indianapolis, 1944). This history of the Southern country store is a mine of information about the life of the country people in the Southern states, especially during the last half of the nineteenth century.

Elmo Howell's "Colonel Sartoris Snopes and Faulkner's Aristocrats," *Carolina Quarterly* (Summer, 1959), pp. 13–19, has some excellent comments upon the country people of the South.

Several years ago, John M. MacLachlan, in an article entitled "William Faulkner and the Southern Folk," *Southern Folklore Quarterly*, 9 (1945), 153–67, argued against taking some of Faulkner's darker pictures of the poor whites as having a literal sociological reference. In his opinion, "the available evidence does not support the idea that the southern regions are in a state of cultural decay. As for the 'little folk,' we have abundant proof that their health, their literacy, their efficiency as farmers and the level of quality of their religious and political behavior have all improved greatly during the present century."

MacLachlan wrote that the fate of the South was not going to be determined by the fact that there are "black sheep among the cultivated people or grasping shysters at large among the little folk." So much, in his opinion, for the decay of the gentry and the appearance of the Snopeses. Like Frank Owsley, MacLachlan has words of praise for "the folk culture of the region" which, he points out, survived with a "remarkable vitality the distress-filled years of the Civil War and the Reconstruction."

3. FAULKNER AS NATURE POET

Man's Innocence and his Harmonious Rapport with Nature

R. W. B. Lewis is very sound in his treatment of this problem in *The Picaresque Saint* (Philadelphia and New York, 1959). The author of *The American Adam* ought to be, and is, sensitive to any possibility that Faulkner may see America as a world of innocence which offers man a new chance. He writes that the "identification of the New World as a divinely offered second chance for humanity after the first opportunity had been so thoroughly muffed in the Old World—the association of America with Eden—has never been more eloquently made" than by Isaac McCaslin in his conversation with Cass Edmonds in "The Bear," but Lewis goes on to say that "Faulkner and Isaac

McCaslin conclude that the mistake was inherent in the myth [of such a new world]; that the New World was not ever devoid of evil, from the moment of its settling," and that what Isaac's ancestors and their kind "brought with them into the New World was themselves; what they brought was the nature of man" (pp. 205–06). Thus the qualities by which Isaac feels he must live are "not given but achieved, by conduct and by art, through discipline and submission" (p. 207).

The Stoicism of Wordsworth and Faulkner

For a discussion of Wordsworth's Stoicism the reader is referred to Jane Worthington's *Wordsworth's Reading of Roman Prose* (New Haven, Yale University Press, 1946), and to Newton P. Stallknecht's *Strange Seas of Thought* (Bloomington, Indiana University Press, 1958). In his 1958 edition (the second), Professor Stallknecht has included an appendix on "Wordsworth and Roman Stoicism." He accepts Miss Worthington's general argument, and comments that "Wordsworth's almost religious emphasis upon the tranquillity and glad confidence that spring from an enduring rational self-control and his suggestion that this way of life is in harmony with the law-abiding system of nature are especially characteristic of Seneca, whom Wordsworth recognized as an author worthy of his attention and respect." But Stallknecht goes on to say that he thinks that the texture of Wordsworth's Stoicism is not wholly of Roman origin: "His philosophy of duty is by no means merely a revival of ancient ways of thought. Wordsworth's Stoicism is modern, even romantic in aspect, just as his Platonism in the *Intimations Ode* is romantic in treatment. This seems true even if we ignore the growing emphasis on Christian attitudes and modes of expression already apparent in *The Excursion*. To be sure, such modern Stoicism, whether we find it in Wordsworth, in Kant, or elsewhere, will resemble in broad outline its ancient counterpart. But it will often develop characteristics of its own." The rest of Stallknecht's appendix elaborates and illustrates some of these developments with their parallels in writers like Shaftesbury and Kant.

Professor John Hunt has kindly allowed me to quote a few passages from his unpublished manuscript "William Faulkner's Theological Center." The following are some of the contrasts between the Stoic view and the Christian view: "Human failure in Stoicism is a failure of nerve, an error in judgment, or a result of ignorance rather than sin; it is a failure because of finitude rather than guilt." Again, "Stoic courage is heroic, while Christian courage is humble; Stoic endurance is a human achievement while Christian endurance is a gift of forgiving love." Such polarities as these, according to Hunt, are evident in Faulkner's work. Indeed "the Stoic and Christian assessments, with Faulkner from the beginning, have formed the poles of a theological tension. If they saw anything religious at all in Faulkner, the early critics could see little else than his Stoicism. But we do not have to wait," writes Hunt, "until the appearance of *Go Down, Moses*, in 1942, in order to find a balance between the visions of a fallen world and a redeemed world." In that novel, Hunt continues, Faulkner shows that "Isaac's diagnosis of the human condition is Christian, but his solution to it is essentially Stoic, essentially one in which the reason and the will remain intact, unaffected by the taint. Isaac assumes he can slough off the sin and act in the heart's truth. That he is unable finally to do so testifies to the accuracy of his diagnosis and to the fallacy of his solution." Hunt concludes by saying that "as a Stoic, Faulkner believes the values in life are posited by men, but as a Christian he sees them to be attainable only in love."

If I understand Hunt's position here, he is saying that unlike the ancient Stoic philosophers, Faulkner, in effect, sees our present world as a fallen world, and yet he does not rely upon grace to extricate man but hopes somehow that man's courage will avail to do so. The kind of courage involved is Christian in its willingness to acknowledge guilt and Stoic in its determination to act in the face of finitude. Hunt sums up by saying: "Faulkner seems unable to tell the Christian story in isolation from Stoic insights, but also unwilling to let his attachment to the traditional Stoic vision obscure the Christian judgment which explains its failure to provide a lasting and meaningful moral order."

Mr. Hunt has allowed me to quote the following excerpt from a recent letter of his on this subject:

> Isaac's relinquishment is Christian only in a limited sense, for though it is heroic in its own way, it is a retreat which assumes the taint is not radical, does not incapacitate the will and the reason. As I understand it, . . . it is precisely a dissociation of love from the will and the reason that is involved in the fall. The more I think about this, the more it seems to me that I am saying Faulkner is not only Christian in his diagnosis (agree-

ing here with Isaac) but also Christian in his understanding of what the cure must be. The human problem is both finitude and guilt; both Stoic and Christian insights are involved. Faulkner's Stoicism is in his confidence in the Stoic virtues—of justice, duty, endurance, resignation, of those human values reflecting the logos, the divine reason. It is, further, in his belief that if man is to be rescued he must rescue himself, and in his hope that with courage he will be able to effect his own rescue. But Faulkner is Christian too, because the only courage which can effect these virtues is a courage founded on love.

If there is a Christian hero of "The Bear" it is Cass. Like Isaac, though perhaps more reluctantly, he accepts the guilt as a burden, but unlike Isaac he is not immobilized by it. Cass takes on responsibility, enters into the stream of life, even though he acknowledges the failure of justice to fulfill love.

In this general connection it may be interesting to note Rudolf Bultmann's treatment of the subject in his *Primitive Christianity in its Contemporary Setting* (New York, Meridian Books, 1957). The Stoic wishes to be free just as the Christian wishes to be free; and, whether we regard them as Christian or Stoical, Faulkner's typical characters yearn for their freedom. But as Bultmann puts it,

> freedom for the Stoics means independence of all reality, external to the human subject. For the Christian on the other hand, the problem of freedom raises the whole question of human nature. Is man left to himself really capable of the Good? Paul can also agree that when a man does evil he is not really doing what he wants to do. But that does not mean that his wrongdoing is simply a mistake. It means that man is radically incapable of doing what he wants to do. . . . For the Stoic, the way to peace and security is to turn away from the world, whereas for the Christian this is precisely to plunge oneself into the disquietude of guilt.
> [pp. 143–44]

Bultmann says that all of this can be expressed in another way: "The Stoic believes that it is possible to escape from his involvement in time. By detaching himself from the world he detaches himself from time. The essential part of man is the Logos, and the Logos is timeless. So the Stoic concentrates exclusively upon his Logos-being, thus rising superior to all obligations in denying himself any future." This would seem to be the posture Gail Hightower attempts to take. It has a special relevance, too, to Quentin Compson of *The Sound and the Fury*, for Quentin, as we shall see, is trying desperately to escape from time, but, as Bultmann puts it, "in thus repudiating the future, he deprives the present and the past of their temporal character as well" (p. 144).

4. THE COMMUNITY AND THE PARIAH

Meaning of the title Light in August

For many years it has been constantly stated that the title of this novel had nothing to do with the quality of daylight in the month of August but rather alludes to a folk idiom for impending birth. A cow that is expected to calve in August will be "light in August." The rather bovine Lena who, at the beginning of the novel, is heavily pregnant, is to become "light" in August. But when Faulkner was asked at the University of Virginia whether "the title *Light in August* came from a colloquialism for the completion of a pregnancy," Faulkner replied "no, I used it because in my country in August there's a peculiar quality to light, and that's what that title means." (See *Faulkner in the University*, p. 74.) He subsequently added:

> In August in Mississippi there's a few days somewhere about the middle of the month when suddenly there's a foretaste of fall, it's cool, there's a lambence, a luminous quality to the light, as though it came not from just today but from back in the old classic times. . . . from Greece, from Olympus. . . . It lasts just for a day or two, then it's gone, but every year in August that occurs in my country, and that's all that title meant, it was just to me a pleasant evocative title because it reminded me of that time, of a luminosity older than our Christian civilization. Maybe the connection was with Lena Grove, who had something of that pagan quality. [p. 199]

Joe Christmas' Flight

There are some very interesting questions that have to do with Joe Christmas' last hour of life. His behavior is so odd that one can understand why Gavin Stevens made his attempt to account for it—

even if one has to discount certain aspects of Stevens' theory. In the first place, why did Joe Christmas break away and run? Was he trying to commit suicide, as some critics have hinted? If he *was* bent on suicide, it is curious that he picked up the pistol in the Negro cabin. In the second place, what was his purpose in going to Hightower's house? And why, after arriving there, did he strike the old man about the head?

The act of snatching the pistol and the attack on Hightower do not look like suicide. But, then, having struck down Hightower, why did Christmas refuse to fire his pistol at Percy Grimm? Though I think that Gavin Stevens' attempt to account for Joe's action is probably wide of the mark, there certainly is a real problem set by his last actions. We can, of course, simply say that toward the end the man was maddened and frenzied and did a great many things compulsively, acts which add up to no coherent pattern. What provides the real problem is something else: we are told on page 401 that Joe Christmas has agreed to plead guilty and take a life sentence. This is on the testimony of the sheriff himself. Why then did Christmas, after he had decided to take the life sentence, break and run?

There is another bit of evidence to be fitted into the pattern. We are told on page 392 that Mrs. Hines saw Joe Christmas in jail and told him something. Stevens thinks that she told him that Hightower could save him. Stevens was also convinced (p. 392) that Joe Christmas believed her. This is why Joe sought out Hightower's house.

Gavin Stevens has an elaborate but fanciful reconstruction of what might have gone on between Joe and his grandmother when she visited him in the jail, and what perhaps passed through Joe's mind during his escape and flight to Hightower's house. Gavin is frankly guessing, and the probability of his account does not concern us here. But the psychology offered by Gavin is sound: that Joe's flight to Hightower's seems purposed, a running with hope, and that this must mean that Joe's grandmother must have given him the belief that in the "presence . . . of that old outcast minister was a sanctuary which would be inviolable . . . *to the very irrevocable past*" (p. 392; italics mine).

But why then did Joe assault the old minister? Gavin, with his elaborate theory of white blood and black blood, accounts for the attack upon Hightower by stating: "I believe that the white blood deserted him for a moment. Just a second, a flicker, allowing the black to rise in its final moment and make him turn upon that on which he had postulated his hope of salvation," etc. If Stevens is simply saying that Joe Christmas at the end is a confused, harried, and desperate man, he is probably right, and perhaps that is as near as we can come to an account of what actually happened; but in that case we don't need the white blood–black blood rigamarole. Whatever Joe's motives were, it is proper *symbolically*, of course, that he should meet his death in Hightower's house, for as Hightower is to realize, he, like Joe, is a murderer and an exile from the human community. The two men are brothers.

The "Lynching" of Joe Christmas

Among the commentators who describe Joe Christmas' death as a lynching are William Van O'Connor (*The Tangled Fire of William Faulkner*, Minneapolis, University of Minnesota Press, 1954); Irving Howe (*William Faulkner: A Critical Study*, 2d rev. and enl. ed. New York, Vantage Books, 1962), and Olga W. Vickery (*The Novels of William Faulkner*, Baton Rouge, Louisiana State University Press, 1959). Mrs. Vickery writes that Joe Christmas is "lynched as 'Negro.' " Through "Percy Grimm the 'young priest' of the occasion, the elect and white of Jefferson castrate and slay the Negro according to ancient custom" (p. 74). In her chapter on *Light in August* she offers many sound insights (some of which anticipate my work), but I think that she is bemused by the Negro-white question and that she errs in trying to interpret the whole of *Light in August* as a study of "myths" got out of hand.

The Sense of the Community

There are plenty of hints in Faulkner's work pointing to the pervasive sense of the community. In "A Rose for Emily" (*Stories*, pp. 119 ff.) the narrator writes: "We had long thought"; "We did not say she was crazy then"; "At first we were glad"; etc. In *The Town* (p. 3) Charles Mallison writes: "So when I say 'we' and 'we thought' what I mean is Jefferson and what Jefferson thought."

Some dozen years ago, in a short article entitled "Notes on Faulkner's *Light in August*," *Harvard Advocate*, *135* (1951), 27, I pointed out the significance of the theme of community for *Light in August*. This aspect of the novel has received considerable development in

Carl Benson's "Thematic design in *Light in August*," *South Atlantic Quarterly*, 53 (1954), 540–55. Benson emphasizes, fully and justly, the place of the community. Curiously enough, however, he calls *Light in August* Faulkner's most pessimistic novel. He seems to me not so fully sympathetic with Joanna Burden as he might be, and I think that he tends to miss the significant point about Percy Grimm.

The Racism of the Burdens

Joanna's grandfather taught his children to hate two things: "hell and slaveholders" (p. 212). But he would seem to hate the slaveholders more than he loves the Negroes. And Joanna's father says that God has put his curse on the Negro race (p. 221). He tells Joanna (p. 222) that the Negro casts a shadow upon every white child: "in order to rise, you must raise the shadow with you. But you can never lift it to your level."

Some readers may feel that Faulkner is being fantastic here in making an abolitionist express such sentiments. If so, they might recall that as late as 1858, Abraham Lincoln stated "that there is a physical difference between the white and black races which I believe will forever forbid the two races living together on terms of social and political equality" (*Complete Works, 4*, J. G. Nicolay and J. M. Hay, eds. [New York, 1894], 89). Certainly there were abolitionists who were racists. For example, see *The Diary of James T. Ayers*, J. H. Franklin, ed. (Springfield, Ill., 1947). Ayers was a Unionist soldier and recruiter of Negro troops. His bitterest reproach, uttered with reference to Jefferson Davis, was that Davis was a "nigger breeder, A negro Equality man mixing his own Blood with niggers" (p. 101). True, he argues that the Negro should be educated. "Educate them," he writes, "set good Examples before them. Let them know they are men and women and are A part and parcel of Gods Creation and I feel Sambo will do tolerably well." But he is aware of the possibility of the Negroes' pushing "into the Northern States" and of the argument that they would then soon "be in every whole and Corner, and the Bucks will be wanting to Galant our Daughters Round." To which his answer is: "Dam the niggers I would Rather Blow there Brains out than they should do this. . . . No man would abhor the sight of A big buck nigger leading my daughter or Any white mans Daughter round [more] than I and yet I think we have ungrounded fears." He is confident that the Negro so much fears the cold and so much craves a southern climate that once the rebellion has been put down and slavery abolished, the Negroes will naturally gravitate to the Southern states. "I shall find myself grossly Disappointed if in fifty years from this time there was not numbers less of the wooleys in the North than now."

The chapter entitled "Along Freedom Road" in Bell Irvin Wiley's *The Life of Billy Yank* (Indianapolis and New York, Charter Books, 1952) indicates that there was a great deal of anti-Negro feeling in the Federal army even among some of the avowed emancipationists. As Wiley puts it on page 109, "One who reads letters and diaries of Union soldiers encounters an enormous amount of antipathy toward Negroes. Expressions of unfriendliness range from blunt statements bespeaking intense hatred to belittling remarks concerning dress and demeanor." This was not the invariable attitude certainly, and some men who began with contempt or hatred toward Negroes apparently changed their minds. But the evidence indicates that it is naïve to suppose that the typical soldier in the Federal army was necessarily in sympathy with Negroes or willing to associate with them as equals.

The Burdens came to Jefferson from Missouri. J. T. Buckley, in an article entitled "Is Oxford the Original of Jefferson in William Faulkner's Novels," *PMLA*, 76 (1961), 447–54, proposes that the character of Calvin Burden might have been suggested by Nelson G. Gill, who came to north Mississippi just after the Civil War to promote education for Negroes. Gill was from Illinois, but his wife was from Missouri. The Gill school for Negroes at Holly Springs, Mississippi, excited much attention in the post-Civil War period.

Buckley's thesis is that Faulkner's Jefferson is not based merely upon Oxford but combines features of several north Mississippi towns—Oxford, Holly Springs, and Ripley—and that the town described in *Light in August* derives special features from Holly Springs. This thesis has called forth an answer from Calvin S. Brown, who argues with great circumstantiality that Jefferson is really Oxford and that "Faulkner habitually thinks of his characters as moving about Oxford and Lafayette County." See "Faulkner's Geography and Topography," *PMLA*, 77 (1962), 652–59.

Joe Christmas as a Christ-Symbol

It has been frequently asserted that Joe Christmas died at the age of thirty-three, and this supposition has had a great deal to do with his being presented as a kind of Christ-symbol. But as William Lamont, in

379

an article entitled "The Chronology of *Light in August*," *Modern Fiction Studies, 3* (1957), 360–61, has pointed out, Joe Christmas actually died at the age of thirty-six. On page 27 we are told that Joe Christmas first appeared in Jefferson three years before he murdered Joanna Burden, and on page 197 we learn that he first came to Jefferson at the age of thirty-three. The death of Joe Christmas can certainly be taken to represent an ironical analogy to that of Christ, whether Joe died at the age of thirty-three or thirty-six; but a realization that at his death Joe was three years past the age of Christ at His death will probably lessen the enthusiasm for seeing him as a Christ-symbol.

The analogies between the life of Joe and the life of Christ have been worked out with great thoroughness by C. Hugh Holman, "The Unity of Faulkner's *Light in August*," *PMLA, 73* (1958), 155–66. Though I find the thesis unconvincing, the article is useful in summarizing the accounts of *Light in August* up to 1957, and it exhibits many sound insights.

Lena Grove and the Female Principle

Faulkner does allow Lena one hard choice in a scene in which she is not completely confident of her position. When the Reverend Mr. Hightower begs her to send Byron Bunch away, Lena is reduced to tears, and she tells him, "with a patient and hopeless abjectness . . . 'And you worry me about if I said No or not and I already said No and you worry me and worry me and now he is already gone. I will never see him again.'" But it is fair to observe that in general Lena knows almost instinctively what she is to do and carries herself forward with a fine and quiet élan. It would not be accurate to call it optimism or cheerfulness or even confidence. Such terms are too self-conscious for Lena's sensibility. But there is usually no agonizing, no painful indecision, no distrust of self on Lena's part. Most of all, she has what can only be called a remarkable confidence in her function. Ilse Lind, in "The Calvinistic Burden of Light in August," *New England Quarterly, 30* (1957), has called this a kind of religious confidence, and that adjective may well be the proper one. But I think it is significant that Lena's religiousness is unself-conscious and that it has very little to do with the kind of stark Protestantism we observe in the other characters.

It may be somewhat nearer the point to say that Lena's assurance is one that Faulkner tends to regard as the natural dower of women and one that can never be a natural attribute of men. To some modern readers his conception of the different roles of the sexes may seem hopelessly old-fashioned and romantic, but the essential distinction that Faulkner makes is one that is deeply rooted in many older cultures, including primitive ones. Some modern readers may actually prefer illustrations drawn from anthropology. Margaret Mead, for instance, in her book *Male and Female* (New York, Mentor Books, 1955), makes Faulkner's *general* point in the following terms. She writes (p. 122) that the boy has to

> face the need to grow, to learn, to master a great variety of skills and strengths, before he can compete with grown males. . . .
>
> But the little girl meets no such challenge. The taboos and the etiquette enjoined upon her are ways of protecting her already budding femininity from adult males. . . . So the life of the female starts and ends with sureness, first with the simple identification with her mother, last with the sureness that that identification is true, and that she has made another human being. The period of doubt, of envy of her brother, is brief, and comes early, followed by the long years of sureness.
>
> For the male, however, the gradient is reversed. His earliest experience of self is one in which he is forced, in the relationship to his mother, to realize himself as different. . . .
>
> The recurrent problem of civilization is to define the male rôle satisfactorily enough—whether it be to build gardens or raise cattle, kill game or kill enemies, build bridges or handle bank-shares—so that the male may in the course of his life reach a solid sense of irreversible achievement, of which his childhood knowledge of the satisfactions of child-bearing have given him a glimpse. In the case of women, it is only necessary that they be permitted by the given social arrangements to fulfill their biological rôle, to attain this sense of irreversible achievement.

This is a way of accounting for the fact that males have to be initiated, face a test which they may well fail, and reach a sense of confidence and sureness only after they have successfully passed the test. Women do not need to undergo any such initiation. Small wonder that to some of the more anxious males—and to many of Faulkner's male characters—women seem to possess a wisdom, a kind of instinctive knowledge of reality, which men must win to by effort.

5. THE OLD ORDER

The Unvanquished *as an Account of the Disintegration of Society*

In an essay-review entitled "The Son of Man: He will Prevail," Andrew Lytle, in the *Sewanee Review, 63* (1955), 114–37, has written one of the most discerning accounts of *The Unvanquished*. He sees the novel as one of Faulkner's "most successful and least understood books" (p. 130). For Lytle *The Unvanquished* represents not only the breakup of a particular society but constitutes a kind of parable of the way in which any society goes to pieces. A society can solve none of the repetitive involvements which are man's plight and inheritance. It can only hold in abeyance the more destructive aspects of these forces, and it does so characteristically "by rules and orders, accepted habits and the convention of property." Through forms such as these the "animal nature of man is transformed" into "what is called civilized behavior."

To say this is, of course, to take an uncompromisingly classical view of man in society, classical in something of the sense in which T. E. Hulme used the term. The general position taken also resembles W. B. Yeats' notion that a civilization requires a constant and necessarily unremitting attempt to maintain balance and control. See also Herbert Butterfield's conception of civilized order in *Christianity and History* (New York, Scribner's, 1949).

Lytle believes that with the Civil War, restricted war for the first time in America gave way to total war, and that with total war our civilization moved toward the dissolution of all forms of order. He sees the breakup of order in this novel in various ways. The "uprooted slaves" represent "the hope of earthly paradise and the loosing of chaos." But Miss Rosa Millard provides a less obvious and more interesting instance of the breakup of society. "To her," Lytle writes, the war "is the usual folly of man raised to its highest power." So we have her absurd journey through the Federal lines to call upon Colonel Dick, and Faulkner, stressing the absurdity of her action, treats the expedition in terms of comedy. But her action points to something very serious too, for the account of what this war really means is grimly realistic.

Lytle, in developing his conception of *The Unvanquished* as a commentary on the nature of the modern world which has no place for a traditional society, is careful not to make Miss Rosa Millard his heroine. He finds that in her own way Miss Rosa is guilty, and he even speaks of "her fall." For as she tries to cope with the engulfing disorder she is "forced," through "the ambiguity of her situation," to violate her own moral code. It is this contradiction between means and ends that finally brings her to her death.

Thus Lytle tends to see Miss Rosa as a tragic protagonist, blind to her fate, guilty of betraying her deeper beliefs, and experiencing defeat in death. Though this is a highly interesting conception and perhaps has its modicum of truth, for my own part I doubt that her character as developed in *The Unvanquished* can sustain quite so much weight. I would prefer to describe her situation in somewhat different terms: Miss Rosa is strong in her courage, her sense of the family, her belief in the basic decencies of life, and her selfless willingness to sacrifice herself for her family and her neighbors. Her limitation is her ignorance of the forces at work in history. For this limitation she is scarcely responsible, but one can point to her religion as defective in that it provides her with a foreshortened view of reality —that is, she relies too much upon her own will; she finds it hard to accept defeat and yet retain confidence in providence; and she underestimates the depths of reality. But how many of us can claim sufficient depth and breadth of insight in such matters?

Hyatt H. Waggoner, in his *William Faulkner: from Jefferson to the World* (Lexington, Ky., 1959), makes an excellent case for *The Unvanquished* as a novel. I think that he overemphasizes the decay of the code and that he too, is somewhat brittle in his treatment of Miss Rosa Millard, but his general account of the novel is perceptive and sensitive.

The Name Sartoris

Most of the names borne by Faulkner characters are family names actually found in the South and more specifically in Mississippi. The name Sartoris is no exception. Miss Brenda Sartoris, of Jackson, Mississippi, writes to me that her father attended high school in Sardis, Mississippi, a town not very far from Oxford. Perhaps Faulkner picked up the name there, though Miss Sartoris believes that the family name occurs elsewhere in the state.

Faulkner Prototypes of the Sartoris Family

For the story of the Sartorises, Faulkner drew rather heavily upon the history of his own family. Colonel John Sartoris derives in some respects from Faulkner's great-grandfather, Colonel John Faulkner, who killed two men while defending himself against assaults and some years later was shot down by a business partner on the streets of Ripley, Mississippi. See Robert Cantwell's introduction to the Signet edition of *Sartoris* (1953). See also Cantwell's "The Faulkners: Recollections of a Gifted Family," *New World Writing*, 2 (New York, 1952), 300–15. This latter account has been reprinted in *William Faulkner: Three Decades of Criticism*, pp. 51–66.

On B. J. Redmond

In *Sartoris* Redmond is named Redlaw. Colonel John Sartoris tells his son Bayard that Redlaw will kill him. The Colonel had just been elected to the state legislature "after a hard and bitter fight," and "doom lay on his brow, and weariness." The railroad in which he and Redlaw had been associated has been finished, but they have now quarreled and so he tells his son: "Redlaw'll kill me tomorrow, for I shall be unarmed. I'm tired of killing men" (p. 23). Surely enough, he is dead the next day.

In *The Unvanquished* (p. 266) Colonel Sartoris tells his son: "I am tired of killing men, no matter what the necessity nor the end. Tomorrow, when I go to town and meet Ben Redmond, I shall be unarmed." But one observes that George Wyatt informs Bayard (p. 268) that his father had been armed, though he had made no attempt to shoot. George says: "John had the derringer inside his cuff like always, but he never touched it, never made a move toward it."

When Faulkner came to write *Requiem for a Nun*, he altered the story once again. In this version Redmond is a carpetbagger from Missouri who settles down in Jefferson after the war and supplies the capital with which Colonel Sartoris and General Compson build "a railroad from Jefferson north into Tennessee" (p. 238). But Sartoris, Redmond, and Compson later quarreled, and "Sartoris and Redmond bought—probably with Redmond's money—Compson's interest in the railroad, and the next year Sartoris and Redmond had quarreled and the year after that, because of simple physical fear, Redmond killed Sartoris from ambush on the Jefferson Square and fled."

6. THE WASTE LAND: SOUTHERN EXPOSURE

An elaborate and, in many ways, searching account of Faulkner's attitude toward the Negro is given by Irving Howe in the fifth chapter of his book *William Faulkner: A Critical Study*. But Howe, concerned to demonstrate Faulkner's "continuous moral growth" in his depiction of the Negro, sees more of a change than perhaps the facts warrant, and trims or squeezes his particular Faulkner episodes to make them illustrate the process of development. He writes (p. 122) that "neither Loosh nor Caspey is conceived in warmth or developed in depth. Both are singled out for an uneasy kind of ridicule, and their rebelliousness is hardly taken seriously." But this is certainly not true of the character Loosh in *The Unvanquished*. (See above, page 85.) Nor does the incident in which Caspey figures quite bear out Howe's remark about him. Caspey, home from the First World War, announces: "I don't take nothin' fum no white folks no mo' . . . War done changed all dat. If us cullud folks is good enough ter save France fum de Germans, den us is good enough ter have de same rights de Germans is. French folks thinks so, anyhow, and ef America don't dey's ways of learnin' 'um." Howe writes that "for such 'sullen insolence' Caspey is knocked down by Bayard Sartoris with a stick of stove wood." Doubtless old Bayard would have resented Caspey's sentiments had he heard them, but what Caspey said that brought on the blow was something rather different. In answer to Bayard's repeated question, "Are you going to saddle that mare?" Caspey answered, "ain't gwine skip it, big boy," and when the half-deaf Bayard could not believe his ears, Caspey repeated, "I says, I ain't gwine skip it." Let us assume that old Bayard was too easily provoked, but it is important to understand specifically what the provocation was.

What makes it most difficult to see a development in Faulkner's attitude, however, is the fact that *Sartoris* (which Howe feels gives us Negro stereotypes) was published in 1929 and that *The Sound and the Fury*, with its portrait of Dilsey, one of Faulkner's most sympathetic Negro characters, surely "conceived in warmth" and "developed in depth," appeared in the same year.

Howe concedes that even in *Sartoris* "there is also a glimpse of another kind of feeling toward the Negro." On the other hand, Howe is uneasy about the way in which even a character like Dilsey may affect the reader. He writes that "no sensitive reader would care to deny her strength and moral beauty," but he registers a dissent from "the effort of certain critics to apotheosize her as the embodiment of Christian resignation and endurance. The terms in which Dilsey is conceived are thoroughly historical, and by their nature become increasingly unavailable to us: a fact which if it does not lessen our admiration for her as a figure in a novel, does limit our capacity to regard her as a moral archetype or model."

The reasoning here is somewhat involved and obscure, but subsequent pages indicate what Howe has in mind. He is concerned lest readers get the impression that Negroes today would want to go on enduring or that resignation and endurance are at the present time really admirable. I think on the whole, however, that it might be better to let the matter rest on our admiration for Dilsey as a figure in a novel, if she is truly admirable in it, and not try to protect the reader from himself. I dare say that few readers are likely to take her as a "moral archetype or model." In any case, this is not a concern with which we have a right to burden the author.

In his first edition Howe wrote: "how the Negroes 'really' feel about Southern society is extremely difficult for any white man to say, though we all know, of course, how they should feel." In his second edition this is altered to read "how Negroes 'really' feel about Southern, or American, society is terribly hard for any white man to say. Serious whites, as they learn more about the hidden, the true life of Negroes, grow hesitant to generalize; they discover how little they know." In this matter Howe might be echoing Faulkner's own remark that because "the white man has forced the Negro to be always a Negro rather than another human being," the "white man can never really know the Negro" (*Faulkner in the University*, p. 211).

When Howe stops worrying about how various readers may possibly get wrong ideas about the Negro from Faulkner's novels, he puts matters very well. He writes: "No other American novelist has watched the Negroes so carefully and patiently; none other has listened with such fidelity to the nuances of their speech and recorded them with such skill; none other has exposed his imagination so freely, to discover, at whatever pain or discomfort, their meaning for American life." This is admirably said and a well deserved tribute.

With reference to the general matter of Negro stereotypes, particularly those of the contented slave, the childlike and happy "Sambo," or the obsequious house servant, the reader might profitably examine the excellent book by Stanley M. Elkins entitled *Slavery: A Problem in American Institutional and Intellectual Life* (Chicago, 1959). Section 3, "Slavery and Personality," is particularly interesting in this connection. Elkins argues that Sambo did in fact exist, though not because of racial characteristics and not even because of the fact of servitude: he did not exist, for example, in the Latin-American slave system.

7. DISCOVERY OF EVIL

Chronology of Events in SANCTUARY (*The year is 1929*)

Horace Benbow leaves his home in Kinston.	Friday, May 3	p. 18
His wife Belle wires Narcissa that Horace has left.	Saturday, May 4	p. 127
Horace arrives at Popeye's.	Tuesday, May 7	p. 14
Horace is back at his sister's, four miles from Jefferson.	Wednesday, May 8	pp. 25, 126
Horace goes to the family home in Jefferson.	Friday, May 10	p. 130
Dance is held at the University.	Friday, May 10	p. 29
The baseball game that Temple was to attend with Gowan is held.	Saturday, May 11	p. 30
Gowan wrecks the car.	Saturday, May 11	pp. 45, 54
Temple is raped and taken to Memphis.	Sunday, May 12	pp. 99, 105, 121, 123, 323
The people in Jefferson view Tommy's body.	Monday, May 13	p. 133
Lee Goodwin is brought to jail.	Monday, May 13 (or perhaps May 12)	p. 135
Horace brings Ruby to his house in Jefferson, but having talked with his sister, takes her to the hotel.	May 13 (or perhaps May 12)	p. 138
Horace goes out to his sister's.	Saturday afternoon, May 18	p. 150

Narcissa has received a letter from Gowan bidding her farewell forever.	Sunday, May 19	p. 154
Horace is summoned by Ruby, who tells him that Temple had been at the Old Frenchman's Place.	Friday morning, May 24	pp. 159, 161, 192
Horace goes to his sister's and reports on Gowan.	Friday night, May 24	p. 197
Horace goes to Oxford inquiring for Temple.	Saturday morning, May 25	pp. 201, 205
Horace meets Clarence Snopes on the train.	Saturday, May 25	p. 208
At the University at Oxford, Horace is told that Temple left school about two weeks ago. (This information is presumably correct. The Jackson newspapers state that Temple has gone to Michigan on approximately the 14th of May, p. 212.)	Saturday, May 25	p. 206
Clarence Snopes meets the two young men who are off to barber college.	Saturday, May 25	p. 214
Horace returns to find that Ruby has been evicted from the hotel.	8:20 P.M., Saturday May 25	p. 215
Horace goes out to his sister's and learns that it was Narcissa who told the church ladies about Ruby.	Sunday, May 26	pp. 218–19
Narcissa asks who the district attorney is.	Monday, May 27	p. 222
Snopes is to go to Memphis.	Monday, May 27	p. 224
Horace finds a place for Ruby.	about May 29	p. 240
Horace has a telephone installed.	about May 30	p. 242
Snopes discovers Temple.	about May 30	pp. 242, 245
Snopes telephones Horace that he has information.	about Sunday night, June 2	pp. 242, 317
Horace visits Miss Reba's.	Monday, June 3	pp. 266, 313, 314
Horace returns to Jefferson at 3 in the morning.	Tuesday, June 4	pp. 266, 313

Snopes starts out for Jackson "for a couple of days."	Tuesday, June 4	p. 313
Narcissa visits Eustace Graham.	Tuesday, June 4	p. 314
Snopes finds Virgil and Fonzo at Miss Reba's.	Saturday, about June 8	pp. 234, 235, 237, 238
Horace telephones Miss Reba and finds that Temple is still there.	about Monday, June 10	p. 321
Red is killed, and Popeye and Temple leave Memphis.	Monday, June 17	pp. 290, 361
Red's funeral is held. Popeye and Temple have fled.	Tuesday, June 18	pp. 298, 307
Snopes emerges from dentist's office talking about a "Memphis Jew" lawyer.	Tuesday, June 18	p. 320
Horace telephones Miss Reba and finds that Temple has left.	Wednesday, June 19	p. 322
The trial of Goodwin opens.	Thursday, June 20	p. 323
Temple appears in court. That night Goodwin is lynched.	Friday, June 21	p. 338

On the Chronology of Events

There are several key dates that peg down the general sequence of events. One of them is the date on which Temple was raped and taken to Memphis. In the court scene on page 343, this is clearly made a Sunday, May 12. The date will fit the year 1929, the year in which we know Faulkner was working on *Sanctuary*. It will not fit 1927 or '28 or '30 or '31, etc. Working back from Sunday, May 12, it is not hard to establish the day on which Horace Benbow left his home or arrived at Popeye's or got back to his sister's near Jefferson, etc.

Another key date is that on which Horace returns to Jefferson at three in the morning from having had his interview with Temple in Memphis the evening before. As the sun rises, he reflects that it was four weeks ago that he saw Popeye watching him across the spring. Since the meeting with Popeye occurred on May 7, the day on which he returned from having seen Temple must have been June 4—that is, if we interpret the phrase "four weeks ago" literally.

Another date which is pegged down quite specifically is the date of Lee Goodwin's trial. We are told on page 321 that the trial was set for the 20th of June.

There is a fourth date which is important in fixing a segment of the chronology. It is the morning on which Horace is summoned by Ruby, whose child has been ill during the night, on which occasion she tells Horace that Temple was out at the Old Frenchman's Place at the time of the murder. Horace is awakened in the morning at 6:30 by a messenger from Ruby. The night before he had reflected that this would be the last night on which the convicted Negro murderer would sing (see p. 159). Now we are told on page 155 that the convicted murderer would be hanged on a Saturday and that one night he would be yelling down out of the soft darkness "of a May night" and the next night would be gone. If the Negro murderer were to be hanged on a Saturday in May, the date would have to be the 4th, 11th, 18th, or 25th. It must be after the 18th, for on page 150 we find that it is Sunday, the 19th of May, and the Negro is still alive, still to be hanged (p. 155). The Saturday for the hanging must then be May 25th. The reference on page 159 to the fact that this night "would be his last night" would appear to make this night the 24th of May; but earlier on the page, apparently on the same day, Horace says "He's only got two days more," which would seem to make the day in question the 23rd of May. (Perhaps the Negro would not be allowed to sing on the night before the execution, May 24th.) At any rate, it is on the day after Ruby tells him about Temple that Horace goes to Oxford to inquire about Temple. He inquires, however (see p. 205), of the clerk at the post office, and the post office would not have been open on a Sunday. It would seem then that we ought to take the date on which Ruby summoned him at 6:30 in the morning as Friday, May 24; that he went out to his sister's that evening to talk about Gowan; and that it was early the next morning, Saturday, May 25, that he came into Oxford by train to inquire about Temple. According to this interpretation, Horace's statement on page 159, "He's only got two days more," would make the date in question Thursday, the 23rd. But whether or not the exact date of Horace's trip to Oxford is the 25th of May, the date is about right, for the clerk at the post office tells Horace that Temple quit school about two weeks ago, and the 25th is two weeks after May 12.

These key dates, along with the other references in the text, allow us to construct the chronology which appears above. There would seem to be only two discrepancies in an otherwise consistent scheme. Narcissa is mistaken in saying that Snopes telephoned Horace "three nights ago"; apparently only two nights had elapsed (see pp. 266, 313, 314, 317). This discrepancy is not very important, but the other one is.

In telling Narcissa that "Court opens the twentieth" (p. 318), the District Attorney obviously refers to the trial of Goodwin on June 20. But when we are told elsewhere that Snopes telephoned Horace "a week before the opening of Court," are we to infer that the call was made on June 13; i.e. one week prior to June 20? If so, how are we to fit into this interval Horace's trip to Miss Reba's, the week that elapsed before he telephoned her, and a later call to her? At the very least nine days are required.

Mr. Charles B. Henley, a member of the Mississippi Bar, has suggested the following solution. He points out that Goodwin's trial could not in any case have occurred on the day that Court opened, for time would be required to empanel a grand jury, get an indictment from the grand jury, and empanel a trial jury. He observes that the "actual practice in the rural counties of Mississippi is to open Court on a specified Monday and to call the docket and dispose of the civil cases during the first term of court. The criminal cases are usually tried the second week. . . ." He thinks it would have been perfectly logical for Goodwin's trial to have been set for Thursday in the second week.

In Faulkner's county, Lafayette, Mr. Henley tells me, Court has always opened on a second Monday, which for June 1929 was the 10th. This would put Snopes' telephone call on June 3—just about the date required by the other evidence in the novel (see p. 388 above).

On Popeye's Name

In concocting the story of Popeye there seems to be some evidence that Faulkner had in mind a Memphis underworld character named Popeye Pumphrey: see Robert Cantwell, "Faulkner's Popeye," *Nation*, *186* (1958), 140–41. It is interesting to note that Faulkner had completed his novel in 1929, over two years before Pumphrey committed suicide. Indeed, *Sanctuary* was published some months before Pumphrey's death in October 1931.

Carvel Collins, in "A Note on *Sanctuary*," *Harvard Advocate*, *135* (1951), 16, tells a very interesting story about Faulkner's having met a girl in a nightclub who came over to his table and told him something about her life—how she had associated with a gangster who was "impotent and with his relations with women . . . was given to substitutions for his impotence. He did keep the girl for a time at a brothel in what might be called semi-privacy." The resemblance to Faulkner's Popeye is obviously close.

Dr. L. S. Kubie's Account of SANCTUARY

Dr. Kubie finds that in the novel itself there is no attempt to explain why Temple does some of the things she does. Her motivations and those of other characters actually lie in their unconscious minds. The key to Temple's conduct, according to Kubie, is the fact that she hates men. As he puts it on page 224, Temple's "career seem[s] to shape itself out of her hate of her father and her four stalwart brothers." It is her hatred of men which is behind her sacrifice of Goodwin, "the potent man," whereas she saves "Popeye, her impotent malefactor."

Dr. Kubie speaks of "Popeye's disguised presence in the courtroom," but I do not know whether he means this literally or is simply thinking of his symbolic presence there. At any rate by the time of the trial Kubie says that "Temple has . . . become an almost automatic engine of destruction." He also would account for Popeye's death through the motivation of Temple. He writes: "it is only indirectly and in the very end that [Temple's] taunts help to drive Popeye himself into a virtual suicide."

It would be impossible to do justice to Dr. Kubie's very interesting essay in a brief note, and I do not pretend to do so here. I must, however, record my disagreement with much that he says as a way of interpreting the story. I find it hard to believe, for example, that Popeye fell into his last lethargy because of Temple's taunts, and I think that Temple's conduct in the courtroom is given a much too simple and therefore less than satisfactory motive in his account. In any case, this article points out very sharply how much Faulkner has left to inference.

The Southern View of Rape

Peter Lisca shows no knowledge of Southern mores when he assumes that the disclosure that Temple had been raped would be a "socially acceptable" account. Temple's family would have made every effort to avoid mention of the rape even though it could be proved that the girl was violated completely against her will and after resisting to the utmost. One notices today the care with which the press in the South still attempts to guard the name of the woman who is raped as compared with the more candid statement of facts in many sections of the press elsewhere in the country. The question at issue here is not which attitude is morally superior but whether it is conceivable that a Mississippi judge, who is supposed to be stage-managing his daughter's testimony, would concoct a story that involved such an admission.

The Memphis Lawyer

Clarence Snopes, it is true, told Horace that he was going down to Jackson (the home of Judge Drake) on what must have been June 4, but if Clarence gave Judge Drake the information then, why did Judge Drake not act to remove his daughter from Miss Reba's? Surely, had he known where she was, he would have tried to do so. But there is no hint in the novel that he did. Perhaps Snopes on his trip to Jackson tried to find out how much Judge Drake knew about the whereabouts of his daughter or merely hinted to him that he might be able to obtain information on Temple. In any case, Snopes seems not to have been paid for his information until two days before the trial (June 18). It is not until then that he turns up with his "sheaf of yellow bills" and his talk of having been paid $100 by "a judge living in the capital of the State of Mississippi."

Mr. Brian E. Cleave, a law student at Manchester University, England, having read my article, "Faulkner's *Sanctuary:* the Discovery of Evil," in the winter 1963 number of the *Sewanee Review,* an article which contains much of the material in this chapter, was kind enough to send me his theory of what happened. His letter, in part, reads as follows:

> As I read it, Eustace Graham, on being given the tip-off by Narcissa that Horace had gone to Memphis as a result of a conversation with [Clarence] Snopes, did not immediately get in touch with Snopes himself, but contacted an underworld lawyer in Memphis to see what he could find out, also telling him that Snopes had information. This lawyer then arranged for Snopes to come to Memphis at short notice, presumably on the promise of a large sum for the information. Snopes, having already received money from two sources for the same information, cancels his trip to Jackson, but does not get quite the reception he expected in Memphis. The "Jew-lawyer" has the information beaten

out of Snopes and gives him a derisive ten dollars. This would mean, of course, that the "Jew-lawyer" is an independent agent, who is brought into the case by Graham and who later does a deal with Popeye after getting the information out of Snopes.

The theory is plausible enough and who can say that it or some other variation on it is not true? But it is impossible to pin it down from anything in the published version of *Sanctuary* or, I might add, in the earlier version of the novel, as represented by the original galley proofs or the manuscript.

SANCTUARY *as the Discovery of Evil*

Aubrey Williams, in his "William Faulkner's 'Temple' of Innocence," *Rice Institute Pamphlet*, 47 (1960), 51–67, makes this general point very decisively. He sums up by saying that

> the true and ultimate shock of the novel is not to be found in the single grotesque episode in which a young girl is raped with a corn-cob. It is to be found in the larger pattern of evil and injustice of which this episode is one mere instance. It is a pattern of evil and a vision of the world which is hardly comparable with any thing else Faulkner has written, though it does have important unexplored connections with the rest of his work. In this novel at least, Faulkner presents us with a bleak assertion that the human body is not a temple of the holy spirit, and with an equally bleak assertion that, for man, there is no sanctuary.

Discrepant Dates in REQUIEM FOR A NUN

In *Sanctuary* Temple Drake is eighteen years old (p. 342), but in *Requiem for a Nun* she is said to have been seventeen at the time of her rape (p. 130). The difference is not terribly important. It may mean that Faulkner had forgotten or that he had changed his mind. But there is a time discrepancy within *Requiem for a Nun* which is due probably to a bit of carelessness or a slip on Faulkner's part. Gavin Stevens (p. 131) refers to Temple's arrival at the Old Frenchman's Place "eight years ago" when Gowan Stevens "took her off the train and wrecked the car at the moonshiner's house." But Temple remarks (p. 274) that this occurred "five years ago that day when I slipped out the back door of that train." Since the events of *Sanctuary* occurred in 1929, those of *Requiem for a Nun* can thus be dated either 1937 or 1934.

On Temple's Alleged Affair with Frank

In her discussion of *Sanctuary* Olga Vickery writes that at seventeen, Temple had "made one very determined effort to break out of [the artificiality of her social life] and to assert her right to choose her own kind of life. Love prompts her to forget her position, to defy her father, and to risk her own life in a futile effort to save her lover. Frank, the intruder in this case, is destroyed, presumably without any legal or social blame being attached to Judge Drake" (*The Novels of William Faulkner*, p. 106). But Mrs. Vickery is here attributing to seventeen-year-old Temple something that had occurred to Ruby, Goodwin's common-law wife. At the Old Frenchman's Place Ruby, in her contempt and disgust—and perhaps fear—of this "nice girl," upbraids her for knowing nothing about love or life, and as proof of it relates to Temple the sort of thing that she herself had been willing to do. When Ruby's father had found out about her lover, Frank, and had threatened to kill him, Ruby had slid down a drain pipe to get out of the upper room in which she had been locked, made her way to Frank, and begged him not to face her father. But Frank insisted on coming anyway, and at the end, when they arrived at her home and saw her father with his shotgun standing on the porch, she tried to interpose her own body between her lover and the death that threatened him, only to be pushed aside and to see her lover killed (see *Sanctuary*, p. 67).

A more careful reading of the passage would have prevented the mistake, and a better sense of the social classifications of the South would have put the reader on the alert against such a mistake. Judge Drake is not the kind of man who strides out on the front porch of his house with a shotgun to blast his daughter's lover, nor could his daughter's lover in 1926 or '27 drive up to the house in a "yellow buggy." Temple is about to descend into the depths, but she is not a young woman who has experienced the more violent and terrible aspects of life: the very point of the novel is the fact that a girl who is going to make her descent into the depths has been heretofore only a bubble playing on the surface.

Needless to say, this misreading of the text thoroughly distorts Temple's character as well as her father's. The same mistake is made by

Elmo Howell in an article entitled "The Quality of Evil in Faulkner's *Sanctuary*," *Tennessee Studies in Literature* (1959), pp. 99–107. Howell's article is, on the whole, informed and sensible. But his mistake in confusing Temple with Ruby allows him to insist much too heavily upon the notion that Temple's whole life is a sham. He writes that before her appearance at the Old Frenchman's Place she "has already had an affair with a young man in Jackson." He also follows Lisca in arguing that Temple's perjury is "directed by her family, who, in order to extricate her from a shameful situation, send an innocent man to his death."

Faulkner's Account of the Writing of SANCTUARY

Faulkner's apparent disparagement of *Sanctuary* in the introduction he wrote for the Modern Library edition has been frequently cited. There he writes that the book was "a cheap idea, because it was deliberately conceived to make money. I had been writing books for about five years, which got published and not bought." Finally, Faulkner writes, "I decided I might just as well make some [money] myself. I took a little time out, and speculated what a person in Mississippi would believe to be current trends, chose what I thought was the right answer and invented the most horrific tale I could imagine and wrote it in about three weeks and sent it to Smith, who had done *The Sound and the Fury* and who wrote me immediately, 'Good God, I can't publish this. We'd both be in jail.' So I told Faulkner, 'You're damned. You'll have to work now and then for the rest of your life.' That was in the summer of 1929."

He did work, taking a job in the power plant on the night shift, and there wrote *As I Lay Dying* "in six weeks, without changing a word." *As I Lay Dying* was published, and Faulkner says that he did not "remember the mss. of *Sanctuary* until Smith sent me the galleys. Then I saw that it was so terrible that there were but two things to do: tear it up or rewrite it. . . . I tore the galleys down and rewrote the book. It had been already set up once, so I had to pay for the privilege of rewriting it, trying to make out of it something which would not shame *The Sound and the Fury* and *As I Lay Dying* too much and I made a fair job."

Most readers have taken to heart Faulkner's statement that *Sanctuary* represented a cheap idea, and they have failed to take into account Faulkner's statement that he thought he made a fair job of rewriting the book into something that would not shame *The Sound and The Fury*. How thoroughly he reworked the original galleys is a matter of record. Linton Massey, in "Notes on the Unrevised Galleys of Faulkner's *Sanctuary*," *Studies in Bibliography* (Papers of the Bibliographical Society of the University of Virginia), *8* (1956), 195–208, has shown in great detail just what Faulkner's revision was. As Massey puts it, "in its original, unrevised form, the story is patently a Freudian study of Horace Benbow, a man who is so much the victim of his half-hidden incestuous fantasies that he has no will of his own, cannot act, and possesses no courage" (p. 202). By bold transpositions, cuts, amplifications, and a great deal of rewriting Faulkner made the book what it is through a "minor miracle of revision" (p. 204).

SANCTUARY *as an Allegory*

One of the seminal pieces of Faulkner criticism is the account of *Sanctuary* published over twenty years ago by the late George Marion O'Donnell ("Faulkner's Mythology," *Kenyon Review*, Summer, 1939; reprinted in *William Faulkner: Three Decades of Criticism*, pp. 82–93). O'Donnell there sees *Sanctuary* as a kind of allegory:

> Southern Womanhood Corrupted but Undefiled (Temple Drake), in the company of the Corrupted Tradition (Gowan Stevens, a professional Virginian), falls into the clutches of amoral Modernism (Popeye), which is itself impotent, but which with the aid of its strong ally Natural Lust ("Red") rapes Southern Womanhood unnaturally and then seduces her so satisfactorily that her corruption is total, and she becomes the tacit ally of Modernism. Meanwhile Pore White Trash (Goodwin) has been accused of the crime which he, with the aid of the Naif Faithful (Tawmmy), actually tried to prevent. The Formalized Tradition (Horace Benbow), perceiving the true state of affairs, tries vainly to defend Pore White Trash. However, Southern Womanhood is so hopelessly corrupted that she wilfully sees Pore White Trash convicted and lynched; she is then carried off by Wealth (Judge Drake) to meaningless escape in European luxury.

This account has proved fruitfully suggestive, but a careful reading of the novel will not, I believe, confirm it. Benbow, for example, is, as we have seen, something more than the formalized tradition. Judge Drake as Temple's father can scarcely be regarded as merely wealth and a means of escape. Besides, this is not what Southern Womanhood has typically escaped into. Popeye (amoral Modernism, itself impotent) uses in fact an instrument other than Natural Lust with which to rape Temple, and though Popeye later does use Red, not as ally but as instrument, Red's affair with Temple actually tends to make her rebel against Popeye. In short, the terms do not quite work out.

True, O'Donnell made it plain that he regretted having had to put Faulkner down as an allegorist, for allegory, as O'Donnell conceived it, was dead (that is, formalized) myth, and Faulkner in writing *Sanctuary* was a "formal traditionalist" rather than the "vital traditionalist" that he showed himself to be in some of his other novels.

Sanctuary is in fact less brittle, less schematized, and infinitely richer than any mere allegory. If, however, we do not "formalize" O'Donnell's terms into a strict pattern, they can be highly useful. They can suggest a great deal about the themes, characters, and social situations in which Faulkner is continually interested. For Gowan Stevens has taken the culture of Virginia at its lowest discount and in its sleaziest terms. Lee Goodwin does represent a very different social class from that to which Horace belongs, and this difference generates some of the difficulties between lawyer and client. Popeye does suggest the kind of modernism which in its brutal efficiency and pure lust for power seems unnatural and inhuman not merely in its violation of the traditional sanctities but also in its monstrous frailties.

8. ODYSSEY OF THE BUNDRENS

Darl's Self-Consciousness

Since the time of the nineteenth-century Romantic poets, the artist has been intensely aware of man's consciousness—as his glory but also as his curse and the source of his troubles. Man differs from his fellow creatures of forest and field by virtue of his consciousness, which means also his self-consciousness. Alone among the creatures, man is able to stand back from himself and view himself as if he were another creature. He can watch himself act and even watch himself watching himself.

Faulkner's treatment of Darl has to be regarded, in part, as a critique of self-consciousness. Darl is self-conscious to the point of madness. His sense of himself in relation to his family is detached in a preternatural way. The other members of the family seem to sense this, and it makes them uneasy. Darl himself is perfectly aware of the alienating force of his self-consciousness. He says: "Jewel knows he is, because he does not know that he does not know whether he is or not" (p. 396)—that is to say, Jewel resembles the natural creature, who, lacking consciousness, never doubts his existence, whereas my very ability to stand aside and look at myself begets doubt within me.

Vardaman as an Idiot

Irving Howe, Harry M. Campbell, Edward Wasiolek, and other commentators have spoken of Vardaman Bundren as an idiot or a child who is crazed. But Vardaman is not an idiot: he has suffered a traumatic experience and in his shock confuses the two exciting events that have occurred so close together: his catching the big fish and the death of his mother. (See *Faulkner in the University*, p. 110–11. See also Floyd Watkins and William B. Dillingham, "The Mind of Vardaman Bundren," *Philological Quarterly*, *39* [1960], 247–51.)

Carl Jung describes cases very similar to Vardaman's. The person involved sees a snake crawling away from a grave and takes it to be the spirit of the person buried there. (See "The Interpretation of Nature and the Psyche," in *Psyche and Symbol*, New York, 1958.) True, this is the mistake of an adult brought up in a primitive society, whereas Vardaman's is the mistake of a child brought up in a society that is simple and rural though not primitive in the anthropological sense; yet the cases are analogous.

Addie and the Experience of Community

Rollo May, in *Existence: A New Dimension in Psychiatry and Psychology* (New York, Basic Books, 1958), makes some comments that seem to have a rather direct bearing on the plight of Addie. On page 56 he writes that one of the "most acute problems of modern human beings" is their sense of having *"lost their world,* lost their experience of community. Kierkegaard, Nietzsche, and the existentialists who followed them perdurably pointed out that the two chief sources of modern Western man's anxiety and despair were, first, his loss of sense of being and, secondly, his loss of his world. . . . Broadly speaking, the symptoms of isolation and alienation reflect the state of a person whose relation to the world has become broken."

On page 57 May goes on to write that "the problem of this loss of world" is not simply

> one of lack of interpersonal relations or lack of communication with one's fellows. Its roots reach below the social levels to an alienation from the natural world as well. It is a particular experience of isolation which has been called "epistemological loneliness." Underlying the economic, sociological, and psychological aspects of alienation can be found a profound common denominator, namely, the alienation which is the ultimate consequence of four centuries of the outworkings of the separation of man as subject from the objective world. This alienation has expressed itself for several centuries in Western man's passion to gain power *over* nature, but now shows itself in an estrangement from nature and a vague, unarticulated, and half-suppressed sense of despair of gaining any real relationship with the natural world, including one's own body.

I am tempted to relate the last phrase to Addie's specific predicament. She is not only alienated from her family but she has lost her own body in the sense that May specifies, and therefore tries to relate her salvation to the body. Though neither Addie nor presumably her creator, William Faulkner, would put the matter in May's terms, May's analysis of this malady of modern man may throw some light upon Addie's need to be assured that her body will be deposited in a grave beside her father's.

The term "existential vacuum," as used by Viktor Frankl in an address delivered before the Academy of Religion and Mental Health in May 1962, would seem to provide a precise definition of Addie's experience as she reports it in the one section devoted to her in *As I Lay Dying*. But Frankl's address has not yet been published, and it is possible that he is using the term to describe a situation of a rather different sort. I have had to rely upon the report of his address as given by *Time*, June 1, 1962, and that given in the *Christian Century, 79* (1962), 722–24.

Faulkner's Debt to Hawthorne

The general resemblance between Addie's lover—the Reverend Mr. Whitfield—and the guilty clergyman in Hawthorne's *The Scarlet Let-*

ter has often been noted. For a very good discussion of this matter see Harold J. Douglas and Robert Daniel, "Faulkner and the Puritanism of the South," *Tennessee Studies in Literature,* 2 (1957), 1–13.

Addie as Heroine

Edward Wasiolek, in *"As I Lay Dying:* Distortion in the Slow Eddy of Current Opinion," *Critique, 3* (1959), 15–23, sharply disagrees with Howe's calling *As I Lay Dying* "the warmest, the kindliest and the most affectionate" of Faulkner's books. On the contrary, before the journey is over with, the Bundrens have "been reduced to a group preying upon one another." Addie's insistence on being buried by her father was motivated he says, by a desire for revenge upon her family. Wasiolek writes that "Addie and Darl are Faulkner's heroes; but Faulkner's tone is bitterly ironic, resigned, and masochistically insistent not only on the bitter condition of man's life, but also on the obtuseness of man's awareness of it. The 'humor' of *As I Lay Dying* grimaces grotesquely through the doomed protest of Addie and Faulkner against the condition of isolation which all men share and against the insensitivity of most to that isolation." But such an account as this reflects a one-sided view of the novel. Darl is far from the hero of the novel, and if there are heroic qualities in Addie, this does not mean that her attitude toward life is Faulkner's. In condemning Howe's view of the novel as too cozy, Wasiolek has surely overcorrected with misapprehensions of his own that see the novel as more bitter than it is.

Home-Made Coffins

The practice of having the coffin made by a local journeyman was widespread in the rural South. Thomas D. Clark's *Pills, Petticoats, and Plows* reveals that the country store, all through the latter part of the nineteenth century, regularly stocked coffin tacks, materials for linings, and other things that would be required by the local carpenter in fitting up the casket. It is hard to date the journey of the Bundrens very exactly, but the reference to the "little spyglass [Darl] got in France at the war" (p. 527) would suggest a date after the First World War. But the poverty of the Bundrens and the fact that Cash was a working carpenter would account for the coffin's being fashioned at home. Poverty (and Anse's niggardliness) would also account for the fact that the body was not embalmed.

9. FAULKNER'S SAVAGE ARCADIA: FRENCHMAN'S BEND

How Ratliff Outsmarted Flem

Faulkner's characters delight in devious negotiations, whether arranging the bets in a poker game, as in the story "Was," or in the horse-trading negotiations that go on in *The Hamlet* between Ab Snopes and Pat Stamper, or in Ratliff's very complicated trading with Flem in the matter of the goats and the sewing machine. Since I have had difficulty in making out precisely what went on in the Flem-Ratliff trade, it occurs to me that some readers might be grateful for a note.

As we can surmise from later developments, Ratliff has planned his strategy very carefully. Presumably he has no interest in selling Mink Snopes a sewing machine except as a means for getting the better of Flem. When Ratliff drives out to Mink's house (p. 74), he puts on quite an act of pretending that Mink has ordered the sewing machine. Mink, it turns out, is not deceived. A little later (p. 77) he says as much. But Ratliff's ploy has achieved its purpose: he has got Mink's wife interested in the machine, and since he has touched Mink's pride and put him on his mettle (obviously stung by some of his wife's bitter comments), Mink prepares to take the machine.

Had Ratliff all along counted on Mink's involving his cousin Flem in the payment? And had Ratliff assumed that Mink would use the threat of barn-burning to force Flem to pay? It would seem so. Ratliff knew that this was the reason for Flem's having been given a job at the Varner store. Clearly, barn-burning is the threat contained in the message that is to accompany the two promissory notes that Mink hands to Ratliff in payment for the sewing machine. Mink wants Ratliff to say to Flem: "Say 'From one cousin that's still scratching dirt to keep alive, to another cousin that's risen from scratching dirt to owning a herd of cattle and a hay barn. To owning cattle and a hay barn.' Just say that to him" (p. 77). Later on Ratliff will tell himself: "I went as far as one Snopes will set fire to another Snopes's barn and both Snopeses know it" (p. 89). The implication is clear: Ratliff had indeed counted on Mink's squeezing money for the sewing machine out of Flem through the threat of burning Flem's barn.

So much for the flank attack on Flem. The frontal attack, of course, involves letting Flem hear that he is in the market for goats so that Flem will corner the goat market. When that is done, Ratliff surprises him by presenting him with the two notes that had been given him by Mink, one for $20, the other for $10 with three years' interest due.

Flem capitulates when Ratliff mentions the message—he does not need to hear it—and gives Ratliff the fifty goats for the $20 note, which is forthwith burned. Flem presumably would also pay off the smaller note of $10 with interest except that Ratliff deliberately forfeits the value of the smaller note and burns it himself. Ratliff, having been introduced to Ike, is appalled at the notion that the idiot's small inheritance should be part of the capital that Flem has at his disposal. By burning the note, he loses its worth of $10 plus interest, but at least Flem will not be allowed to trade in it further.

What had Ratliff originally expected to gain? First, a $5 profit on the goats—he will sell them for $37.50; for his contract which cost him $12.50 and the $20 it cost him to acquire them from Flem will amount to $32.50. However, by connecting the goat transaction to Mink's purchase of the sewing machine, Ratliff had expected to gain another $10, his commission on the sale of the sewing machine. His total anticipated profit then amounts to $15. If he could extract from Flem three years' interest on the $10 note, perhaps he would gain a little more. Three years' interest on $10 at 6 per cent amounts to $1.80, and $5 plus $10 plus $1.80 amounts to $16.80—which we find out later in the story to be exactly the amount of money that Ratliff had turned over to Mrs. Littlejohn for the benefit of Ike (p. 205).

Ratliff might presumably have bought the goats from Quick for $12.50—this is probably what Flem paid for them—and thus made a profit of $12.50 without bothering to involve Flem in the transaction at all. In fact, Ratliff had deliberately sacrificed $7.50 of his profit in order to involve Flem, but by using Flem to supply most of the money for Mink's sewing machine, Ratliff had hoped to gain something more—indeed, the sum of $16.80.

The whole transaction is typical of Ratliff. He likes a devious game: Mink, or at least Mink's wife, will be benefited by acquiring the sewing machine; Ratliff will make a little more money himself and, most of all, can get the better of the inhumanly successful Flem. Such limited aims are typical of Ratliff: he is not greedy, and he is willing to sacrifice something ($7.50 of his potential goat profit) in order to win a larger sum (the $10 commission on the machine plus $1.80 interest on the $10 note) and the reputation for having bested Flem in a trade.

What Ratliff does when he discovers Ike's plight is again completely typical. He makes over the whole of his contemplated profits to Ike and thus contents himself with the moral victory. Ratliff also does something else. In order to pay the worth of the burned note ($11.80) to Mrs. Littlejohn for Ike's benefit, he has to reach down into his own pocket.

Flem, though defeated in the contest, has actually benefited monetarily. The goats cost him something less than $20, one supposes, and very likely $12.50 for the lot—25 cents per goat. Since he trades the title to the goats to Ratliff for the $20 note that Ratliff holds against him, Flem has actually lost only $7.50. And when Ratliff burns his IOU, now worth $11.80, Flem registers a positive gain in the cancellation of this $11.80 debt.

Hervey C. Lewis has, in the following note to me, put the more complicated parts of the transaction into bookkeeping entries. He writes:

> Perhaps the simplest way to illustrate the various "deals" is by the use of "T" ledger accounts. Let us employ a short-cut bookkeeping method that is not necessarily proper or legal but which gives the net results. The left, or debit, side will show assets, expenses, and losses. The right, or credit, side will show capital, liabilities, and profits.
>
> To set the stage, first of all, the accounts of Flem, Mink, and Ike each showed a capital of $10, resulting from the gift of $10 each from their grandmother. However, Flem, having first given a note to Ike for his (Ike's) $10 and then, as Ike's guardian, having sold the note to Mink for his (Mink's) ten dollars, now had $30 in cash. This $30 is offset by a $10 note payable to "Isaac Snopes or bearer," plus a $10 "loan" from Ike (the $10 received from Mink), plus Flem's original $10 capital. Ratliff, meanwhile, has a capital of $32.50, consisting of a sewing machine which cost him $20 and a contract to deliver goats which cost $12.50.
>
> Ratliff sells the sewing machine to Mink for $30, taking in payment a new note, for $20, made by Mink, plus the $10 note payable to "Isaac Snopes or bearer":

MINK		RATLIFF	
Sewing Machine $30.00	Capital $10.00	Goat Contract $12.50	Capital $32.50
	Note Payable $20.00	Note Receivable $20.00	Profit $10.00
		Note Receivable $10.00	

Ratliff's paper profit at this point is $10.

Flem buys 50 goats from Quick, paying $12.50 in cash:

FLEM		QUICK	
Cash	Capital	Cash	Capital
$17.50	$10.00	$12.50	$12.50
50 Goats	Note Payable		
$12.50	$10.00		
	Loan Payable		
	$10.00		

Ratliff buys the goats from Flem, giving in payment the $20 note made by Mink. Flem thus shows a profit of $7.50:

FLEM		RATLIFF	
Cash	Capital	Goat Contract	Capital
$17.50	$10.00	$12.50	$32.50
Note Receivable	Note Payable	Note Receivable	Profit (Sewing
$20.00	$10.00	$10.00	Machine)
	Loan Payable	50 Goats	$10.00
	$10.00	$12.50	
	Profit	Loss (Goats)	
	$7.50	$7.50	

Ratliff shows a net profit of $2.50 so far:

RATLIFF	
Goat Contract	Capital
$12.50	$32.50
Note Receivable	Profit
$10.00	$2.50
50 Goats	
$12.50	

Flem, wishing to avoid a possible scorched-earth policy on the part of Mink, burns the $20 note, thus sustaining a loss of $12.50:

FLEM		MINK	
Cash	Capital	Sewing Machine	Capital
$17.50	$10.00	$30.00	$10.00
Loss	Note Payable		Profit
$12.50	$10.00		$20.00
	Loan Payable		
	$10.00		

Ratliff now burns the $10 note originally given by Flem to Ike. This changes his profit of $2.50 to a loss of $7.50. Flem now shows a loss of only $2.50:

FLEM		RATLIFF	
Cash	Capital	Goat Contract	Capital
$17.50	$10.00	$12.50	$32.50
Loss	Loan Payable	50 Goats	
$2.50	$10.00	$12.50	
		Loss	
		$7.50	

Ratliff sells the 50 goats for $37.50, realizing a gain on *that* transaction of $12.50, but showing a net profit so far of only $5:

RATLIFF	
Cash	Capital
$37.50	$32.50
	Profit
	$5.00

If Flem had paid the $10 note plus $1.80 interest, Ratliff would have made a total profit of $16.80.

FLEM		RATLIFF	
Cash	Capital	Cash	Capital
$5.70	$10.00	$49.30	$32.50
Loss	Loan Payable		Profit
$14.30	$10.00		$16.80

Instead Ratliff gave Mrs. Littlejohn $16.80 to hold for Ike:

IKE		RATLIFF	
Loan Receivable	Capital	Cash	Capital
$10.00	$10.00	$20.70	$32.50
Cash	Profit	Loss	
$16.80	$16.80	$11.80	

Flem still owes Ike the $10 he (Flem) received from Mink when the latter bought the $10 note. (It seems unlikely, of course, that Ike will ever see the $10 again.)

Mrs. Littlejohn's Moral Superiority to Ratliff

Florence Leaver, in her "Structure of *The Hamlet*," *Twentieth Century Literature, 1* (1955), 77–84, argues that Mrs. Littlejohn is morally superior even to Ratliff. Does her superiority consist in her willingness to allow the idiot to carry on his couplings with the cow, whereas Ratliff, in his self-righteousness, insists on stopping poor Ike's "love" affair? If so, we have come a long way in the twentieth century toward a pure permissiveness: compassionate understanding applies to anything.

There is no doubt that this is the point made by T. Y. Greet in his "The Theme and Structure of Faulkner's *The Hamlet*," *PMLA, 72* (1957), 775–90; reprinted in *William Faulkner: Three Decades of Criticism*, pp. 330–47. Greet writes that "Mrs. Littlejohn suggests that Ratliff is guilty of the same fear of convention which has sacrificed Eula; he, though acknowledging the injustice of his attitude, nonetheless embraces it. Ratliff, the rational, the conventional, overbears Ike, the passionate, the natural" (p. 785).

Greet has taken too literally Ratliff's self-deprecation. Ratliff is acutely sensitive to the fact that he may seem to take on the "holier than thou" air of a Pharisee. He tells the crowd who have been watching the idiot's shame: "I aint cussing you folks. I'm cussing all of us." And he dismisses the crowd by saying "That's all. It's over. This here engagement is completed" (p. 199). A little later, when Mrs. Littlejohn proposes to Ratliff that his real objection is that "somebody named Snopes . . . is making something out of it" or that perhaps his objection is simply that "folks come and watch? It's all right for it to be, but folks mustn't know it, see it," Ratliff answers that he knows that this pleasure is the only one that the idiot has and he knows, too, that "it aint any of my business" (p. 201). But he means to stop the exhibition just the same. Ratliff then goes on to put the case against himself even more sharply: "I know that the reason I aint going to leave him have what he does have is simply because I am strong enough to keep him from it. I am stronger than him. Not righter. Nor any better, maybe. But stronger."

This is the speech of a man who, in spite of his country upbringing, is thoroughly aware of the relativity of morals in the modern world and the difficulty of proving that any act is right or wrong. But the fact that Ratliff, in repudiating any righteousness, states the case against himself so vigorously, hardly constitutes a reason for the reader taking him at his word. There is evidently no doubt in Ratliff's own mind what has to be done, just as I take it there was no doubt in Faulkner's mind. The doubt, I suspect, will come only from readers who have become so habituated to the modern world of the lunatic irrational that the only crime is the inhibiting of one's own or someone else's self-expression, and the only virtue is a kind of sentimental good will that calls itself love.

Greet, I gather, sees *The Hamlet* as a sort of symbolic poem in which one incident answers analogically, and sometimes ironically, to another: the idiot's cow melting into Eula, for example. The thwarting of Ike's passion has its parallel in the murder of Houston, and the horse becomes a "symbolic barrier" against man's love for woman. Because Greet's article is typical of much current Faulkner criticism and because it takes its method to extremes—and it does possess a kind of crazy logic—I should like to make a few further comments here.

When Houston out of pity gives the idiot, Ike, a coin and Ike loses it, Greet writes that Ike "refuses to search for it," and "this un-Snopeslike rejection" marks him as "a courtly lover who accepts no material compensation" (p. 784). But at this point common sense hammers loudly on the door: Ike is an idiot. He doesn't know what the coin means or signifies, and since this is the obvious explanation for his refusal to hunt for the coin after he lost it, how much symbolic meaning will the incident carry?

In his criticism of Ratliff's insistence upon stopping the exhibition of the idiot with the cow, Greet writes that "Ratliff is as humane, perhaps as good, as a man may be, but the ravished land will be redeemed by an act of love, not of righteousness. Rain is described but once in *The Hamlet:* it falls on Ike and his beloved" (p. 785). Yoknapatawpha County is thought of here as a kind of waste land, lying under a curse and waiting for the rain which will restore its fertility. But the country that we are asked to view in Faulkner's novel is not at all the haunted land of the Grail legend. It may be that the fall of rain is described only once in the novel, but water is coming from somewhere: Frenchman's Bend is no desert. There is plenty of reference to rivers and creeks.

If the county is a ravished land, it is very plain who has ravaged it: Flem Snopes and the spirit of ruthless mercantilism he represents. If we are to regard poor Ike's encounter with a cow a redemptive "act of love"—though this is to mix up *eros* and *agape* rather scandalously—that kind of redemptive act has been practiced for some time without abating the Snopes menace. What would Greet have Ratliff do? See to it that Ike is allowed to continue to practice his "act of love" as a kind of sympathetic magic? Take Ike and his beloved cow on tour throughout the county?

Greet is aware of the association that Faulkner—and perhaps many other people—makes between horses and the masculine principle, and cows and the feminine principle, and mindful of the fact that when Ike rushes through the smoke to rescue the cow from a grass fire, a terrified horse charges out of the smoke and leaps over him, and mindful also of Eula's rather bovine quality, Greet extends the symbolism as he sees it in these terms: "Faulkner leads us to expect that Eula merits reverence as the embodiment of fertilty. Proper understanding of this symbol demands, however, a sloughing off of such accretions as traditional morality and destructive individualism. [Why "traditional morality" should be lined up with destructive individualism is puzzling.] Thus Labove fails because the instinctive rightness of his desire [for Eula] is repudiated by his overly developed rational will. Thus the horses rise again and again as barriers between man and woman, as sources of catastrophe" (p. 789). Now Labove is, as was pointed out earlier, one of Faulkner's Puritans, and he has his own problems, but he does not fail to reverence Eula as a kind of fertility goddess and insofar as Eula is able to elicit from him an almost overbearing masculine response, there is no repudiation of his desire by an overly developed rational will. Eula simply regards him as an unattractive Ichabod Crane. Labove's rational will does nothing to prevent the "act of love" that Greet thinks will redeem the ravished land. Nor is "the goddess [that is, Eula] betrayed because she exists in a world predominantly self-conscious." The rural world depicted in *The Hamlet* is a peculiarly unself-conscious world. If Frenchman's Bend is too self-conscious to provide a proper abode for the fertility goddess, what hope has she in the rest of the Western world?

Eula, the fertility goddess, is thus profaned. Greet writes that "the result of this profanation is chaos. Eula is transformed into the cow and love becomes perverse. . . . [But Eula is transformed into the cow only in Greet's consciousness, not in Labove's or in Ike's.] the fist fights of Eula's suitors become a murderous quarrel between Mink and Houston. [But they do not become so in the novel. The murderous quarrel between Mink and Houston occurs over a bull yearling that Mink has illegally pastured on Houston's land and at Houston's expense. If Eula is allegorically a cow, her suitors ought to be young bulls. The transformation from fact to symbol and back is a kind of sleight of hand.] Even the earth, in the grip of winter, becomes sterile; and finally the humane, objective Ratliff shares the guilt of the Varners as he works the destruction of the cow, the last vestige in the land of 'the shape of love.' "

But it just isn't true to say that the cow beloved by Ike is the last vestige in the land of the shape of love. Eula is still in the land and so are a good many things, including other cows. As for the earth sterile "in the grip of winter," no redemptive act of love needs to be performed. Nature will take care of that: "If winter comes, can spring be far behind?"

10. PASSION, MARRIAGE, AND BOURGEOIS RESPECTABILITY

Warren Beck's Account of the Trilogy

Warren Beck's *Man in Motion* (Madison, University of Wisconsin Press, 1961) considers *The Hamlet, The Town,* and *The Mansion* not merely as separate works but also in their interrelations. Taken together, they make up, for Beck, "a unique and imposing work of art." I have my own disagreements with a good many details of Beck's study and even with some of his general emphases, but *Man in Motion* is a sensitive and intelligent work, and should be consulted by any reader seriously concerned with Faulkner's trilogy.

Leslie Fiedler on the Subject of Faulkner and Sex

In his *Love and Death in the American Novel* (New York, Criterion Books, 1960), Fiedler gives a good deal of attention to Faulkner's attitude toward women. He has some very just insights, but often makes his points overemphatically, and in his anxiety to make out his thesis, he sometimes reads passages in Faulkner's fiction carelessly.

In general, Fiedler believes that Faulkner echoes in his fiction a great deal of the American male's typical antifeminism. Faulkner indicts women for possessing "neither morality nor honor," for their willingness to betray "without qualm or quiver of guilt," although he concedes that they are also capable of "inexplicable loyalty." Fiedler tells us that "no Jiggs and Maggie cliché of popular anti-feminism is too banal for [Faulkner] to use" (p. 309).

Whatever the merits of these generalizations, Fiedler is clearly over-simplifying when he writes (p. 314) that in *The Town* "Faulkner carries Eula's refurbishing even farther than he had Temple's, actually rewriting Eula's past history as he pretends to recapitulate it, and turning her into the very model of female courage and endurance." He goes too far when he describes Judith Sutpen as a child "leaning over the edge of a loft and screaming with the blood-lust her brother does not share . . . while her father wrestles, naked and bloody, with one of his Negro field hands" (p. 325). The screams of blood-lust are the product of Fiedler's own imagination. What we are told in *Absalom, Absalom!* is that Judith was seen "looking down through the square entrance to the loft" (p. 30). Again, Fiedler describes Joe Christmas' mother in *Light in August* trying to "convince the doctor who attends her that the man who had fathered her bastard was a Mexican. When old Doc Hines could see in his face the black curse of God Almighty" (p. 395). One would scarcely infer from this passage that we learn of the incident only through the mad old Doc Hines himself, and that the person whom the girl tries to convince is Doc Hines, her father. There was no attending physician (see *Light in August,* pp. 331–32).

Fiedler has little sympathy with the hunting tradition which informs so much of the early American fiction and which is so prominent in Faulkner's work. He writes: "In the forest rather than brothel or bedroom, through murder rather than sex, the child enters manhood, trembles with nausea over the broken bird or lifeless rabbit rather than the spread-eagled whore" (p. 355). But in Faulkner's work boys like Isaac McCaslin or Charles Mallison do not regard the lifeless rabbit with nausea, and obviously do not equate killing an animal with murder.

Fiedler's book has to be read with some caution, therefore, but it has its uses, and on occasion Fiedler makes some very sensible observations. On page 449, for example, he writes that "the European has unfortunately tended to read Faulkner's gothic and symbolic distortion of life in Mississippi as literal sociological reporting; and Jean-Paul Sartre's *The Respectful Prostitute* provides a classic (and ridiculous) example of what happens when complex art is taken as simple fact."

11. FAULKNER'S REVENGERS' TRAGEDY

Discrepancies among the Three Novels in the Trilogy

There are a good many discrepancies as we move from *The Hamlet* to the end of *The Mansion*. Some are the result of conscious rethinking of character and event; some are due to carelessness; and some can evidently be put down to forgetfulness. In *The Hamlet*, for instance, the Varners have sixteen children, the youngest of whom is Eula, the ninth of whom is Jody, but we never hear anything more of the other fourteen children, and the ending of *The Mansion* definitely suggests that Jody and Eula are the only heirs to old man Varner. In *The Hamlet* the girl whom Jack Houston marries is named Lucy Pate, but in *The Town* she has become Letty Bookwright. (The Vintage edition paperback of *The Town*, 1961, has changed her name back again to Lucy Pate.) In *The Hamlet*, after Mink has shot Houston, we are told that Mink would have liked to leave a printed placard on the dead man's breast reading: "This is what happens to the men who impound Mink Snopes's cattle" (p. 222). But in *The Mansion* Mink actually speaks to the dying man, saying, among other things, "That aint why I shot you. I killed you because of that–ere extry one-dollar pound fee" (p. 39.)

Recognizing that readers would note such discrepancies, Faulkner appended to *The Mansion* a brief note which ends with the following statement: "The author has already found more discrepancies and contradictions than he hopes the reader will—contradictions and discrepancies due to the fact that the author has learned, he believes, more about the human heart and its dilemma than he knew thirty-four years ago; and is sure that, having lived with them that long time, he knows the characters in this chronicle better than he did then."

Mink Snopes' Religion

On page 5 of *The Mansion* it is said of Mink that he "had simply had to trust *them*—the *Them* of whom it was promised that not even a sparrow should fall unmarked. By *them* he didn't mean that whatever-it-was that folks referred to as Old Moster. He didn't believe in any Old Moster. He had seen too much in his time that, if any Old Moster existed, with eyes as sharp and power as strong as was claimed He had,

He would have done something about." Irving Howe (*William Faulkner: A Critical Study*, p. 292), says that Mink "sees existence as an unending struggle between Old Moster (God) and Them (the world), with Them forever and even rightly and naturally triumphant, always in control of events as they move along, yet with Old Moster standing in reserve, not to intervene or help but to draw a line." But *them* cannot mean the world. On page 6 Faulkner tells us that Mink "meant, simply, that *them—they—it*, whichever and whatever you wanted to call it, who represented a simple fundamental justice and equity in human affairs, or else a man might just as well quit; the *they, them, it*, call them what you like, which simply would not, could not harass and harry a man forever without some day, at some moment, letting him get his own just and equal licks back in return." The word *they* must refer to something like "the powers that be," though the concept is so vague and indeterminate in Mink's mind that he is willing to say either "they" or "it." The main point seems to be that Mink does not believe in a personal God but in a kind of impersonal power of justice. By the end of the book, however, Mink has come to a belief in Old Moster. Either he has experienced some kind of conversion or he is willing now at last to accept the name "Old Moster" as the proper term for "they" or "it," for he tells himself on page 407, as he contemplates his rusty gun: "It will have to [shoot]. . . . Old Moster jest punishes; He dont play jokes."

Table of Events in THE . MANSION

12. THE STORY OF THE McCASLINS

Earlier Versions of "The Bear"

"The Bear," in the form in which it appeared in *Go Down, Moses,* was fashioned out of two earlier stories plus some additional material. In December 1935 Faulkner published in *Harper's Magazine* (*172*, 67–77) a story entitled "Lion." It is told in the first person by a boy of sixteen, though the boy is not Uncle Isaac, for Uncle Isaac is mentioned elsewhere in the story.

"Lion" has to do with the hunt for the bear named Old Ben. Boon Hogganbeck occupies a prominent place in the story. He is very fond of Lion and tries to get him to sleep on his pallet. On the day of the hunt Lion (who in this story is part Walker hound, part mastiff) brings Old Ben to bay. Boon pulls the dog back after the bear has him on the ground. The dog, undaunted, lunges again at Old Ben and Boon climbs on the bear's back and finally kills him with his hunting knife.

Boon turns up at the camp badly mauled by the bear and carrying in his arms, wrapped in a blanket, the disemboweled Lion. Apparently none of the other hunters witnessed the death of the bear. Boon, beside himself with grief, insists on making the journey for the doctor. He brings the doctor back to the camp, Lion's wounds are sewed up, but Lion dies the next day.

The story ends with an account of how the sixteen-year-old narrator went back to the scene of the hunt sometime later and found that the grave of Lion had been obliterated by the spring floods, though the wooden cross with Old Ben's mutilated paw nailed to it was still there to mark the place. The last three or four paragraphs of the story give an ending that resembles that of section 5 of "The Bear" in *Go Down, Moses*.

In the March 9, 1942, issue of the *Saturday Evening Post*, Faulkner published a story entitled "The Bear." It has to do with a boy, ten years old, who learns the woods under the tutelage of Sam Fathers. The boy is anxious to get a glimpse of Old Ben, and finally manages to do so. Still later, he decides to use a little fyce dog, because he realizes it is the courage of the dog, and not its size, that is important. His plan works almost too well, for the fyce runs at the bear and will not stop. The boy has to rush in to rescue the dog and later realizes, when Sam Fathers asks him why he didn't shoot the bear, that Sam, too, has been unwilling to shoot. The last eight or ten paragraphs of this story give us substantially the passage that we find in section 4 of "The Bear" as published in *Go Down, Moses*. Later on in the story, the boy is again asked why he did not shoot the bear, but in the *Post* version, it is his father (not McCaslin Edmonds) who puts the question. The father, trying to help the boy understand his motive, reads to him a passage from Keats' "Ode on a Grecian Urn." The last short paragraph is interesting. It reads: "Sam, and *Old Ben* and *Nip* [the small dog] he thought. And himself too. He had been all right too. His father had said so. 'Yes, sir,' he said."

When Faulkner came to put together *Go Down, Moses*, he incorporated portions of the two stories and then added as fresh material the long discussion between Isaac and his cousin concerning Isaac's decision to repudiate his inheritance. It is in this version of the story that we have for the first time any mention of the wickedness of Isaac's grandfather and the story of his incestuous relationship with his daughter.

Faulkner told an inquirer at the University of Virginia that when "The Bear" was published as a short story (presumably in *The Portable Faulkner*), the publisher mistakenly used the whole of the *Go Down, Moses* version. He had been quite rightly unwilling to tamper with Faulkner's text. But if the publisher had asked him in time, Faulkner indicates, he would have been told that the material in the long section 4 of that version had been put there to tie the story into the novel and was not part of "The Bear," considered as a story in its own right. In the collection entitled *Big Woods* (1955) Faulkner's wishes were followed, and the story consists of only four sections, sections that correspond to 1, 2, 3, and 5 of the narrative as given in *Go Down, Moses*.

Isaac McCaslin's Wife

For Faulkner's statement that Isaac McCaslin's wife had the ethics of a prostitute, see *Faulkner in the University*, pp. 275–76. Andrew Lytle's discussion is to be found in "Faulkner's *A Fable*," *Sewanee Review, 63* (1955), 127–28. Lytle's general discussion of Isaac McCaslin is very interesting. For Lytle, "Young Ike is the exemplum of the Puritan hero, who holds in fee simple the body of the world, and who is incapable, as are all men, of this responsibility. To this is owed his unconscious guilt which makes him reject the inheritance."

Faulkner and the Hunting Tradition

Modern man has already got so far away from the woods and fields and from a hunting tradition that he is likely to misunderstand the story that Faulkner is telling because of his lack of this experience. The urban reader may need to be told that it is the hunter who loves the game that he pursues, and that his code of sportsmanship embodies— however inadequately and however crudely—a regard for his prey which is probably much deeper than that of those citizens who have no first-hand concern for the animals of the wilderness and who would be perfectly happy to have all the creatures of the world eliminated except for such stock as might be kept for scientific purposes in properly appointed zoos.

Archibald Rutledge makes some pertinent observations in an article entitled "Who Knows Nature Best?" (*Sports Afield,* Aug. 1949):

> Every hunter who has a heart will find himself wondering especially after the shooting seasons have closed and some wild winter weather has come, how the game is faring in the deep and snowy woods . . . "How are they making it?" he keeps asking himself as, from the safe harbor of his heated house, he looks out on a blizzard or a cold midwinter rain. *He feels real concern for the birds and animals that he was lately trying so hard to kill.*
>
> [p. 38; italics mine]

> There are two classes of men only who really know much about nature; the scientific experts and the real woodsmen. I do not say that all men who hunt understand nature. Some are densely ignorant of it; some are superstitious; some are in the woods merely to kill *and not to learn;* and many are afield only rarely and for short periods. But now and then you will find an inveterate hunter *who is constantly seeing, studying, and understanding things.* When you find him, you have found a man who knows as much as anybody about nature as it really is.
>
> Who haunts the lonely woods at daybreak, and sometimes lingers far in the forest until the first stars appear? Usually only the hunter does this; *and by constantly pitting his intelligence against that of wild things in the wilderness, he comes to a just appreciation of their character and their ability. . . . Let others read the books that have been written about nature; he reads the Book itself.*
>
> [p. 80; italics mine]

Faulkner makes a similar point when he observes in "The Old People" that "perhaps only a country-bred [child] could comprehend loving the life he spills" (p. 181).

The Morality of Isaac McCaslin

The indictment of Isaac for "compromises with segregation" is made by Leonard Casper, "The Square Beatific," *America, 103* (1960), 515. See also in this general connection Melvin Backman, "The Wilderness and the Negro in Faulkner's 'The Bear,' " *PMLA*, 76 (1961), 595–600; Stanley Sultan, "Call Me Ishmael: the Hagiography of Isaac McCaslin," *Texas Studies in Literature and Language*, 3 (1961), 50–66; O'Connor, *The Tangled Fire of William Faulkner*, pp. 133–34; and Vickery, *The Novels of William Faulkner*, pp. 133–34. All of these critics, in varying degrees, express their disappointment with Isaac McCaslin, particularly with the old man who in "Delta Autumn" tells the girl upon whom Roth has begotten a child to go North. Isaac is too passive, too easily willing to make an accommodation with injustice, too resistant to any acceptance of miscegenation. Because Isaac McCaslin has been presented sometimes in the past with emphasis on his saintly character, recent critics have, in reaction, insisted on how poorly he comes off if one applies absolute standards, and particularly when one looks at him in the light of the burning issues of the 1950s and '6os. As a reaction against a too-exalted notion of Isaac, the sharp moral questioning of him is probably to the good and may redress the balance toward a view which answers to Faulkner's conception of the character all along. Isaac has throughout *Go Down, Moses* been presented as a limited being, the product of his own time and culture, who could not transcend all his inherited values, and who, in any case, by the time that he meets Roth's paramour, is an old man who has long ago divested himself—through his very act of renunciation—of any real power to right a wrong.

Yet it behooves the critic to understand Isaac and not to attribute to him acts and motives which are not his. Mrs. Vickery is surely wrong when she writes that what Isaac "could not forgive in Carothers McCaslin, he accepts without hesitation in Roth Edmonds" (p. 134). I take it that he is bitterly disappointed with Roth Edmonds—his disagreements with Roth had been suggested throughout "Delta Autumn" —but knows in his despair that there is nothing he can do that will exert any influence upon Roth at all.

O'Connor writes that Faulkner's "treatment of the theme of the wilderness in the first version of 'The Bear' is moving, almost hallucinatory in its power to convince us of the existence of a world of no sin, no evil, no injustice. . . . But Faulkner is not willing, apparently, to allow the implications of the wilderness theme, its power to purify, to work as a leaven inside the subject of injustice to the Negro." What right have we to assume that Faulkner ever felt that the wilderness theme had any ultimate power to purify? Could the very point of *Go Down, Moses* be the fact that in spite of the beauty of the wilderness and what man can learn from it, we are not to believe in "the existence of a world of no sin, no evil, no injustice?"

Sultan writes that "the alternatives are clear to [Isaac], and they are absolute: either he can 'kill the doe' in the story's terms, send the girl away and . . . repeat himself the sin of Carothers, repeat it even to symbolically paying Carothers' conscience money, which the girl's grandfather had refused half a century before in a gesture of moral outrage; or he can help Roth to accept the proffered love and so, in the love child, end the long history of the curse and perhaps even expiate it." But is the second alternative a real option? What possible reason is there for thinking that the old man "can help Roth to accept?" He has no power to force him, and our acquaintance with Roth as he appears elsewhere in *Go Down, Moses* ought to make perfectly plain how little influence his aged relative has over him.

Sultan also writes that

> with the rejection of the love child, union of Beauchamp and Edmonds, the author presents the other McCaslin of the seventh generation, Samuel Worsham Beauchamp, originally rather blatantly named "Carothers Edmonds Beauchamp." He is the last male descendant of Carothers, is called "Benjamin" in the Negro-spiritual idiom of his grandmother's mourning rather than "Joseph," because Benjamin was Jacob's youngest son. He is the end of the line.
>
> Samuel, the heir to the plantation had there been no injustice, is exiled from it by Roth. . . . He goes to Chicago . . . shoots a policeman, and meets his death in the electric chair; the last chance for expiation passed, Carothers' curse is fulfilled.

This is a very neat rounding off of the story and has the virtue of providing a kind of contrast to "Delta Autumn" by juxtaposing Samuel against the nameless paramour of Roth. But if it is neat, it is also rather brittle in its reasoning. The notion that property should descend to illegitimate as well as to legitimate children belongs to one kind of moral world; but the careful insistence that property should descend only to males belongs to quite another. In any case, Samuel Worsham Beauchamp's heirship of the McCaslin plantation, however appropriate it may seem symbolically, simply cannot be made out in fact. Even if we ignore the possibility of male heirs that may descend from Tennie's Jim, Samuel descends from Lucas Beauchamp through a female line and has an uncle Henry, who by Sultan's reasoning, should be the heir to the plantation.

Sultan is on much firmer ground when he makes the very sensible point that "Ike fails to be the sainted redeemer, even of himself"— a point with which Faulkner would have been happy to agree—"and if he is thereby a less convenient example of the heartening spirit of Faulkner's Stockholm speech, he is a more valid and tragic character."

See also John Hunt's comments on Isaac McCaslin's act of renunciation, quoted above, p. 373.

Benjamin Sold into Egypt

As someone has pointed out, Faulkner nodded when he made Benjamin the brother sold into Egypt. It was Joseph, of course, who was sold into Egypt. (See Genesis 37:27–28.) Faulkner may have been confused by the fact that Benjamin was for a time held by the Egyptians. After Joseph had become Governor of Egypt, in order to test his brethren who had come in search of food, he had his silver cup put into the sack belonging to Benjamin and then had Benjamin arrested as a thief. Until Joseph discloses himself, the brothers think that Benjamin will have to remain in Egypt. (See Genesis 44, 45:1.)

13. THE COMMUNITY IN ACTION

The speeches of Gavin Stevens, which have proved a stumbling block to some readers, amount to about ten pages in all. Gavin right away gets off to a bad start by using the term "Sambo," a term that seems to point contemptuously to a racial stereotype. But a little concern for the context would show that Gavin is not using the term in disparagement of the Negro. He associates Sambo with Lucas Beauchamp, for example, and he does this after he has come to believe that Lucas is innocent of the murder and has come to admire Lucas' conduct. Moreover, he praises Sambo for possessing virtues better and more important than those of the white man. Indeed, Gavin never says anything disparaging about Sambo in the course of his three extended pronouncements on the state of the South. He seems, then, to be using the term to emphasize the following point: the Negro taken at his lowest discount is nevertheless a man who "has a better homogeneity than we have" and with whom we "should confederate," etc. Presumably Gavin is using the term Sambo to indicate that his praise of the Negro is said in perfect awareness of all the usual disparagements of him, past and present. We may feel that Gavin's rhetorical device is strained or in bad taste, but we misread if we say that he uses Sambo in order to deprecate Lucas Beauchamp and the race he represents.

So much for the tone. What of the argument? Gavin's first contention (pp. 153–56) is that the Southerners and the New Englanders are the only homogeneous people in the United States, though the old homogeneous New England culture has already been obliterated along the industrial coast and survives only inland. Gavin values this homogeneity and acknowledges that the Negro possesses the same quality. Indeed, he "has a better homogeneity than we have." The Southern white man and the Negro should "confederate." The white man should "swap him the rest of the economic and political and cultural privileges which are his right, for the reversion of his capacity to wait and endure and survive." So allied, Gavin says, "we would dominate the United States; we would present a front not only impregnable but not even to be threatened by a mass of people who no longer have anything in common save a frantic greed for money and a basic fear of a failure of national character which they hide from one another behind a loud lipservice to a flag" (p. 156).

The last are bitter words, and Gavin has not been thanked for this comment on the North, or for his earlier reference to "the coastal spew of Europe which this country quarantined unrootable into the rootless ephemeral cities" (p. 153). But if it is worth quarreling with Gavin Stevens, it is worth trying to understand what he is saying. For me the main difficulty is in his choice of the word *homogeneity*. Gavin cannot mean by the term a sameness in racial stock though this is what the term will suggest to most readers. Gavin is aware that the white Southerners represent a blending of somewhat different racial stocks, as his own references in this book make clear. And the "confederation" of two "homogeneous" peoples, the Negroes and the white Southerners, for which he asks is certainly not the uniting of two branches of the same racial stock. In calling a people homogeneous Gavin can only mean that they have a community of values that is rooted in some kind of lived experience. For example, he contrasts the remnant of homogeneous New England with the "rootless ephemeral cities," and he says that the Negro has proved his homogeneity by "finding himself roots into the land where he had actually to displace white men to put them down" (p. 156).

It may be that Gavin overrates the value of community. He certainly has the country-bred man's distrust of urbanization and industrialism, and he has evidently been irritated by the guff of Madison Avenue. But wiser men than Gavin were appalled in the 1940s by the inability of our spokesmen, including some of our statesmen, to present clearly the positive ideals of the nation. The reiteration of platitudes aside, a careless reader might have thought that we were fighting World War II to provide better refrigerators and automobiles.

In his second pronouncement (pp. 203–06) Gavin resumes a theme that he had touched on earlier, a fear that the "outlanders" from the North, East, and West will worsen the Negro's case "by forcing on us laws based on the idea that man's injustice to man can be abolished overnight by police" (p. 203). The "injustice," he concedes, "is ours. . . . [and therefore] we must expiate and abolish it ourselves, alone and without help nor even (with thanks) advice" (p. 204). This theme is continued in Gavin's third and last harangue (pp. 215–17). He attacks once more the use of "federal laws and federal police to abolish Lucas' shameful condition" because he fears that such action risks dividing the country at a time when it needs unity. Moreover, instead of setting against the Southern whites all the rest of the country plus all the Negroes, he fears that it may instead produce another kind of division which may bring down upon the Negro, even in the great cities of the North—"your Chicagoes and Detroits and Los Angeleses" —the bitterness of "ignorant people" who "fear the color of any skin or shape of nose save their own" (p. 216).

In general, Gavin argues (in both his second and third disquisitions) that if the Negro's equal status is to be more than an abstraction —if it is to be a living reality—it must be acknowledged and accepted by the community in which the Negro leads his life. It must be regarded as something which is his just due—because he has earned it or because he does not need to earn it, it being his by natural right. But in any case, as far as the Southern Negro is concerned, that status must be conceded by the South itself, not imposed from without, for until it is conceded it will have to be defended by artificial safeguards.

Gavin Stevens is obviously caught between his concern for justice for Lucas and his people and his concern for the life and continuity of a real community whose values are rooted in a lived history. The reader is likely to be impressed more with Gavin's inner conflicts than with the force of his arguments. But his arguments do reflect a very real cultural situation, and the reader could learn from them a great deal about the problem of the South. David Potter, writing as a student of Southern history, has put the matter very ably in a review-article entitled "A Minority Within a Minority," *Yale Review, 46* (1957). He discusses "the South's acute sense of insecurity because of its minority position, and its conviction that, as a minority, it must be both united and militant" (p. 264). If the Negro represents a minority vis-à-vis the whites, the Southern whites constitute and react as a minority vis-à-vis the rest of the nation. "Thus the Southern situation presents the unique spectacle of a minority within a minority."

This "minority status," Potter goes on to say,

> holds important and relatively neglected implications, for the mental stance of a majority and a minority are essentially different. . . . minority status impels the group to present a united front and to act defensively. This is what has always occurred in the South. The so-called Southern gradualists would urge the Southern whites, acting as a majority toward the Negroes, to exercise rational judgment and liberality. But it always happens—with the abolitionist movement, as with integration—that before the gradualists can move the great load of inertia which they are trying to stir, the Yankee—not without reason—repudiates such glacial progress and takes a hand. Thereupon the Southern white majority reverts to regarding itself as a persecuted sectional minority with the duty to practice the minority virtues of resistance and group solidarity.
>
> [pp. 264–65]

Professor Potter goes on to mention another facet of the matter which also throws light upon Gavin Stevens' argument. He remarks that "Southern culture remains, to a considerable extent, a folk culture. . . . It is characteristic of a true folk—rural and unsophisticated—that its ways are traditional rather than rational, and that its processes are group processes rather than individual ones. . . . Where such a genuinely communal basis for social action and such a commitment to traditionalism exist, the group, when it finds itself challenged as a minority by the forces of change, will offer resistance in a far more acute degree than would a minority of individuals of urban culture" (p. 266).

Potter's analysis is based upon a total study of Southern culture, and has no special reference to Faulkner's novels, but it accords perfectly with Gavin's feeling that his culture is being threatened from without, and accords, too, with Gavin's suspicions of an "ephemeral," rootless urban society.

To sum up: Gavin's speculations on the Negro problem are scarcely calculated to please the modern American intellectual, and of course they do not. But Gavin ought not to be accused of intentionally disparaging the Negro, whom he admires; and even the reader who pooh-poohs his thinking might give him top marks for urging the South to grant the rights to which Gavin admits Lucas and his fellows are entitled. Moreover, even the citizen who wants the rights of the Negro to be secured for him at once by Federal pressure must agree that the law is finally an expression of community values, and until, in fact, it becomes such, its enforcement remains in jeopardy.

How much do Gavin's arguments reflect those of William Faulkner, at least the views Faulkner held in 1947–48? It would be hard to say. Faulkner had taken a number of positions from time to time on the Negro question. He certainly shared some of Gavin's doubts about Federal laws and the risk of breaking down a traditional society by trying to right certain wrongs too fast. See, for example, "A Talk with William Faulkner," *Reporter, 14* (1956), 18–20. But he has also taken positions rather at variance with those of Gavin Stevens in *Intruder in the Dust*. See, for example, his article "On Fear: the South in Labor," *Harper's, 212* (1956), 29–34. For opinions expressed in 1958 one might consult *Faulkner in the University,* pp. 209–27. In any case, Gavin Stevens is not Faulkner's mouthpiece. As we have already seen, he is treated by Faulkner with great detachment. His theories and arguments are not privileged utterances, but have to take their chances in the total artistic context.

14. HISTORY AND THE SENSE OF THE TRAGIC

Chronology and Genealogy of ABSALOM, ABSALOM! *as given in the Modern Library Edition*

There are in these two lists a number of errors and discrepancies that require correction.

Ellen Coldfield was not born in 1818 but on October 9, 1817, if the dates on her tombstone are to be credited. Moreover, she died not in 1862 but on January 23, 1863 (see p. 188). The errors occur in both the genealogy and the chronology.

Charles Bon's year of birth as given in the chronology is 1829, and the place, Haiti. But Judith Sutpen had inscribed on his tombstone: "Born in New Orleans, Louisiana. Died at Sutpen's Hundred, Mississippi, May 3, 1865. Aged 33 years and 5 months." She is clearly in error as to his birthplace and, since his age as given would put his birth in *1831*, presumably wrong also as to his birth date, in spite of the circumstantial "5 months." (On p. 313 Henry is described as "almost ten years [Bon's] junior." See also p. 265.) The error in dating the tombstone, if it is an error, can be interpreted as meaningful: Judith's knowledge of her fiancé is so slight that she does not know his age and birthplace.

Judith is said (in both the chronology and the genealogy) to have been born in 1841. The date on her tombstone (p. 211), October 3, 1841, confirms this, and her aunt Miss Rosa, who had the stone lettered, should know the correct date. Yet in 1860 Judith is said to have been a girl of seventeen (p. 70), and when her father was killed (in 1869), she is said to have been a woman of thirty (p. 185).

The year date of the last two entries in the chronology, 1910, clearly should be 1909. Quentin and Shreve entered Harvard in the fall of 1909, and Quentin's ride out to Sutpen's Hundred took place shortly before he left home for school. The burning of Sutpen's Hundred took place three months later (p. 373) in December, as the chronology correctly puts it, but the year, of course, is 1909. Since Henry and Clytemnestra Sutpen perished in the fire, their death dates, given as 1910 in the Genealogy, should be corrected to 1909. Since Jim Bond disappeared after the fire, the date of his disappearance noted in the genealogy might more properly be given as 1909 rather than 1910. One more item might be added to the chronology: Miss Rosa's death on January 8, 1910.

In both the chronology and the genealogy Thomas Sutpen's birth is given as 1807 and this is presumably correct. Shreve (p. 220) has him born in 1808; however, he is not taking months into account but simply rounding off to the nearest year. There is one further item in the genealogy that raises a question. Sutpen's first wife is three times referred to as Eulalia Bon. Now when Mr. Compson on page 265 conjectures that Sutpen himself named Charles Bon, the implication is that he bestowed not only the Christian name but the surname Bon as well: "Charles Bon. Charles Good." Indeed, Mr. Compson goes on to say that Sutpen, knowing the tainted lineage, would not allow the "child, since it was a boy, to bear either his name or that of its maternal grandfather." Taken literally, this would mean that the woman Sutpen married did not have Bon as her surname. Does the name Eulalia Bon in the genealogy indicate that Mr. Compson's conjecture was simply wrong? Or is it to be accounted for as merely an instance of Faulkner's forgetfulness?

Sutpen as the Typical Southerner

Olga Vickery has evidently read my essay, *"Absalom, Absalom!:* the Definition of Innocence," *Sewanee Review, 59* (1951), and though she makes no specific reference to it, she obviously takes some pains to try to refute its thesis that Sutpen is not so much "Southern" as "American," with his confident self-assertion, his "schedule," and his "innocence." She devotes a good deal of space to arguing that Sutpen's "design" is really "a microcosm of the South" (*The Novels of William Faulkner*). Sutpen is simply carrying out the Southern scheme a little more brutally and without the courtly gestures of the Sartorises. In making her point, however, she has to romanticize a little about the mountain home of Sutpen's boyhood: that home which, "however lacking elegance . . . had stressed certain fundamental values—the man rather than his possessions" (p. 93), etc.

Ilse Devoir Lind ("The Design and Meaning of *Absalom, Absalom!,*" *PMLA, 70* [1955]; reprinted in *William Faulkner: Three Decades of Criticism*) concerns herself with the same argument and encounters the same problem. She too points up the contrast between the mountain "innocence" of Sutpen's youth and the "spiritual depravity of a slave society" (*Three Decades*, p. 297) into which he descends. To her, too, the primitive society recommends itself by its lack of concern for social status and property rights. But I find Faulkner in his estimate of this society to be quite as close to Hobbes as to Rousseau. That "mountain paradise" is the home of a society in which the test of manhood is "lifting anvils and gouging eyes or how much whiskey you could drink." If the statement that "the land belonged to anybody and everybody" smacks of a charming Arcadian commonalty, the succeeding statement, "everybody had just what he was strong enough or energetic enough to take and keep" sounds like a dog-eat-dog society, one in which might makes right. In fact, it sounds like the ethic that Sutpen retained after he had adopted the plantation society's system of slavery. He even retained the eye-gouging. Miss Lind numbers among Sutpen's admirable qualities "his establishment of man-to-man superiority over his slaves in sportsmanlike physical combat" (p. 298), but in the one scene in which we see him in hand to hand encounter with a slave (p. 29) the two men are "gouging at one another's eyes."

The curse of slavery is so obvious and brought so much destruction on the South—on all classes of the South—that one does not really need to beat at it further. But in any case, one can find a more serviceable stick than Sutpen's "mountain paradise."

There are several marked resemblances between Sutpen and the founder of the McCaslin line, old Carothers McCaslin. Old Carothers is described as a "strong and ruthless man." Like Sutpen, he gets possession of part of the wilderness and uses his slaves to tame it, building a great plantation house. Like Sutpen too, he has a son of mixed blood. In his disregard for all laws, either of man or God, he begets a child upon his own daughter, whose mother was the slave woman Eunice. The child is a boy named Terrel (known in "The Bear" as Tomey's Turl). Unlike Sutpen, however, Carothers does make a kind of left-handed acknowledgment of this son. He leaves him a $1,000 legacy which his much older white half-brothers are to pay. Carothers is thus morally both better and worse than Sutpen. He differs sharply from him in lacking "innocence." He is a cynical man. We are told also that he has something of "a contempt for all his get." He cares nothing for the opinion of his neighbors or the community.

Powerful and ruthless men certainly did appear on the American frontier and certainly must have appeared in the frontier South. (Mississippi was still very close to the frontier in the early nineteenth century.) What is at issue here, however, is not whether hard and ruthless men were to be found in Yoknapatawpha County, but the sense in which they typify something specifically Southern as opposed to frontier America in general, so that the downfall of one of them could constitute a kind of symbolic downfall of the old South.

What makes Thomas Sutpen special is his optimism, his abstraction, and his innocence. His specifically "Southern" values are appropriated in typical bourgeois fashion from the community in which he has settled. They are not inherited values, and he has no ultimate concern for them. By contrast, Old Carothers is the true aristocrat who scorns any notion of keeping up with the Joneses. He sets his own standards and is prepared to defy those of society.

Carothers McCaslin is, I suppose, in some respects, a more wicked man than Thomas Sutpen, but he sustains no special downfall: he dies in bed. He has no "design" and no interest in founding a dynasty.

Presumably he would have been amused to learn that his two white sons had turned out to be Southern abolitionists, and that his grandson, the hero of "The Bear," had repudiated the whole McCaslin inheritance, preferring to live as a poor carpenter.

Faulkner's Later Comments on Thomas Sutpen

It is fascinating to read what Faulkner said some twenty years after the publication of *Absalom, Absalom!*, because one can see the mind of the born artist at work on the materials, still speculating, revising, shifting; but it is also disconcerting to realize how much Faulkner had forgotten about the detail of the novel. In *Faulkner in the University* (p. 46) one questioner inquires as to how Sutpen acquired the money he brings back to Jefferson. Faulkner answers: "He very likely looted his Caribbean father-in-law's plantation when he married the daughter." And then he adds: "I don't know that I ever decided myself just how he did it but very likely he looted and wrecked the whole place." Yet this account hardly squares with the scrupulous sense of justice which induced Sutpen to leave the money to his first wife when he rejected her. He was careful to see that she was well provided for. General Compson reported that Sutpen said: "I made no attempt to keep . . . that which I might consider myself to have earned [and] resigned all right and claim to this" (p. 264).

Faulkner made another curious remark at the University of Virginia: "I think that Bon knew all the time that his mother was part Negress, but during Bon's childhood that was not important. He grew up in the Indies or in New Orleans where that wasn't too important. His mother was a wealthy woman. She could have called herself a Creole whether she had Negro blood along with the French or not. It became important only when Bon realized that it was important to his father" (p. 272). This comment throws an interesting light upon some of the matters about which Shreve and Quentin conjecture. But Quentin says flatly (p. 269) that "nobody ever did know if Bon ever knew Sutpen was his father or not," and Shreve assumes (p. 321) that Bon did not know "whatever it was in [his] mother's [blood] that [Sutpen] could not brook." Later on, Quentin and Shreve are to *conjecture* that Bon did know that Sutpen was his father and that on his mother's side he inherited some Negro blood. It is amusing to see Faulkner, many years after publishing the novel, continue the game of conjecture and speculation. Note that Faulkner does not say "Bon knew all the time" but rather "I think Bon knew all the time."

When he was asked whether Sutpen acknowledged Clytemnestra as his daughter, he first said no and then added, "Well, that would not have mattered because Clytemnestra was a female. The important thing to him was that he should establish a line of dukes, you see" (*Faulkner in the University*, p. 272). Faulkner's comment deals with the important issue. But his preliminary denial that Sutpen did acknowledge Clytemnestra as his daughter is at variance with what we are told in the novel (see pages 61, 109, 163–64).

Sutpen's Innocence

See the discussion above, p. 380. In Faulkner's world the male is expected to lose his innocence in a discovery of the true nature of reality. There is little disposition in Faulkner to see the "American" experience as involving a radical and persistent innocence in contrast to the European. By this measure, too, Sutpen is less "Southern" than "American."

What We KNOW about Thomas Sutpen and His Children

All the information the reader has comes through Quentin directly or through Quentin's conversations with his father, Mr. Compson, and with Miss Rosa Coldfield. The information from General Compson comes to Quentin presumably through Mr. Compson, for though the General did not die until Quentin was ten years old, there is no indication in *Absalom, Absalom!* that the General discussed the matter with his grandson, nor is it likely that he would have done so.

FACT OR EVENT	ULTIMATE AUTHORITY	PAGE
Sutpen's life in Jefferson from 1833 until 1860.	Gen. Compson and Miss Rosa	p. 8 and passim
Sutpen in 1834 tells Gen. Compson about his early life; stops with his engagement; then waits 30 years to go on with it.	Gen. Compson	pp. 219–58
Bon's friendship with Henry and Judith.	Gen. Compson and Miss Rosa	p. 67 and passim
Charles Bon visits Henry (Christmas, 1859, and summer, 1860).	Gen. Compson	p. 70

Fact or Event	Ultimate Authority	Page
Sutpen visits New Orleans summer (or late spring), 1860.	Gen. Compson	p. 70
Henry brings Bon home (Christmas, 1860), quarrels with his father, and leaves home with Bon.	The Negro servants at Sutpen's Hundred (as reported by Gen. Compson)	pp. 78–79
Charles Bon and Henry enlist. Bon is soon made a lieutenant.	Gen. Compson	pp. 122–24
Henry and his father meet and talk in Carolina, 1865.	Gen. Compson	p. 276
Bon's letter to Judith in 1865, telling her that he is coming back to marry her.	The letter was preserved by Gen. Compson	pp. 129–32
Judith makes her wedding gown.	Gen. Compson	p. 132
Judith finds on Bon's dead body the picture of the octoroon woman and her child.	Gen. Compson, who presumably learned this from Judith (Miss Rosa probably went to her grave believing that the picture was of Judith).	pp. 90, 95 p. 142
Sutpen returns (autumn, 1864) with the gravestones and tells Gen. Compson about his first marriage and his "design."	Gen. Compson	pp. 188, 270
Sutpen's return from the war (Jan. 1866) and his subsequent life at Sutpen's Hundred.	Miss Rosa and Gen. Compson	p. 158 and passim
Sutpen refuses to join the Ku Klux Klan.	Miss Rosa	p. 161
Sutpen makes his proposal to Miss Rosa.	Miss Rosa	pp. 164–68
Sutpen sets up his little store.	Gen. Compson	p. 180 and passim
Gen. Compson overhears Sutpen and Wash talking about Milly.	Gen. Compson	pp. 283–84
Wash kills Sutpen.	The Negro midwife	pp. 185, 285–88

Fact or Event	Ultimate Authority	Page
Wash kills his daughter and is killed.	Gen. Compson	pp. 291–92
Judith buries her father.	Gen. Compson	pp. 185–86
Bon's octoroon mistress visits his grave (summer, 1870).	Gen. Compson	pp. 192–95
Etienne Bon is brought to Sutpen's Hundred (Dec. 1871).	Gen. Compson	p. 195
The piece of mirror is found under Etienne Bon's bed.	Gen. Compson (from information presumably communicated by Judith)	p. 199
Etienne Bon's indictment.	Gen. Compson	p. 203
Etienne Bon marries.	Gen. Compson	p. 205
Judith nurses Etienne Bon.	Gen. Compson	p. 210
Judith and Etienne die (1884).	Gen. Compson	p. 210
Henry returns to Sutpen's Hundred (1905).	Quentin	p. 373
Quentin learned something on his visit to Sutpen's Hundred (Sept. 1909) which altered his notion of the Sutpen story.	Quentin	p. 373
Clytie sets fire to Sutpen's Hundred; she and Henry die (Dec. 1909).	Mr. Compson	pp. 374–76

What Miss Rosa and General Compson Did Not Know

Miss Rosa did not know that the picture that Judith found on Bon's body was that of his octoroon mistress.	p. 142
Gen. Compson did not know that Bon was Henry's part-Negro half-brother.	p. 274
Neither did Miss Rosa know this, unless she learned it at the same time that Quentin did, in Sept. 1909.	p. 18

*The More Important Conjectures Made about Thomas
Sutpen and His Family*

CONJECTURE	MADE BY	PAGE
Sutpen named all his children including Charles Bon.	Gen. Compson (see the revision of the chronology, p. 425).	p. 61
	Mr. Compson	pp. 265–66
Miss Rosa hated her father.	Mr. Compson	p. 83
During the war Judith knew where Henry and Bon were.	Mr. Compson	p. 87
Bon must have learned of Sutpen's visit to New Orleans when he himself returned to New Orleans in the summer of 1860.	Mr. Compson	p. 92
Sutpen told Henry of Bon's "marriage" to the octoroon woman.	Mr. Compson	p. 90
Bon brought Henry to see the octoroon woman in New Orleans.	Mr. Compson	pp. 108–18
Henry's objection to the marriage of Bon and Judith was the fact that Bon had gone through the ceremony with the octoroon woman.	Mr. Compson	pp. 118–19
Henry and Bon hoped that the war would settle the dispute by removing one of them.	Mr. Compson	p. 120
Judith did not ask her father what his objection was to Bon.	Mr. Compson	p. 120
Henry and Bon returned to Oxford only long enough to enroll in the company being formed at the university.	Mr. Compson	p. 122
Bon was wounded at Shiloh and carried back to safety by Henry.	Mr. Compson (Or does Mr. Compson *know* this? Shreve questions it on p. 344.)	p. 124

CONJECTURE	MADE BY	PAGE
Sutpen's first wife was in New Orleans and Sutpen journeyed there in 1860 to buy her off.	Mr. Compson conjectures this after Quentin had seen Henry. The "Genealogy" printed at the back of the Modern Library edition states that "Eulalia Bon died in New Orleans," and thus provides auctorial sanction for this conjecture. Mr. Compson's first conjecture had been that Sutpen went to New Orleans to check on Bon's octoroon mistress.	pp. 268–69
The conversation between Judith and her father when he returned in 1864.	Quentin	p. 271
At Christmas Sutpen told Henry that Bon was his brother and that Bon knew this; but Bon did not know it.	Shreve (On p. 303 it is said that Shreve was speaking though "it might have been either of them and was in a sense both." But it is clearly Shreve who is speaking from p. 303 to p. 333, from p. 336 to p. 345, from p. 350 to p. 351, and from p. 358 to p. 359. Moreover, save for a dozen or so words, nothing in section 7 is *specifically* assigned to Quentin.)	pp. 293–96
There was a lawyer in New Orleans counseling Sutpen's first wife.	Shreve	p. 304
Perhaps Bon's mother discovered that he had an octoroon mistress and child.	Shreve	p. 307
Bon's mother had made the lawyer promise not to tell Bon who his father was.	Shreve	p. 309
The lawyer discovered where Sutpen lived and that Henry attended the University of Mississippi.	Shreve	pp. 309–10

433

Conjecture	Made by	Page
The lawyer wrote to Henry; Henry showed the letter to Bon; and Bon suspected that Henry might be his brother.	Shreve	p. 313
Bon accepted Henry's invitation to visit him, thinking that he might see his father.	Shreve	p. 319
Bon did not know "whatever it was in mother's [blood that Sutpen] could not brook."	Shreve	p. 321
Bon wanted only a hint of recognition from his father; he would not even demand to know "what it was my mother did that justified his action toward her and me." (Shreve evidently assumes at this point that Bon knew nothing of his possession of Negro blood.)	Shreve	p. 327
Bon believed that Sutpen had gone to New Orleans to make sure that Bon was truly his son.	Shreve	p. 329
Bon having returned to New Orleans did not learn whether Sutpen had seen his mother, but continued to believe that he had.	Shreve	p. 331
Sutpen told Henry on the second Christmas visit that Bon was his brother.	Shreve	p. 334
Henry and Bon visited Bon's mother and heard her say "So [Judith] has fallen in love with [Charles]," and Henry "knows" that Bon is indeed his brother.	Shreve ("that drawing room of baroque and fusty magnificence which Shreve had invented and which was probably true enough" and "this slight dowdy woman . . . whom Shreve and Quentin had likewise invented and which was [a construction] likewise probably true enough.")	pp. 335–36

Conjecture	Made by	Page
The lawyer congratulates Bon and Bon forces an apology.	Shreve	pp. 338–39
In 1862, when Bon was recovering from his wound, he received his octoroon mistress' picture and an appeal for money: she wrote that the lawyer had fled and that she could not find Bon's mother.	Shreve	p. 339
Henry wrestled with his horror of incest and asked Bon: "must you marry [our sister]?"	Shreve	p. 341
Bon did not know what he meant to do though he pretended he did. Henry knew what he meant to do, but had to say that he did not know.	Shreve	p. 341
Henry allowed Bon to write one letter to Judith.	Shreve	p. 342
It was Henry, not Bon, who was wounded at Shiloh.	Shreve	p. 344
In 1864 Bon asked Henry whether he had his permission to marry Judith, and Henry told him to write to Judith.	Shreve or Quentin?	p. 349
In 1864 Sutpen met Henry and told him that he had seen Charles Bon. (But p. 352 seems to contradict this. Compare also with the conjecture that Bon would have abandoned his courtship of Judith if he had had only a nod of recognition from his father, p. 327.)	Shreve or Quentin?	p. 353
Sutpen also told Henry that Bon's mother was part Negro.	Shreve or Quentin?	pp. 354–55
Bon said to Henry: "So it's the miscegenation, not the incest, which you can't bear." Does this conjecture imply that	Shreve or Quentin?	p. 356

435

Conjecture	Made by	Page
Henry proceeded to tell Bon what his father had just told him (pp. 354–55)? As late as p. 327, Quentin and Shreve take for granted that Bon did not know that he had Negro blood.)		
Bon told Henry that mere recognition could have stopped him, but now "I am thinking of myself."	Shreve or Quentin?	p. 357
Bon offered his pistol to Henry, but Henry hurled the pistol away.	Shreve or Quentin?	p. 358
Bon's motive in substituting the picture of his octoroon mistress and child for that of Judith was to say to Judith— if Henry did kill him—"I was no good; do not grieve for me."	Shreve	p. 358–59

Bon's Negro Blood

Ilse Lind's essay on *Absalom, Absalom!* has one notion that is so curious as to deserve comment. She tells us that the information that Bon was Sutpen's son has been told to Quentin by his *grandfather,* who had not, however, divulged it to Quentin's father. But nowhere in this novel is there any account of General Compson's telling Quentin anything. When the novel opens on a September afternoon in 1909, General Compson has long been dead. Moreover, there is in the novel no cutback to a scene in which Quentin has a conversation with his grandfather. One cannot say that the notion that Quentin was given the Sutpen secret by his grandfather is completely impossible. If we are to trust the genealogy of the Compson family published by Faulkner in the Modern Library edition of *The Sound and the Fury,* General Compson did not die until 1900, and since Quentin was born in 1890, the old man in his late eighties conceivably could have confided the secret to his ten-year-old grandson. But this theory is a highly improbable way of accounting for the facts. Actually, if one will look at pages 181 and 266–74, he will find that Quentin must have learned the secret of Bon's birth on his night visit to Sutpen's Hundred with Miss Rosa, that he did tell his father about it, and that this knowledge altered his father's view of the meaning of the story.

On this matter of how Quentin learned of Bon's Negro blood, Olga Vickery's *The Novels of William Faulkner* is not very satisfactory either. She gives a kind of blanket comment on the way in which the three basic accounts of the Sutpen story are molded by the personalities of the people who frame them. But she does not face the fact that the versions of General Compson and Miss Rosa show no knowledge of Bon's Negro blood, whereas that of Quentin and Shreve does. Nor does she tell us whether this element in the Quentin-Shreve version was a guess or was based on information that Quentin discovered. (But in writing [p. 92] that Quentin "has introduced" the "element of miscegenation," she may mean to say that it is mere guess or inference.)

Faulkner has made it quite plain, however, that Bon's possession of Negro blood was more than a mere conjecture made by Quentin and Shreve. It was evidently something that Quentin discovered. In Mr. Compson's earlier talks with Quentin, in which he tells him what General Compson knew about Thomas Sutpen and what he himself had known, it is plain that Mr. Compson does not know what the secret was. He knows that Clytie was Thomas Sutpen's part-Negro child, and he knows, what perhaps a good many people knew, that Thomas Sutpen named Clytie and Judith and "all his own get and all the get of his wild niggers" (p. 61), but in mentioning that Clytie was Sutpen's part-Negro child, it is significant that Mr. Compson, the evening before Quentin rode out to Sutpen's Hundred, does not include Charles Bon among Sutpen's children. Months later, at Harvard, when Quentin is relating to Shreve what his father had told him about Sutpen, the matter of Thomas Sutpen's naming his children comes up again, and with reference to the young Creole whom Henry brought home to visit the Sutpens at Christmas time. Quentin says: "Father said he probably named him himself. Charles Bon. Charles Good." At this point, Mr. Compson obviously does know that Charles Bon was Sutpen's son, and he talks as if he knew what the secret was, for Quentin quotes him as saying that Sutpen would not allow his first wife "and the child any place in the design even though he could have closed his eyes and, if not fooled the rest of the world as [his wife's parents] had fooled him, at least have frightened any man out of speaking the secret aloud—the same conscience which would not permit the child, since it was a boy, to bear either his name or that of its maternal grandfather" (p. 266). This rather clearly implies that Mr. Compson knows that the impediment is a trace of Negro blood.

Naturally Shreve seizes upon the discrepancy between Mr. Compson's former ignorance and present knowledge, and protests to Quentin: "Your father . . . seems to have got an awful lot of delayed information awful quick, after having waited forty-five years." Quentin concedes that his father had got new information, information that could not have come from General Compson, since, as Quentin remarks, "Sutpen never told Grandfather quite all of it." Then Quentin makes the surprising disclosure that it was he who supplied the information and that he gained it on the evening on which he and M´ s Rosa went out to Sutpen's Hundred. (See also Quentin's remark on p. 181.)

The holograph manuscript of *Absalom, Absalom!*, now in the University of Texas library, does not contain the important passage beginning " 'Your father,' Shreve said," and ending "And father said—" on page 266 of the Modern Library edition. Instead it reads: "he chose the name himself grandfather said, just as he named them all— the Charles Goods and Clytemnestras and Henrys and Judith and all of them—that entire fecundity of dragon teeth, as father called it. And father said how he must have stood there on the front gallery that afternoon and waited for Henry and the friend Henry had been writing home about to come up the drive." The Texas manuscript, on page 172, is dated January 31, 1936, the date on which it was finished. *Absalom, Absalom!* was published in October 1936. The added passage, then, is a late and deliberate insertion. The author makes it very plain that what Quentin learned at Sutpen's Hundred constituted information that his father had never had and that for the first time made sense, to Mr. Compson, of the conversation between Sutpen and General Compson so many years before.

The care with which Faulkner reworked *Absalom, Absalom!*, particularly the closing pages, is illustrated by comparing the University of Texas manuscript with the published text. In the following passage from pp. 375–76 of the Modern Library edition, the matter that Faulkner added in his revision is printed in italics; changes are indicated in brackets.

But the ambulance could not go fast in that drive; doubtless Clytie knew, counted upon, that; it would be a good three minutes before it could reach the *house, the* monstrous tinder-dry rotten shell seeping smoke *through the warped cracks in the weather-boarding as if it were made of gauze wire* and filled with roaring *and beyond which somewhere something lurked which bellowed, something human since the bellowing was in human speech, even though the reason for it would not have seemed to be.* And [MS reads "and"] the deputy and the driver would [MS reads "could"] spring out and Miss Coldfield would [MS reads "could"] stumble out [MS reads "stumble to the ground"] and follow them, running too, onto the gallery too, *where the creature which bellowed followed them, wraith-like and insubstantial, looking at them out of the smoke, whereupon the deputy even turned and ran at him, whereupon he retreated, fled, though the howling did not diminish nor even seem to get any further away. They ran onto the gallery too,* into the seeping smoke, *Miss Coldfield* screaming harshly, "The window! The window!" to the second man [MS reads "to the deputy"] at the door. But the door was not locked; it swung inward; the blast of heat struck them. The entire staircase was on fire. Yet they had to hold her; Quentin could see it: the light thin furious creature making no sound at all now, struggling with silent and bitter fury, clawing and scratching and biting at the two men who held her, who dragged her back and down the steps as the draft created by the open [MS reads "draft of the opened"] door seemed to explode like powder among the flames as the whole [MS reads "so that the whole"] *lower* hall vanished. He, Quentin, could see it, could see the deputy holding her while the driver backed the ambulance to safety [MS reads "ambulance clear"] and returned [MS reads "returned on foot, and"], the three faces all a little wild now since they must have believed her—[MS reads "her;"] the three of them staring, glaring at the doomed house [MS reads "burning house"]: and then for a moment maybe Clytie appeared in [MS reads "appeared at"] that window from which she must have been watching [MS reads "have watched"] *the gates* constantly day and night for three months—the tragic gnome's face beneath the *clean* headrag, against a red background of fire, *seen for a moment between two swirls of smoke,* looking down at them, perhaps not even now with triumph and no more of despair than it had ever worn, possibly even serene above the melting clapboards [MS reads "serene as the clapboards melted and peeled away. Then her face went

439

away, vanished;"] *before the smoke swirled across it again—and he, Jim Bond, the scion, the last of his race, seeing it too now and howling with human reason now since now even he could have known what he was howling about. But they couldn't catch him. They could hear him; he didn't seem to ever get any further away but they couldn't get any nearer and maybe in time they could not even locate the direction any more of the howling.* They—*the driver and the deputy*—held Miss Coldfield [MS reads "Coldfield as she struggled, still making no sound and foaming a little now at the mouth. The whole enormous house seemed to collapse"— all cancelled] as she struggled: he (*Quentin*) *could see her, them; he had not been there but he could see her, struggling, and fight- ing like a doll in a nightmare, making no sound, foaming a little at the mouth, her face even in the sunlight lit by one last wild crimson reflection* [MS reads "wild glare"] *as the house* [MS reads "the entire enormous house"] *collapsed* [MS reads "collapsed."] *and roared away, and there was only the sound of the idiot negro left.*

Chronology of Quentin's Night Visit to Sutpen's Hundred

On page 88 it is said that Miss Rosa expected on this evening to be away from her house for about six hours. Since it was twelve miles from town to Sutpen's Hundred and a good buggy horse—presumably the Compsons' horse was a good one—could travel the twelve miles in less than two hours, Miss Rosa's planning to be gone some six hours means that she was allowing something like two hours to go, two hours to be spent at Sutpen's Hundred, and two hours to return. We know that Quentin waited for dark (p. 88) before setting out, and in north Mississippi in mid-September dark falls not much before 8 P.M.

We are not told the hour of their return. But the lights are out in Quentin's house and it is presumably sometime after midnight, per- haps much later. Yet even if we allow a full two hours for the visit, it is not easy to find explicit indications showing that there was any lengthy talk between Quentin and Henry Sutpen. Miss Rosa and Quentin got out of the buggy and walked up the half-mile-long drive to the house—a matter of ten or fifteen minutes—and they took a little time to get into the house. Once in, Miss Rosa does go right up the stairs, but how long she stays in the room with Henry we do not know —in terms of the events noted by Quentin, not very long. Yet his sense of the action is so tranced and his attention so rapt that it is hard to say how much time actually does elapse. For her stay, short or long, must have seemed to the excited Quentin a period when time appeared to stand still.

So perhaps also with his own visit to Henry's room, though there is a hint by which to measure Quentin's stay in the room: by the time Quentin catches up with Miss Rosa, she has not had time to walk as far as the buggy. True, Miss Rosa is an old lady and would walk slowly, and indeed she has fallen and is lying on the ground when Quentin comes up to her. At the least, however, Quentin probably had ten minutes to talk with Henry—although their conversation *may* have been much longer. The fragment of it that keeps running through Quentin's head does not pretend to give more than the awesome confrontation. There is no warrant for concluding that it represents all that was said.

What about Miss Rosa's conversation with Henry? What questions would she have put to him? And how freely would he have talked? (Did Miss Rosa talk further with Clytie while Quentin was upstairs?) As for Quentin's conversation with Henry, what would Henry have told—if anything—to a young man whom he had never seen before? And would Quentin have dared to put to the pallid man on the bed any other questions than those which we know he did put: Who are you? How long have you been here? Why did you return?

These are problems that are not easy to solve. Faulkner has been willing to leave the matter to his reader's imagination. He has withheld from us all of Miss Rosa's colloquy with Henry and all but a fragment of Quentin's. But in the chronology of the events of this particular evening, one can find time enough for Henry to pass on the information about Charles Bon's birth to Miss Rosa (who then passed it on to Quentin on their ride home) or perhaps to Quentin directly. (The latter possibility is the more likely: Miss Rosa's dazed condition as Quentin helps her to the door of her cottage suggests that she may well have sat in dazed silence during the whole of the ride back to Jefferson.)

Sutpen's Downfall and the Defeat of the South

Some readers may need to be reminded that if the South had won the Civil War and achieved its independence, Sutpen's design would still have failed—that is, a Southern victory would not have removed

Henry's dilemma. Presumably he still would have had to shoot Bon at the gates of Sutpen's Hundred and flee. Thomas Sutpen would still have found himself seeking a male heir in order to complete his design, and though a wealthier Sutpen might have had a somewhat easier time finding a mate willing to accept the arrangement he proposed to Miss Rosa, that would have been his only advantage. No one could guarantee that his third wife would produce a male heir. (What the aging Sutpen really needed to improve his chances was an easy and quick system of divorce which would allow him to change wives legally once or twice more, if need be, in order to get a male heir.)

Judith and Bon's Son

The commentators on *Absalom, Absalom!* have a good deal of difficulty in remembering what is not fact but mere conjecture, and in then giving it its proper weight. For example, Olga Vickery blames Judith for telling Etienne that he is a Negro. But if one reads pages 196–201 with a little care, one realizes that it is simply General Compson's conjecture that Judith or Clytie told Etienne that he was a Negro. It is not, in fact, at all clear that Judith told the boy, or even that Clytie did so. Mrs. Vickery is literally correct in saying that Etienne's situation in relation to his aunts is dramatically rendered by the sleeping arrangements made for him midway "between Judith's bed and Clytie's pallet." But the hasty reader is to be warned against concluding that Judith commanded sleeping arrangements that assume the boy's possession of Negro blood. He sleeps in a trundle bed (a "white child's bed," p. 200). It is Clytie who, with "a sort of invincible spurious humility," insists upon sleeping on a pallet on the floor. It is not surprising that a boy growing up in this special community and sensitized by this strange household should notice the difference between Clytie and Judith, as well as that between the Negroes and whites around him, and finally come to feel that he himself was a Negro, thus accounting for his general sense of alienation. His concealment of the shard of broken mirror (p. 199) hints of such puzzled speculations. In any case, it is perfectly clear to General Compson that Judith did not drive Etienne to consort with Negroes and that even Clytie tried to prevent his having anything to do with them. As we have seen, Quentin (whose conjectures are at least as sound as his grandfather's) believes that Judith begs the boy to call her aunt and tries to persuade him to go North and live as a white man. If we are to judge from

Judith's kindness to Bon's mistress and her care for his child, her love for Charles Bon was apparently not shaken—though she must have been puzzled—by her discovery on his body of the picture of his mistress and child. Ilse Lind has her own interpretation of Bon's act of removing Judith's picture from his wallet and replacing it with that of his octoroon mistress. She calls it an act of "defiance and counter-retaliation." Bon means to show the Sutpens that "if he is to be none of theirs, they will be none of his." Maybe so, and she has a right to enter the game with Shreve, Quentin, and the rest of us and make her own interpretation. But on the showing of such evidence as we have in the novel, Charles' gesture was singularly inept. For if Bon wanted to strike at Judith, to her his blow could only seem wanton and not an act of retaliation. For Judith knows nothing of his Negro blood and presumably never does know of it. She has worked him no injury, has remained faithful to him, and means to marry him.

If Bon meant by his gesture to retaliate against Henry, it was still inept. For there is no evidence that Henry was ever aware that Bon had swapped the pictures. Besides, Bon, since he knew Henry well, must have known that by forcing Henry to kill him, he had visited upon him the worst punishment that he could invoke. The switched picture to be found on his dead body would be a mere fleabite as *retaliation* compared to the Cainlike murder for which he made Henry responsible.

15. MAN, TIME, AND ETERNITY

Patterns of Guilt and Innocence in THE SOUND AND THE FURY

For example, Lawrence E. Bowling, in "Faulkner and the Theme of Innocence," *Kenyon Review, 20* (1958), 466–87, sees the novel as "an exploration of the idea of innocence." Benjy illustrates one kind of innocence ("want of knowledge and intellect"); Quentin illustrates the Puritan view of innocence ("moral purity"); and even Jason, though he does what "he knows to be immoral and vicious," is innocent in the sense that "he remains ignorant of basic human principles" (p. 475). This account is ingenious and Bowling has some excellent observations to make incidentally as well as on the main theme of his essay; but I think that his case for regarding Jason as "innocent" might be rendered more effective by an appeal to the example of Thomas Sutpen.

The two men are very different in personality, but Jason's failure to understand other human beings or even himself is related to Sutpen's brittle rationalizing and his confidence in blueprints and designs.

Events Referred to in Benjy's Section

It has long been recognized that there is considerably more order to Benjy's section than a merely casual reading would suggest. His mind constantly recurs to events important in the family's life such as Caddy's wedding, the death of the grandmother, or the day on which his name was changed. There have been various attempts to distinguish separate experiences or scenes or levels. Sumner C. Powell, "William Faulkner Celebrates Easter, 1928," *Perspective*, 2 (1949), 195–218, finds fifteen divisions; in an essay entitled "Primitivism in *The Sound and the Fury*," in *English Institute Essays*, A. S. Downer, ed. (New York, 1952), I distinguished eleven various experiences, and Carvel Collins, in "The Interior Monologues of *The Sound and the Fury*," published in the same volume, distinguished thirteen scenes scattered over a "twenty-nine year period." The most elaborate attempt to sort out the various elements in Benjy's monologue is to be found in the essay by George R. Stewart and Joseph M. Backus, "'Each in its Ordered Place': Structure and Narrative in Benjy's Section of *The Sound and the Fury*," *American Literature*, 29 (1958). Thirteen levels are distinguished, and these are dated and keyed to the "units" of the monologue that refer to them. The authors have also provided a plan of the Compson house and a map of the Compson property down to the woodpile, the pigpen, and the ditch in which Nancy's bones repose. Students of *The Sound and the Fury* will find this material interesting and in many ways useful. The speculations of the authors, as in the matter of possible incest between Benjy and Caddy, are less happy. (See above, p. 7.)

Faulkner on the Subject of Quentin

Some years ago one of my students showed me a copy of a letter from Faulkner in which he replied to another student who had asked him whether Caddy and Quentin ever did commit incest. Faulkner writes that they did not: "Caddy was highly sexed but no nymphomaniac, was monogamous and even moral in her fashion. Her sexual affinity was never Quentin but a tough, hard, soul-less man, vide the casual soldier who got the child on her, and the German general." Quentin, on the other hand, according to Faulkner's letter, was undersexed. He did not really want his sister's body but wanted "the world to believe he had [committed incest with her], yet his own conscience would not let him tell the actual lie."

The sentiments expressed here are obviously fairly close to those expressed in the appendix that Faulkner later furnished for *The Sound and the Fury.* Since I unfortunately did not make more careful notes at the time that this copy was given me and therefore cannot compare my copy with the original, I forbear to quote the whole letter in detail. But it does have the ring of truth, and I have no doubt in my own mind that it represents Faulkner's feelings about Quentin around the year 1950.

Mrs. Compson and Caddy

One of the most curious revelations about the neurotic Mrs. Compson is given by Jason, who relates that once when she happened to see a beau of Caddy's kissing her, "all next day she went around the house in a black dress and a veil and even Father couldn't get her to say a word except crying and saying her little daughter was dead and Caddy about fifteen then" (p. 247). The mother's extravagantly neurotic exaggeration of the seriousness of what Caddy had done would be humiliating and bewildering to the girl. No wonder that Caddy soon does worse things than kissing, and no wonder that, as soon as she can, she gets away from home.

Benjy's Compulsive Orderliness

Rollo May writes that certain

> brain-injured patients—chiefly soldiers with portions of the frontal cortex shot away—have specifically lost the ability to abstract, to think in terms of "the possible." They were tied to the immediate concrete situation in which they found themselves. When their closets happened to be in disarray, they were thrown into profound anxiety and disordered behavior. They exhibited compulsive orderliness—which is a way of holding oneself every moment rigidly to the concrete situation. . . . It was as though they were threatened with dissolution of the self unless they re-

mained related at every moment to the immediate situation, as though they could "be a self" only as the self was bound to the concrete items in space.

In calling attention to the resemblance of Benjy here, I am not attempting to diagnose his brain ailment. The use that Faulkner has made of his orderliness in the closing paragraphs of *The Sound and the Fury* does not depend in the least on how we account for Benjy's psychic disability, but the parallels are interesting.

16. THE WORLD OF WILLIAM FAULKNER

Parsham as Grand Junction, Tennessee

When *The Reivers* appeared, it was apparent to anyone familiar with west Tennessee that Parsham was almost certainly Grand Junction in Hardeman County, Tennessee, where the Southern Railroad crosses the Illinois Central, and where, on what used to be old plantation country, the field trials for bird dogs are held each year.

The Reverend Rowan Greer, who has family connections with this part of Tennessee, writes me that

> Parsham in *The Reivers* is unmistakably Grand Junction—the reference to railroads and to the Grand National trials prove that. The trials, as you may know, are held on the Ames Plantation (and I believe always have been since some time in the 1870's or 80's). The Horace Lytle mentioned on p. 166 and p. 194 was an advertising executive in Dayton, Ohio, an old friend of my father and grandfather, my own godfather. The story about him on p. 166 is a true one, but Faulkner has altered the details. Uncle Horace never owned Mary Montrose and it was another dog he was asked to sell. I am not sure of the price, either. As a small boy I used to hunt with Dad and Uncle Horace and I remember hearing the story.

COMPSON GENEALOGY

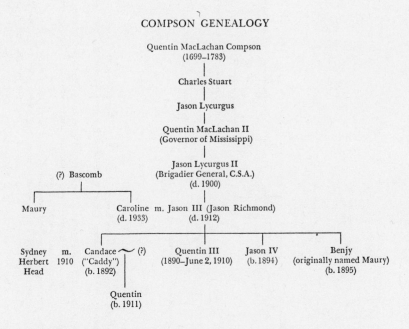

Quentin MacLachan Compson
(1699–1783)

Charles Stuart

Jason Lycurgus

Quentin MacLachan II
(Governor of Mississippi)

Jason Lycurgus II
(Brigadier General, C.S.A.)
(d. 1900)

(?) Bascomb

Maury

Caroline m. Jason III (Jason Richmond)
(d. 1933)   (d. 1912)

Sydney   m.   Candace ～ (?)   Quentin III   Jason IV   Benjy
Herbert 1910 ("Caddy")   (1890–June 2, 1910)   (b. 1894)   (originally named Maury)
Head   (b. 1892)   (b. 1895)

Quentin
(b. 1911)

NOTE: The symbol ～ is used to indicate a union which resulted in an illegitimate birth.

The evidence for the birth dates of Caddy and her brothers comes from various sources. In *Absalom, Absalom!* (p. 294) we learn that in January 1910 Shreve was nineteen and Quentin Compson some months older. This means that Quentin was born in 1890 and perhaps in the earlier or middle part of the year. In the appendix that Faulkner furnished for the Modern Library edition of *Absalom, Absalom!*, he says that Quentin was born in 1891, but as the appendix has a number of other errors, I prefer to follow the text of the novel.

In the story "That Evening Sun," Quentin tells us that he was the oldest: "I was nine and Caddy was seven and Jason was five" (p. 294). This dating would make Caddy's birth year 1892, and the date agrees with what we are told in the appendix to the Compson genealogy. Jason, then, would have been born in about 1894, and since we are told in the Compson genealogy that Benjy was thirty-three years old in 1928, his birth year should be 1895. It is curious that in "That Evening Sun," Benjy is never mentioned.

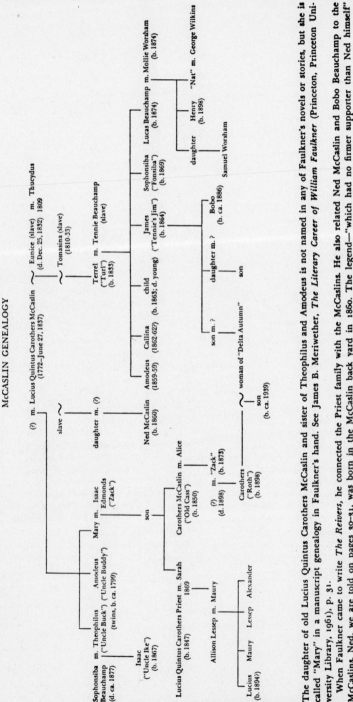

McCASLIN GENEALOGY

The daughter of old Lucius Quintus Carothers McCaslin and sister of Theophilus and Amodeus is not named in any of Faulkner's novels or stories, but she is called "Mary" in a manuscript genealogy in Faulkner's hand. See James B. Meriwether, *The Literary Career of William Faulkner* (Princeton, Princeton University Library, 1961), p. 31.

When Faulkner came to write *The Reivers*, he connected the Priest family with the McCaslins. He also related Ned McCaslin and Bobo Beauchamp to the McCaslins. Ned, we are told on pages 30–31, was born in the McCaslin back yard in 1860. The legend—"which had no firmer supporter than Ned himself" —was that "his mother had been the natural daughter of old Lucius Quintus Carothers himself and a Negro slave."

Ned's relationship to the McCaslin family is obviously an afterthought. So also is the ancestry of Bobo Beauchamp. On p. 22 of *The Reivers* we are told that Tennie's Jim was the grandfather of Bobo Beauchamp, but "grandfather" must be a slip for "father." In 1905 Bobo must have been at least 20 (see *The Reivers*, pp. 13, 229), but in 1905 Tennie's Jim, if still living, would have been only forty-one. Incidentally, since Tennie's Jim left Mississippi in 1885 and apparently never came back, one supposes that Bobo was begotten before 1885; in any case, he was left in Mississippi for his grandmother to bring up (*The Reivers*, p. 229).

STEVENS GENEALOGY

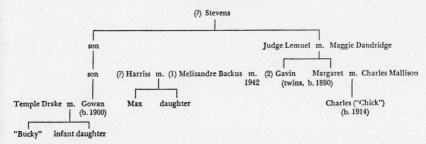

According to *Knight's Gambit*, Gavin Stevens was fifty years old in 1939, which would make his birth year 1889. But in *The Mansion* we are told that he was a year younger than Eula Varner Snopes, and *The Town* indicates that Eula was born in 1889. Accordingly, I have dated Gavin's birth as 1890.

Faulkner seems to have had two quite different notions about the age of Charles Mallison, Jr. *Knight's Gambit* and *Intruder in the Dust* point to his birth year as 1924, but in *The Town* it would seem to be 1915, and in *The Mansion*, 1914. On the genealogical chart I have put it down as 1914, in line with Faulkner's latest conception of the character. But I remind the reader that this date will apply only to the Charles that we see in the last two novels of Faulkner's trilogy.

It may be useful to set down here a brief chronology of Gavin Stevens' actions as a young man. (The dates are drawn from references in *The Mansion*.) Gavin was at Harvard in 1909. After he had returned to Jefferson he fell in love with Eula Varner Snopes. She offered herself to him in 1913. A few months later, early in the spring of 1914, Gavin went to Heidelberg. In 1915–16 he served in the American ambulance service in France as a stretcher-bearer. He returned to Jefferson in 1916, and a year later went back to France as a YMCA man. He came back to Jefferson to practice law in 1919. But it ought to be pointed out that these dates do not necessarily apply to the stories included in *Knight's Gambit*, where Gavin does not come home until 1924.

In *The Town* (p. 3) it is made plain that Chick Mallison and Gowan Stevens are second cousins, and this is the relationship that I have depicted on the genealogical chart; but in *Requiem for a Nun* (p. 127) Gavin Stevens says that Gowan is his nephew.

449

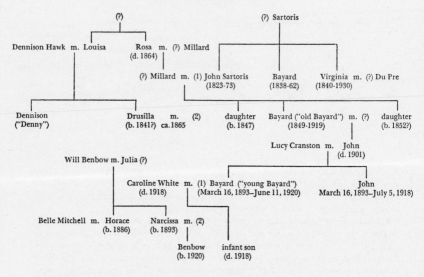

In *Sartoris* (p. 375) Colonel John Sartoris dies in 1876; in *Requiem for a Nun* (p. 238) in 1878. In *The Unvanquished* his death occurs when his son Bayard is twenty-four years old, and therefore took place in 1873 or 1874, depending upon whether Bayard was born in 1849 or 1850.

The problem of old Bayard's age is not easy to settle. The several inconsistent references to it in *The Unvanquished* are as follows: on page 5 of *The Unvanquished* we are told that Bayard was twelve when Vicksburg fell—that is, in July 1863. On page 216 of *The Unvanquished* we are told that he was fifteen just before Christmas of 1864. On page 253 we are told that four years after his father remarried, he was twenty. All the indications are that Colonel John Sartoris married Drusilla very shortly after the war had ended, in 1865, which would make Bayard twenty years old in 1869. Bayard was twenty-four when he was recalled in October on the occasion of his father's death. The second, third, and fourth of these references would suggest that Bayard was born in 1849, but the first of them points to a later date. If Bayard is right in saying that he was twelve years old in July of 1863, he had to be born in 1850, and possibly was born as late as 1851. (Had Faulkner forgotten that Vicksburg fell in 1863?) In view of three other references that point to the year 1849, one is inclined to say that this was when Bayard was born.

Yet it must be pointed out that on page 271 of *The Unvanquished* we are told that Aunt Jenny came to Mississippi on a cold January day "six years ago." The year, if we are to trust *Sartoris*, was 1869. This would point to the year of Colonel Sartoris' death as 1875 or possibly 1874. On this reckoning Bayard's birth year goes up to 1850 again. The truth of the matter is that one cannot construct a chronology which will make all the references consistent with each other. Faulkner was careless or perhaps simply did not attach very much importance to exact dates—though he *was* carefully exact in indicating the day of the month and the year of the deaths of the twins John and Bayard, and Bayard's first wife, Caroline. It is not really of great consequence whether the climactic event in *The Unvanquished* took place in 1873, 1874, or, as *Sartoris* has it, 1876, or even, as in *Requiem for a Nun*, 1878. In the interests of simplicity I have decided to set down Bayard's birth date as 1849 and so adjust all the other dates keyed to it. But the reader is warned to give or take a year or two for all of them.

In "There Was a Queen" young Bayard is said to have died at the age of twenty-six rather than at twenty-seven, as indicated in the genealogical chart.

SUTPEN GENEALOGY

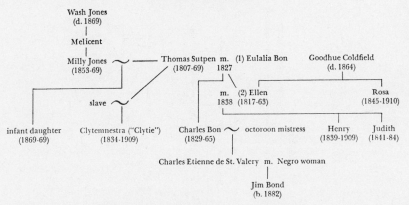

For notes on this genealogy, see p. 424 above.

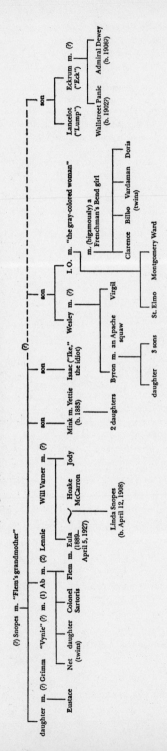

SNOPES GENEALOGY

"... they were just Snopes, like colonies of rats or termites are just rats and termites" (*The Town*, p. 40).

Character Index

FOR THE STORIES AND NOVELS
OF FAULKNER

I HAVE NOT INCLUDED characters from *New Orleans Sketches* (1958) or from stories which were later absorbed into the novels. The exceptions are certain stories that Faulkner reprinted in *Collected Stories* ("Barn Burning," "Centaur in Brass," "Mule in the Yard," and "Wash"). I have included the characters in both versions of "A Bear Hunt" (see *Stories* and *Big Woods*). Numbers refer to pages in the editions listed on p. xiii above. Family relationships are indicated in parentheses directly after the character's name.

I had completed the Index before I learned of Mr. Robert Warner Kirk's unpublished doctoral dissertation (University of Southern California, 1959) entitled "An Index and Encyclopedia of the Characters in the Fictional Works of William Faulkner," but I have been fortunate enough to secure a copy before my own Index has had to go to the printer. Mr. Kirk's index and mine differ considerably in plan, and we do not always agree as to the identity of certain characters or their relation to each other; but it has been a great help to check my page references against his, and, because of the thoroughness of his cataloguing, I have been able to add to my list a good number of minor characters that I had missed and some of the more obscure appearances of major characters. This help I gratefully acknowledge.

BENBOW, JULIA (mother of Horace and Narcissa) *Sartoris*, 174

BENBOW, NARCISSA (sister of Horace and second wife of "Young Bayard" Sartoris) *Mansion*, 189; *Sanctuary*, 25 and passim; *Sartoris*, 29 and passim; "There Was a Queen," *Stories*, 727 and passim; *Town*, 117

BENBOW, PERCY (son of Judge Benbow) *Absalom*, 212

BENBOW, WILL (father of Horace and Narcissa) *Sartoris*, 170–80

BERRY, BEN "An Error in Chemistry," *Knight's Gambit*, 117

BERRY, LOUIS "Red Leaves," *Stories*, 313 and passim

BEST, HENRY *Town*, 86

BIDET, GEN. ——— *Fable*, 23–55

BIDWELL, ——— "Hair," *Stories*, 138, 145–47 (storekeeper), keeps Starnes house keys for Hawkshaw)

BIGLIN, LUTHER *Mansion*, 206, 408–10, 428 (guards Flem's house)

BILLY, UNCLE See Varner, Will

BINFORD, ——— *Mansion*, 119 (one of Eula Varner's suitors)

BINFORD, DEWITT (relative of the Snopeses by marriage) *Town*, 365–66

BINFORD, MRS. DEWITT *Town*, 366–67

BINFORD, LUCIUS *Mansion*, 72, 117; *Reivers*, 99, 114; *Sanctuary*, 185, 306 ("landlord" at Miss Reba's)

BIRD, TOM-TOM "Centaur in Brass," *Stories*, 152 and passim; *Mansion*, 164; *Town*, 15–29, 83–85, 142 (daytime fireman at power plant)

BIRD, "UNCLE" *Sartoris*, 270 (in church delegation recovering funds from Simon)

BIRDSONG, ——— *Moses*, 153–57 (watchman whose throat is cut by Rider)

BIRDSONG, "PREACHER" *Town*, 183 (sometimes boxes with Matt Levitt)

BISHOP, EPHRIAM *Mansion*, 370 and passim (sheriff at time of Flem's murder)

BISHOP, ——— *Fable*, 88–89, 112, 120 (British fighter pilot)

BLACK, MR. ——— "Death Drag," *Stories*, 189

BLAIR, HARRISON "Fox Hunt," *Stories*, 588 and passim

BLAIR, MRS. HARRISON "Fox Hunt," *Stories*, 588 and passim

BLAIR, JOHN "Artist at Home," *Stories*, 629, 642–45

BLAKE, JIM "Hand upon the Waters," *Knight's Gambit*, 68 (helps with burial of Lonnie Grinnup)

BLAND, ——— "Ad Astra," *Stories*, 407 and passim (in the R.A.F.—was a Rhodes Scholar before war)

BLAND, GERALD *Sound and Fury*, 109–84 (student at Harvard)

BLAND, MRS. ——— (Gerald's mother) *Sound and Fury*, 110–84

BLEDSOE, ——— *Wild Palms*, 326 (at the penal farm)

BLEDSOE, SERGEANT ——— *Fable*, 317–19

BLEYTH, CAPT. ——— *Soldiers' Pay*, 9 (R.A.F. pilot)

BLUM, MAJOR ——— *Fable*, 279–82

BOBBIE See Allen, Bobbie

BOGARD, CAPT. H. S. "Turnabout," *Stories*, 475 and passim (American flyer)

BOGGAN See Corporal

BOLIVAR, UNCLE DICK *Hamlet*, 347, 351 (treasure-dowser)

BON, CHARLES (son of Thomas Sutpen by his first wife) *Absalom*, 67 and passim

BON, CHARLES ETIENNE DE SAINT-VELERY (son of Charles Bon by his octoroon mistress) *Absalom*, 191 and passim. On p. 191 the name is given as Charles Etienne Saint-Valery Bon; on p. [380], as Charles Etienne St. Velery Bon; on p. [383] as Charles Etienne de Saint Velery Bon.

BON, EULALIA (Charles Bon's mother and first wife of Thomas Sutpen) *Absalom* (where she is not named), 252, 272, 335. In the genealogy of the Modern Library edition, 381, she is called Eulalia Bon.

BOND, JIM (son of C.E.S.-V. Bon and his Negro wife) *Absalom*, 215, 371

BONDS, JACK "A Bear Hunt," *Stories*, 63 (former member of Provine gang)

BOOKRIGHT, LETTY (daughter of Calvin) *Town*, 78 (marries Zack Houston). In *The Hamlet*, 218, Houston's wife is named Lucy Pate; also Lucy Pate in paperbound ed. of *The Town*.

BOOKRIGHT *See* Bookwright

BOOKWRIGHT, CALVIN *Mansion*, 170, 231; *Reivers*, 13; "Tomorrow," *Knight's Gambit*, 85-86, 89-90, 105 (or perhaps this is Homer Bookwright); *Town*, 78 (where, in the first edition, it is spelled "Bookright")

BOOKWRIGHT, HERMAN *Mansion*, 118, 126 (one of Eula Varner's suitors)

BOOKWRIGHT, HOMER *Mansion*, 63; "Shall Not Perish," *Stories*, 102; "Shingles for the Lord," *Stories*, 27 and passim

BOOKWRIGHT, ODUM *Hamlet*, 62, 69, 347 and passim; *Mansion*, 138, 142 (joins Ratliff and Henry Armstid in buying the Old Frenchman's Place)

BOSUN, THE "Divorce in Naples," *Stories*, 877 and passim

BOUC, PIERRE *Fable*, 339-40, 355

BOWDEN, MATT *Unvanquished*, 208 (associated with Grumby)

BOWEN, CAPT. ――――, U.S.A. *Unvanquished*, 132

BOYD, MR. ―――― (father of Howard) "The Brooch," *Stories*, 647

BOYD, MRS. ―――― (mother of Howard) "The Brooch," *Stories*, 647 and passim

BOYD, AMY (wife of Howard) "The Brooch," *Stories*, 648 and passim

BOYD, HOWARD (husband of Amy) "The Brooch," *Stories*, 647 and passim (kills Amy and himself)

BRADLEY, ―――― *Wild Palms*, 99, 106-09

BRANDT, DR. ―――― *Sartoris*, 240 (Memphis specialist consulted by Old Bayard)

BRECKBRIDGE, GAVIN *Unvanquished*, 101, 219, 263 (Drusilla's fiancé, killed at Shiloh)

BRIDESMAN, CAPT. ―――― *Fable*, 89 and passim

BRIDGER, ―――― *Unvanquished*, 205-07 (associated with Grumby)

BRIGGINS, LYCURGUS (grandson of Parsham Hood) *Reivers*, 247

BRIGGINS, MARY (daughter of Parsham Hood) *Reivers*, 248

BROUSSARD, ―――― *Mosquitoes*, 34, 37 (proprietor-waiter in restaurant)

BROWN, JOE *See* Burch

BROWNLEE, PERCIVAL *Moses*, 263-93. He was renamed Spintrius: see *Moses*, 265

BRUMMAGE, JUDGE ―――― *Mansion*, 40-43 (judge who sentences Mink)

BRZEWSKI, ―――― *Fable*, 277 (one of the names by which "the Corporal" is known)

BUCHWALD, ―――― *Fable*, 372-81 (American soldier)

BUCK *See* Conner, Buck

BUCKNER, "BUCK" *Wild Palms*, 179 and passim (manager of mine where Wilbourne works)

BUCKNER, MRS. BILLIE (Buck's wife) *Wild Palms*, 179-209

BUCKWORTH, ―――― *Wild Palms*, 326-31 (deputy warden)

BUD, "UNCLE" *Sanctuary*, 301-12 (small boy, with the "ladies" at Miss Reba's)

BUFFALOE, MR. ―――― *Reivers*, 25, 27; *Town*, 12-30 (city electrician; owns first automobile in Jefferson)

BUFORD, ―――― *Light in August*, 256, 286, 401 (deputy sheriff)

BULLITT, R. Q., "BOB" *Pylon*, 31-33, 52, 60 (in air race)

BULLITT, MRS. ―――― (wife of Bob) *Pylon*, 31

BUNCH, BYRON *Light in August*, 21 and passim

BUNDREN, MRS. ―――― (Anse's second wife) *As I Lay*, 512, 532

BUNDREN, ADDIE (wife of Anse, mother of Cash, Darl, Dewey Dell, Jewel and Vardaman) *As I Lay*, 340 and passim

BUNDREN, ANSE (husband of Addie) *As I Lay*, 344 and passim

BUNDREN, CASH *As I Lay*, 340 and passim

CASSE-TÊTE, "Horse" *Fable*, 357–61, 384–86 (executed by firing squad)

CAVALCANTI, SIGNORA "Mistral," *Stories*, 870, 875

CAYLEY, MISS ——— *Knight's Gambit*, 184–91, 226 (Max Harriss and Capt. Gualdres are supposedly rivals for her)

CAYLEY, HENCE (father of Miss Cayley) *Knight's Gambit*, 184

CHANCE, VIC *Pylon*, 47 (wants to build an airplane for Shumann)

CHANCELLOR, THE *Moses*, 127 (presides at Lucas' divorce proceeding)

CHARLES *See* Mallison, Charles

CHARLEY *Light in August*, 105–06 (Miss Atkins' lover)

CHARLEY, "UNCLE" "Dr. Martino," *Stories*, 584–85 (porter at hotel)

CHARLIE *Sound and Fury*, 66–68 (Caddy's "date")

CHAUFFEUR OF MRS. BLAIR "Fox Hunt," *Stories*, 593 and passim

CHAUFFEUR OF MRS. MAURIER *Mosquitoes*, 21, 31

CHLORY "Beyond," *Stories*, 782–83

CHRISTIAN, MRS. ——— (wife of Uncle Willy Christian) "Uncle Willy," *Stories*, 236–38

CHRISTIAN, WALTER *Town*, 155 (Willy Christian's janitor)

CHRISTIAN, UNCLE WILLY *Mansion*, 55–56, 134, 201; *Town*, 60, 154–62; "Uncle Willy," *Stories*, 225 and passim (druggist)

CHRISTMAS, JOE *Light in August*, 28 and passim

CHURCH, MRS. ——— "That Will Be Fine," *Stories*, 274

CINTHY *Light in August*, 416–18, 424 (Negro servant in Hightower household)

CLAIBORNE, GOVERNOR WILLIAM C. C. *Requiem*, 106, 108

CLAPP, WALTER *Reivers*, 241, 290 (Mr. van Tosch's horse trainer)

CLAY, HENRY *Requiem*, 109

CLAY, "SIS" Beulah *Sound and Fury*, 52

CLEFUS *Town*, 357 (cleans Gavin's office)

CLYTIE *See* Sutpen, Clytemnestra

COFER, ——— *Wild Palms*, 11, 17 (real estate agent)

COLBERT, DAVID "A Courtship," *Stories*, 363 and passim (chief Man of the Chickasaws)

COLDFIELD, MRS. ——— (wife of Goodhue) *Absalom*, 59 (dies when Rosa is born)

COLDFIELD, ELLEN *See* Sutpen, Ellen

COLDFIELD, GOODHUE *Absalom*, 42 and passim; *Requiem*, 109

COLDFIELD, ROSA (daughter of Goodhue) *Absalom*, 7 and passim

COLEMAN, MRS. ——— *Soldiers' Pay*, 233

COLLIER, ——— "Turnabout," *Stories*, 491, 494 (American flyer)

COLLYER, ——— *Fable*, 93 and passim

COMPSON, MRS. ——— *Unvanquished*, 52 and passim

COMPSON, BENJAMIN, "Benjy" (born Maury, son of Jason III and Caroline) *Mansion*, 322; *Sound and Fury*, 9 and passim

COMPSON, CANDACE, "Caddy" (daughter of Jason III and Caroline) "A Justice," *Stories*, 343, 358, 360; *Mansion*, 322; *Sound and Fury*, 8 and passim; "That Evening Sun," *Stories*, 290 and passim

COMPSON, CAROLINE BASCOMB (wife of Jason III) *Sound and Fury*, 11 and passim

COMPSON, CHARLES STUART (father of Jason I) *Sound and Fury*, 4–5

COMPSON, JASON LYCURGUS I *Requiem*, 9–45, 215–20; *Sound and Fury*, 6 (a founder of Jefferson)

COMPSON, GEN. JASON LYCURGUS II (grandfather of Quentin and Candace) *Absalom*, 13 and passim; "A Bear Hunt," *Big Woods*, 145; *Intruder*, 93; "A Justice," *Stories*, 343–60; *Moses*, 164 and passim; "My Grandmother Millard," *Stories*, 675; *Reivers*, 18; *Requiem*, 237–38; *Sound and Fury*, 95; *Town*, 69; *Unvanquished*, 282

459

DAVIES, RHYS *Fable*, 88, 120 (British fighter pilot)

DAVIS, JEFFERSON *Requiem*, 109

DAVY "The Leg," *Stories*, 823 and passim (young American at Oxford)

"DEACON" (1) *Sound and Fury*, 101, 115–20

"Deacon" (2) *Sartoris*, 125–28, 145

DEFRANCE, ABRAHAM *Requiem*, 106 (laid out the city of Jackson, Miss.)

DELPHINE *See* McCaslin, Delphine

DEMARCHI, ——— *Fable*, 99, 117 (British fighter pilot)

DEMONT *See* Marthe's husband

DE MONTIGNY, ——— *Fable*, 282 (French officer)

DE MONTIGNY, PAUL "Elly," *Stories*, 207 and passim

DENNISON, UNCLE *See* Hawk, Dennison (2)

DENNY, COUSIN *See* Hawk, Dennison (1)

DEPRE *See* Du Pre

DEPUTY, THE FEDERAL *Fable*, 158–89

DE SPAIN, ——— (sister of Manfred, and Allison, her daughter) *Mansion*, 422, 428–29

DE SPAIN, LULA (wife of Major de Spain) "Barn Burning," *Stories*, 11, 16; "A Bear Hunt," *Stories*, 63; *Hamlet*, 15

DE SPAIN, MAJOR ———, C.S.A. (father of Manfred) *Absalom*, 291; "Barn Burning," *Stories*, 12, 18–19, 23; "A Bear Hunt," *Big Woods*, 145–46; *Hamlet*, 14, 17; *Intruder*, 93; *Moses*, 164 and passim; *Reivers*, 18, 58; *Town*, 43, 58, 362

DE SPAIN, MANFRED (son of Major de Spain and sometimes himself called "Major") "A Bear Hunt," *Big Woods*, 145 and passim and *Stories*, 63 and passim; *Mansion*, 34, 62 and passim; *Reivers*, 21, 25; "Shall Not Perish," *Stories*, 103 and passim; *Town*, 10 and passim. In *The Town* and *The Mansion* he is unmarried.

DE SPAIN, MRS. ——— (wife of Manfred) "A Bear Hunt," *Big Woods*, 145 and *Stories*, 63

DESPLEINS, JULES *Pylon*, 27, 142, 229 (stunt flyer)

DE VITRY, CHEVALIER SŒUR-BLONDE "A Courtship," *Stories*, 363; *Moses*, 165; "Red Leaves," *Stories*, 317–20

DEVRIES, COL. ——— *Mansion*, 308–20 (runs for Congress against Clarence Snopes)

DICEY "Wash," *Stories*, 544 (midwife attending Milly, but in the corresponding passage in *Absalom* she is not named)

DICK, COL. NATHANIEL G., U.S.A. *Unvanquished*, 34–38, 88–89, 124–25, 145–46

DILSEY (wife of Roskus, mother of Luster, Frony, Versh, and TP) *Sound and Fury*, 8 and passim; "That Evening Sun," *Stories*, 290 and passim

DISTRICT ATTORNEY *Mansion*, 46–47

"DOC" (1) *Sanctuary*, 34–38

"DOC" (2) *Pylon*, 97

DOCTOR, THE (husband of Martha) *Wild Palms*, 3–22, 289–93 (rents house to the Wilbournes)

"DOCTOR" JONES *Sartoris*, 219 (old Bayard's janitor at the bank)

DODGE, GRANBY ("cousin-in-law" of Anselm Holland, Sr.) "Smoke," *Knight's Gambit*, 6 and passim

DOLLAR, ——— *Light in August*, 312–13 (storekeeper in Mottstown)

DON "Mistral," *Stories*, 843 and passim

DOOM (see also Ikkemotubbe) "A Justice," *Stories*, 344 and passim; "Red Leaves," *Stories*, 313 and passim; *Reivers*, 73

DOSHEY, ——— (wife of Eustace Grimm) *Hamlet*, 367

DOUGH, JAMES *Soldiers' Pay*, 189–95, 201 (injured in World War I)

DOWNS, MRS. ——— *Intruder*, 71 (an old white woman who tells fortunes, sells charms, etc., to Negroes)

DRAKE, JUDGE ——— (father of Temple) *Sanctuary*, 62, 212, 320, 342 and passim

DRAKE, HUBERT (brother of Temple) *Sanctuary*, 63, 347

461

EWING, IRA, SR. "Golden Land," *Stories,* 702 and passim

EWING, MITCH "Hair," *Stories,* 142–43 (depot freight agent)

EWING, MRS. —— (wife of Ira, Jr.) "Golden Land," *Stories,* 703 and passim

EWING, MRS. SAMANTHA (mother of Ira, Jr.) "Golden Land," *Stories,* 702 and passim

EWING, SAMANTHA, "April Lalear" (daughter of Ira, Jr.) "Golden Land," *Stories,* 705 and passim

EWING, VOYD (son of Ira, Jr.) "Golden Land," *Stories,* 705–09

FAIRCHILD, DAWSON *Mosquitoes,* 27 and passim (novelist)

FALLS, "OLD MAN" *Sartoris,* 1 and passim

FARMER, —— (father of Cecilia) *Requiem,* 229 (jailer)

FARMER, CECILIA *Requiem,* 229

FARINZALE, GIULIO "Mistral," *Stories,* 848–51

FARR, GEORGE *Soldiers' Pay,* 77 and passim

FATHERS, SAM, "HAD-TWO-FATHERS" (son of Ikkemotubbe and a slave) *Intruder,* 93; "A Justice," *Stories,* 343–45, 358–60 (where his father is said to be Craw-ford); *Moses,* 163 and passim; *Reivers,* 21–22

FAULKNER, WILLIAM *Mosquitoes,* 145. Though the first name is not given, this is evidently a self-portrait.

FEINMAN, COL. H. I. *Pylon,* 12 and passim

FENTRY, "MRS." *See* Thorpe, Two Brothers

FENTRY, G. A. (father of Stonewall Jackson) "Tomorrow," *Knight's Gambit,* 90, 92

FENTRY, JACKSON AND LONGSTREET (Stonewall Jackson Fentry's adopted son) "Tomorrow," *Knight's Gambit,* 85 and passim. He is later known as Buck Thorpe.

FENTRY, STONEWALL JACKSON "Tomorrow," *Knight's Gambit,* 89 and passim

FFOLLANSBYE, —— "All the Dead Pilots," *Stories,* 513–18; "Thrift," *Saturday Evening Post,* 16–17, 78, 92

FITTIE, AUNT *Reivers,* 143 (Everbe Corinthia once lived with her)

FLINT, —— *Wild Palms,* 34–45 (an intern)

FLINT, ELLIE PRITCHEL (wife of Joel) "An Error in Chemistry," *Knight's Gambit,* 109 and passim

FLINT, JOEL "An Error in Chemistry," *Knight's Gambit,* 109 and passim. His professional name is Signor Canova.

FONSIBA *See* Beauchamp, Fonsiba

FONZO *See* Winbush, Fonzo

FOOTE, MR. —— "Two Soldiers," *Stories,* 89–92 (policeman)

FORREST, GEN. BEDFORD, C.S.A. *Moses,* 263; "My Grandmother Millard," *Stories,* 688; *Requiem,* 231, 233

FORTINBRIDE, "BROTHER" *Unvanquished,* 152 and passim (acting pastor at Methodist church)

FOTHERGILL, ZEB *Sartoris,* 224

FOX, MATT "Hair," *Stories,* 132 and passim

FRANK *Sanctuary,* 67 (former lover of Ruby Lamar Goodwin)

FRANKIE *Sartoris,* 183–92 (friend of Belle Mitchell)

FRANZ "Ad Astra," *Stories,* 418–20 (German officer)

FRASER, —— "Monk," *Knight's Gambit,* 42–47 (old whiskey-maker with whom Monk lived)

FRASER, MR. —— "A Bear Hunt," *Big Woods,* 158 and *Stories,* 73

FRASER, ADAM *Intruder,* 27–41, 219–29 (owns store)

FRASER, DOYLE (son of Adam) *Intruder,* 20, 37

FRAZIER, JUDGE —— "Tomorrow," *Knight's Gambit,* 88 (presiding at Bookwright's trial)

FRED, COUSIN (Georgie's cousin) "That Will Be Fine," *Stories,* 267, 275–76

tendent of Jefferson power plant)

HARKER, OTIS *Town*, 25, 194 (has succeeded Winbush as night marshal)

HARPER, ———— "Turnabout," *Stories*, 484, 509 (aviation gunner)

HARRIS, MR. ———— (1) "Death Drag," *Stories*, 205 (man from whom car was rented)

HARRIS, ———— (2) "Honor," *Stories*, 559–60 (owner of flying circus)

HARRIS, ———— (3) "Barn Burning," *Stories*, 3–5; *Hamlet*, 9–10 (has Ab Snopes arrested)

HARRIS, ———— (4) *Sanctuary*, 315–16 (owns livery stable)

HARRIS, ELMER "Black Music," *Stories*, 819 (chief of police)

HARRIS, MELONEY *Sartoris*, 27, 183–84, 370 (Negro servant)

HARRISON, SERGEANT ———— *Unvanquished*, 34 (Yankee sergeant searching Miss Rosa's house for Bayard and Ringo)

HARRISS, ———— (first husband of Melisandre Backus) *Knight's Gambit*, 146 and passim; *Mansion*, 195, 196

HARRISS, MISS ———— (daughter of Mrs. Melisandre Harriss) *Knight's Gambit*, 135 and passim; *Mansion*, 196, 255

HARRISS, MAX (son of Mrs. Melisandre Harriss) *Knight's Gambit*, 135 and passim; *Mansion*, 196, 255

HARRISS, MRS. MELISANDRE BACKUS (widow of Mr. Harriss, later wife of Gavin Stevens) *Knight's Gambit*, 144 and passim; *Mansion*, 194 and passim. *See also* Backus, Melisandre (2)

HARRY, "MR." *See* sentry

HATCHER, LOUIS *Sound and Fury*, 112, 133–34

HATCHER, MARTHA (wife of Louis) *Sound and Fury*, 133

HAWK, "COUSIN" DENNISON (1) (brother of Drusilla) *Unvanquished*, 98 and passim

HAWK, "UNCLE" Dennison (2) (husband of Louisa, father of "Denny") *Unvanquished*, 15, 97, 230

HAWK, DRUSILLA (second wife of Col. John Sartoris) *Unvanquished*, 100 and passim

HAWK, AUNT LOUISA (mother of Drusilla) *Unvanquished*, 105 and passim

"HAWKSHAW," Henry Stribling "Dry September," *Stories*, 169 and passim; "Hair," *Stories*, 131 and passim

HEAD, SYDNEY HERBERT (husband of Candace Compson) *Sound and Fury*, 112–30, 216–38

HELMSMAN ON YACHT *Mosquitoes*, 74, 79, 99, 101

HENDERSON, MRS. ———— *Soldiers' Pay*, 31 (a nosy old lady)

HENRY (1) *Soldiers' Pay*, 15–16 (pullman porter)

HENRY (2) *See* McCallum, Henry

HENRY (3), "Uncle Henry" *Sartoris*, 283–85

HENRY (4) *Sanctuary*, 74 (bailiff)

HET, OLD "Mule in the Yard," *Stories*, 249 and passim; *Town*, 231–56

HIGHTOWER, ———— (father of the Rev. Gail) *Light in August*, 409–16

HIGHTOWER, GAIL (grandfather of the Rev. Gail) *Light in August*, 412 and passim

HIGHTOWER, MRS. GAIL (wife of the Rev. Gail) *Light in August*, 53 and passim

HIGHTOWER, REV. GAIL *Light in August*, 43 and passim

HIGHTOWER, HIRAM *Reivers*, 75 (one of Gen. Forrest's chaplains)

HILLIARD *Unvanquished*, 250 (runs livery stable in Oxford)

HINDS, GEN. THOMAS *Requiem*, 105

HINES, MRS. ———— (wife of Eupheus) *Light in August*, 299 and passim

HINES, EUPHEUS, "DOC" (grandfather of Joe Christmas) *Light in August*, 119–24, 323 and passim

HINES, MILLY (mother of Joe Christmas) *Light in August*, 325 and passim

HIPPS, BUCK *Hamlet*, 276 (the Texan who auctions the spotted horses)

HOAKE, ———— (father of Alison Hoake McCarron) *Hamlet*, 135

position in Jefferson corresponds very closely to that of the younger De Spain in *Town* and *Mansion*

HUB *Sartoris,* 138–59

HUGHES, MANNEY *Idyll in the Desert,* 13–14

HULE "Mountain Victory," *Stories,* 764 and passim (son of mountaineer family)

HULETT, MR. —— *Moses,* 128–29 (clerk at Lucas' divorce proceeding)

HUME, —— "Ad Astra," *Stories,* 414 (British flyer)

HUMPHRIES, GOV. BENJAMIN (HUMPHREYS) *Requiem,* 109

HURTZ, —— *Pylon,* 270 (marries reporter's mother)

"IKE" "Hand upon the Waters," *Knight's Gambit,* 68 (apparently supervising burial of Lonnie Grinnup). *See also* McCaslin, Isaac and Snopes, Ike.

IKKEMOTUBBE, "DOOM" (father of Issetibbeha, but, in "A Courtship" and *The Town,* the nephew of Issetibbeha) *Absalom,* 44, 54; "A Courtship," *Stories,* 361 and passim; "A Justice," *Stories,* 344 and passim; *Moses,* 165 and passim; "Red Leaves," *Stories,* 313 and passim; *Requiem,* 13, 45, 215–29; *Reivers,* 73; *Sound and Fury,* 3, 6; *Town,* 307, 316

INGERSOLL, ROBERT "Beyond," *Stories,* 791

INGRUM, WILLY *Intruder,* 136 and passim

IOWAN, THE *Fable,* 371–81

IREY *Fable,* 170

ISHAM *Moses,* 348–61 (cook on hunt for Old Ben)

ISOM "All the Dead Pilots," *Stories,* 529; *Sanctuary,* 145 and passim; *Sartoris,* 8 and passim; "There Was a Queen," *Stories,* 728 and passim (servant of Sartoris family)

ISSETIBBEHA (son of Ikkemotubbe [Doom] and the father of Moketubbe) "The Bear," *Moses,* 259; "A Courtship," *Stories,* 361 and passim; *Moses,* 165–66; "Red Leaves," *Stories,* 313 and passim; *Reivers,* 73; *Requiem,* 8–21; *Town,* 307, 316. In "The Bear" he is the father, in "A Courtship" and *The Town,* the uncle of Ikkemotubbe.

ISSETIBBEHA'S BODY SERVANT "Red Leaves," *Stories,* 316 and passim

JABBO *Town,* 68 (called to fix Major de Spain's tire)

JABBO, "CAP'M" *Mansion,* 97 (penitentiary guard)

JACK "Honor," *Stories,* 552–53

JACKSON, AL *Mosquitoes,* 66, 86–88, 276

JACKSON, ANDREW *Requiem,* 196; *Sound and Fury,* 3

JACKSON, ART *Pylon,* 39, 264, 282, 295–96 (parachute jumper)

JACKSON, CLAUDE *Mosquitoes,* 87, 278–81

JACKSON, GEN. "Stonewall" *Requiem,* 108, 233, 240, 259

JACKSON, OLD MAN (father of Al and Claude) *Mosquitoes,* 277–80

JAKE (1) "Beyond," *Stories,* 782–83, 797 (Negro servant)

JAKE (2) "Death Drag," *Stories,* 196 and passim (drives car in "Demon Duncan" act)

JAMES, LT. COL. —— *Fable,* 64 (British officer)

JAMESON, DOROTHY *Mosquitoes,* 27 and passim (portrait painter)

JARROD, HUBERT "Dr. Martino," *Stories,* 565 and passim

JASON *See* Compson, Jason IV

JEAN *Fable,* 16 and passim (one of the Corporal's band)

JEFFERSON, THOMAS *Requiem,* 106

JERRY "Turnabout," *Stories,* 483–84 (American officer)

JESUS (Nancy's husband) "That Evening Sun," *Stories,* 290 and passim

JIGGS *Pylon,* 7 and passim (airplane mechanic)

JIM (1) *Hamlet,* 260 (deputy sheriff)

Virginius) *Sartoris*, 315–36; "The Tall Men," *Stories*, 50 and passim

McCALLUM, VIRGINIUS *See* McCallum, Buddy and McCallum, old Anse

McCANNON, SHREVLIN *Absalom*, 173 and passim (Quentin Compson's Harvard roommate as he is named in the genealogy for *Absalom*). *See also* Mac-Kenzie

McCARRON, ———— (father of Hoake) *Hamlet*, 134–36 (elopes with Alison Hoake)

McCARRON, ALISON (mother of Hoake) *Hamlet*, 134–36

McCARRON, HOAKE (father of Eula Varner's child) *Hamlet*, 136–38; *Mansion*, 4, 115–75; *Town*, 100 and passim

McCASLIN, MRS. ———— (wife of Isaac) *Moses*, 4, 311–15, 352

McCASLIN, AMODEUS, "UNCLE BUDDY" (son of L. Q. C. McCaslin) *Moses*, 4 and passim; *Unvanquished*, 52–57. Faulkner consistently uses this form rather than the expected Asmodeus.

McCASLIN, DELPHINE (wife of Ned) *Reivers*, 30, 299

McCASLIN, ISAAC, "UNCLE IKE" (son of Theophilus) "A Bear Hunt," *Big Woods*, 145; and *Stories*, 69 and passim; *Hamlet*, 9, 358; *Intruder*, 93; *Mansion*, 31–32; *Moses*, 3 and passim; "Race at Morning," *Big Woods*, 177 and passim; *Reivers*, 14; *Town*, 12, 58

McCASLIN, LUCIUS QUINTUS CAROTHERS, "OLD CAROTHERS" (father of Amodeus and Theophilus) *Intruder*, 17, 69, 226; *Moses*, 36 and passim; *Reivers*, 22, 31; *Requiem*, 9; *Town*, 58

McCASLIN, NED (husband of Delphine) *Reivers*, 30 and passim

McCASLIN, THEOPHILUS, "UNCLE BUCK" (son of L. Q. C. McCaslin, father of Isaac) *Absalom*, 152; *Hamlet*, 16; *Moses*, 4 and passim; *Reivers*, 96; *Unvanquished*, 52 and passim

McCASLIN, MRS. THEOPHILUS *See* Beauchamp, Miss Sophonsiba

McCASLIN, THUCYDIDES, "THUCYDUS" (husband of Eunice) *Moses*, 266–67 (McCaslin slave)

McCASLIN, TURL *See* Tomey's Turl (1)

McCORD, ————, "MAC" *Wild Palms*, 88 and passim

McCUDDEN, ———— *Fable*, 88–89, 91, 119–20 (British fighter pilot)

McDIARMID, MR. ———— *Reivers*, 235 (judges the horse race)

McEACHERN, MRS. ———— (wife of Simon) *Light in August*, 125–47, 181–82

McEACHERN, SIMON *Light in August*, 124–90 (adopts Joe Christmas)

McGINNIS, LT. DARREL "Turnabout," *Stories*, 485 and passim

McGOWAN, SKEET *As I Lay*, 517–23; *Intruder*, 66 (works in the drugstore); *Mansion*, 187–88; *Town*, 156 and passim (Uncle Willy Christian's soda jerker)

MACK *See* Gillespie

McKELLOG, COL. ———— "Two Soldiers," *Stories*, 98

McKELLOG, MRS. ———— (the Colonel's wife) "Two Soldiers," *Stories*, 97–99

MacKENZIE, SHREVE *Sound and Fury*, 96–103. *See also* McCannon, Shrevlin

McKIE, ———— "Crevasse," *Stories*, 472

McKINLEY *See* Grove, McKinley

McLAN, ———— "Victory," *Stories*, 449

McLENDON, CAPT. JACKSON "Dry September," *Stories*, 171 and passim; *Light in August*, 76; *Mansion*, 183–87; *Town*, 104, 116

McWILLIAMS, ———— *Knight's Gambit*, 243 (railroad conductor)

McWILLIE *Reivers*, 225 and passim (Negro jockey)

McWILLIE'S FATHER *Reivers*, 283

MACWYRGLINCHBEATH, ———— "Thrift," *Saturday Evening Post*, 16 and passim

MADAM OF SAN ANTONIO BROTHEL *Wild Palms*, 211–13

MADDEN, RUFUS *Soldiers' Pay*, 173 and passim

MAHON, DONALD *Soldiers' Pay*, 25 and passim (badly injured in World War I)

473

MAHON, REV. DR. (father of Donald)
Soldiers' Pay, 56 and passim

MALLISON, CHARLES, JR., "CHICK" (son of
Charles, Sr. and Maggie) *Intruder*, 3
and passim; *Knight's Gambit*, 39 and
passim; *Mansion*, 109 and passim;
Town, 3 and passim. He is apparently
the narrator of several of the stories in
Knight's Gambit—certainly of "An Error in Chemistry," "Monk," and "Tomorrow."

MALLISON, CHARLES, SR. (husband of Maggie Stevens Mallison) *Intruder*, 32,
105, 124, 127; *Mansion*, 109 and passim; *Town*, 3 and passim

MALLISON, MAGGIE (wife of Charles, Sr.,
sister of Gavin Stevens) *Intruder*, 15
and passim; *Knight's Gambit*, 163;
Mansion, 215 and passim; *Requiem*,
67, 96, 204; *Town*, 46 and passim

MAME *Light in August*, 167–69, 190 and
passim

MANDY (1) *Sartoris*, 310–37 (cook in Mc-
Callum household)

MANDY (2) "That Will Be Fine," *Stories*,
274–76, 284 (grandpa's cook)

MANNIE (Rider's wife) *Moses*, 135–51

MANNIGOE (MANIGAULT), NANCY *Requiem*, 50 and passim

MANNOCK, —— *Fable*, 88, 91, 112
(British fighter pilot)

MARCHAND *Pylon*, 212 and passim
(works for Ord)

MARDERS, MRS. SARAH *Sartoris*, 183–202
(friend of Belle Mitchell)

MARION, GEN. FRANCIS *Requiem*, 218

MARKEY, ROBERT *Knight's Gambit*, 192–
222 (Memphis lawyer)

MARSH (Mrs. Res Grier's brother) "Two
Soldiers," *Stories*, 84

MARSHAL, THE *As I Lay*, 488–90

MARSHAL, THE OLD *See* the Generalis-
simo

MARTEL, GEN. —— *Fable*, 269

MARTHA (1) *See* Hatcher, Martha

MARTHA (2) *See* Armstid, Martha

MARTHA, "MISS" *Wild Palms*, 6–12, 289–
93 (Doctor's wife)

MARTHE *Fable*, 214 and passim (half
sister of the Corporal)

MARTHE'S HUSBAND *Fable*, 396 and passim

MARTINO, DR. —— "Dr. Martino,"
Stories, 571 and passim

MARYA *Fable*, 214 and passim (older
sister of Marthe and half sister of the
Corporal)

MATRON OF THE ORPHANAGE *Light in
August*, 123–27

MATTHEW "Hand upon the Waters,"
Knight's Gambit, 68 (contributes to
burial expenses of Lonnie Grinnup)

MAURIER, MR. —— (deceased husband
of Patricia Maurier) *Mosquitoes*, 323–
26

MAURIER, HARRISON *Soldiers' Pay*, 99

MAURIER, MRS. PATRICIA (aunt of Patricia
and Theodore Robyn) *Mosquitoes*, 12
and passim

MAURY, UNCLE *See* Bascomb, Maury

MAXEY "Hair," *Stories*, 131 and passim
(proprietor of barber shop)

MAXEY, MR. —— *Light in August*, 76

MAYCOX, JUDGE —— *Intruder*, 110

MAYDEW, —— *Moses*, 154–58 (sheriff)

MAYES, WILL "Dry September," *Stories*,
169 and passim (Negro who is lynched)

MEADOWFILL, MR. —— (father of Essie)
Mansion, 327–48, 361

MEADOWFILL, MRS. —— (mother of
Essie) *Mansion*, 348

MEADOWFILL, ESSIE (wife of McKinley
Smith) *Mansion*, 329–48, 361

MEEK, MELISSA *Sound and Fury*, 11–16
(librarian who sees Caddy's picture)

MELISANDRE *See* Backus, Melisandre (1)
and (2)

MELONEY *See* Harris, Meloney

MERRIDEW, MRS. —— "Uncle Willy,"
Stories, 228 and passim (helping look
after Uncle Willy)

METAL-DETECTOR SALESMAN *Moses*, 78–96
(from whom Lucas buys money finding machine)

METCALF, —— *Light in August*, 309–
10 (Mottstown jailer)

RHODES, MISS ———— *Reivers*, 303 (Lucius Priest's schoolteacher)

RICHARD *Sartoris*, 314–17 (a Negro on the McCallum place)

RICHARDSON, DR. ———— *Wild Palms*, 294, 301–07

RIDEOUT, ———— (brother of Aaron) *Hamlet*, 370

RIDEOUT, DR. ———— *Moses*, 125 (summoned when Molly is found in the woods)

RIDEOUT, AARON (cousin of V. K. Ratliff) *Hamlet*, 370 (owns restaurant in town).

RIDDELL, ———— *Town*, 310–11, 337, 362 (boy who has polio)

"RIDER" *Moses*, 135–59

"RINGO," MARENGO (grandson of Louvinia) "My Grandmother Millard," *Stories*, 667 and passim; *Unvanquished*, 3 and passim

RITTENMEYER, ANN (daughter of Charlotte and Francis) *Wild Palms*, 124 and passim

RITTENMEYER, CHARLOTTE (wife of Francis) *Wild Palms*, 5 and passim

RITTENMEYER, CHARLOTTE (daughter of Charlotte and Francis) *Wild Palms*, 124 and passim

RITTENMEYER, FRANCIS, "RAT" *Wild Palms*, 38 and passim

RIVERS, LEE *Soldiers' Pay*, 190–209 (local bachelor)

RIVERS, MISS REBA *Mansion*, 72–82; *Reivers*, 98 and passim; *Sanctuary*, 170 and passim

ROBERT, UNCLE "Uncle Willy," *Stories*, 239

ROBINSON, ———— "Thrift," *Saturday Evening Post*, 78

ROBYN, HENRY, "HANK" (father of Pat, brother of Mrs. Maurier) *Mosquitoes*, 124–25, 191, 256

ROBYN, PATRICIA (daughter of Henry, twin sister of Theodore) *Mosquitoes*, 16 and passim. She and her twin call each other "Gus."

ROBYN, THEODORE, "JOSH," "GUS" (son of

Henry, twin brother of Patricia) *Mosquitoes*, 45 and passim

RODNEY, MR. ———— (uncle of Georgie) "That Will Be Fine," *Stories*, 265 and passim

ROEBUCK, JOHN WESLEY *Town*, 54–55, 130 (friend of Charles Mallison)

ROGERS, ———— *Sartoris*, 158; *Sound and Fury*, 228, 233 (runs cafe in Jefferson)

ROGERS, HOWARD "Honor," *Stories*, 553 and passim (an airplane pilot)

ROGERS, MILDRED (wife of Howard) "Honor," *Stories*, 556–59

RONNIE *See* Smith, R. Boyce

ROSA COLDFIELD'S AUNT *Absalom*, 51–56, 176 (elopes with horse trader)

ROSCIUS, "ROSKUS" (husband of Phoebe, father of "Thucydus") *Moses*, 263 (McCaslin slave)

ROSIE "That Will Be Fine," *Stories*, 265 and passim (servant in Georgie's family)

ROSKUS (husband of Dilsey) "A Justice," *Stories*, 343; *Sound and Fury*, 29–90

ROSS, FRANK "The Brooch," *Stories*, 660

ROSS, MARTHA (Frank's wife) "The Brooch," *Stories*, 654–56, 660

ROUNCEWELL, MR. ———— *Reivers*, 47 (local oil company agent)

ROUNCEWELL, MRS. ———— *Mansion*, 128; *Reivers*, 24; "Tomorrow," *Knight's Gambit*, 89; *Town*, 70–77, 122 (runs boarding house, later, flower shop)

ROUNCEWELL, WHIT (son of Mrs. Rouncewell) *Mansion*, 59; *Moses*, 373; *Town*, 160, 212

ROXANNE, AUNT "My Grandmother Millard," *Stories*, 675 (Sartoris slave)

ROY *Mosquitoes*, 144–47 (Thelma's friend)

RUNNER, THE *Fable*, 60–322

RUSSELL, ———— *Light in August*, 309–10 (deputy sheriff)

RUSSELL, AB *Sound and Fury*, 257, 260

RUST, EVERBE CORINTHIA (daughter of Simon) "The Leg," *Stories*, 823 and passim

Gowan and Temple) *Requiem* 51 and passim

STEVENS, BUCKY (son of Gowan and Temple) *Requiem,* 64 and passim

STEVENS, GAVIN (son of Judge Stevens, second husband of Melisandre Backus Harriss) "An Error in Chemistry," *Knight's Gambit,* 111 and passim; "Hair," *Stories,* 144 and passim; "Hand upon the Waters," *Knight's Gambit,* 65 and passim; *Intruder,* 3 and passim; *Knight's Gambit,* 135 and passim; *Light in August,* 388–94; *Mansion,* 55 and passim; "Monk," *Knight's Gambit,* 46 and passim; *Requiem,* 40 and passim; "Smoke," *Knight's Gambit,* 13 and passim; "The Tall men," *Stories,* 56; "Tomorrow," *Knight's Gambit,* 85 and passim; *Town,* 3 and passim

STEVENS, GOWAN (cousin of Gavin, husband of Temple) *Requiem,* 51 and passim; *Sanctuary,* 26 and passim; *Town,* 3 and passim. In *Requiem,* 127, Gowan is referred to as Gavin's *nephew.*

STEVENS, JUDGE LEMUEL (father of Gavin and Margaret Stevens Mallison) *Mansion,* 130; *Reivers,* 15–16; "A Rose for Emily," *Stories,* 122; *Town,* 48–49, 97–99. He is called Captain Stevens in "Tomorrow," *Knight's Gambit,* 91.

STEVENS, TEMPLE DRAKE *See* Drake, Temple

STILLWELL, SHUFORD H. *Mansion,* 96, 100 (threatens to kill Mink)

STONE, PHIL *Town,* 326–28

STOKES, —— "A Justice," *Stories,* 343–44, 358, 360 (manager of Compson farm)

STOVALL, —— "That Evening Sun," *Stories,* 291 (bank cashier)

STRAUD, DR. —— *Sartoris,* 378

STRIBLING, HENRY *See* Hawkshaw

STROTHER, SIMON (1) (son of Joby and father of Ringo) *Unvanquished,* 18–19, 277–79

STROTHER, SIMON (2) (grandson of Joby)

Sartoris, 2 and passim; "There Was a Queen," *Stories,* 727

STRUTTERBUCK, CAPT. —— *Mansion,* 75–81

STRUTTERBUCK, Q'MILLA (wife of the Captain) *Mansion,* 81

STUART, GEN. J. E. B. *Sartoris,* 10

STUDENMARE, CAPT. —— "A Courtship," *Stories,* 366 and passim (owns the steamboat)

SUBADAR, THE "Ad Astra," *Stories,* 407 and passim; "Honor," *Stories,* 562

SUBALTERN, THE "Crevasse," *Stories,* 466 and passim

SUE (Hub's sister) *Sartoris,* 165

SURATT, V. K. *As I Lay,* 478, 512, 530; "Centaur in Brass," *Stories,* 149–50; *Sartoris,* 135 (sewing machine dealer). He becomes V. K. Ratliff in subsequent novels and stories.

SUTPEN, CLYTEMNESTRA, "Clytie" (daughter of Thomas and a slave) *Absalom,* 61 and passim

SUTPEN, ELLEN COLDFIELD (second wife of Thomas) *Absalom,* 9 and passim; "Wash," *Stories,* 537

SUTPEN, HENRY (son of Thomas and Ellen) *Absalom,* 18 and passim

SUTPEN, JUDITH (daughter of Thomas and Ellen) *Absalom,* 15 and passim; "Wash," *Stories,* 541

SUTPEN, THOMAS (father of Henry, Judith, Clytie, and Charles Bon) *Absalom,* 11 and passim; *Moses,* 191, 255; *Reivers,* 20; *Requiem,* 9, 37–45, 214, 225, 238; *Unvanquished,* 255–56; "Wash," *Stories,* 536 and passim

SUTTERFIELD, REV. TOBE *Fable,* 141–207, 310–22 (also known as Tooleyman)

SWAMP-DWELLER, THE *Mosquitoes,* 213–15, 263

SWAMPERS, THE SEVEN *Moses,* 222–23

SYLVESTER'S JOHN "A Courtship," *Stories,* 363, 365, 369–70

TALLIAFERRO, ERNEST *Mosquitoes,* 9 and passim. He was born "Tarver."

WUTHERSPOON, JAMIE "Turnabout," *Stories*, 479

WYATT, ———, "OLD LADY WYATT" (great-aunt of Emily Grierson) "A Rose for Emily," *Stories*, 123, 125

WYATT, AUNT SALLY *Sartoris*, 68 and passim (for a time, companion of Narcissa Benbow)

WYATT, GEORGE *Unvanquished*, 237 and passim

WYATT, HENRY *Moses*, 347–48

WYATT, MISS SOPHIA (Aunt Sally's elder sister) *Sartoris*, 181

WYOTT, DR. ——— *Town*, 306 (president emeritus of the Jefferson Academy)

WYOTT, MISS VAIDEN *Town*, 127–28, 145–46 (schoolteacher)

WYOTT, MR. ——— *Reivers*, 69, 73 (a friend of the Priests)

WYLIE, ASH, JR. "A Bear Hunt," *Big Woods*, 145 and passim and *Stories*, 67 and passim. Both Wylies are referred to as Old Man Ash and it is not clear whether the Ash of *Stories* is the father or the son.

WYLIE, ASH, SR. "A Bear Hunt," *Big Woods*, 145; *Moses*, 175 and passim (cook in hunting camp)

WYLIE, CAPT. ———, C.S.A. *Sartoris*, 13

WYLIE, JOB "Uncle Willy," *Stories*, 226 and passim (Uncle Willy's servant)

ZILICH, MRS. ——— "Pennsylvania Station," *Stories*, 617 and passim (neighbor of Mrs. Gihon)

ZILPHIA (daughter of Zilphia Gant and her second husband) *Miss Zilphia Gant*, 28–29

ZSETTLANI *Fable*, 16 and passim (one of the Corporal's band)

General Index

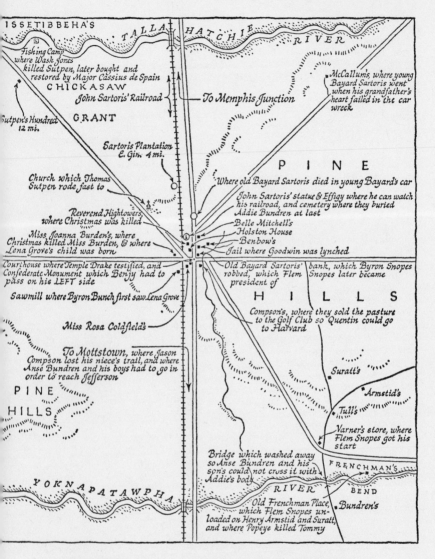

JEFFERSON, YOKNAPATAWPHA COUNTY, MISSISSIPPI

Area, 2400 square miles. Population: Whites, 6298; Negroes, 9313.
William Faulkner, sole owner and proprietor.

(From *Absalom, Absalom!*, New York, Modern Library,
Random House, 1951. By permission of the publisher.)